THREE GENRES ✳ ✳ ✳

The Writing of
Poetry,
Fiction,
and Drama

PRENTICE-HALL INTERNATIONAL, INC., *London*
PRENTICE-HALL OF AUSTRALIA, PTY. LTD., *Sydney*
PRENTICE-HALL OF CANADA, LTD., *Toronto*
PRENTICE-HALL OF INDIA PRIVATE LIMITED, *New Delhi*
PRENTICE-HALL OF JAPAN, INC., *Tokyo*

THREE GENRES ✳✳✳

The Writing of Poetry, Fiction, and Drama

SECOND EDITION

STEPHEN MINOT

Trinity College
Hartford, Connecticut

PRENTICE-HALL, INC., ENGLEWOOD CLIFFS, NEW JERSEY

ACKNOWLEDGMENTS

I am indebted to Dick Tuttle for his invaluable illustrations and to William Ritman for permission to reproduce his set design for Pinter's *The Collection*. I am grateful to George E. Nichols III, Robley Wilson, and Richard P. Benton for their helpful suggestions, and to Hilda Tauber of the Prentice-Hall editorial staff. And I remain indebted to the late Frederick L. Gwynn who had faith in this work when it was in the planning stage.

My thanks to the authors, publishers, and individuals mentioned below for permission to reprint or to quote from the following works.

"The Sandbox" by Edward Albee is reprinted from his volume *The Zoo Story, The Sandbox and The Death of Bessie Smith*, by permission of Coward-McCann, Inc. Copyright © 1960 by Edward Albee. "The Sandbox" is the sole property of the author and is fully protected by copyright. It may not be acted either by professionals or amateurs without written consent. Public readings, radio and television broadcasts likewise are forbidden. All inquiries concerning these rights should be addressed to the agent, William Morris Agency, 1350 Avenue of the Americas, New York, N. Y.

The Theatre of the Absurd by Martin Esslin. Copyright 1961 by Martin Esslin. Used by permission of Doubleday & Company, Inc.

"Sausage and Beer" by Stephen Minot, copyright © 1962 by The Atlantic Monthly Company is reprinted with permission of the publisher.

"Hello Out There" by William Saroyan is reprinted from his volume *Razzle-Dazzle*, copyright 1942, by permission of the author. This play may not be acted, broadcast, televised, or presented to an audience in any way without permission in writing from the author.

"Friends from Philadelphia" by John Updike. Copyright © 1954 by John Updike. Reprinted from his volume *Olinger Stories* by permission of Alfred A. Knopf, Inc. First appeared in *The New Yorker*.

"The Use of Force" from William Carlos Williams, *The Farmers' Daughters*. Copyright © 1938 by William Carlos Williams. Reprinted by permission of New Directions Publishing Corporation.

"A Tribute to the Founder" by Kingsley Amis, used by permission of the author.

"Elegy Just in Case" by John Ciardi, used by permission of the author.

"The Language" (Copyright © 1964 Robert Creeley) is reprinted by permission of Charles Scribner's Sons from *Words* by Robert Creeley. First appeared in *Poetry*.

"Buffalo Bill's" by E. E. Cummings. Copyright 1923, 1951 by E. E. Cummings. Reprinted from his volume *Poems 1923–1954* by permission of Harcourt Brace Jovanovich, Inc.

"The Love Song of J. Alfred Prufrock," "The Hollow Men," and "The Waste Land" from *Collected Poems 1909–1962* by T. S. Eliot, copyright 1936 by Harcourt Brace Jovanovich, Inc. Copyright © 1963, 1964 by T. S. Eliot. Reprinted by permission of the publisher and Faber and Faber Ltd.

"Dove Sta Amore" from *A Coney Island of the Mind* by Lawrence Ferlinghetti. Copyright © 1958 by Lawrence Ferlinghetti. Reprinted by permission of New Directions Publishing Corporation.

"Fire and Ice" and "Mowing" from *The Poetry of Robert Frost*, edited by Edward Connery Lathem. Copyright 1923, 1934 by Holt, Rinehart and Winston, Inc. Copyright 1953, © 1962 by Robert Frost. Reprinted by permission of the publisher.

"Howl" from *Howl and Other Poems* by Allen Ginsberg. Copyright © 1956, 1959 by Allen Ginsberg. Reprinted by permission of City Lights Books.

"Lizards and Snakes" from *The Hard Hours* by Anthony Hecht. Copyright © 1967 by Anthony Hecht. Reprinted by permission of Atheneum Publishers.

Haiku translations by Harold G. Henderson from his *An Introduction to Haiku*. Copyright © 1958 by Harold G. Henderson. Reprinted by permission of Doubleday & Company, Inc.

"Another Song" from *The Summer Anniversaries* by Donald Justice. Copyright © 1954 by Donald Justice. Reprinted by permission of Wesleyan University Press. First published in *The New Yorker* under the title "Tune for a Lonesome Fife."

"Trees" by Joyce Kilmer, used by permission of Jerry Vogel Music Co.

"To the Snake" from *With Eyes at the Back of Our Heads* by Denise Levertov. Copyright © 1958 by Denise Levertov Goodman. "A Solitude" from *The Jacob's Ladder* by Denise Levertov. Copyright © 1961 by Denise Levertov Goodman. Both poems reprinted by permission of New Directions Publishing Corporation.

"Local Places" copyright 1965 by Howard Moss, used by permission of the author.

"In a Station of the Metro" from *Personae* by Ezra Pound. Copyright 1926 by Ezra Pound. Reprinted by permission of New Directions Publishing Corporation and Faber and Faber Ltd.

"Like This Together" by Adrienne Rich is reprinted from her volume *Necessities of Life, Poems 1962–1965*. Copyright © 1966 by W. W. Norton & Company, Inc. Reprinted by permission of the publisher.

"The Still Voice of Harlem" by Conrad Kent Rivers is reprinted by permission of Cora Rivers. First appeared in the *Antioch Review*.

"The Sloth" copyright 1950 by Theodore Roethke, from *The Collected Poems of Theodore Roethke*. Reprinted by permission of Doubleday & Company, Inc.

"The Division of Parts" and "The Farmer's Wife" from *To Bedlam and Part Way Back* by Anne Sexton, copyright 1960. Used by permission of Houghton Mifflin Company.

"To the Western World," copyright 1957 by Louis Simpson, from *A Dream of Governors* by Louis Simpson. Used by permission of Wesleyan University Press.

"American Primitive" from *Poems 1947–1957* by William Jay Smith, copyright 1953 by William Jay Smith. Reprinted by permission of Atlantic-Little, Brown and Company, Publishers.

"A Flat One" from *After Experience* by W. D. Snodgrass. Copyright © 1960 by W. D. Snodgrass. Reprinted by permission of Harper & Row, Publishers, Inc. First appeared in *The Quarterly Review of Literature*.

"Fern Hill" from *Collected Poems of Dylan Thomas*. Copyright 1946 by New Directions Publishing Corporation. Reprinted by permission of the publisher, J. M. Dent & Sons Ltd, and the Trustees for the Copyrights of the late Dylan Thomas.

"On a Maine Beach" by Robley Wilson. Copyright © 1965 Commonweal Publishing Company, Inc. Reprinted by permission of the author and publisher.

To Ginny
who supplied coffee, criticism, and enthusiasm
throughout the preparation.

PREFACE

This book ends with the statement that "creative work is a way of life, and the effort to publish is an important but not a central portion of that life." The statement explains why I wrote the book and who should use it. It is the link between the first edition and this, the second.

Creative work covers a lot more than writing, of course. Many people find it in music, painting, acting, or even in a nonapplied science. What all these individuals share is a sense of satisfaction in sharpened awareness, in skills that are practiced for their own sake, and in productivity as an end in itself. The creative life requires a kind of controlled instability in which the individual is constantly growing.

Many authors, poets, and playwrights share these values. Yet until recently about the only texts available for the apprentice writer were the "How To..." books which solemnly promised hard cash sales in two to three weeks or, on the other hand, critical works and anthologies designed for the student of literature rather than for the writer.

A text was needed which would deal with all three genres strictly from a writer's point of view, treating each as a genuinely sophisticated art form. In working toward this goal I have used those concepts which my students have found valuable in the process of developing their own individual styles, and I have tried to avoid all those which are of interest mainly to the literary critic.

I have had three types of readers in mind. The first is the student in a college or university who is taking a course in creative writing. The second is the writer who is working on his own. Third is the reader who, although not an active writer, constantly explores the intricacies of literature simply for the pleasure of it.

Students taking writing courses are often puzzled about why that type of course seems to require an annual defense in the pages of *Atlantic, Harpers,* or *Saturday Review.* So am I. It is an odd fact that those who have to be reassured about the value of these courses are perfectly prepared to accept the legitimacy of courses in painting, sculpture, or aspects of musical composition. The question which concerns me is not whether these courses should exist but whether they can be made more effective. I think they can.

A good writing course has, among other characteristics, a rapid and provocative interchange of ideas. By *interchange* I mean that the students talk to their classmates and their instructor fully as much as he talks to them. More significant, students should not simply answer questions but be willing and able to initiate discussion. This is what distinguishes a seminar from a lecture course; and most writers who teach creative writing find that the seminar is an ideal approach.

There are, however, certain basic concepts which the instructor must explain each year to each new class; this is why many seminars need occasional lectures. The function of an analytical text in a creative writing seminar is not to bring the course closer to the traditional methods of teaching literature but to preserve the *flexibility* of the informal seminar. The text should intensify the student-instructor relationship by increasing the time devoted to discussion.

The writer who is working on his own has a different problem: isolation. His friends tend to give criticism which is highly subjective, and the publishers to whom he submits are usually too busy to say much more than "yes" or "no." As a result, it is difficult for him to evaluate his own work. Eventually he may repeat the same style and even the same thematic concerns without being aware of it. No amount of determination will compensate for lack of growth or development.

A text like this one does not provide specific techniques and rules. Those methods are effective only when working with very rigid conventions such as greeting-card verse or pulp-magazine fiction. But if the independent writer applies each chapter of this work both to his own writing and to the literature he has read and respected, the process should awaken a wide variety of new reactions. What the independent writer needs most of all is refertilization. Writers' clubs are often stimulating, and some summer conferences can be helpful too, but only through a text can one re-evaluate one's basic literary values at leisure.

The third group I have in mind is made up of nonwriters for whom literature is more than a means of escape. Most of these have taken a few English courses in college but no longer have a way of sharpening their literary perceptions. Like the independent writers, these readers run the risk of going stale.

They will find that *Three Genres* differs from the purely critical text and the critical anthology which were assigned in literature courses. The primary concern here is not so much the final literary creation as the methods used to create it. This approach is in some respects like Homer's description of the design on a shield which he presented in temporal sequence, describing each step of the craftsman. This text describes literature in terms of process.

During the five years that the first edition has been in use at many colleges and universities, I have received many valuable suggestions from my own students, from other teachers, and from individual writers working on their own. Their response has been most gratifying.

The major change in this new edition is the addition of a collection of poems, three short stories, and two plays, all in their entirety. These works—most by well-known contemporary writers—now serve as the touchstones for each section. In addition, almost every page of the original text has been revised so that the analysis is linked directly with the examples. In this way, no critical concept is left suspended in the abstract; each is illustrated by a specific work or passage in this same volume.

The principle which has guided me from the beginning and which remains unchanged in this edition is that a text on writing has no business telling a reader *how to write*; its single task is to help readers to *develop individually as writers*. There is a crucial difference. The first strives for uniformity. A "How To..." book, for example, is distinctly proscriptive. "Technique" becomes a restrictive term—even a set of prohibitions. But a sophisticated writer develops the way a work of art does: individually. "Technique" sets him free by giving him a range of options.

A student who has been restricted to meter, for example, is apt to feel that it is only a limitation. But those who understand that it is only one of about six highly distinctive methods of creating rhythmical effects in language will want to include it as one of their options. In this-way, technique becomes liberating.

 A writer develops by discovering the full range of what is possible in his genre. Much of this is done by reading. An equal amount is done by practice writing. Both have to be active, conscious efforts. Later, this familiarity will be internalized in what might be called "a feel for the medium." The goal of this text is to speed the transition.

S. M.

CONTENTS

PART ONE ✶✶✶
The Writing of Poetry

1	The Distinction of a Poem	3
2	The Source of a Poem	14
3	The Sound of Words	25
4	Rhythms of Stress	38
5	Rhythms of Free Verse	47
6	Images	56
7	Diction	73
8	Poetic Tension	83
9	From Units to Unity	95
10	Revising a Poem	105
11	Poems for Study	110

PART TWO ✶✶✶
The Writing of Fiction

12	The Scope of Fiction	125
13	The Sources of Fiction	136
14	"Friends from Philadelphia," a story by John Updike	148
15	Structure: From Scenes to Plot	156

16 "The Use of Force," a story by William
    Carlos Williams   164
17 Viewpoint: The Means of Perception   168
18 "Sausage and Beer," a story by Stephen Minot   183
19 Characterization   194
20 Narrative Tension   209
21 Orientation: Place and Time   224
22 Literary Concerns: Theme, Tone, Symbol,
    and Style   234
23 Revising Fiction   248

PART THREE ✳✳✳
The Writing of Drama

24 Theater: A Live Performance   257
25 *Hello Out There,* a play by William Saroyan   266
26 Dramatic Impact   283
27 *The Sandbox,* a play by Edward Albee   293
28 Suggestion and Statement   301
29 Realism and Expressionism   315
30 Dramatic Dialogue   326
31 Visual Effects: Action   336
32 Visual Effects: Set and Costume   350
33 Revising a Play   366

PART FOUR ✳✳✳
Appendices

A Submission of Material for Publication   373
B Glossary-Index   381

THREE GENRES ✳✳✳

The Writing of
Poetry,
Fiction,
and Drama

PART ONE ∗∗∗

The
Writing
of
Poetry

1

THE DISTINCTION
OF A POEM

The value of basic *definitions;* defining *literature; verse* distinguished from prose by its use of *the line,* the *sound* of words, the *rhythm* of phrases, and *compression* of suggestion; *sophisticated* poetry distinguished from simple verse by complexity of suggestion and the employment of poetic *conventions.*

Writers do not wrestle with definitions of literary terms as constantly as critics do. A writer's first obligation, after all, is to write.

But a poet who does not have the vocabulary to describe his own work and that of others is in trouble. He may "have a feeling" about a poem, but unless he can express it accurately in words, his ability to evaluate and to revise is crippled.

There are several alternatives for a writer like this—some more profitable than others. He may develop his own critical terminology and use it so freely and with such assurance that at least the gullible will assume that he is brilliant. Or he may turn sullen, muttering darkly about how critical terms destroy the spontaneity of literature.

But in either case, he will probably remain a "first draft writer." And an amateur.

A third approach is to study and use whatever basic terms seem to be helpful when writers talk among themselves about their work. This is actually easier. Anyone who has been forced to talk in vague, evasive terms about someone's poem knows how exhausting it is—and how pointless.

Analyzing specific aspects of a work accurately is one of the ways writers develop their own abilities. Subjective evaluation ("I don't like the second stanza") is of limited value. It may reflect nothing more important than the speaker's personal preference for one color over another or city images over nature settings. But precise analysis ("This vehicle has the wrong overtones for its tenor") leads to understanding and usually to revision. And it is through understanding his own work and that of others that a writer continues to develop.

What is
Literature?

Answering this is the never-ending task of literary critics. But writers need to share a general, working definition of *literature* if they are going to understand each other. A great deal of time can be wasted if this term is used as a synonym for *good*. "I like your poem," a self-proclaimed critic says, "but is it literature?" And the next four hours are then spent trying to define the term.

For practicing writers, the most useful definition is the one proposed by Northrop Frye (see *Anatomy of Criticism,* Princeton University Press). He divides all writing into two categories, *descriptive* and *literary*.

In *descriptive writing* "the final direction of meaning" is tied to the real world about us. That is, its primary purpose is to describe or interpret some aspect of man's "real" environment. This category includes such forms as the essay, thesis, editorial, article, or a text such as this. When we evaluate such works we use terms like *valid, true,* and *helpful* (or *false* and *useless*), each of which implies that such writing should reflect accurately the world about us.

Literary writing, on the other hand, creates its own world. The poem, the story, the novel, and the play are judged largely by internal criteria: unity, consistency, complexity, and fresh use of literary conventions. Such works may also make suggestions about the "real" world, but the primary concern of the writer is not to convince or inform, it is to create. Viewed this way, the poem is closer to a sculpture than it is to utilitarian writing such as an essay. Even when literary writing becomes highly thematic—satiric poetry, for example—it tends to be not so much an argument as a human response. It is possible, of course, to thrust poetry, fiction, or drama directly into the area of argumentation in the form of advertising jingles, propagandistic fiction, and political skits. But then we judge them for their "message," treating them quite correctly as descriptive writing.

This definition of literary writing is particularly helpful for the poet. It describes how his work is related to fiction and drama. It is more precise than phrases like *creative writing*. And it avoids value judgments. There is an enormous difference, of course, between the verse of Edgar Guest and that of Ezra Pound, but it does not help a writer to understand his art to shrug off Guest's work as "nonliterary."

Most important of all, Frye's precise use of this term reminds the poet that his work is not just an elaborate way to present a philosophical truth. It provides an antidote to the emphasis on "theme" and "message" which has dominated many English classes. After all, we can listen to a song without demanding that it give some philosophical truth. And we study a painting in the same spirit. A poem also exists for its own sake, a pleasure in itself.

The Characteristics
of a Poem

All literary writing is composed either in verse or in prose. What is the difference? There is only one absolute distinction: in poems, the length of the line is a part of the art form. This is one distinguishing factor which is found in all poetry regardless of the period.

Prose, on the other hand, is continuous. That is, the length of a line has nothing to do with the form. It varies according to the size of the page on which it is being printed. The author leaves this up to the typist or the linotype operator because it is not an aspect of his art.

The poet does not allow the printer to make the slightest change in the length of his lines because in most cases he has used them to create rhythmical effects or sound patterns. It is a part of his language —an element which simply is not present in prose.

This is more than a technical distinction. The poet tends to *think* in lines, using them as a base for the construction of images, rhythms, and sound patterns. It is for this reason that many poems are begun with what eventually may become the fifth, the twelfth, or the last line. The poet adds lines by association, far removed from the prose writer's concern for chronology.

By controlling the line length, the poet also controls the shape of his poem. Whether he is using traditional meter or free verse, he can make his poem snake down the page in brief lines or have it fill the page with long ones. And by extreme use of typography, which is rare, the shape of the poem can be made pictorial in itself.

The writer of prose has only one typographical device, the paragraph. With the exception of that, his work will fill the page in a simple block. The poet, then, becomes far more concerned with the visual aspect of his work. Through typography he can influence the meaning, the tone, and the rhythmical patterns of his work.

There are three additional characteristics of poetry each of which will be treated in a separate chapter. I mention them here as an overview so that each can be kept in perspective. They are *sound devices, rhythmical patterns,* and the *compression of statement.* None of these is as absolute as the use of the line—individual poems can be found which fail to use one or even two of these devices. But a great majority of poems contain all four characteristics.

The use of sound is enormously important to most poets. Generally this is a matter of linking two or more words by matching final sounds (rhyme), initial consonants (alliteration), or sounds within words (assonance and consonance). In addition, the sound of the word itself may echo what it describes (onomatopoeia) as in "buzz," "cuckoo," and "hiss."

Analysis and examples of all these devices appear in Chapter 3, but it is worth noting here how intense the element of sound can become even when buried within words. In the first stanza of Dylan Thomas's "Fern Hill," for example, the poet describes how as a child he felt like a young prince among the trees and in the sunlit fields. These three lines ripple with assonance. I have italicized only the most obvious examples—six pairs in three lines!

> And once be*low* a *time I lord*ly had the *trees* and *leaves*
> *Trail* with d*ai*sies and b*ar*ley
> Down the *rivers* of the w*i*ndfall light.

It is possible, of course, to write a poem which contains no sound devices whatever. It is still a poem. But the use of sound is a significant part of most poetry regardless of period.

The third characteristic of verse is the use of rhythm. In simplest terms, rhythm is a systematic variation in the flow of sound. All speech varies the flow of sound, of course; otherwise it would be a steady hum. But the key word here is "systematic." Such systems vary enormously. Traditional meter, a fairly regular repetition of stressed and unstressed syllables, is the most common form. A looser method involves counting just the stressed syllables in a line. *Beowulf* was written in this way, as is a good deal of contemporary verse. Quantitative meter, rarely used in English, depends not on stress but on the length or duration in the pronunciation of a syllable. Varied as these approaches are, they all constitute systematic variations in the flow of sound.

But there are also nonauditory rhythms. Striking effects have been achieved by patterning the number of syllables in each line regardless of stress (Marianne Moore), by balancing syntactical elements (Walt Whitman), by repeating key words and phrases (Allen Ginsberg), and by arranging the length of lines (E. E. Cummings). The reader responds to these signals from what he sees on the page as well as through what reaches his ear as he reads the poem aloud. Rhythm in poetry is like a heartbeat, giving this genre a special kind of life.

Prose can also contain samples of rhythm, as seen in the fiction of Thomas Wolfe and Dylan Thomas. Such rhythms, however, tend to be more fragmentary and are often created from the sentence structure. They are never based on line length.

The fourth and final characteristic of poetry is compression of statement. Poems usually say a lot in a few words. That is, most poems have a range of suggestion with subtle shadings of feeling. Often they require several readings.

This does not mean, of course, that poems have to be short. But within even the most sweeping epics like the *Iliad* or *Beowulf* there are stanzas which reverberate with implications. And now that story telling is so closely identified with prose fiction and the film, the tendency for poets is to concentrate on the subtleties of personal experience, packing their lines with varied implications. Even when poems make blunt social or political statements, they usually are distilled from one man's experience.

This compression—drawing broad implications from specific details or images—is achieved partly through similes but mostly by metaphors and symbolic suggestion. In Chapter 6 I will analyze how a poet like

Dylan Thomas can build a simple word like "green" into a symbol which would require pages of prose to explain.

Verse, then, is distinguished from prose by its special use of the line, the sound of words, the rhythm of phrases, and compression of suggestion. There is no law which forces a poet to develop all four in every poem; but a writer is not a poet in the full sense until he *can* use all when he choses.

Sophisticated
vs. Simple Poetry

So far, I have been describing poetry, not evaluating it. But we make value judgments all the time. Teachers of writing classes occasionally give an "F" or a "D" for what they consider inferior work, and this is only a gentle prelude to the "F" grades which editors hand out regularly in the form of rejection slips. A poet spends a lifetime being publicly "graded" by reviewers. But just what do we mean by "good" and "bad"?

Standards obviously vary from person to person. Many sane adults really prefer greeting-card verses about ideal mothers and dear old dads; others reject work on that level as "rubbish" but secretly believe that the last "genuine poetry" was written by Tennyson. And then there are those who with equal sincerity admire the song lyrics of Bob Dylan or the poetry of LeRoi Jones. How does one develop as a poet with so many conflicting standards?

The solution comes from two terms used in science. To a biologist, simple forms of life are *simple* and complex forms are *sophisticated*. Thus, the bird is not *better* in any objective sense than the jellyfish, but it is far more sophisticated in that the potential of living matter has been developed much further.

As an individual, the biologist may prefer a canary to a jellyfish as a pet or may feel that the jellyfish is *better* as an example of living tissue; but acting as biologist, his use of the terms *simple* and *sophisticated* are objective.

Does all poetry have to be sophisticated? Of course not. Judging by the verse on greeting cards, far more people prefer their poetry simple—regular meter, conventional sentiments, and the cozy familiarity of time-tested clichés. Writing simple verse is a craft and there are books that teach it. But this is not one.

Sophisticated literature is the subject of this text. It is by definition complex, but it is not necessarily cluttered or obscure. A fly's eye, for example, is in some ways more complex in structure than a human eye, but as an instrument of sight it is far from sophisticated. It cannot see as well. In the same way, a sestina with its highly complex system of repeated words may be more complicated than, say, a three-line haiku; but in many cases the haiku is more sophisticated because it *does* more—has a wider, more subtle range of suggestion.

Varieties of *complexity* can be created in any of the four characteristics already discussed: use of the line (Herbert, Thomas, Ginsberg), sound devices (Poe), rhythmical effects (Vachel Lindsay), and compression of statement (an example of Ezra Pound appears later in this chapter). And in addition, complexity may involve refashioning an old convention, such as Coleridge's use of the ballad form in "The Rime of the Ancient Mariner," Dylan Thomas's ironic use of the elegy in "Refusal to Mourn...," or Ginsberg's use of syntactical rhythm, which has its roots in Biblical prose.

In some cases, complexities such as these have resulted in sophisticated verse. But in others they have become ends in themselves and the poem becomes more of a trick, a stunt—and simple.

Joyce Kilmer's "Trees" has been used many times in battles over what is and what is not "good" poetry. I cite it here not for one last hatchet job but to illustrate what makes a poem *simple*. Here are the first three of its six stanzas:

> I think that I shall never see
> A poem lovely as a tree.
>
> A tree whose hungry mouth is pressed
> Against the earth's sweet flowing breast;
>
> A tree that looks to God all day
> And lifts her leafy arms to pray;...

Setting aside all concern for evaluation, we can see certain specific characteristics which, first, indicate that it is indeed verse and, second, that it is simple verse. It uses lines, but the lines are arranged in rhyming couplets that soon become monotonously regular. There are three samples of sound devices, but each is an end rhyme which lands bluntly on a stressed, one-syllable word. This mathematical regularity is not softened by assonance, consonance, double rhyme, slant rhyme, or any other sound device.

The rhythm is based on a simple, unvaried use of iambic tetrameter. No attempt has been made to integrate rhythmical patterns with tone or statement. In this respect, it resembles the simple chants used by children ("Eeny meeny miny mo / Catch a tiger by the toe"), but there is no indication that Kilmer's work is intended to be chanted.

The degree of compression varies. The first stanza contains none. It is denotative, direct, and without any figure of speech. It is a good prose sentence. But the second and third stanzas do use metaphors: The tree's roots are likened to one suckling at a breast; and the branches, to one lifting arms upward in prayer. Since only an un-weaned contortionist could manage this, we must assume that we are not dealing with an extended metaphor. The use of two separate, visually unrelated metaphors in two adjoining couplets intensifies the separation between stanzas already established by the meter and the rhyme. Further, the images themselves are essentially unchanged and undeveloped borrowings from two well-used metaphors: Mother Nature and a tree as a man reaching toward heaven.

By way of contrast, here is Ezra Pound's two-line poem, "In a Station of the Metro":

> The apparition of these faces in the crowd;
> Petals on a wet, black bough.

Because this is so short, many readers are tempted to make a quick judgment and pass on. But my concern here, as with Kilmer's poem, is not evaluation; the poem can be examined with the same objective sense the biologist uses when dissecting.

As with "Trees," the line is an intentional part of the form and can't be changed by the typesetter. The title sets the scene—assuming that the reader knows that "Metro" refers to the Paris subway. The first line presents a more or less literal description of the faces in the subway, and the second offers a metaphorical association—a comparison which intensifies our view of the scene.

But the first line is not entirely denotative in the sense that Kilmer's first stanza was. The word "apparition" has overtones which we do not normally associate with subway stations. First, it suggests that something has appeared suddenly or unexpectedly; further, it has the meaning of ghosts or phantoms. In some way, then, the faces of those in a crowded subway station remind the poet of apparitions.

The second line develops this in an intricate fashion. The image is one of petals presumably torn loose in a rain storm and plastered on a black bough. Each word is significant. "Petals" has a conventional association with youth (spring) and innocence; "wet" is our only clue that there has been a storm; "black bough" not only establishes a contrast with the lightness of petals but provides the picture of faces in the black subway car which rushes in with the suddenness of an apparition when viewed from the platform.

There is no moral here and not even a "message" such as some school children are taught to seek in every poem. But there is the sense of suddenness when the subway car rushes into a station, a touch of fear, and a highly original suggestion about the relationship between that solid, black metallic product of modern society and the faces one sees through the window, pale and fragile.

The first reason for calling this poem sophisticated, then, is the complex use of imagery and the subtlety of the suggestions which result. But the rhythm is also complex. The first line is iambic through-out. The second breaks the pattern with a trochee which stresses the first syllable (*Pet*–als) and then abandons meter for the sake of those three heavy stresses which demand a pause between them: ". . . wet, black bough." Just why iambic followed by a trochaic foot moves the poem from light to heavy tone is a matter for Chapter 4, but it is enough to point out here that in this poem, rhythm, with all its variations, is bound quite consciously with meaning and tone.

There is no true rhyme in this brief poem, but there are other samples of sound devices. The final words in each line are bound with similar vowel sounds (cr*ow*d and b*ough*) in what is called a slant rhyme or assonance. The second line is constructed with two linked pairs: p*e*tals and w*e*t joined with assonance, and *b*lack and *b*ough with alliteration.

Beyond the technicalities of composition, these two poems differ considerably in their apparent function or purpose. Kilmer's poem is predominantly assertive: It states at the beginning that trees are "lovely" and ends with the proposition that "only God can make a tree." Pound, on the other hand, presents no clear proposition. He makes use of what appears to be a fleeting and personal observation. The reader's concern is not so much whether he agrees or disagrees with a proposition but whether he sees what is described and feels what is suggested. And if he does, his reactions and insights may grow the more he reads the poem. If one begins with the sense of certain visual relationships coming abruptly (like an apparition), one has drawn a good deal from the poem. Later, however, the implication of these people who look like petals may emerge as a major concern. Or one may work out some of the implications of the "black bough" —the subway train and all it represents. In short, one does not "learn" a poem like this in the way one quickly memorizes a popular song; it is more like a Beethoven quartet in its ability to draw the trained and interested listener back for repeated and expanding interpretations.

Poetry, like every other art form, has its factions, and these two poems happen to represent two of the most militant. My analysis, however, is not intended as a battle cry. I wish only to suggest that beneath all the squabbling about the "value," "worth," and "spiritual significance" of poetry, there are certain objectively definable differences between composition which is, on the one hand, simple and unimaginative use of poetic techniques and, on the other, complex, original, and penetrating use of the genre.

Conventions vs.

Individuality
A poetic convention is any pattern or device which is repeated in a large number of poems. Rigid adherence to restrictive conventions (themes such as love for Mother, Christmas, and small dogs; rhythm such as the unvaried use of iambic tetrameter) leads to simple verse. But all poetry—even the most sophisticated—is based on conventions, as we have already seen in the use of the line, the techniques of sound, patterns of rhythm, and the methods of establishing compression.

A poet's first task, then, is to master the basic conventions of his genre. Only in this way can he achieve freedom as a writer, for only when he is at ease with a particular technique is he free to decide whether to use it.

Take, for example, the various systems of creating rhythm. Students of poetry sometimes spend valuable time arguing about whether meter, rhythm of stress, or free verse is "best." Best for what? And for whom? The practicing poet bases his decision partly on personal preference and partly on the needs of a particular poem. He can do this only when he is at home with each system.

But mastering conventions is largely a matter of craft. Any poet who is committed (as is this text) to sophisticated work must learn to use the language of poetry to reflect what is unique in himself: his special insights and reactions. The second task of the poet, then, is to go beyond mastery of conventions and to make his "voice" as individual as he is himself.

The following ten chapters will deal with the conventions of verse and with the ways poets use these techniques to create work which is sophisticated and unique.

2

THE SOURCE
OF A POEM

The danger of broad *abstractions;* the use of *sense perception:* sight, sound, touch, smell, and taste; the recall of specific *emotions;* the fragmentation and magnification of *experience;* the pleasure of *sound* and *meaning* of words.

If this were a text for fourth- or fifth-grade students, a chapter on where to look for poetic material would not be necessary. Children may be limited in their range of experience and in their vocabulary, but most of them know intuitively where to look for material. Like the mature, practicing poet, they make use of what they have seen, what they have felt, what they have done, and what they discover accidentally about the sound of words.

By the time a student reaches college, however, he has begun to associate all writing with the process of intellectual analysis. This is natural: Compare the hours he has put into writing "themes" as opposed to those, if any, devoted to composing verse. And in most cases, his study of published poetry has centered on the "message," "theme," or "central concern" as if the function of a poem were essentially the same as that of an essay.

It is no wonder, then, that some students tend to hang their poems on such broad abstractions as love, death, nature, war, peace, brotherhood, hypocrisy, God, beauty, social justice, and truth. "Love," we are told, "turns the sour taste of life to sweet." A satisfactory slogan, that, but is it really rooted in genuine experience? If so, it doesn't show. The pronouncement is still about love as an abstract state. Notice how the same metaphor ("turns the sour taste...to sweet") can be plugged into nature, peace, brotherhood, God, beauty, and truth. And with a simple inversion (to "turns the sweetness of our lives to sour") the metaphor can serve equally well for death, war, and hypocrisy. The poet has thus produced ten different poems without once revealing the smallest portion of himself.

Established poets tend to be more honest. This often requires revealing more of oneself. Here is an example from Adrienne Rich's "Like This Together," the first of six stanzas:

> Wind rocks the car.
> We sit parked by the river,
> silence between our teeth.
> Birds scatter across islands
> of broken ice. Another time
> I'd have said "Canada geese,"
> knowing you love them.
> A year, ten years from now,
> I'll remember this,
> this sitting like drugged birds
> in a glass case—
> not why, only that we
> were here like this together.

Miss Rich is not here concerned with Love in the abstract; she is dealing with a specific relationship between two people at a specific moment in time. She recalls the scene through very precise memories —the feel of a car shuddering in the wind, the look of a bay in winter. And then she develops the *unique* quality of that relationship at that particular stage: the chill of the landscape, the couple sitting "like drugged birds / in a glass case..." There is love here, but it is a part of a complex set of emotions and its future is uncertain.

Student poets often miss the stuff of poetry when it is that close to them. Here are four basic sources from which poems often develop.

Sense

Perception The human being is trapped in the dark confines of his own mind and makes contact with the outside world in five specific ways: by seeing, by hearing, by touching, by smelling, and by tasting. Many people somehow get through life with very little contact with this outside world, seeing and hearing only what is necessary, feeling nothing but pain, smelling only that which is unpleasant or dangerous, and tasting nothing whatever. If there is any meaning to terms like "poetic sensitivity" or "poetic inclination," it is rooted in the ability—perhaps the compulsion—to see, hear, feel, smell, and taste more in this world than the average human. Usually this is coupled with a desire to share this awareness—poetry as communication. Occasionally there is no such desire—poetry as pure expression. For most poets there is a balance.

While the writer of fiction looks for events which might be rearranged into a full narrative, the contemporary poet seeks shorter, more fragmented units of experience. Most often these come in the form of things seen: birch trees bent over from winter storms, a dead colt, a Yiddish newspaper lying in a gutter, a grassy river bank remembered from childhood, black faces staring out of tenement windows on an oppressive August night, cracks in a concrete playground, patterns of frost on a window, the veins in a maple leaf or an old man's hand, or an abandoned spider web.

Rarely is the poet content to describe the object as an end in itself. The original image is selected because it has certain qualities—feelings, associations, implications, and the like—which develop as the artist expands his first conception.

Occasionally a city serves as the poet's starting point. Sandburg's use of Chicago and Williams's study of Paterson, New Jersey are good examples. Or the poet may turn to specific scenes of his childhood. Of the poems included in this text (see Chapter 11), Dylan Thomas's "Fern Hill" is a fine example. Although the phrasing is dreamlike ("About the lilting house and happy as the grass was green"), the origin is clearly the farm on which the poet was raised. The poem is filled with precise visual details from that scene—wagons, apple trees, daisies, barns, foxes, horses, owls, and the like.

But that is a big scene to work with. More often, poets draw on places that they have visited—specific scenes which have lingered in their memories for some reason. This is the origin of Robley Wilson's

"On a Maine Beach" (see p. 112). Written in Iowa, the poem draws on an earlier summer. It doesn't indulge in generalities about the Maine coastline the way travel ads usually do; instead it focuses on specific details, drawing a pattern from them. Almost every line contains a precise visual image which the poet eventually uses to link this scene with broader, more abstract suggestions. I will return to this poem in a later chapter on images, but it would be helpful to read it now as an example of how a relatively simple experience can serve as the genesis for a highly sophisticated poem.

Occasionally sounds may also serve as sources for the poet. In "Fern Hill," for example, the boy imagines that the calves "sang" to his horn like a pack of hunting dogs, and he hears the foxes bark "clear and cold," and the sound of distant church bells mingled with that of the brook is described with the phrase, "The sabbath rang slowly"—all this in one stanza!

In using sounds, the poet has to go further than generalities. "The roar of traffic" doesn't give the reader enough to work with; and besides, the metaphor is worn out with overuse. The poet searches his memory for those specific elements which created the general effect—the sounds of pneumatic drills, police whistles, car and truck horns, and the like. Or if the scene is in the country, he may try to isolate exactly how the wind sounds in a pine grove or through wheat fields.

It is annoying, of course, when the sound which actually initiated a poetic sequence is sufficiently overused to be considered a cliché. Brooks babbling, gulls crying, and wind whistling in the rigging have all reached the level of song lyrics. That is the end of the line. If the sound is truly an individual experience, one can include it in the early drafts and decide later whether to delete the image altogether or to revitalize it, as Howard Moss did in "Local Places" where the potentially dangerous babbling brook became "the stream's small talk at dark."

The other senses—touch, smell, and taste—serve less frequently as sources for the poet. But when one does experience such a sense perception, it is well worth a moment of contemplation, such as Proust gives to his taste of a madeleine dipped in tea. These may be mild reactions, such as the feel of grit on a dirty kitchen table, the coarse lick of a cow, the smell of a pine grove in August, the odd mixture of oil and hops outside an urban brewery, the taste of potato chips combined with the smell of sweat, or the exhaust of a Diesel bus. Or they may take more severe forms such as the burning sensation of tear gas or the sharp pain of a knife wound or of childbirth.

Once one has caught a specific piece of sense data in the memory and translated it into words, one has, by definition, an image. Whether to use it directly, employ it as a simile or metaphor, build it into a symbol, or expand it as the core of an image cluster is the subject of Chapter 6. I am concerned here with the poet's need not only to keep his eyes open but to keep the other four senses alert and receptive to every stimuli about him—or as much as he can stand.

How does one do this? Not by waiting passively for inspiration. It is true that accomplished poets rely heavily on chance observations, but those with less experience must make a special effort to use all five senses. It helps, for example, to go on solitary walks in unfamiliar areas—city or country—and look for visual associations and contrasts: the texture of brick resembling the reddened skin of an old farmer; a row of parked automobiles looking like a toy counter; a shabby man offering a sharp contrast with a new storefront. Or one can concentrate on sounds. Sit on a park bench or on a curb or in a cafeteria and mentally list all the sounds—*all* of them, mechanical, human, animal, natural. How many of these would have been noticed by a non-observer?

Personal

Emotions   The stress here is on *personal*. As was pointed out at the beginning of this chapter, only when the poet is dealing with feelings close to his heart can he develop the nuances, the overtones, and the ambivalences of the emotion.

Take love, for example. Over the centuries it has remained one of the most popular poetic topics, yet it is artistically one of the most dangerous. The risk comes from the fact that no subject has a greater collection of poetic conventions. When Shakespeare begins "Sonnet 18" with the question, "Shall I compare thee to a summer's day?" he quickly answers it negatively, not just because his love was in fact "more lovely and more temperate," but because the comparison between love and summer had become even then a thoroughly overused convention. Yet three centuries later college sophomores are still linking their loves with summer days.

It is a mistake—or at least cowardly—to avoid a subject merely because it has been widely used. But one should be aware of the fact that it takes more skill to make it a fresh work. One solution is to instill in the love such high ambivalence that a tension is created between the love and the hate. W. D. Snodgrass's "A Flat One" (p. 116), for example, is in one sense a kind of love song to an old soldier who has spent months dying in a hospital. Through seventeen stanzas the speaker, an attendant at the hospital, voices the resentment and even hatred which many of them felt toward the ungrateful patient. But in the very last two lines he reveals their underlying devotion:

> No. We'd still have to help you try. We would
> Have killed for you today.

Love and hate, however, are not the only emotions. Consider loneliness: in childhood, in a foreign country, in a crowd. Think of the ambivalences involved in dependence: on one's family, a friend, a group. Almost everyone has experienced loss: a friend, a parent, a familiar neighborhood, childhood. And then recall those moments of discovery: of nature, the city, fear. Closely connected are those sensations of wonder: at the extraordinary growth of a sunflower, the strength of an old man, one's own prejudices. Looking forward, there are aspects of anticipation which may be pleasurable or grim: the prospect of adulthood or age, war, love, parenthood, dying.

These are, of course, all described here in the abstract. The poet is concerned with what he can make concrete through the use of vivid and fresh imagery. His first question might be, "Did I really feel this?" Such a query would eliminate a great many unconvincing love lyrics. The next question should be, "Were there any complexities, ironies, ambivalences in this emotion?" If there are none, it might be wiser to drop that subject and go on to another. The emotion which most naturally lends itself to poetry is not necessarily intense, but for most poets it must be genuine and fairly complex.

The Sweep of

Experience Basically, both sense perception and specific emotions are forms of experience. But I am concerned here with those broader portions of one's life, whole episodes including events and dialogue.

This is, of course, the material of fiction. But whereas poet and

short-story writer may seize upon similar episodes for literary treatment, the two usually move in opposite directions from the very start.
The writer of fiction dwells on characterization and event, combining
the two to create some sort of dramatic tension. For this reason he is
concerned with the whole episode, often enlarging or expanding on
what may have been a rather simple sequence of events. He builds
out from the central incident, adding scenes, characters, and background information.

The poet tends to work the other way, reducing an incident to its
essentials. In a sense, he chips away at an experience as if he were
a sculptor working on a block of marble. He has less need for a narrative sequence, so he looks for the most significant emotions and the
most effective images with which to express them. The actual experience may have been metamorphosed—fundamentally altered—as
thoroughly as it would have been by a short-story writer, but the
poetic concern for incident usually involves fragmentation and concentration on the fragments.

In Chapter 11 there are a number of poems based on personal
experience. One of the most striking is Anthony Hecht's "Lizards and
Snakes" (p. 110). Read it now and examine those characteristics which
make it similar to a short story.

It has, first, a vivid setting. Notice the visual details. There are also
tactile images ("hot...enough to scorch / A buzzard's foot"). Next,
there are three main characters clearly designated: Aunt Martha, Joe,
and the narrator. And there is a plot which serves as the organizing
principle of the piece. Finally, there is a theme which elevates the
narration from the level of simple anecdote to a relatively sophisticated
poem: Fear of lizards and snakes, the poem suggests, can be funny on
one level, but it also can have deep psychological and religious roots
which we can't laugh off.

It is, of course, a poem and not a story. Reviewing the characteristics outlined in the first chapter, it is clear that Hecht is making
artistic use of the line (it is the basis of his meter and his rhyme
scheme). He is also concerned with sound devices (alliteration in addition to rhyme), and compression of statement. Even though the treatment is distinctly poetic, the source of the work is a specific incident—
similar to that in most stories.

Now compare this poem with "A Flat One" by Snodgrass (p. 116).

Give the poem two careful readings and ask yourself to what degree and in what ways this poem is *less* like a short story than "Lizards and Snakes."

Essentially, the difference between the poems is the degree to which each makes use of plot. Snodgrass also has a specific scene, a narrative sequence of action, and at least one well-defined character; but in his poem many lines and entire stanzas are analytical. In Hecht's poem the lizards take on a supernatural, Satanic quality through the aunt's dialogue; in the Snodgrass poem there is no dialogue and we learn about the situation through the narrator's description of the equipment and the human effort which went into keeping the old man alive. The poem relies increasingly on direct, analytical statement—particularly in the last two stanzas.

Now turn to a third poem, Adrienne Rich's "Like This Together" (p. 113). Notice how the first stanza has all the ingredients of narrative poetry: a scene, characters, certain events. But she soon moves off into a complex set of metaphors suggesting loss of closeness (razed buildings, misunderstood words, winter, a severed hand), ending with a reaffirmation: "hold fast to the / one thing we know."

Reread the last two stanzas, pretending that they are the entire poem. Notice that the intent would be more difficult, more obscure, but not totally hidden. The first stanza may not be essential, but it leads us into the poem. And it is our clue that this poem, like the other two, had its origins in a segment of personal experience.

**Delight
in Words**   This final source of poetry is perhaps the most significant. If there is any one characteristic which separates poets from writers of fiction, it is their particular fascination with words in themselves. Poetry is normally written more slowly, more painstakingly than fiction and the finished work is intended for careful, repeated reading. It is natural for the poet to place a special emphasis on the overtones, the rhythmical effect, and the sound of words.

Students who have been taught poetry with a heavy hand sometimes miss the fact that many poems are written with a sleight of hand. The wordplay in Shakespeare's sonnets, for example, is often more enjoyable than the theme or "message" of the poem. And how many readers remember that Hamlet was a compulsive punster? John

Donne's early poetry may not have won over any more women than his later work won converts, but both continue to dazzle readers with verbal gymnastics.

Several modern examples of wordplay are included in Chapter 11. Turn first to Lawrence Ferlinghetti's "Dove Sta Amore" (p. 115), and read it aloud a couple of times.

Why is it a pleasure to read? Partly because "dove sta amore" (Italian for "where lies love") can also be read as the English words *dove* and *star;* partly because of melodic repetition; and partly because of the way the opening and closing lines of the poem echo each other. In a sense, the poem builds outward from the center like an onion (read it from the center line up, and then from the center line down). And what does all this prove? It is odd that we ask this question of a poem but not of a song. Clearly this is a type of song and "proves" nothing more than music does.

Now try Donald Justice's "Another Song" (p. 111). Again, read it aloud.

This too is a "song" as the title suggests. Like simple melodies, it gives pleasure mainly through the balance of its parts. The recurrent refrain at the end of each stanza is one way of achieving balance, and so is repeated phrasing in lines like "merry the green, the green hill shall be merry." Both techniques were used in old English ballads just as they are today in song lyrics. These familiar elements plus the echo of the nursery rhyme about Jack and Jill put us off guard.

But unlike "Dove Sta Amore," this poem has a darker thread woven through all three stanzas. There is continual seeking and a lack of fulfillment. The young owl looks for food, the young man looks for love, the traveler looks for shelter, and the soldiers march on to another weary war. Summer in the first stanza becomes winter in the second; the green hill becomes a withered hill. The conventions of light, lyrical verse have been used to suggest a stark theme.

Finally, turn to "Fern Hill" by Dylan Thomas (p. 118). More will be said of this poem later. For now, read just the first stanza, underlining the phrases in which a whimsical distortion is used. The poem is more sophisticated than "Another Song" (just as it, in turn, was more sophisticated than "Dove Sta Amore"), but in line after line one can see the poet's delight in playing with words.

Responding to
Oona and Kepick
Where should a student poet begin? Not, I would suggest, with a pronouncement about the world or life or love. But it is not always easy to "turn on" lines about sense responses, emotional reactions, or personal experience. Sometimes word play helps to loosen one's imagination. This is where Oona and Kepick may help.

Study these two shapes:

If each shape had a name, which one would be Kepick and which Oona? Now think of them as a couple. Which is the girl? Assume that one of them is a brand of gasoline and the other a type of oil. Which is which? Suppose one is a melon and the other a lemon? And now listen to them: one is a cymbal and the other a violin. Too easy? One is a saxophone and the other a trumpet; one is the wind and the other a dog's bark. It is a curious and significant fact that nineteen out of twenty people will give identical answers. This is the "language" of association, of connotation, which is the special concern of the poet both consciously and subconsciously.

Thinking of them once again as a couple, give each of them four more nonsense names. Now try a few lines of very free verse describing Oona and Kepick, using their other names as adjectives or verbs. (Surely you think of Oona looking feenly in the shane, but what happens when Kepick kacks his bip and zabots all the lovely leems?)

There is no end to this. It won't lead directly to sophisticated poetry, but it does help to link language with music. The two should not be confused, but poems often have more to do with sound, rhythm, and overtone than they do with pronouncement.

From verbal games like these, it is an easy route to such personal experiences as the memory of things seen, felt, heard, and emotional responses, and those longer episodes from one's life which nourish a poet's imagination.

3

THE SOUND
OF WORDS

The value of listening to language; nonrhyming devices of sound including alliteration, assonance, consonance, and onomatopoeia; the sound of true rhyme and its use in rhyme schemes; the need for variety in sound; composing verse for the ear.

It is hard to imagine a musical composer who hasn't spent a good portion of his waking hours listening to music. Yet some would-be poets hesitate to read and listen to poetry on the grounds that they don't want to be overly influenced by any one style. This is perfect nonsense. There is no danger of becoming imitative if one reads a wide variety of works; and one can't begin to be an accomplished poet until one has "heard" (by ear or by imagination in silent reading) an enormous body of poetry.

Listening to one's language requires more than time; it also requires discrimination. There is little on television or in films which will help the developing poet. Contemporary audiences require dramatic plots and bizarre situations, and care little for the word play which delighted even the illiterate portion of Elizabethan audiences.

25

The lyrics of folk and country-style music, however, sometimes contain subtleties of sound. This is particularly true when the singer is also a composer. It is no coincidence that Bob Dylan named himself after Dylan Thomas. But impressive as his complex rhyme scheme and metrical systems often are, on the cold page they read more like the verbal gymnastics of Poe than the subtleties of Dylan Thomas. This is not surprising. Lyrics written to be accompanied by one or more instruments have always tended to be less subtle, less sophisticated as language, than poetry which must stand alone on the page. For proof of this one need only to read the librettos of such operas as *La Traviata* or *Tannhäuser*. In such cases, it is the *combination* of music and lyrics which results in a sophisticated art form. The poet must develop his "music" from language itself. To achieve this, he should spend twice as much time listening to poetry as he does listening to song lyrics.

One way to hear poetry is to read it slowly and aloud. Some people can achieve this same effect by mouthing the lines silently. If the book is one's own, it is helpful to mark those letters and syllables which echo the sounds in neighboring words. These may appear at the beginning, in the middle, or at the ends of words.

Another way is to listen to records of poets reading their own work. Most large libraries have collections, and some will allow those with portable tape recorders to record specific selections for their own use.

Nonrhyming

Devices of Sound   There is a tendency to think of rhyme as the primary method of linking the sound of one word with another. Actually, it is only one of many techniques. To place it in perspective, I shall begin with a sample of prose which is highly lyrical in spite of the fact that it by necessity contains no rhyme scheme.

The selection is from Dylan Thomas's "August Bank Holiday." It describes a summer holiday at the beach not through plot but, in the manner of poetry, through a succession of vivid images. The first paragraph is typical of them all. It is reprinted here with the linking sounds italicized.

> August Bank Holiday.—A tune on an ice-cream cornet. A *s*lap of *s*ea and a tickle of *sand*. A *fanfare* of sun*sh*ad*es* opening. A *wince* and *whinny*

of bathers *d*ancing into *d*eceptive water. A tuck of dresses. A rolling of trousers. A compromise of paddlers. A sunburn of girls and a lark of boys. A silent hulla*baloo* of *balloo*ns.

There are two levels of sound present here. The first, a primary list, is clear, definable, unarguable, and graced with specific literary terms. The secondary list is vague, arguable, and without terminology; but it constitutes a significant part of what we commonly call lyricism in both prose and poetry.

Starting with the primary list of sound relationships, it is clear that words can be linked in only three ways: by the initial sound, by some sound within each word, and by a final sound. In addition, these can be based on consonants or on vowels. Moving in this order, we can group the sound relationships according to type.

Alliteration is the repetition of consonants, particularly those at the beginning of words. There are three groups of these:

slap—sea—sand
wince—whinny (a similarity, not an identity of sound)
dancing—deceptive

Assonance is the repetition of similar vowel sounds regardless of where they are located in the word. Some good examples are:

w*i*nce—wh*i*nny
sunb*u*rn—g*i*rls (similarity of sound, not spelling)
hullabal*oo*—ball*oo*ns

Consonance is the repetition of consonantal sounds. Since *alliteration* is used to describe similarity in initial sounds, *consonance* usually refers to sounds within the words. Often the two are used in conjunction. There are three sets of consonance in this passage:

wi*n*ce—whi*nn*y
gir*ls*—*l*ark
si*l*ent—hu*ll*aba*l*oo—ba*ll*oons

Onomatopoeia is often defined as a word which sounds like the object or action which it describes; but in point of fact, most onomatopoetic words suggest a sound only to those who already know what the meaning is. That is, we are not dealing with language which mimics life directly; it is usually just an echo. There are three good examples in Thomas's paragraph:

slap of sea (the sound of a wave on the beach)
whinny (an approximation of the horse's sound)
hullabaloo (the derivation of this coming from "hullo" and "hello" with
an echo of "babble")

This single paragraph of prose contains most of the sound devices available to the poet. And yet there are still more relationships present in this passage. These so-called secondary sound combinations will be missed by many readers. Like subtle harmonies in music, they are difficult to detect.

In general, they take the form of related vowel sounds which are not close enough to be called assonances but which, when taken as a group, echo each other. The first group includes the cluster of sounds around *a* and *e;* the second link the "rounder" sounds of *u, o,* and *ou.*

Representing the first group we have "sl*a*p of s*ea a*nd a tickle of s*a*nd." Here "and" and "sand" are clearly linked by assonance; but Thomas has also added the related sounds of *ee* in "sea" and the short *a* of "slap." This would be of no significance if we did not find other examples. We do in "*fanfare* of sunsh*ades*" where the sounds *an, air,* and *aids* are clearly not identical but distinctly related. As a third example of the *a* and *e* cluster we have "b*a*th*e*rs d*a*ncing into d*ece*ptive w*a*ters."

The second cluster, that of *u, o,* and *ou* sounds is seen first in "t*u*ne . . . c*o*rnet." It is then seen in "r*o*lling of tr*ou*sers." And it appears once again in "h*u*llabal*oo* of ball*oo*ns," which is primarily a sample of assonance (*oo* and *oo*) but which also links the *u* sound with the *oo.*

Secondary relationships in the form of sound clusters like these are not essential to poetry—though they were to Thomas both in his prose and his poetry. I stress them here to indicate that sound in literature is not just a matter of mastering certain technical terms and struggling to sprinkle one's work with a representative sample for critics to play with. Sound is for most poets an integral part of composition, and the manipulation of sound takes place both consciously and unconsciously.

Analyses like this tend to remain abstract and theoretical until one tries the technique in actual composition. Stop now and think of a scene, a friend, or a piece of music which comes to you with the soft, gentle contours you associated with the Oona figure in the last chapter. Now try a paragraph of descriptive prose in which you make use of as many sound devices as possible. Remember that this is prose, so there is no need to worry about rhythm or a regular rhyme scheme.

It might help to circle the linkages in sound. The point of this exercise is merely to help you find and use sound clusters.

Now, by way of contrast, think of a place, a person, or a piece of music which more closely resembles the Kepick figure. Again, work out one or two prose paragraphs. This is to poetry what preliminary sketches are to a finished painting.

The Sound
of Rhyme Here is one sound device which by definition is the exclusive property of poets. Prose may contain scattered rhymes, but only when the composition makes use of prescribed line length can one have a rhyme *scheme* or system.

This is not to suggest, of course, that all poetry makes use of rhyme or even that it should. The choice is up to the poet on the basis of an individual poem. But rhyme is still a primary sound device in a great deal of contemporary verse, so only those poets who have mastered the technique can be sure that they are making a truly free choice. Ignorance in this case is highly limiting.

Definitions of true rhyme can reach levels of incredible complexity. None which I have seen, however, contain more than this three-sentence description: *True rhyme* is an *identity* in *sound* in accented syllables. The identity must begin with the *accented vowel and continue to the end*. The sounds preceding the accented vowel must be *unlike*.

I have italicized the key concepts which seem to give the most trouble. First, we are talking here about true rhyme as opposed to slant rhymes or off rhymes, which are respectable and will be discussed shortly. True rhyme is not a general similarity in sound as are assonance and consonance, but an actual identity. Thus "ru*n*" and "co*me*" are not true rhymes nor are "see*n*" and "crea*m*."

Second, rhyme is a matter of sound, not spelling. "Girl" and "furl" rhyme, but "to read" and "having read" obviously do not. It is often necessary to repeat the final syllable aloud several times before one is sure whether the rhyme is true or not—as do composers when testing the relationship between chords.

Next, there is the matter of continuing identity which must begin with the accented vowel and run through to the end of each word. This is only a problem with two-syllable rhymes (known as feminine rhymes). In "running," for example, the accented vowel is *u* and the only words which rhyme with it end with *unning* as in "sunning."

The word "jumping" has the *u* sound, but the *mp* keeps it from rhyming with "running."

Finally, the sound which comes before that accented vowel must differ from its rhyming partner. Thus, "night" and "fight" rhyme since the accented vowel (*i*) is preceded by *n* in one case and *f* in the other. But "night" and "knight" do not. These are technically known as identities.

Since rhyme, like meter, is based on the sound of syllables and has nothing to do with the division of words, the same principles apply when more than one word is involved in each rhyming end. "Bind me" and "find me" rhyme (the accented vowel is *i* in each case, and the rhyming sound is *ind me*), but neither rhyme with "kindly" because of the *l*.

Rules like these take on the artificiality of grammar when first met, but like grammar they become absorbed once one is used to working with them. An easy way to check each rhyme (and also review the principles of rhyme) is to ask these three questions of each potential rhyme:

1. What is the accented vowel sound?
2. Is the sound in each word identical from that vowel through to the end of each?
3. Is the consonantal sound preceding that vowel different?

These three questions become automatic; one's eye moves first to that key vowel, then forward to the end of each word, then back to the preceding sound. And in each case the eye is translating what is seen into what would be heard if the word were sounded—a fact which makes it almost impossible to work with rhyme without muttering.

It is important to move as rapidly as possible from the rules to application. The best method, of course, is actual composition. But the table on the next page may also provide a way of making unconscious what must begin as conscious effort.

After studying these examples, move as quickly as possible from theory to actual practice. Those who have never worked extensively with rhyme should try some light-hearted lyrics in which rhyme is the primary device. Theodore Roethke's "The Sloth" (p. 112) is a delightful example and can serve as a model. Turn to it now and read it twice, once for enjoyment and once to study the form. Notice that each line has four stressed syllables and that each stanza is made up

RELATED WORDS	ACCENTED VOWEL SOUND	ACTUAL RELATIONSHIP AND EXPLANATION
1. night fight	*i*	True rhyme (meets all three requirements)
2. night knight	*i*	An identity (preceding consonants are identical)
3. ocean motion	*o*	True rhyme (*oean* and *tion* have the same sound)
4. warring wearing	*or* and *air*	Consonance or off rhyme (accented vowel sounds do not match)
5. lyrical miracle	*y*	Off rhyme (the *i* in "lyrical" does not match the *a* sound in "miracle")
6. track to me back to me	*a*	True rhyme (a triple rhyme used by Hardy)
7. dies remedies	*i* and *em*	Eye rhyme (similarity only in spelling)
8. bear bare	*a*	Identity (preceding consonants are identical)
9. balloon hullabaloo	*oo* and *u*	Consonance and assonance (vowel sounds do not match nor do the endings)
10. then you see us; when you flee us	*e*	Quadruple rhyme—true (rare and usually appears forced—often comic)

of three rhyming lines. Examine his rhymes carefully, testing each one with the three-stage analysis described earlier in this chapter.

In writing your own verses, choose some other animal. Don't be ashamed of the fact that you are writing *simple* verse; let yourself go as Roethke did. Work like this should be enjoyable in the writing as well as in the reading. And it is also an excellent way to master the technique of rhyme.

The Rhyme Scheme

as a System in Sound   Most poets who use rhyme use it regularly in a specific rhyme scheme. *Scheme* implies a recurring cycle. And the basic unit of that cycle is the stanza.

Stanzas in general use today vary from two to eight lines, though they occasionally run even longer as in Adrienne Rich's "Like This Together." It is helpful to be able to refer to the seven more common types by name—couplet, triplet, quatrain, quintet, sestet, septet, and octave. Stanzas are also linked with metrical systems (next chapter) and with the structural organization of a poem (Chapter 9), but our concern here is limited to systems of sound.

The *couplet,* of course, offers only one ryhme pattern. If it is to be rhymed at all, it must be in pairs, *aa, bb, cc.* Popular as this was in the eighteenth century, it is only occasionally used today because of the difficulty of muting the sound of the rhyme. It is only a matter of taste, but poets in our own century have tended to keep the sound relationships subtle and unobtrusive.

The *triplet* (also called a *tercet*) is the shortest stanza form which permits a noncontiguous rhyme: *aba, cdc, efe,* and so forth. This also allows the poet to leave one third of his lines unrhymed, further muting the sound. Only very rarely (and usually for a comic effect) is the triplet rhymed *aaa, bbb, ccc* as in "The Sloth."

An effective variation of this stanza form is the *terza rima,* used by Dante, Shelley, and some contemporary poets. In this, each stanza is linked to the next one forming an interlocking rhyme in this fashion: *aba, bcb, cdc,* and so forth.

The *quatrain* is often rhymed in the loose manner of the traditional ballad, *abcb.* Here, only two out of four lines are rhymed, but the form has its origin in a rhyming couplet made up of two unusually long lines. By breaking each line in half (as was natural in reading or singing), the result was a four-lined stanza with the rhymed ending appearing in the second and last line.

More demanding but equally common is *abab.* Rarely are quatrains grouped in pairs, *aabb,* since this retains the obviousness of rhyming couplets.

The *quintet* (or *cinquain*) is an odd-numbered stanza which is sometimes rhymed with a couplet at the end, *ababb.* Although Swinburne's "Hertha" is a fine example, the quintet has not been popular in rhymed verse.

The *sestet* (or *sextet*) is often thought of in connection with the second portion of a sonnet which I will come to later in this chapter. Notice that as the length of the stanza grows, the number of possible rhyme schemes increases at a rapid rate—particularly if you include systems which leave certain lines unrhymed.

The *septet* is famous for the *rhyme royal* which is *ababbcc.* And the *octave* develops this further with the *ottava rima, abababcc.* Notice how both these forms resemble the Elizabethan sonnet in their use of a final rhyming couplet which can be employed as either a summary or a counterpoint to the rest of the stanza.

Rhyme schemes do not, however, have to fit a pattern which has already been made famous. Some poets prefer to let the first stanza of a new poem work out its own rhyme scheme—largely a chance process of finding rhymes. This then becomes the model for the following stanzas. In doing this, it is important to maintain the system through to the end of the poem. Letting a regularly rhymed poem slide into random rhyme at the end gives the impression of being incomplete— like having the left portion of a painting done in oils and the right side left as charcoal sketching.

It is also important to keep in mind just how the rhyme will affect the reader. Contiguous rhymes tend to highlight those lines—particularly when they appear at the end of a stanza. Rhyme endings which are more than three or so lines apart tend to serve only as an unconscious echo for the reader. In Snodgrass's "A Flat One," for example, his sestets are generally rhymed *abbcac*. Where he does not have true rhymes, he allows himself slant rhymes. Lines two and three are clearly linked, but the connection between the first and the fifth remains as a kind of half-heard resonance.

For those who enjoy form, the sonnet offers a real challenge. All sonnets (as we use the word today) consist of fourteen lines, and in all cases we can refer to the first eight as the octave and the last six as the sestet. In the Italian version, one can also think of those fourteen lines as divided into two quatrains and two triplets: *abba, abba; cde, cde*. Another version substitutes a sestet of *cdc, dcd*. The Elizabethan sonnet is often thought of as three quatrains and a final rhyming couplet: *abab, cdcd, efef, gg*. Shifts in mood or tone may come after any of the quatrains or after the octave (as with many Italian sonnets) or as one turns from the final quatrain to that rhyming couplet.

The real pleasure in the sonnet form both for the reader and for the writer lies in that fusing of the form and the content. In reading a sonnet, it helps to mark out where the divisions in mood or attitude come and to see if these coincide with the structural elements of the poem. In writing, such blending of form and statement eventually becomes unconscious. When one experiences the pleasure of this interplay, one has moved from the mechanical assignments many of us recall from the eighth grade to the level of sophisticated and rewarding composition.

Variety in
Sound Devices
The use of rhyme in triplets or even couplets often seems blatant. But this obviousness is not due to the *number* of sound combinations; it is due to their placement and their

lack of variety. In Roethke's "The Sloth," for example, the use of matching sounds occurs only at the ends of lines and never within the line. The device used is always rhyme and never assonance. And to heighten this effect (helping to make it comic rather than merely tedious), he weights each rhyming word by having it a single syllable, stressed, and often capitalized.

Turn now to Snodgrass's "A Flat One" (p. 116) and read once again the opening stanza.

Most readers feel that this sounds less musical, less dominated by rhyme than the light verse sample, "The Sloth." Some readers may even be unaware that the Snodgrass poem is rhymed at all. But the fact is that every line rhymes with another and the same rhyme scheme is maintained throughout all eighteen stanzas.

His rhyme is muted in two ways. First, most rhymed lines are separated from each other. The first line, for example, rhymes with the fifth. The gap is too great for most readers to hear at first reading. It is only an echo. Although the second line rhymes with the third, the most blatant pair, the fourth line is paired with the sixth. As I pointed out earlier, this pattern is *abbcac*.

His second method of muting sound devices is the use of slant rhymes (similar but not identical sounds) and eye rhymes (look alike but sound different). In the first stanza, all but one set of rhyming pairs are true. But in the second, the freest stanza of all eighteen, there is only one true rhyme. "Shut" and "brought" are slant lines and so are "iron" and "turn." The link is through consonance since the final consonantal sounds are the ones which match. There is an eye rhyme in the fourth stanza where "blood" and "food" (also an example of consonance) are placed in the position where he normally has rhyming words.

Notice that while some stanzas contain more variations than others, the general proportion of true rhymes to slant remains more or less constant. There is a tendency among novice poets to begin with a formal rhyme scheme and then, as the hour grows late and enthusiasm wanes, turn to freer and freer verse. Sometimes the defense is made that the theme has become "discordant" or "less structured," but rarely is this convincing. The form a poem begins with—whether metered and rhyming or free—is like a "language" established for the length of that poem. Notice that Snodgrass caps his eighteen stanzas with a final one made up of *all* true rhymes.

Not all rhymes are arranged in regular schemes. Scattered rhymes are often used in metered verse, and Robley Wilson's "On a Maine Beach" (p. 112) is a good example of this. Turn to it now and study the sound linkages in the first four lines.

Only two lines rhyme here, the first with the fourth. And at first reading this doesn't appear to be a repeated pattern. It helps, however, to divide the poem into four "stanzas" of four lines each. The rhyme in the second "stanza" is in the second and third lines—"dumb" and "sum." The next "stanza" takes the same form, but the last one is *abba.*

Read this way, the poem appears to have a scattering of rhymes without any consistent pattern. But if one examines the slant-rhyme endings and adds these to the true rhymes, each "stanza" turns out to be *abba.* The casual reader may only half hear these sound devices, but to the practicing poet they suggest another approach to patterned sound.

Although the rhyme in this poem is far freer than that in the Snodgrass poem, Wilson makes greater use of the other devices of sound. It is more valuable for a reader to pick them out for himself rather than be given a list, so turn now to the first four lines and circle all the samples of alliteration. Then underline examples of assonance.

There are alliterative pairs in lines two, three, and four; and two of these are extended into an alliterative run of three words. Notice that only one pair is contiguous. The others are separated by at least one word and sometimes several. Contiguous alliteration can become highly obtrusive just as rhyming triplets can. Spacing them out tends to mute the effect—again just as spacing rhymed endings does. Of course, if the distance between the alliterative words is too great, the reader will no longer hear it.

Assonance is less precisely defined. In the first line, for example, there is a cluster of *o* sounds which are similar but in no case really the same. "Look, in these pools, how rocks are like worn change / Keeping the ocean's. . . ." Abstracting these sounds, we have *ook, ool, ock, orn, oh*—a wide range of related sounds which the English language designates with the letter *o.* There is no precise division between assonance and that broader association of sounds referred to earlier in this chapter as "secondary relationships" or "sound clusters." But regardless of terminology, it is clear that there are more linkages in sound here than in the more formally rhymed poem by Snodgrass.

A third approach to sound in poetry ignores rhyme altogether and depends entirely on assonance, consonance, and alliteration. One example is seen in the prose selection from Dylan Thomas's "August Bank Holiday" quoted at the beginning of this chapter. For a poetic version of the same approach, turn now to Thomas's "Fern Hill" on page 118. Mark the sound devices in the first stanza.

Although Thomas does not use rhyme here, he employs either assonance or alliteration in every line except the third, and several have two pairs in a single line. The best way to appreciate subtle sound relationships like this is to read each stanza three times, once out loud merely for the pleasure of it; once slowly and analytically, marking each sound device; and a final time for pleasure again. This way, one combines that subjective response which should go into the reading of any poem with the analysis which is necessary if one wishes to understand its inner workings.

Composing

For Sound   The four examples used in this chapter represent four different points on a spectrum. At one end is doggerel with its dependence on unvaried rhyme. The other three are progressively freer. Snodgrass in "A Flat One" uses a regular rhyme scheme which is consciously muted. Wilson in "On a Maine Beach" mutes his rhymes still further, and Thomas, who normally rhymes his work, avoids it altogether in "Fern Hill." When a poet is able to use any of these approaches, he can allow the poem itself to suggest a form. To argue which is "better" is as pointless as it would be for painters to debate whether to use broad or narrow brush strokes.

In order to achieve this freedom of choice, many beginning poets find it helpful to imitate the sound devices of a particular poet or even a specific poem. There is nothing dishonest in this as long as one doesn't publish it as original work. Each of the examples referred to in this chapter could be used in this way, and they are varied enough to give a good range of skills. A second method of practice is to develop the same subject matter in two different poems, each with a different style. A third is to begin with a sound-packed stanza of, say, five or six lines, and then attempt to develop the poem with stanzas which repeat the same form. Notice that both "A Flat One" and "Fern Hill" are closely guided by the pattern established in the first stanza.

Sound, of course, is not the only concern in the composition of a poem; it is merely one important element. But composing primarily for sound is often a rewarding way for a novice to begin. It serves, first, as a reminder of how much a poet depends on his ear. Equally important, it may help him to discover that the act of poetic composition does not have to be an agonizing attempt to solve the world's problems. It can be a pleasure.

4

RHYTHMS
OF STRESS

Rhythm as a psychological need in humans; *stress* as one method of achieving rhythm in language; *meter* as a development of stress with the addition of metrical *feet* and metered *lines;* the value of *staying loose* with metrics; the reasons for the *continuing popularity* of meter.

Rhythm is a surprisingly basic need in human beings. Some babies thump their cribs rhythmically long before they are introduced to language. Children throughout the world adopt traditional schoolyard chants long before they are introduced to sophisticated poetry. And adults who do not enjoy contemporary poetry usually complain that it lacks the rhythmical patterns they are used to.

Rhythm is found in all kinds of writing—often where one least expects it. In Harold Pinter's plays, for example, there is a rhythm in the silences. And in those dull legislative resolutions which introduce each clause with "Whereas..." and end with a traditional, "Therefore let it be resolved..." there is a rhythm of syntax which is as old as the Old Testament and as new as Ferlinghetti and Allen Ginsberg.

It is poetry, however, which lays special claim on verbal rhythms. This is partly due to the close affinity between poetry and music. It is significant that the word *lyric* has its roots in *lyre* and that even today the word *verse* is used interchangeably for metered poetry and lines to be sung. This is no mere historical accident. Poetry makes fuller use of verbal rhythms than fiction or prose drama mainly because the poet is able to maintain control over the length of the line he writes. As we shall see, all meter is based on the length of the line, and most free verse systems of rhythm also rely heavily upon this control.

The study of rhythm should never be thought of as a constricting or limiting aspect of writing. There are six widely used methods of creating rhythmical patterns in English and an infinite number of variations possible within each. Some are fairly simple to master, and others (like meter) require learning certain terms. But those who have at least tried all approaches are then free to choose their own individual style, and this freedom is for most poets extremely important.

Rhythm of Stress

English is a language of stress. That is, most words in our language are pronounced with a heavier emphasis on one syllable than on the others. So important are these stresses that in some cases an error in stress alone makes the word unpronounceable —much to the frustration of foreign students.

This is in sharp contrast with French. Take the words *animal* and *nation,* for example. Although they are spelled the same way in each language, English places a special stress on the first syllable of each word, *an*imal and *na*tion. In French, on the other hand, there is a tendency to place more nearly even weight on each syllable, particularly in verse.

Partly because of this factor, French poets began early with a complex set of rhythmical systems based on the division of syllables, while the Old English poets merely counted the number of stresses in a line. *Beowulf,* for example, is based on a line containing two stressed syllables, a pause, and two more stresses. No attention was paid to the number of unstressed syllables. By French standards, this was a rather crude system of composing verse.

Here is a passage where Beowulf pursues the sea monster down into her underwater lair. Read the selection a couple of times and underline the stresses.

> Then bore this brine-wolf, when bottom she touched,
> the lord of rings to the lair she haunted,
> whiles vainly he strove, though his valor held,
> weapon to wield against wondrous monster
> that sore beset him; sea-beasts many
> tried with fierce tusks to tear his mail

It is obvious that the poet never counted syllables. He was concerned only with having four stresses in each line. He concentrated on this simple beat, and in *Beowulf* it is so clear that one can pound on the table while the song is chanted or sung—which is probably just what the ancients did.

Notice, in passing, how alliteration was often used to emphasize those stressed syllables: "Then *b*ore this *b*rine-wolf, when *b*ottom she touched."

This is a simple system of rhythm. A much more subtle (and literarily *sophisticated*) use of stress was developed by Gerard Manley Hopkins. Like the poet of *Beowulf,* he based his rhythms on the spoken language, usually with a given number of stresses per line. He often paid no attention to the number of unstressed syllables, calling his method "sprung rhythm" in the sense of "freed rhythm."

Turn to his "Pied Beauty" on page 113. For a comparison with the *Beowulf* passage, underline what you feel are the four stressed words in each line, and circle words which are emphasized with alliteration. There is a sample on every line!

Hopkins, writing in the late nineteenth century, was both a link with the past in this respect and also an innovator for the twentieth century, because systems of stress have become popular with many contemporary poets.

From Stress to Meter

Historically, meter came to English verse when French was imposed on Anglo-Saxon after the Norman invasion. And it has been here ever since. From a writer's point of view, the real significance of this is that meter is a rhythmical system which combines the simple concept of stresses with a more subtle system of identifying groups of stressed and unstressed syllables. These groups are called *feet*. And since a metrical foot is made up of either two or three syllables, there are only four basic types in general use.

The *iamb* is the most popular foot in English. It consists of an unstressed syllable and a stressed one, ta-*tum*. Many two-syllable verbs fall naturally into this pattern: ex*cept,* al*low,* dis*rupt,* ad*ore;* and there is a tendency for sentences and lines of verse to begin with an unstressed syllable. Notice in the selection from *Beowulf,* which is not written to any meter, that most lines begin with an unstressed syllable: "Then bore...," "the lord...," "that sore...."

The *trochee* is simply the reverse of the iamb, *tum*-ta. Since the metrical system is determined from the beginning of each line, position is all-important. "The lord of rings" is clearly two iambic feet (ta-*tum* ta-*tum*); but we can shift these to trochees by starting the line with a stressed syllable: "Lord of rings and master" (*tum*-ta *tum*-ta *tum*-ta).

The stress in these cases is based on normal speaking patterns. Notice how if we shift the natural stress in "the lord" to "*the* lord" by adding italics, we actually change the meaning.

Trochees can be used as the basic foot for an entire poem. But more often they are used as a substitution for an iambic foot in an iambic poem. As we shall see, this can give a special emphasis to a word or phrase particularly if it is done at the beginning of a line.

The other two feet each consist of three syllables. The *anapest* has two unstressed syllables followed by a stressed syllable, as in "disap*point*" and "lower *down*." The *dactyl* is the reverse of this, as seen in "*hap*pily," "*mer*rily," and "*sing* to me."

These basic four feet are common enough so that familiarity with them is sufficient to scan (analyze and classify) almost any sample of metered verse in English and related languages. And they provide enough flexibility for the poet to do almost anything he wishes without knowing some of the thirty other combinations used by classical poets. Conscientious scanning occasionally requires familiarity with the *spondee*—two equally stressed syllables, as in "heartbreak"—and the *pyrrhic foot*—two equally unstressed syllables, such as "in the" or "but the"; but the practicing poet normally reads these as softened versions of iambs or trochees.

As review, the table on the next page shows the four basic metrical feet, with the stress pattern and examples of each.

In addition to the types of feet, there is the matter of how many feet are used in each line. By far the most popular length in English is five feet, known as pentameter. Unrhymed iambic pentameter,

TYPE OF FOOT	ADJECTIVE	STRESS PATTERN	EXAMPLES
iamb	iambic	ta-*tum*	except; she might
trochee	trochaic	*tum*-ta	Midas; lost it
anapest	anapestic	ta-ta-*tum*	disappoint; lower down
dactyl	dactylic	*tum*-ta-ta	happily; sing to me

known as blank verse, was Shakespeare's favorite form; pentameter is also the line used in the sonnet; more recently, Frost and such younger poets as X. J. Kennedy have made extensive use of this line.

The four-footed line, tetrameter, is a close second. And trimeter is also used widely. Lines which are longer than pentameter and shorter than trimeter are used far less frequently, but for the purpose of clarity, here is a list of types:

One foot to each line (very rare)   *monometer*
Two feet to each line (rare and usually comic)   *dimeter*
Three feet to each line (fairly common)   *trimeter*
Four feet (sometimes combined with trimeter)   *tetrameter*
Five feet (most common in English)   *pentameter*
Six feet (less used in this century)   *hexameter*
Seven feet (rare)   *heptameter*
Eight feet (a heavy, very rare line)   *octometer*

Doggerel often provides a good example of simple, unvaried meter. In fact, it is this lack of variation which often adds to the humor. This is certainly the case in "The Sloth" (p. 112). For practice mark the stresses and the divisions between the feet, following this model:

In móv|ĭng slów |hĕ hás |nŏ Péer.

A poem like this serves well as a basic example of meter just as it did for rhyme. And at this point, it would be helpful to try about eight lines of rhyming, unvaried iambic tetrameter. Then, forgetting the rhyme, shift the meter to trochaic tetrameter ("Moving slowly is his habit," for example). Next, shifting the topic, perhaps, to something lighter, try a few lines of anapests like, "In a leap and a bound, the gazelle in delight welcomes spring!"

Most writers find the iamb the easiest to work with. The trochee has added punch, thanks to that initial stress in each line. The anapest usually has a lilting quality. And the dactyl, least used of the three, tends to have some of the heavy quality of a trochee and the length of an anapest.

Iambs and anapests are similar in that they both end on a stressed syllable. This is called *falling meter*. Trochees and dactyls, on the other hand, end on unstressed syllables and therefore are *rising meters*. This becomes an important distinction when one begins to use substitutions for variety and special effects.

Staying Loose
with Metrics   Until now, I have been working only with skeletal outlines. They may appear to be as far from the actual creation of lyrical poetry as the study of notes and clefs appear to be from musical composition. But the process of absorption is similar in these two cases. What appears at first to be a set of arbitrary rules eventually becomes—even for those who may then depart from them—an internalized influence.

There are three widespread misconceptions about meter which have to be cleared away before one can use metrics effectively. The first is the belief that a strong metrical beat is somehow a primary goal. In point of fact, most poets try to mute their metrics. The second is that meter to be "good" must be unvaried. Actually, about the only samples of contemporary meter which are unvaried turn out to be doggerel. Finally, there is the belief that meter is the key to reading the finished poem. In most cases, however, it is used only as an underlying rhythm or a kind of counterpoint to the normal pace of reading.

Strong, unvaried meter is still found in greeting-card verse and in doggerel. But when it is serious, it is to the rhythms of sophisticated meter what a Sousa military march is to a Bach concerto.

Turn now to W. D. Snodgrass's "A Flat One" (p. 116) and try scanning the first stanza, marking each foot as you did for "The Sloth." Remember that you are looking for a general pattern, and it may take a few tries before you find the basic foot and line length of the poem as a whole. If one line seems particularly difficult, you may wish to compare it with the corresponding line of other stanzas.

A careful reading of the poem reveals that the basic meter is iambic tetrameter. But it is clear that the impact of his meter has been consciously muted. One rather unusual method of muffling the regularity of the beat is to have a more-or-less regular variation in the length of the last two lines of each stanza: the fifth line has five feet, pentameter; and the sixth has only two or three feet. He signals these changes by regularly indenting these lines differently.

A second and more common method of varying the meter is substitution. In almost every line he substitutes some other type of foot for at least one of the iambs. In the first stanza, for example, there is only one line of unvaried iambic tetrameter: "For seven wasted months you lay." The third line contains a trochaic substitution and an incomplete final foot: "Unfit to move, shrunken, gray." Here "*shrunk*en" is highlighted by arranging it as a trochee. And "gray" is given additional weight by allowing it to stand alone.

Often this system of trochaic substitution is used at the beginning of a line where the unexpected initial stress has the effect of underlining the word or writing it in capital letters. Snodgrass uses this device twice in the final stanza:

> ... and so we kept
> You; because we need to earn *our* pay.
> No. We'd still have to help you try. We would
> Have killed for you today.

The stress here on "you" and "no" is achieved partly by the use of dactyls and partly by the syntactical trick of having the sentence end after the first word of each line.

There are two other methods of muting the regularity of meter. One is by using *run-on lines*. A run-on line (not to be confused with a run-on sentence) is one in which both the grammatical construction and the sense are continued directly to the next line. It is opposed to the *end-stopped* line in which there is a natural pause—usually the end of a sentence. Line 8 is a true run-on:

> We set pads on your bedsores, shut
> Your catheter tube off ...

Line 5 ends with a period and is a true end-stopped line. Most stanzas end this way, but occasionally a poet may wish to thrust the reader forward into the next. Turn to the poem again and notice the difference between the endings of the first, third, and fourth stanzas on the one hand and the ending of the second stanza on the other.

There are many degrees between a true run-on and an end-stopped line. These often consist of slight pauses such as those at the ends of clauses or phrases.

The final method of placing the meter in perspective is by reducing the number of words which are in themselves iambic feet. Even in lines of unvaried iambs, splitting words between two feet softens the regular beat. Notice the difference between these two selections, each of which is unvaried iambic tetrameter:

> And then, before he says a Word
> There, upside down (unlike a Bird)

> Old man, these seven months you've lain
> Determined—not that you would live—

If the first draft of a poem seems too regular, too "sing-songy" and monotonous, these are four different ways to create interest and variations without destroying the meter. Careless or arbitrary substitutions will begin to make the poem sound just that: careless and arbitrary. And excessive variations (particularly using lines of different length) will cause the reader to lose the beat completely. It takes time to create meter which is subtle and effective.

In spite of the effort it takes, meter is about as popular today as are the various methods of free verse rhythms which are described in the next chapter. Editors, of course, have their preferences, and sometimes studying one particular collection will seem to indicate that all younger poets are in one camp or the other. Thus Donald Hall's *New Poets of England and America*—both first and second selections—is dominated by poets working with meter. *A Controversy of Poets* (Paris Leary and Robert Kelly) and *The New American Poetry* (Donald Allen) tend toward varieties of free verse. These are all excellent collections, but they ignore the fact that meter and free verse systems are equally popular today.

There are several reasons for the continuing use of meter; two can be most easily understood by an analogy with music. First, it is difficult to have variations on a theme if there is no theme. When, for example, a jazz group (or a single instrument) begins to depart freely from a well-known melody, those who know the tune are actually listening to two compositions: the original melody (which may be only touched on from time to time) and the variations. In metered verse, the meter is like the original melody which runs in the background; the actual rhythms of the spoken poem may serve as a counterpoint from time to time, and periodically the work will return to the familiar. It does, of course, require knowing the original version if one is to appreciate the work fully.

The other reason meter remains popular has to do with achieving emphasis. In a metered poem, certain types of departure from the basic structure can, as we have seen, place emphasis on a particular word, a phrase, or an entire line. True, one can underline words or use multiple exclamation marks as young girls often do in correspondence. Or one can use some of the more sophisticated devices of free verse. But for many poets, there is a subtle freedom in being able to highlight a word simply by casting it as an initial trochee, or adding a lilt to a phrase by making it an anapest, or shouting a particular line in each stanza by regularly making it shorter.

Seen in this way, meter is not some external system added to a poem; it is a method of composition, a way of making the poem do more than it could have otherwise.

5

RHYTHMS
OF FREE VERSE

Using *typography* to establish rhythms; *syntactical rhythms* of Whitman and others; *syllabics,* the counting of syllables; *breath units;* methods of *developing a facility* in the full range of rhythmical techniques.

Free verse abandons meter for other rhythmical devices and it avoids regular rhyme in favor of looser sound systems. But it is not a revolution in poetry. It is not even new. It is a continuing tradition with some of its roots reaching back to the verse of the Bible.

Essentially, it refers to all those methods of creating rhythmical patterns which are *not* based on stress and meter. It is essential to remember that *free verse* does not suggest the absence of rhythm; it is merely the use of other rhythmical systems.

There are in general use today four ways of creating free verse rhythms: typography, syntax, syllabics, and breath units. It is important to remember, however, that varied as these are, they do not represent separate, unrelated systems. They are often used in conjunction with each other.

There is a tendency for novice poets to establish a personal "style"

47

by adopting a single rhythmical system and staying with it. Accomplished poets, however, usually vary their method from poem to poem so that the requirements of a particular work, not the limitations of the poet, become the determining factors. Dylan Thomas, for example, was equally at home with rhymed meter and alliterative syllabics. Once again, familiarity with a wide range of methods gives the poet the artistic freedom he needs.

Using
Typography

This method of creating rhythmical effects is not strictly a matter of sound. Since it depends heavily on how the poem looks on the printed page, it is often called visual rhythm. But actually there is no clear separation between visual and auditory rhythms. The way a poem is arranged on the page is going to effect a reading in some way. *Typography,* then, refers to the arrangement of words on the page, but it is linked closely with the sound of a poem.

Before considering the varieties of effects which are possible, read E. E. Cummings's "Buffalo Bill's" on page 121. Go through it once or twice for pleasure. Then study it carefully, looking for the ways in which he controls the speed of your reading and provides elements of surprise.

There are two ways in which Cummings appears to speed up one's reading of this poem: by running words together and by using long, fairly uncluttered lines which can be read as fast as prose. In some cases, however, this may only be an illusion of speed—particularly in the first reading. It often takes longer to puzzle out lines which are printed without spaces. But once one is used to the poem, these lines seem to ripple by as if they were moving.

>   and break onetwothreefourfive pigeonsjustlikethat
>   Jesus
>   he was a handsome man

Here the word "Jesus" appears to be linked syntactically with Buffalo Bill's shooting ability; but then it leaps forward to become linked with how handsome he was. It is essentially a visual trick, tripping our expectations through an unexpected shift in rhythm. Of course, the same device of syntactical ambiguity can be used in metered verse, but the effect is heightened here by literally hanging the word between the two lines.

Notice, too, the way he uses line length. In many cases it is clear that he has kept a line short to highlight a certain phrase or even a word. But remember that one cannot find a rational explanation for every typographical element. Like the brush strokes of a painter, a majority of decisions which go into a poem are intuitive.

Occasionally, typography becomes the major ingredient of a poet's style. Turn to Robert Creeley's "The Language" on page 111 and consider the advantages and disadvantages to the extraordinarily short lines he uses.

This is a tricky little poem in which the phrase "I love you" is used as a single entity as if it were something which could be "located" in the body or in our minds. Thus, a phrase, a part of "language," becomes a metaphor for love to be seized wherever one can find it. In the second half of the poem, love (using the same metaphor) fills the "emptiness" which occurs when one is not in love in the same way words (or a poem) fill a silence. With verbal ingenuity like that, one can argue that typographical brevity—lines no longer than three words —helps the reader follow the poem. Creeley urges the reader to take the poem in small "bites," piece by piece.

There is nothing wrong with this explanation. But it is also true that using short lines running down the page like this has been for a number of years one of Robert Creeley's stylistic preferences. Just as Cummings's work is often scattered across the page, Creeley's clings to the left column. Both men produced a great variety of verse, but the work of each is usually identifiable merely by the typography.

One extreme form of typography is the "shaped poem" which molds the shape of the work into the object it is describing. This was particularly popular in the seventeenth century and is well illustrated by Herbert's "The Altar" and "Easter Wings," as well as by Herrick's "The Pillar of Flame," each of which resembles the object suggested in its title. More recently, contemporaries like Allen Ginsberg have published poems in the shape of atomic clouds and, with the aid of punctuation, rockets. And certain painters have moved in from the other end, arranging the letters in a single word like *LOVE* as their composition. Here, of course, the written word becomes painting just as, in the case of the chant, it becomes a form of music.

Where are the limits to what one can do with typography? They are not, as some think, in tradition. As we have seen, some of the most experimental work is now more than three hundred years old. But there are limitations within the form itself. As a poem begins to rely more and more on visual shape, it generally becomes less and less concerned with sound devices, rhythmical systems, and even metaphorical language. It is as if concern for the visual composition drains all other aspects. The most extreme experiments in shaped poetry are remembered for their curiosity value rather than their literary worth.

Even nonpictorial use of typography has its internal limitations. Sophisticated poetry depends at least in part on maintaining unity and flow—concerns which I will return to in Chapter 9. As one increases the rearrangement of words and lines on the page, the poem becomes proportionally fragmented and, as a result, less of an organically unified work.

The use of typography, therefore, continues to be a part of the poetic tradition, but it has its own set of limitations.

Syntactical

Rhythms In essence, syntactical rhythm is merely the patterning which one achieves through the sentence structure itself. It is one device which poetry shares with prose. Here elements of the sentence—grammatical units—are arranged to create relationships. This is not strictly visual rhythm—one can respond to it without seeing the work on the page; but it is not rhythm of sound either—unlike meter it cannot be detected by one who does not know the language. This last sentence, by the way, is an example of syntactical rhythm in prose which can be described as: "statement—amplification; but second statement—amplification." Note that this involves both meaning and grammatical sequence.

Walt Whitman made full and varied use of syntactical rhythms. Here is a sample from his "Passage to India":

> Ah who shall soothe these feverish children?
> Who justify these restless explorations?
> Who speak the secret of impassive earth?
> Who bind it to us? what is this separate Nature so unnatural?
> What is this earth to our affections? . . .

This is rhythm by syntactical repetition. The repetition of the word "who" is only a cue; the full interrelationship among these quoted lines has to do with the echo of each question with the one which precedes it. The key verbs are "soothe," "justify," "speak," "bind," and "is." One can see from these highly varied verbs that the *statement* is not repetitious; it is only the *form*. Whitman has replaced rhythm of metrical units with rhythm of grammatical units.

Allen Ginsberg wrote "Howl" in 1959, one hundred and four years after Whitman first published "Leaves of Grass," and his indebtedness is clear. Here is a sample:

who broke down crying in white gymnasiums naked* and trembling before the machinery of other skeletons,
who bit detectives in the neck and shrieked with delight in police-cars for committing no crime but their own wild cooking pederasty and intoxication,
who howled on their knees in the subways and were dragged off the roof waving genitals and manuscripts
who let themselves be ... in the ... by saintly motorcyclists, and screamed with joy. . . .

Ginsberg is clearly influenced by Whitman, but both of them drew on a still earlier source, the Bible. Although Whitman's version was in English, the King James translation, and Ginsberg's was in the original Hebrew, both men were strongly influenced by the rhythmical patterns found there. Compare, for example, the selections quoted from these two poets with this passage from *Job* 38: 34:

Canst thou lift up thy voice to the clouds,
    that abundance of waters may cover thee?
Canst thou send lightnings, that they may go
    and say unto thee, Here we are?
Who hath put wisdom in the inward parts?
    or who hath given understanding to the heart?
Who can number the clouds in wisdom?
    or who can stay the bottles of heaven,

Here too, it is the entire syntactical unit which is repeated to achieve the rhythm. The repeated words are merely cues which signal the repeated form. For further examples, read over the rest of the *Book of Job* and review *The Psalms*. Then go back and study the enormously complex system of syntactical rhythms in *Genesis*. Doing this makes one far more open to the rhythms not only of Whitman and Ginsberg but Ferlinghetti, Gregory Corso, John Ashbery, LeRoi Jones, and many others writing today.

After one has absorbed a variety of samples—ancient, nineteenth century, and contemporary—one is ready to try the form. It may help to select some topic about which one feels strongly since the chant-like aspect seems to lend itself to moods of indignation, rage, exultation, and derision.

Start with a strong line which has some complexity and length. Then try to match the syntactical form in the second and third lines.

At this point, shift the sentence pattern and repeat this one or two more times. The poem might then be rounded out with a seventh line which returns to the pattern of the first. The variations, of course, are endless. One is bounded only by these two extremes: a lack of rhythm which is so complete that the piece becomes fragmentary (and therefore *simple*) prose; and on the other hand a regularity of rhythm which becomes monotonous and sounds like a childish (and literarily *simple*) chant.

Syllabics
and Breath Units
The two systems of creating rhythm which were discussed in the previous chapter, stress and meter, are closely related. Meter is both a refinement and an elaboration of stress. And the two rhythmical systems already discussed in this chapter, typography and syntax, are also closely linked. They are often used in conjunction with each other. These next two systems, however, are in no way related to each other. They are the "et cetera" in this list of six methods of creating verbal rhythms.

Syllabics, quite simply, involves counting syllables. A haiku is a simple form of syllabics since its definition calls for lines of five, seven, and five syllables in that order. More sophisticated forms of syllabics create a pattern in the first stanza which is then followed in each of the succeeding ones. Thus, the first lines of each stanza match in number of syllables regardless of the number of words or stresses, and the second lines match, and so forth.

The effect is highly muted. Often one is only aware that there is a certain similarity between one stanza and the next. In reading "Fern Hill," for example, it is clear that each stanza has lines of varying length and that the poem is not based on a unified metrical system. Only a close analysis reveals that Thomas has maintained an internal order by imposing a tight system of syllabics. Counting syllables in each stanza reveals this pattern (italics indicate the variations):

1st stanza: 14,14, 9, 6, 9, *15*,14, 7, 9
2nd   ″   : 14,14, 9, 6, 9, 14,14, 7, 9
3rd   ″   : 14,14, 9, 6, 9, 14,14, *9, 6*
4th   ″   : 14,14, 9, 6, 9, 14,14, *9, 6*
5th   ″   : 14,14, 9, 6, 9, 14,14, *9, 6*
6th   ″   : 14,14, 9, 6, 9, 14,*15*, 7, 9

Notice how regular his syllable count is. Even his variations take on a certain order. And this in a poem which on first reading appears to be a free, lilting lyric without form.

But the structure is no mere trick. Each stanza becomes an echo of the others, and often the phrases or specific images in one line match or are contrasted with those in the corresponding line of the following stanza. The second lines of each stanza, for instance, match unvaryingly in numbers of syllables and each serves to announce the scene for that stanza: the "lilting house," the "happy yard," the "fields," and so forth. In this way the form is wedded to the content. In reading the poem we are given the *sense* of structure even though the mechanics of the form are not immediately apparent.

Breath units are about the loosest form of rhythm in poetry today. Essentially, the poet breaks the line at that point where he expects the reader to take a breath. Poets like Charles Olson who defend this approach argue that it emphasizes the oral aspect of verse and provides greater freedom for the poet. Others feel that the lack of structure reduces the range of effects possible and thus is actually restrictive.

Developing a
Facility in Rhythm   I have urged that the reader work with each type of rhythmical system as he progresses, combining technical familiarity with practice. The two must be constantly blended to achieve a real understanding.

A second approach is to take a single work and convert it into various rhythmical systems, both those of stress and those of free verse. By working with all rhythmical systems in this way, one is reminded that there is no "right" approach. The goal is to find what rhythmical system is appropriate and effective for a particular poem.

Take, for example, these first four lines from Shakespeare's "Sonnet 2."

> When forty winters shall besiege thy brow
> And dig deep trenches in thy beauty's field,
> Thy youth's proud livery so gazed on now,
> Will be a tattered weed of small worth held.

This sample of iambic pentameter is unusual in that there is not one substitution. For this reason, it serves as a fine base for rhythmical doodling. One might begin, for example, by converting it to iambic trimeter. There are many ways of doing this, but here is one:

> When forty winters shall
> Besiege thy brow and dig
> Deep trenches in thy face
> Thy youth's proud livery
> Will be a worthless weed.

The point of this exercise is not to improve on Shakespeare but to improve one's own ability to work with meter and one's inner *sense* of pentameter and trimeter. Line-length conversions are easy; shifting from iambic to trochaic requires a little more effort. It might come out like this:

> Forty winters shall besiege thy lovely
> Brow and dig deep trenches in thy beauty's
> Field and youth's proud livery loved so fully
> Soon will be a tattered weed of little worth.

The perceptive reader will notice that I have slurred "livery," a three-syllable word, to "liv'ry," two syllables; I also allowed an extra stressed syllable at the end of the fourth line. If this reader is also a poet, perhaps he can devise a more perfect rendering.

Moving from meter to visual rhythm, any number of translations might be tried. Here is one sample:

> When forty winters shall
>   besiege
>   starve
>   torment
> The rounded beauty of your brow,
>   then
> Your light step will
>   limp
>   pause
>   trembling before the last descent.

This, of course, verges on syntactical rhythm in that "shall" is followed by a series just as "will" is; but the relationships are high-lighted by typography. If we shift to almost purely syntactical concerns, we might come out with something like this:

> Now your youth's proud livery
>   is our envy
> Now your smile's light courage
>   is our delight.
> But then some forty years will
>   wear you threadbare

And then your darkened eyes will
    show our fear.

All of this doodling requires enough terminology to see what one is doing and to describe what one has done. But with surprisingly little technical training, one is ready for both the reading and the composition which is essential if one is to feel at home with varieties of rhythm. Since almost all poetry contains rhythmical patterns of some sort, every anthology and little magazine serves as a source for study. It takes both extensive reading and random experimentation before rhythm in poetry ceases to be a burden and becomes—often with surprising speed—one of the most liberating aspects of the genre.

6

IMAGES

The *image* defined; images of *sight* as the dominant
type; *sound* images; images of *touch, smell,* and *taste;*
images used in *figures of speech,* including *similes* and
metaphors; the use of *symbol;* a *schematic view* of
imagery; *thinking* in images.

In its purest sense, an image in poetry is any significant
piece of sense data. Although we tend to think of images as objects
seen, the term also covers sounds heard, textures felt, odors smelled,
and objects tasted.

As I pointed out in Chapter 2, sense perception is a major source
of poetic creation. For this reason alone, the image becomes one of
the most significant elements in the construction of a poem. But images
are also the foundation of similes, metaphors, puns, hyperbole, and
other types of figurative language as well as symbolic suggestion.

Because the term *imagery* is used so frequently in conjunction with
similes and metaphors, it is sometimes taken to be a synonym for
figurative language. In this text, however, *image* is used to mean any
unit of sense experience regardless of whether it is employed literally,
figuratively, or symbolically.

Images, then, tend to be concrete nouns or phrases which are readily identifiable through the senses. Much depends on how specific they are. "Bird," for example, is an image and "crow" a sharper one; but a vague term like "thing" is not. "Babbling brook" is an auditory image and also a cliché; "the stream's small talk" is a fresher image. "The sounds of nature" is not, nor is "the clutter of city noises." "A rotting fish" is a highly odoriferous image, but neither "odoriferous" nor even "stink" is.

Images
of Sight

Of the five senses, sight is by far the most popular for the poet. This is natural enough when one realizes how much human beings depend on their ability to see. Blindness is a more severe loss than deafness, and the loss of touch, smell, and taste are mild oddities not even honored with words in common usage. When we understand something, we say, "I see"; and if we are baffled, we are "left in the dark."

Our language gives us far more subdivisions in the area of sight than any of the other senses. We may speak of intensity (brilliant, bright, dull, dark), color (red, blue, aqua), shape (organic or geometric, the latter with many subdivisions), and we have a particular name for almost every object seen. This may not seem so remarkable until one contrasts it with the limited vocabulary with which we describe sounds. There are a few specific terms like "whistle," "bang," "crack," and "sigh," but soon we turn to similies such as "like a song," "like a screech owl." And smells, even lower on our scale, are almost wholly described by association. It is only from whimsy or frustration with the language that we refer to "a blue smell" or a "round smell"; even such distinct odors as oil or flowers do not have words separate from the object that produces it.

Returning from the psychology of perception to the use of images, we can see how natural it is for the poet to seize upon something seen as the core of a particular work. Often it is a specific place which the poet knows well. One famous example is Wordsworth's "Tintern Abbey." The full title of that poem is "Lines Composed a Few Miles Above Tintern Abbey, on Revisiting the Banks on the Wye During a Tour." This is rarely remembered even in oral examinations, but it does indicate how heavily the poet depended on a specific place not only for the original conception but for the development of the poem. Clearly he did not start with such abstract conceptions as "tranquil restoration" or "holier love" or even "Nature." He began, simply, by revisiting the banks of a river called the Wye.

Although the poem is too long to be included here in its entirety, it is widely anthologized and is worth a review not only for Wordsworth's use of visual details, but also for his comments about the effect on a poem (or on any sensitive individual) of familiar places remembered in absence. What one recalls, he suggests, is not merely the physical details which one could report to others in descriptive prose, but a wide range of subtle sensations which require a highly sophisticated language, poetry, to evoke. He is particularly interested in how the unconscious recall of "unremembered pleasure" can have an influence on one's memory—and on one's poem. Here is how he puts it:

> ...These beauteous forms,
> Through a long absence, have not been to me
> As is a landscape to a blind man's eye:
> But oft, in lonely rooms, and 'mid the din
> Of towns and cities, I have owed to them,
> In hours of weariness, sensations sweet,
> Felt in the blood, and felt along the heart;
> And passing even into my purer mind,
> With tranquil restoration:—feelings too
> Of unremembered pleasure: such, perhaps,
> As have no slight or trivial influence
> On that best portion of a good man's life

These lines serve as an effective introduction to a more recent example of poetic recall, "Fern Hill." In these scenes from his childhood, Dylan Thomas recalls the house, the groves at night ("dingle starry"), the apple orchard, fields of daisies, streams, stables, the night sky, and a dazzling array of minor details. It is rich in overtones which suggest what Wordsworth described as "those unremembered pleasures." And the danger of sentimentality (always present in poems recalling childhood) is cut at the very end of the poem with that stark reminder than even in the freedom of one's early years one is bound by mortality.

> Time held me green and dying
> Though I sang in my chains like the sea.

The use of place, of course, does not have to be rooted in a rural scene. Sandburg's "Chicago" describes that city as the "Hog Butcher for the World"—a strong visual image. Hart Crane's "To Brooklyn

Bridge" makes complex use of its mechanical image, and William Carlos Williams makes full use of an unlikely poetic topic in "Paterson, New Jersey."

More recently, Watts, Chicago's South Side, and Harlem have become sources of strong visual impressions for black American poets like Lucy Smith ("Face of Poverty"), David Henderson ("Sketches of Harlem"), and the prolific LeRoi Jones. Included in this text is Conrad Kent Rivers's "The Still Voice of Harlem (p. 120). In this poem, Harlem is personified and becomes the speaker, calling out to "the glory of fruitless souls."

When one uses the countryside or an entire city as one's source of visual images, one is painting with broad strokes. Another approach is to take some minute scene and to see in it universal implications. This is called describing the macrocosm (universe) through a microcosm (world in miniature). Robley Wilson's "On a Maine Beach" (p. 112) is a fine example of this approach. The visual images are drawn from a close-up examination of a rock pool in which barnacles, snails, and "groves of weed" become the images which help us to understand the broadest cycles of life—including our own.

It should be clear from these varied examples that poets are almost as dependent on visual patterns as are photographers. And also like photographers they can choose whether they will use a wide lens or a microscopic one.

Still another approach to visual imagery is what one might call episodic. Here the poet shifts rapidly from one scene to the next as if presenting a series of slide projections. This is essentially what Adrienne Rich does in "Like This Together." Turn to it now (p. 113) and notice how each of the first four stanzas is given a different setting. After identifying the scene, pick out the specific visual images which help the reader to "see" it.

This poem moves from the intensely visual to the speculative. The stanzas are increasingly less dependent on a scene. But notice that separate visual images are still employed in the last two stanzas.

Another approach is using visual fragments. Rather than developing a single scene or an experience, the poet compiles a series of details which he presents in rapid sequences sometimes like a slide projector gone wild. Much of Ginsberg's work is like this, and the excerpt from "Howl" (p. 51) is a good example. Study it again and see how abrupt and violent each scene is. Further examples of this style can be seen in the works of men like Gregory Corso, John Ashbery, and Frank O'Hara.

Images
of Sound
Sound images are far less used than sight, but they are extraordinarily effective both in the development of a poem and in its inception. Frost's "Mowing" is a good example. Note how five of the following six lines make use of the single image of a scythe's sound.

> There was never a sound beside the wood but one,
> And that was my long scythe whispering to the ground.
> What was it it whispered? I know not well myself;
> Perhaps it was something about the heat of the sun,
> Something, perhaps, about the lack of sound—
> And that was why it whispered and did not speak.

In the next seven lines, not one reference is made to sound—either directly or metaphorically. But the image returns again with this final line:

> My long scythe whispered and left the hay to- make.

There are two incidental points in this selection which are worth noting. First, the word "sound" is both abstract and vague and frequently represents poetic laziness—the poet settling for the - general because it takes time and effort to find the exact word needed. Editors and teachers grow weary of "sounds of the night," "sounds of the street," and "sounds of the sea" which recur with deadening regularity. But although "sound" is used twice in the six quoted lines, it is vividly contrasted with a single and highly specific sound image of the scythe "whispering," a metaphor which is used three times. This portion of the poem, then, is rooted in a single sound, not in the generality suggested by the word in the abstract.

Second, it is significant that Frost returns to the image at the end of the poem. This is a common practice, for it adds to the verbal (not necessarily logical) unity of the poem.

This same pattern is seen in Louis Simpson's "To the Western World." He begins this fifteen-line poem with:

> A siren sang, and Europe turned away
> From the high castle and the shepherd's crook.

The following nine lines are based almost exclusively on visual images, leading naturally from "castle" and "shepherd's crook" in line two. But the last four lines of the poem return once again to a sound image, new but linked by opposition to the first one:

> In this America, this wilderness
> Where the axe echoes with a lonely sound,
> The generations labor to possess
> And grave by grave we civilize the ground.

Using Touch,
Smell, and Taste   These three remaining senses are "lower" in the hierarchy of human experience in that we are not able to make as subtle differentiations in these areas. But their use in poetry is often highly effective. Occasionally they appear as single, isolated images which serve to amplify relationships already established. No matter how hidden they may be in the final version of the poem, they may have been the poet's starting point.

Another approach is combining several types of images in a single passage. The result is "sensual" in that sense data are being used with great variety and, usually, intensity. The poem "Local Places" by Howard Moss provides a fine example. The following stanza is the first of five and the italics, mine, have been added to stress the use of sound, sight, and touch.

> The song you *sang* you will not *sing* again,
> Floating in the spring to all your local places,
> Lured by archaic sense to the wood
> To *watch* the frog jump from the mossy rock,
> To *listen* to the stream's small talk at dark,
> Or to *feel* the springy pine-floor where you walk—
> If your green secrecies were such as these,
> The mystery is now in other trees.

The italicized words are not, of course, the images themselves but verbs which introduce and emphasize such images as song, frog jumping, mossy rocks, the sound ("talk") of a stream, and the like. Three of the five senses are used in this single stanza; only taste and smell are missing. The second stanza introduces the desert cactus, which is allowed "To perfume aridness," adding one more dimension of sense experience.

Each stanza of this poem is unified by a dominant visual image:

the trees for the first, the desert for the second, the ocean for the third, and the rocks for the fourth. In the final two lines of the poem Moss recalls each of these visual images and links them with the same sound image used in the first line quoted above:

> The tree, the sand, the water, and the stone,
> What songs they sing they always sing again.

There is, of course, a logical development in this poem; and there is a "theme" or "statement" and something which might be called a "message." But what concerns us here is the degree to which the poet as artist has conceived of his work as the expression of sensation. These images of sight, sound, touch, and smell are not mere turrets and gargoyles added to an otherwise solid piece of logic; they are the bricks and timbers with which the piece is constructed.

Images as Figures of Speech

To this point, I have been describing images used simply as descriptive detail. Images also serve as the heart of any figure of speech.

Figurative language most commonly takes the form of the simile or metaphor. These are both comparisons, the first linking the two elements explicitly with "like" or "as" and the second implying a relationship. Here are three similes from three poems included in Chapter 11.

From Rich's "Like This Together":

> ... sitting like drugged birds
> in a glass case

From Snodgrass's "A Flat One":

> We watched your lean jaws masticate
> As ravenously your useless food
> As thieves at hard labor in their chains chew
> Or insects in the wood.

From Thomas's "Fern Hill":

> About the lilting house and happy as the grass was green

It should be clear from these examples that similes are not simple comparisons. When we compare, for example, a starling with a grackle, we imply that *in most respects* the two objects are similar. But when Rich compares the couple sitting silently in the car with "drugged birds" in a "glass case," she certainly does not want us to picture them as beaked and feathered. They are alike *only in certain respects*—in this case, their dulled mood and their isolation from the natural world outside the car. As with most similes, the area of similarity is far narrower than the area of differences. Its impact depends on how sharply it can make the reader see a new relationship.

Study, for example, the two similes in the selection from "A Flat One." Clearly the old patient is not literally in chains nor does he resemble in size, shape, or intelligence an insect. But as a dying patient he is *as if* chained and he eats even though the food will do him no good just *as if* he were a condemned prisoner. Further, there is an instinctually ravenous quality about his hunger, like that of certain insects. Notice how narrow and specific the area of similarity is and how broad the dissimilarities.

A metaphor, one learns in the ninth grade, is a simile that doesn't use *like* or *as*. Actually, the difference is far more subtle than that. In choosing to use a metaphor one shifts from an explicit to an implicit or implied comparison. It is a shift from a statement which is literally true to one which is literally untrue but figuratively effective. Hence, the metaphor demands more of the reader than the simile. And it is generally stronger.

In the lines quoted from "Fern Hill," Thomas used one simile, "happy as the grass was green." But the other three figures of speech are all metaphors. To convert the passage so that it contains all similes requires more than the addition of "like" or "as." It might come out in this awkward fashion:

> Now as I was young and living *as if* all things in
> life were easy and *as if* I spent all my time in the
> orchard looking up through the branches, the house and
> the entire area of my childhood were *like* a gay and
> rhythmical song and I was *as* happy *as* the grass is green.

It should be clear from this brutal translation that a metaphor is not necessarily a simile with "like" or "as" removed. The metaphor is often highly compressed, carrying overtones which require entire phrases or clauses to explain. This should also serve to explain why the simile is the dominant form of comparison in prose whereas the metaphor is far more frequently used in poetry.

This is a particularly important point for the writer who, having spent most of his literary effort writing prose, tries to shift to poetic composition. The tendency is to inflate his lines with needlessly explicit similes and the result is a lack of compression which is apt to sound prosaic. The solution is to remember that the intelligent reader of poetry moves slowly and is prepared to make extraordinary leaps in his perception of imagery. Further, he is willing to go over the poem several times. Those first two lines from "Fern Hill," for example, don't truly reach the reader until after the entire poem has been read —preferably aloud—two or three times.

There are two terms which are extremely helpful in analyzing any figure of speech—including one's own. I. A. Richards has suggested *tenor* as the poet's actual subject of concern and *vehicle* as the image by means of which the subject is being presented. "Happiness," then, is the tenor in Thomas's simile and he presents this feeling with the vehicle, "green grass." Grass becomes a vehicle in the sense that it "carries" the subject to the reader.

In the metaphor, the tenor is often left out. Thus, "a house as gay and rhythmical as a lilting song" becomes "the lilting house." Those qualities of joy which he intends the reader to recognize have been implied rather than stated. Sometimes those implications become very complex. Because of this, it is often helpful when revising one's own work to separate tenor from vehicle and to question whether that particular vehicle contains the overtones one has in mind.

Most other figures of speech are forms of the metaphor, and their technical names are more important for the critic in his work of analysis than for the writer in his task of composition. Hyperbole, for example, is commonly defined as extreme exaggeration, but in most cases it is a metaphorical exaggeration. Andrew Marvell's "To His Coy Mistress," for example, is filled with hyperbole.

> My vegetable love should grow
> Vaster than empires and more slow;
> A hundred years should go to praise
> Thine eyes. . . .

Transposing this back to a simile, we would begin, "My love would be *like* a vegetable which *like* an empire would grow. . . ."

Synecdoche is also a specialized form of metaphor. In this case a portion of something (the vehicle) represents the whole (the tenor). In common speech we still hear the phrase, "A town of four hundred souls"; in poetry it can reach the complexity of Dylan Thomas's "The lips of time leech to the fountain head" (from "The Force That

Through the Green Fuse Drives the Flower"). Here the intent is "time clings," but time is first personified and then one part of that personification is taken to stand for the action of the whole, adding the overtones of the bloodsucking leech.

Even the pun can be seen as a form of metaphor when one is able to separate the tenor from the vehicle. In Thomas's "A Refusal to Mourn..." he has a play on "grave":

> I shall not murder
> The mankind of her going with a grave truth. . . .

The tenor here is "solemn truth," and he has, in effect, added "*as if* spoken at the grave-side." He uses essentially the same device in "Do Not Go Gentle into that Good Night" with the line, "Grave men, near death, who see with blinding sight. . . ." Once again, we have only to convert the pun to a simile in order to see it as a part of metaphorical construction.

The Strength
of Image Clusters   Although many metaphors are used only once and then dropped, there is a special strength which one can build by compounding them either through extending a single metaphor or by using similar vehicles. It is helpful in reading a new poem to look for and identify such clusters or groups of related details even when the central theme is not yet fully clear. And it is equally valuable for the poet to think in terms of clusters as he writes, drawing full use from all the associations which a simile or metaphor might suggest to him.

In Robley Wilson's "On a Maine Beach" there are two such clusters. That is, in addition to the beach images which one would expect, there are two sets of metaphors which are "clustered" in the sense that their vehicles are similar. Turn to the poem now (p. 112) and read it through carefully, identifying the images and marking the lines on which they appear.

The first of these image clusters is coins. Metaphors in which some form of money is used as the vehicle appear in lines 1, 2, 3, 13, and 14. In some cases these are direct as in "worn change" and "mint-mark." And sometimes they are somewhat indirect as in "miser on them" and "counting them"; but the series runs down through the length of the poem.

The second cluster has to do with circles and spirals. They appear on lines 5, 6, 15, and 16 in direct, unmistakable form like "mainspring" and "pinwheeling." But in a broader sense, circles and spirals are seen in the "small equations" whose "sum" is the end of life, in the shape of the pools, in the shape of the coins, and most significantly in the ebb and flow of the tide. The phrase "beach rhythms" (line 15) becomes the dominant pattern for the entire poem.

As the last line suggests, watching these cycles of living and dying within the rock pool help us to see our own mortality in perspective. In this way, the life and death of the reader is included in the dominant image cluster of circles and cycles.

The Image
as Symbol

Turning now to image as used in symbolic language, we shift to a different emphasis altogether. In brief, the symbol is any detail—an object, action, or state—which has a range of meaning beyond and usually larger than itself. Our language is filled with public symbols, like Madison Avenue (commercial values), the flag (nation), the cross (church), which are widely accepted. But the poet more generally constructs his own private symbols. The process is a form of teaching in which "instructions" are given either in the course of a single poem or in several. Anyone familiar with Dylan Thomas's poetry, for example, has learned that "green" is not just a color but a symbol for youth, vitality, growth, and the like. Thus, the phrase from "Fern Hill" quoted above, "happy as the grass was green" is coupled with other uses of the word in the same poem such as "I was green and carefree," "And fire green as grass," "the whinnying green stable," and "the children green and golden." Once the symbolic association is made, any reference to the word (the vehicle) brings to mind the intended meaning (the tenor).

This private symbol of Thomas's is in sharp contrast, of course, with the public symbol of wealth as seen in the term "greenbacks" and developed so vividly by Fitzgerald in *The Great Gatsby,* where green lawns and the green light are the very opposite of youth and innocence. It is often difficult for a poet to reject public symbols like youth—spring, winter—age, nature—mother, God—old man. But when he does, as in Francis Thompson's "The Hound of Heaven" in which God is perceived as a pursuing bloodhound, the result is often startling and effective. More often, the poet selects an image not already strongly identified as a public symbol and builds it to suit his needs.

Symbol is often confused with simile and metaphor. It helps to remember that both similes and metaphors tend to be more literal and in this respect closer to prose. The real subject of the phrase—the tenor—is either directly stated or clearly implied. The vehicle is like an elaborate modifier.

In Wilson's "On a Maine Beach," for example, it is clear that within the context of the first line "rocks" is the tenor and that "like worn change" is the vehicle, forming a simile. And when he writes that "barnacles / Miser on them," we know that "barnacles" is the tenor of the metaphor and that "miser" is a vehicle which describes how they cling to rocks.

With symbol, on the other hand, it is the vehicle which receives all the attention. Often it is only after finishing the poem that one realizes just what is the true tenor of the poem. A careless reader, for example, might assume that Wilson's intent was merely to describe a Maine beach. Actually those rocks and pools and barnacles which were the tenors of individual metaphors are used collectively as the vehicle for a symbol. The overall tenor of the poem is life itself.

Wilson has made this symbol explicit by direct statement in lines 8 and 16. In other poems, however, the tenor may be left unstated. One way to do this is to repeat a metaphor several times in the same poem so that whenever the vehicle is mentioned, the larger meaning comes to mind. This is the case in Thomas's use of "green." Line by line, these phrases are mere metaphors. But as we have seen, the color green eventually takes on a permanent association in our minds, and what began as repeated metaphors takes on the strength of a symbol.

Must a poem have a symbolic suggestion? Certainly not. A great deal of verse is written about a particular place or event (commemorative poetry) or an occasion like a birthday, a coronation, or an election (occasional poetry) or merely for pleasure. The subject of these poems may take on no greater meaning than itself. In general, these are *simple* in the literary sense. But if the subject itself is complex, as in the case of Sandburg's "Chicago," the poem may be relatively sophisticated.

But imagine Wilson's poem if it did nothing but describe an

interesting aspect of nature. It might serve to illustrate a book of nature photographs, but by itself it would be too *simple* to hold the interest of anyone who enjoys the sophisticated use of language.

In the case of "Fern Hill," one of the reasons it is enjoyed by such a wide range of readers is that it can be read as simple verse—a happy poem about a happy childhood. But this is only a small portion of the poem. The key to the larger set of suggestions comes in the closing lines. There "green" becomes more than just the metaphorical suggestion of the vitality of youth; it is the life force itself. The exuberance is life, and all living is limited by mortality just as the sea is limited by its tide. His childhood, then, becomes a symbol for life itself. And in writing poetry he, as an adult, is "singing" in his "chains like the sea." The sophistication of the poem is built on that tension between the love of life and the awareness of certain death.

In the poem "Lizards and Snakes," by Anthony Hecht (p. 110), there is another example of how a potentially sentimental subject matter is given a range of suggestion—literary sophistication—through the use of symbol without losing the relatively light tone. The impact of the poem comes when one realizes that *for the aunt* the lizard was a strong symbol suggesting death and Satan himself. Review it again and pick out the turning point. Notice how the tone changes there as well.

The boys in the poem also recognize the symbol, for they never play a trick on her again. And we, as readers, take the symbol seriously in that we stop smiling at what seemed to be an as-if-told bit of reminiscence and we take the aunt's vision seriously. The treatment here is similar to that which is often used in fiction: our moment of recognition comes through the sudden discovery of a character. What concerns me here, however, is the dramatic moment when the reader discovers that what he thought was the tenor (the "lizards and snakes" of the title) is really only a vehicle for a greater and more ominous tenor, the devil and all the forces of evil he represents.

To see the distinction between these forms, it is helpful to convert symbols to metaphors and metaphors to similes. In the case of "Lizards and Snakes," for example, one would have to imagine a poem which began with lines about the fear of death. After establishing the concern (the tenor), one might use such lines as, "He can crack us like lice with his fingernail." In this case "he" becomes a personification of evil and death, a vehicle intended to dramatize the tenor.

The image used for its own sake, non-figuratively.		"The green grass"
Comparison of two Items. The area of agreement (shaded) is broad.		"Grass is like wheat"
Simile: A linking of essentially dissimilar items to highlight certain similarities.	T V	"Happy as the grass was green" (Thomas) **Paraphrase** (italics indicate the tenor): *Happy* in a vital, vibrant way like the green grass of early spring.
Metaphor: An implied simile. (The example from Thomas contains three separate metaphors.)	T V	"Time held me green and dying" (Thomas) **Paraphrase:** I was mortal as if I was a child held by Time; *I was also alive and growing* as if I were a young blade of grass. Yet even then *I was approaching death* as if I were literally dying.
Symbol: An item presented as if for its own sake which then takes on a broader, implied meaning.	V≡ T	"Fern Hill" The entire farm becomes a vehicle suggesting aspects of life itself: birth, rapid growth; the certainty of death at the end of the "season" —an endless cycle.

The difference is not entirely a matter of establishing the tenor first. The distinguishing characteristic of all metaphors (and similes as well) is that the vehicle is clearly there *only* because it amplifies or dramatizes the subject at hand. It is a literary device. This is why a passing reference to one who "can crack us like lice" in a poem which is explicitly about death would be described as a metaphor, not a symbol.

From that point, it is an easy step back from metaphor to the most literal form of figurative language: the simile. "Death is so all-powerful that it is *like* some devil who can crack us like lice with his fingernail."

A Schematic
View of Imagery

The distinctions between a simple comparison, a simile, a metaphor, and symbols are subtle, but they are enormously important for anyone who reads or writes poetry. For some, a diagrammatic presentation is more helpful than a description in words. The schematic representation on page 69 is a review of these relationships.

The letter T represents the tenor or principal subject, and V is the vehicle, the word or phrase being used to "carry" the subject to the reader's consciousness. I have included a set of examples from "Fern Hill," but the outline will prove more helpful if one adds a set of examples from another poem.

Thinking
in Images

As I mentioned earlier, the school experience with its emphasis on exposition tends to discourage thinking and writing in images. The beginning poet may have to make a conscious effort to find the language of the senses. One mechanical approach is to spend time composing conversions from image to simile to metaphor to symbol. Some writers like to keep these in a journal.

Here, for a start, is a list of five images. Three of these are visual (two static and one dynamic), one auditory, and one tactile.

1. A fat, lazy cat
2. A city street on a hot summer's day
3. The way a particularly graceful girl walks
4. The sound of good jazz
5. The warmth of an open fire in winter

The simplest sort of conversion is to make each one into a vehicle for a simile. For example: "After winning the Pulitzer Prize, he looked like a fat, lazy cat."

Now that I have used a person as the tenor, try using the image to describe a section of a city or the society. Be careful to avoid clichés.

After composing one simile with each image, try converting them to metaphors. In each case, remember, the item in the list serves as the vehicle for something else, the tenor, such as the man who won the Pulitzer Prize or, in the case of the hot city street, a career as a newspaper editor.

Now reverse the process, using each item as the tenor. Try, first, to find an image which would serve as a vivid simile for a fat, lazy cat. Let your mind go free. How about a cat lying in the sun "like a pool of molasses"? Go through each of the others like this.

Next, convert these to metaphors. In some cases, there will be little difference except for the loss of the "like" or "as." But in other cases there will be a surprising boost in strength. Notice how often the metaphorical version will read more like a line of verse than the simile did.

The final step is most difficult. Try writing a brief prose paragraph in which a description of the image becomes, through suggestion, symbolic. Try not to mention the tenor. Here is an example for the lazy cat.

> The cat, Mod, lay peacefully in his Puss-A-Bye bed in his corner of the family room. There had been a time when he had prowled the house constantly in search of mice. But what was the point now that such a perfectly balanced, protein-packed meal was brought to him each day? And there was a time when he purred as soon as the drafty chill of winter passed and he could lie in the spring sun. But since they moved to the new home, winter was indistinguishable from summer. There was no need now to prowl nor to purr. Life was, if he thought about it, just perfect. But why should he think about it?

All this is for one's journal. Where does it affect the working poet? The selection or rejection of images is at the heart of composition. Some of the decisions are made unconsciously, but even these can be judged and revised consciously.

In some cases an ailing poem may be revived by converting metaphorical treatment into symbolic or vice versa. If, for example, a poem is begun with a feeling of strong ambivalence toward the city, the poet may come across an image such as the subway which would capture elements of his pleasure and his disgust. Such a poem would probably develop as an extended metaphor. It would be well worth considering the possibility, however, of beginning with the image itself and adding to it symbolic significance. And conversely, if a poem has begun with something seen which only after several drafts begins to take on real significance, it might be worth beginning with the new-found tenor and employing the image as metaphor.

The use of the image in poetry is so basic that it is infinitely vari-able. The poet must exercise his imagination in two areas if he hopes to make full use of this potential: First, there is the matter of respond-ing to the kind of stimuli most people shrug off as inconsequential. He should stop and examine what others have missed, whether it be veins on a leaf or the surge of a mob; he should hear what others miss —not just skylarks but the breath of an old man or sleet against the window; he should respond to the feel of a rusted iron railing, a cut, or a gull's feather; he should identify the variety of city smells and country odors and consider what it is that makes an unoccupied house different from one lived in; and he should taste not only food but pine gum and smog.

But all this is only half a poet's training in the use of the image. The other half is what other poets have done. This requires analysis —reading poetry critically and even competitively, not as verbal Muzak. It is worth lingering over a complex metaphor to determine not only the similarity but the differences between the tenor and the vehicle; it requires converting metaphors into similes, similes into metaphors, and both into symbols; it demands a constant search for the overtones in every image.

7

DICTION

Poetic diction: restrictive or free? The *four dangers* to fresh diction: *Clichés* described as dying metaphors, *hackneyed language* as "soft" expression, *sweeping generalities* as alien to the poet's language, and *archaisms* as needless aids to meter; fresh diction seen as the *stimulant* in poetry.

The question often arises as to whether there is such a thing as poetic diction. Is there a difference between the kind of words which lend themselves to poetry and those which we tend to use in prose? The only valid answer to this question is that some poets do make such a distinction and others vehemently do not.

When, for example, one reads the works of Richard Wilbur, it is difficult to find words which are colloquial and almost impossible to find samples of what might be described as base or vulgar. Although these descriptive terms are all highly relative, one has the feeling that there is within this poet either consciously or unconsciously a censor who passes judgment on each word used. Writing in *Mid-Century American Poets* (John Ciardi, ed., 1950), Wilbur insists that he has "no special theory of diction." But he does suggest a personal preference when he writes: "The Auden school of the thirties, which gave poetic language a refreshing infusion of slang and technical terminology, has also been aped quite enough now." And this feeling is reflected in his work.

John Ciardi, on the other hand, opens his poetry to a wider variety of words. Writing in the same anthology, he states his position without qualification: "There is no subject not fit for poetry and no word not fit for poetry." And to make his point perfectly clear he adds: "...the language of common speech is preferable to enlarged rhetorical constructions, and the 'pretty' should be approached willingly but with caution." We are not, then, surprised to hear him pay poetic tribute to the human race by comparing it to that extraordinary insect which avoids extinction by perfectly resembling a "bird turd," nor are we unprepared for the opening lines of his "Elegy Just in Case":

> Here lie Ciardi's pearly bones
> In their ripe organic mess.

or his brutal fourth stanza:

> Here lies the sgt.'s mortal wreck
> Lily spiked and termite kissed,
> Spiders pendant from his neck,
> Beetles shining on his wrist.

It is interesting to note that, although Ciardi has described the Beat Poets as "unwashed eccentricity" and "not only juvenile but certainly related to juvenile delinquency," he has shared with them this militant demand for the poet's right to use whatever diction he chooses.

The fact is that for the past forty years there has been no "academy" dictating standards of diction any more than there has been one enforcing or restricting the use of meter and rhyme. For better or for worse, the literary scene has been highly fragmented for almost a half-century, with the extremes finding a voice in publications that are as varied as *Wings* on one hand and *Pocket Poets* (in which Ginsberg's poems appeared) on the other. This is disturbing for those who would like to have a single literary standard—and there are those in both camps who editorialize for this under the banner of "freedom"; but for the serious poet who is primarily concerned with developing his own art, it provides the luxury of exploration and experimentation.

The first rule of diction, then, is that there is no general rule demanding a single level of usage. One can concentrate on what John Frederick Nims described as "the language of men as used by the expert in men's language"; or one may employ language which is, as

Ginsberg put it in "Howl," "obscene odes on the windows of the skull." The choice is an individual one.

Beneath this individuality and disagreement, however, is a shared belief in Ezra Pound's dictum: "Keep it fresh." This is no truism; it is one of the essential differences between poetry on the amateur level and genuine literary composition. It is not a matter of taste; it is a concern which is rooted in the definition of poetry.

The ambition shared by most poets is to break through to the consciousness of the reader or listener. To achieve this, the diction—like other aspects of the poem—must startle the reader either by its ingenuity, its beauty, or merely its effectiveness. This goal is in sharp contrast to such subliterary forms as greeting-card verse, which is designed to lull the reader by murmuring the familiar in much the same way that Muzak is selected to soothe the restaurant patron without disturbing his meal or even his thoughts.

With this in mind, the poet must be on guard against diction which allows the reader to skip words or phrases without a single reaction. Regardless of whether the verse is light or serious, each element must make contact on some level—and preferably on several.

There are many pitfalls between the novice poet and this ideal. These four are the most dangerous:

The Cliché The cliché is equated with sin from the seventh grade on, yet it remains a constant problem long after one's schooling is over. Part of the difficulty lies in the fact that few people bother to analyze just what it is about the cliché which makes it a literary sin. They memorize the tabooed expressions as if they were profanities—and revert to them in much the same way.

The cliché, as George Orwell pointed out in "Politics and the English Language," is actually a dying metaphor, that is, an expression which was once fresh enough to create a clear picture in the reader's mind but has now lost its vitality. Thus, "sharp as a tack" has become dull; "free as a bird" no longer takes flight; "clean as a whistle" sets the reader wondering—if at all—whether he is to picture one of those bright penny-whistles or the sound of a "wolf"; and, as Orwell points out, "to toe the line" has drifted so far from the original metaphor that it is now frequently seen in print as "to tow the line."

Yet when these metaphors finally die—that is, become built into the language as single words which no longer appeal to a visual comparison—they occasionally regain respectability as utilitarian words. Thus a "current" of electricity has moved from metaphor to an independent word in its own right. In the same way, "stereotype" has moved from a metaphor based on the printer's term for the metal duplicate to an abstract meaning. The fact that it no longer serves as metaphor is proved by the number of people who use the word without having the slightest idea of its original sense. The tenor has been detached from the original vehicle and becomes good usage, just as "limelight" is freely used by individuals who are unaware of the fact that the word was once a metaphor referring to stage lighting which placed an oxyhydrogen flame against a cylinder of lime.

The most dramatic example of a dead metaphor is the word "cliché" itself. Originally a French word for a stereotype printing plate, it was an effective metaphor for standardized phrasing. Yet for those not in the printing business the word now clearly denotes the tenor without the slightest echo of its original metaphorical use.

The reader's attention is caught by a fresh simile or metaphor, and it is also held by words which have become denotative in their own right. The cliché is a word or phrase which is midway between these two—so overused that it no longer serves as suggestive language and not yet condensed into an independent, denotative word.

The cliché weakens a line of poetry because the reader skips over it rapidly without response. He draws from it neither the visual impression of a metaphor nor the denotative impact of a well-selected word. Further, because such expressions are associated with writing which makes no demands, the reader is lulled rather than awakened. The cliché, then, is a literary sin not because it is "bad taste" but because it converts intense, compressed, highly suggestive writing into that which is loose and bland.

There are three different ways of dealing with the clichés which appear in one's first draft. First, one can work hard to find a fresh simile or metaphor which will force the reader to see (hear, taste, and so on) the vehicle and make the startling association with the tenor. Second, one can merely drop the comparison completely and deal with the subject directly. Finally, one can twist the cliché so that it is reborn in some slightly altered form. This final choice is more frequently associated with comic verse, but there is no reason why it cannot be used with serious intent.

For example, if a poet discovers he has allowed "blood red" to slide into his verse, he can avoid this most ancient cliché with such alternatives as "balloon red" or "hot red" or "shouting red," depending on the overtones he wishes to establish. If none of these will do, he should consider going back to just "red." Should the tone of the poem be whimsical, however, he might twist the cliché into "bloodshot red."

A good way to improve one's skill in dealing with clichés is to apply these three techniques to "sea blue," "rosy dawn," "tried and true," "mother nature," and "strong as an ox."

Hackneyed
Language   This is a general term which includes not only the cliché but the far more dangerous area of phrases which have simply been overused. Whereas clichés usually consist only of conventionalized similes and are easily identified, hackneyed language also includes direct description which has been seen in print too long to provide impact. A seventh-grader can compile a list of clichés as readily as he can recall names of birds; but only one who has read literature extensively can identify that which is literarily hackneyed. This is one reason why vocabulary lists which are emphasized so heavily in secondary schools are no substitute for wide and varied reading.

Certain subjects seem to generate hackneyed language like maggots. Take, for example, sunsets. The "dying day" is a true cliché, but perfectly respectable words like "golden," resplendent," "magnificent," and even "richly scarlet" all become hackneyed when used to describe a sunset. It is not the word itself which should be avoided—one cannot make lists; it is the particular combination which is limp from overuse.

In the same way, smiles are too often "radiant," "infectious," or "glowing." Trees tend to have "arms" and frequently "reach heavenward." The seasons are particularly dangerous: Spring is "young" or "youthful," suggesting virginity, vitality, or both; summer is "full blown"; and by autumn many poets slide into a "September Song" with only slight variations on the popular lyrics. Winter, of course, leads the poet to sterility and death, terms which too often describe the quality of the poem as well.

Our judgment of what is hackneyed depends somewhat on the age. That which was fresh and vivid in an earlier period may have become shopworn for us. Protesting "But Pope used it" does not make a metaphor acceptable for our own use. But standards of fresh language are far less tied to period than most students believe. It is difficult to find lines in, say, Shakespeare's sonnets which would even today be considered hackneyed. Conversely, many of the conventions which he attacked as stale and useless have continued in popular use and reappear like tenacious weeds in the verse of college freshmen.

In "Sonnet 130," for example, he protests that

> My mistress' eyes are nothing like the sun;
> Coral is far more red than her lips' red....
> And in some perfumes is there more delight
> Than in the breath that from my mistress reeks.

The poem is directed not so much at his mistress as at those poets of his day who were content to root their work in conventions which were even then thoroughly stale. Yet more than three hundred years later poetry is produced not only for class but for publication in which eyes sparkle like the sun, lips are either ruby or coral red, and breath is either honeyed or perfumed.

Hackneyed expressions can, of course, be twisted into new life in the same way that clichés can. This is what Shakespeare did in the sonnet which begins with a most contemporary question: "Shall I compare thee to a summer's day?" His decision in that poem was, as I have pointed out earlier, to shift the conventionalized comparison into a series of contrasts, stressing not the traditional associations of the season but the reverse. Thus, his next line inverts what would have been hackneyed:

> Thou art more lovely and more temperate.
> Rough winds do shake the darling buds of May,
> And summer's lease hath all too short a date.

The same inversion of a conventionalized association appears in Eliot's opening to "The Waste Land."

> April is the cruellest month, breeding
> Lilacs out of the dead land, mixing
> Memory and desire....
> Winter kept us warm, covering
> Earth in forgetful snow, feeding
> A little life with dried tubers.

In both cases the poet has relied on our familiarity with the convention, but in neither case was he content merely to reinforce that familiarity. The vitality comes from drawing unexpected patterns from potentially hackneyed conventions.

Abstractions and
Sweeping Generalities   In the chapter on the sources of poems, I warned against beginning with a broad, abstract principle like love, death, nature, and the like. It is equally dangerous to allow a poem which was originally inspired by some genuine experience or personal reaction to slide into sweeping generalities. Last stanzas are particularly vulnerable. There is a temptation to "explain" one's poem in a concluding stanza which too easily turns into a truism.

If the origin of a poem is a specific love, try to deal with the details as precisely as possible. There will be, of course, aspects which would mean nothing to another reader without a great deal of background material, and these should be avoided. But if the relationship is dealt with honestly, the reader will be able to draw universals from the specific you provide.

Adrienne Rich's "Like This Together" is a particularly good example. The relationship she describes is unique, but most of us have at some period felt the desperate need to "hold fast to the / one thing we know." She has defined an aspect of love, but she has done it by sharing with the reader the personal details of an apparently real relationship.

The same is true of death. When a novice poet deals with it in the abstract, one wonders why he did not turn to assertive writing in the form of the essay. Before it becomes poetically manageable, the poet must find a set of images which will make the familiar abstraction fresh and convincing. John Donne's well-known "Death Be Not Proud" uses personification. In a very different way, so does Anthony Hecht's "Lizards and Snakes." Robley Wilson gets at an aspect of death in his treatment of cycles in "On a Maine Beach." And even Dylan Thomas is concerned with death in "Fern Hill." Notice that in each case the poet has avoided the abstraction and concerned himself either with people or, in the case of Wilson, sea creatures.

Other abstractions like patriotism, liberty, and peace contain the same dangers death does; but in addition they have a special tendency to attract clichés. The mind is so rutted with the language of unimaginative orators that what may have started out on an original course is apt to slip into one of these deep grooves and end, both figuratively and literally, in a political convention.

One solution is to shift the theme and attack rather than support all these concerns. I am convinced that at least some of the violently anti-everything poetry which we all wrote as college sophomores was not so much a political or even an emotional rebellion as it was a desperate search for fresh language. But this is no final solution; the anti-convention soon becomes conventional.

The more mature approach is breaking up the abstraction into manageable parts, reducing it from "concept" to images, and constructing figurative language which will give it life.

Broadly speaking, the generality is that which the reader, critic, and the writer of texts uses to *describe* patterns in poetry. The poet, usually, has not started with the high-level abstraction but a particular river near Tintern Abbey, a news item about a girl killed by fire in a London air raid, a bit of conversation in a Boston cocktail party, or a walk through a birch grove. From these he makes certain implications which, as we analyze them, are categorized as "nature," "death," "sterility," or "life."

The poet who begins with "Life is. . ." or "Love is. . ." should stop right there and ask himself just what a poet is and what a critic is, for he may well have confused the working procedures of each.

Archaic

Diction   This is the last in this list of four threats to fresh language. Quite often it takes the form of time-honored but dated contractions such as "o'er," and "oft" as substitutions for "over" and "often." But there are other words which now have the same musty quality: "lo!" "hark!" "ere," and even "O!" are the most frequently used.

The majority of poets writing today need no such warning, and some may be surprised that it must be included here. Yet the practice is seen repeatedly in college writing classes and is well represented in some of the less distinguished poetry journals.

There are two explanations for the persistent use of diction which the poet would never consider in speech or even in his prose. First, for one not used to the feel of meter there is a strong temptation to use any device which will allow the line to come out "correctly." Thus, if his first inclination is to work with a simple image like "The gull wakes the day before the sun," he may be bothered by the metrical confusion. Assuming that he is working with iambs, he has just produced a line which, after the initial iambic foot, is followed by four trochees.

It is at this point that some writers start reaching into the grave of archaic diction to force the meter back into line. If the poet is not careful, he may end up with something like, "Ere sun arises, lo the noble gull, , , ." He may be pleased that he has produced a line of perfect iambic pentameter, but his pleasure will be snuffed out as soon as he reads his work to a contemporary audience.

Were he a little more ingenious, he might have noticed that merely shifting "wakes" to "awakes" would also shift the entire line into iambic meter: "The gull awakes the day before the sun."

The second temptation which leads some poets to archaisms is far more serious because it appears to be based on logic. The syllogism runs like this: "Wordsworth used this sort of diction; Wordsworth was great; archaic diction is great." If one substitutes Keats and Shelley for Wordsworth, one has a valid explanation for the fact that many American poets manage to work skylarks and nightingales into their poems even when they have neither seen nor heard these creatures.

These would-be poets have forgotten the essential fact that words have overtones. There is nothing "wrong" with any word *per se*. But if one uses words which are heavily associated with the nineteenth or eighteenth century, one must be prepared to have the reader's associations move back as well. Spenser used this technique effectively in "The Faerie Queene," and his readers are, if they are sensitive to language, moved back to an earlier period. But it is a difficult technique. In most cases, archaisms defeat the intent of the poem by establishing associations which are completely extraneous.

These, then, are the four practices which most frequently defeat the goal of fresh diction: clichés, hackneyed language, sweeping generalities, and archaisms. They are not absolute taboos. Each may, in certain cases, be used to create a particular effect. To succeed, the poet must be both conscious of the dangers he is running and skillful enough to avoid them.

Fresh diction, however, is not achieved merely by remembering the danger areas. The poet must be determined to prod the reader's consciousness. His goal is stimulation, be it intellectual, spiritual, or merely pleasurable.

In addition, he must probe the reader's unconscious rather than skim over it. To achieve this penetration, the poet must select each word on the basis of its denotative meaning, its connotations, its sound, its contribution to rhythm, and its capacity to establish an internal tension. This process is as necessary for the ballad as it is for the lyric, as essential to metered verse as for free.

If poetry is to be something more than a narcotic, then diction must serve as a stimulant.

8

POETIC TENSION

Direct contrast presented without irony as in differing moods, logical alternatives, arguments, and protests; *irony* as tension in phrasing, in paradoxes and puns; *satire:* the absurd played against the "reasonable" either with or without irony.

A dull poem is a failure by any standard. Yet a good deal of technically competent work is unquestionably dull. What is one to do with a poem which was well conceived and developed with a good sense of rhythm, sound, images, and fresh diction, and yet bores not only the readers but the poet himself? It is easy enough to blame such failures on the subject matter and to send the poet back to his typewriter. But in most cases the boredom was not due to a weak theme but to a lack of internal tension.

There are many ways to create tension in a poem, but generally speaking they take one of three forms. The first utilizes some kind of thematic conflict, argument, or protest. The second is based on irony. And the third—which often is combined with the first two—is satire.

It is helpful to explore these individually, but it is also important to remember that they are closely related. Argument often involves irony and sometimes is presented as satire. Some poems contain all three. The point to remember is that almost every sophisticated poem depends upon at least one of these approaches because it is through tension that poetry draws its strength.

Direct
Thematic Contrast   In fiction and drama, the basic contrast is often based on conflict, a struggle between characters. And it can take this form in poetry—particularly in epics such as the *Odyssey* and *Beowulf*. But the contrasts developed in nonepic poetry tend to lie within the theme or themes rather than between characters. That is, the tension is in contrasting moods, ideas, convictions, or feelings.

By "direct" I mean nonironic. That is, a simple contrast is the primary structural device of the poem. Many of Shakespeare's sonnets are constructed this way with the first eight lines, the octave, taking one "side" and the remaing six lines, the sestet, presenting the alternative. In "Sonnet 29," for example, he begins with an accounting of despair:

> When in disgrace with fortune and men's eyes
> I all alone beweep my outcast state,
> And trouble deaf heaven with my bootless cries

The shift comes, as it so often does in the sonnet, at the beginning of the sestet:

> Yet in these thoughts myself almost despising,
> Haply I think on thee,—and then my state,
> Like to the lark at break of day arising
> From sullen earth, sings hymns at heaven's gate

Although this sort of division between octave and sestet is more generally associated with the Italian sonnet, it appears in a surprising number of Shakespeare's as well. Significantly, thirteen of his sonnets begin the sestet with "but" or "yet."

The thematic conflict in these poems is locked into the sonnet form itself. The tension can be described equally well as being the opposition of the poet's two moods or as a tonal shift between the octave and the sestet.

A more recent example of thematic conflict in the form of alternatives is seen in Frost's "Fire and Ice." Turn to it now (p. 121) and study how the alternatives which are so blatantly presented in the title are developed subtly in the context of the poem.

The poem has more to it than is seen by those who like to remember Frost as a friendly, simple, rural philosopher. A careful reading reveals that the poet *has* been destroyed by love (having "favored" fire) and, in the last five lines, *will* be destroyed by hate, elevating a casual bit of rural philosophy into an intense personal experience. But what concerns us here is the tension which is established between the destructive quality of love on the one hand and hate on the other. By eliminating the alternatives, one reduces the poem to a flat statement linking either love with fire or hate with ice, both of which have been done in any number of unimaginative song lyrics.

This same technique appears frequently in Frost's poetry and is worth study because of the fact that what would otherwise be bland observation is given strength through such tension in thematic alternatives. "The Road Not Taken," for example, begins and ends with a choice, and the poem is equally concerned with each of these two paths. "Stopping by Woods..." would be nothing but a Grandma Moses print complete with quaint little pony were it not for the fact that the poet is caught between a longing for death (seen in such images as "frozen lake," "darkest evening of the year," and "woods... lovely, dark and deep") and the much less emphasized commitment to life ("have promises to keep" and the somewhat fatalistic "And miles to go before I sleep.").

This type of tension can be found in a majority of poems, for it is almost as fundamental to the genre as conflict is to fiction. But often it is less directly stated than it is in the samples given above. Take, for example, Denise Levertov's "To the Snake." In the first stanza she describes what it is like to hang a green snake around one's neck, feeling its scales and hearing its hiss. It is vivid but purely descriptive without a hint of thematic tension or even a suggestion of theme. Then the poem shifts as she opens the second stanza with these lines:

> Green Snake—I swore to my companions that certainly you were
>   harmless! But truly
> I had no certainty, and no hope, only desiring to hold you, for
>   that joy, . . .

Because this is the point at which one is first aware of how the snake is to be used symbolically, one is apt to miss the fact that this is also the introduction of tension into the poem: fascination for the snake and all it represents played against a kind of fear ("I had no certainty"). This ambivalence is made more complex by the fact that the fear itself becomes a desire: She had "no hope" that the snake was harmless.

On the simplest level, then, there appears to be a tension established between the woman and the snake. But actually, the voltage of the poem comes through the internal struggle within the woman. Now turn to the poem in its entirety (p. 120) and try answering the question of exactly what the snake represents.

There is in the symbolic use of the snake an intentional ambiguity. Although the poem makes sense on a nonsymbolic level, it becomes far more highly charged when one sees in the snake the suggestion of sexuality. One does not have to be familiar with the Freudian implications of snakes to sense the overtones here.

Other readers, however, may prefer to make use of the "public symbol," the snake as the one who introduced Eve to the fruit of knowledge. The fear and the desire here—strong ambivalence—are reminiscent of Eve's emotions as described in *Genesis* and in greater detail by Milton. Which is "correct"?

This is a case of intentional ambiguity. It is not simply a carelessness of the poet, nor does it suggest that the poet has decided that her work can "mean all things to all people." She still has control of her work. And she respects it.

The difference between this example of controlled ambiguity and careless writing is that we can link the two readings, drawing from them a still more highly sophisticated suggestion. The woman of the poem handles the snake with a mixture of desire, uncertainty, and fear which is similar to sexual confrontation and in a larger sense like one's introduction to any new phase of experience.

Opposing moods, emotions, and attitudes generate the tension in a majority of poems. But arguments and protest have also been a part of the poetic tradition since the beginning. Some of the strongest examples come from the Hebrew prophets. They tended to stand outside the mainstream of their own cultures, and they were highly critical of the societies of their day. Their language was blunt and direct. Take this brief sample from *Isaiah* 3:24:

> And it shall come to pass, that instead of sweet smell
>   there shall be stink; and instead of a girdle, a rent;
> And instead of well set hair, baldness; and instead of
>   a stomacher, a girding of sackcloth;
> And burning instead of beauty.

> Thy men shall fall by the sword,
>   and thy mighty in the war.

The following (*Isaiah* 33:1) is an attack on those in power. It is not far in spirit from the attacks made today by poets like Allen Ginsberg, Gregory Corso, and others.

> Woe to thee that spoilest, and thou wast not spoiled;
>   and dealest treacherously, and they dealt not treacherously with thee!
> When thou shalt cease to spoil, thou shalt be spoiled;
> And when thou shalt make an end to deal treacherously,
>   they shall deal treacherously with thee.

In this country, black Americans have struck the same note. For generations, slaves in this country identified themselves with the oppressed Jews of the Old Testament and this link is reflected in the spirituals. The protest poetry of today, however, is released from the sense of resignation which characterized most of the spirituals. In many respects, these are closer to the bitter sense of outrage which is so much a part of the works of Isaiah, Jeremiah, and Ezekiel.

Turn now to Conrad Kent Rivers's "The Still Voice of Harlem" (p. 120) and study the pattern of tensions there. Notice how the harshness of life for black Americans is contrasted with the sense of serenity within the "gardens" of Harlem. Obviously this is not intended to suggest literally that life in Harlem is easy; the "hope" is the sense of identity found there. This poem has many parallels in Biblical verse where the Jews looked to Israel as a source of identity—the brutality of the world pitted against the solidarity of the group.

The Tensions
of Irony   All forms of irony are based on a reversal of expectations. We expect a certain logical order in our world and are jolted when, say, the fire truck catches fire or the Olympic swimming champion drowns in his backyard pool. Since these involve our assumptions about the world around us, they are called examples of *cosmic irony*.

Or irony can appear in the form of a statement which unwittingly suggests future events either directly or indirectly. "I bring good news" the messenger in *Oedipus Rex* says, and the audience shudders, knowing that disaster is at hand. Since this is most closely associated with plays, it is called *dramatic irony*. More will be said about this in the chapters on drama.

The type of irony most frequently found in contemporary poetry is *verbal* or *conscious* irony. The terms are used interchangeably. *Verbal* differentiates it from a turn of *events* which characterize cosmic irony. Verbal irony is usually based on a turn of a phrase or on tone. *Conscious* differentiates this type of irony from statements given by innocent speakers as is the case in dramatic irony.

A full examination of these three types of irony appears in Chapter 20. I am concerned here with the varieties of verbal irony because the poet generally employs an ironic line or phrase knowing that it will trip or startle the reader by switching his expectations in some way.

Often poetic irony can be achieved with a single word or brief phrase. Anne Sexton, for example, when writing of her mother's death in "Division of Parts" plays outward appearance against reality with these lines:

> ...I trip
> on your death and Jesus, *my stranger*
> floats up over
> my Christian home....

The italics here are hers, thrusting the irony at the reader blatantly. Actually there are two samples of verbal irony in these lines. First, the phrase "Jesus, my stranger" is a jarringly effective reversal of the conventional "Jesus, my savior." She relies on the reader's familiarity with the conventional phrase just as Eliot relies on the reader's knowledge of the Lord's Prayer in "The Hollow Men" with the lines:

> For thine is
> Life is
> For Thine is the
>   This is the way the world ends

The second irony involves a tension between the same phrase and one actually stated: "my stranger" and "my Christian home." Here the first phrase represents an inner truth and the latter, while no less "true," represents outer appearance.

These two examples from Sexton's poem and the one from Eliot's all establish tension through paired phrases which are, on the one hand, intimately related and, on the other hand, vividly opposed. In this connection it is worth noting that every example of irony involves a pair of items which are both linked and opposed even if one of these two items is implied rather than stated.

These examples are direct and clear, but often irony in poetry is so

subtle that it is easy to miss. Take, for example, these lines from Denise
Levertov's "A Solitude" in which she is describing a blind man in
a subway:

> ...He doesn't care
> that he looks strange, showing
> his thoughts on his face like designs of light
>
> flickering on water, for he doesn't know
> what *look* is.
> I see that he has never seen.

There is a clear ironic contrast in the last line in which she *sees* his
lack of sight. More subtle, however, is the example earlier which works
as a kind of faint pre-echo: The face of a man whose world is total
blackness is described as "designs of light."

Poets do not usually add irony to a poem the way a cook adds
seasoning to a bland recipe—though the results may be similar.
Instead, ironies suggest themselves to the poet either in the original
conception or in the revisions.

Yet the poet cannot be entirely passive. He must be willing to probe
his own ambivalences honestly, looking for elements of hate in love,
hidden longings in hatred, or subtle desires buried in fears. He should
consider potential reversals in each image he uses. Just as April is in
some ways cruel and old age is in some ways beautiful, so also a love
for the good life can be deadly, a war might be soothing, a serene
dawn could be a deadly threat, and the roar of a jet a lullaby.

Closely related to the reversal of expectations in irony are the
apparent contradictions and ambiguous meanings in the paradox and
the pun. A paradox is a statement which at first appears to be a
contradiction but which on a second level makes a specific point by
implication. Some paradoxes have been embalmed in the form of
clichés. "The trouble with women," comedians tell us with monotonous
regularity, "is that you can't get along with them and you can't get
along without them."

But the paradox need not be comic. John Donne, for example, in
his sonnet "Death Be Not Proud" ends with these well known lines:

> One short sleep past, we wake eternally,
> And death shall be no more; Death, thou shalt die.

The core of the paradox, of course, lies in the last clause. It is
illogical to state that death can die, yet there is a poetic validity to

the statement which rises beyond absurdity. It is worth noting that in this case the paradox is not simply a trick of logic added for entertainment; it provides the thematic core for the entire poem.

Even more dramatic is the paradox in his Sonnet 14, "Batter My Heart." At the end of this poem God is pictured as a violent suitor and the poet himself as the woman. Speaking directly to God, Donne ends the poem with these three extraordinary lines:

> Take me to you, imprison me, for I
> Except you enthrall me, never shall be free,
> Nor ever chaste, except you ravish me.

There are actually two paradoxes here, both charged with high voltage. The first suggests that he cannot be "free" unless he is "enthralled," a word which was then synonymous with "enslaved." Stronger yet is the final suggestion that he cannot be "chaste" unless he is "ravished."

Paradox is really a form of irony in that a tension is established between the apparent or literal meaning on the one hand and the intended meaning on the other. But what irony in its conventional sense does to tone and expectations, paradox does to logic. Effective paradox is a clash of logic from which some richer, fuller insight rises.

The pun also creates a strain between two elements. In this case they are made up of two or more uses of the same word. Dylan Thomas, remember, uses the same pun in two major poems: "I shall not murder / The mankind of her going with a grave truth" in "A Refusal to Mourn..." and "Grave men, near death, who see with blinding sight" in "Do Not Go Gentle into that Good Night." This particular pun was also used by Shakespeare in *Romeo and Juliet* when Mercutio, a wit even while dying, says "Ask for me tomorrow and you shall find me a grave man."

Quite frequently the pun is not made up of perfect equivalents but approximations in sound, like this opening of Anne Sexton's "The Farmer's Wife":

> From the hodge porridge
> of their country lust

The pun here, which links their married life with a hodgepodge and a bland bowl of porridge, is particularly interesting because of the fact that "hodgepodge" comes from the Walloon "hosepot," which literally meant "house-pot" or the daily stew eaten by simple farming people such as those described in the quoted poem. Whether Miss Sexton was aware of this is of no importance; the point is that the much maligned pun can be made to reverberate with echoes of etymology and suggestive overtones.

The Tensions
of Satire
In satire tension is established by playing an exaggerated view of characters, places, or institutions against the "reasonable" view. Poetic satire is in this respect like the political cartoon—if there is not enough exaggeration we lose the humor and treat it as a simple sketch; and at the other extreme, if we can't identify the figure being ridiculed, we merely shrug and the cartoon has failed.

Satire and irony can, of course, be used independently from each other. All the examples of irony above are nonsatiric, and the first example of satire below does not use irony. But ridicule is particularly effective when it is presented "with a straight face." That is, the cutting edge of satire is sharpest when the poet gives the illusion of presenting an unbiased view. It is the tension between the poet's apparent honesty and his actual intent which makes satire almost invariably ironic. In fact, when satire is presented without irony the result often appears rather crude. Such is the case with Kingsley Amis's "A Tribute to the Founder." In this first of four stanzas, the intent to ridicule is clear, but because the material is presented directly rather than ironically the attack lacks subtlety:

> By bluster, graft, and doing people down
> Sam Baines got rich, but mellowing at last,
> Felt that by giving something to the town
> He might undo the evils of his past.

There is, of course, irony in the title since "tribute" is not intended literally. But the first line destroys all chance of sustaining subtlety. As soon as we see the words "bluster, graft, and doing people down" we know exactly where the poet stands, which is no sin in itself unless one asks more of poetry than one does of a good newspaper editorial.

William Jay Smith describes essentially the same sort of individual in his poem "American Primitive," and he also is satiric. But notice how different the effect is when irony is sustained.

> Look at him there in his stovepipe hat,
> His high-top shoes, and his handsome collar;
> Only my Daddy could look like that,
> And I love my Daddy like he loves his Dollar.

The lines flow like the ripple which runs silently down the length of a bull whip; and with his final word comes the "snap" which is sharp enough to make the most sophisticated reader jump. This is still fairly light verse, but the satire, sharpened with irony, draws blood. The tension here lies in the contrast between the *apparent* tone of sentimental tribute and the *actual* tone of cutting protest.

Moving further—much further—in the direction of subtlety and complexity, we have a third example of satire in Eliot's "The Love Song of J. Alfred Prufrock." The poem is an entire course in satire and deserves much more careful scrutiny than I can give it here. One brief selection from 131 lines will have to serve as appetizer.

Like the other two poems, this one aims its attack at an individual who represents a general type. Unlike the other two, the attack comes not from the poet directly but from the character himself. As in the case of Browning's "My Last Duchess," the narrator damns himself. But unlike Browning's characters, Prufrock recognizes at least some of his weaknesses. He veers constantly from self-deprecation to self-defense, employing both in a pattern of self-deceit which almost deceives us, the readers, until we notice that in even a brief description of the man the word "self" is constantly repeated.

Take, for example, these lines in which Prufrock reflects on his own worth:

> Should I, after tea and cakes and ices,
> Have the strength to force the moment to its crisis?
> But though I have wept and fasted, wept and prayed,
> Though I have seen my head (grown slightly bald) brought in
>   upon a platter,
> I am no prophet—and here's no great matter;
> I have seen the moment of my greatness flicker,
> And I have seen the eternal Footman hold my coat, and snicker,
> And in short, I was afraid.

The tension here is established in the strain between his apparent modesty and his extraordinary egotism; a more subtle form of tension is seen in the satiric irony of a man who reveals his conceit through the very phrases which he intends to be self-deprecating.

Specifically, we are tempted to see him as he sees himself: a man who recognizes the superficiality of his own society ("tea and cakes and ices"), a man who has tried to rise above it ("wept and fasted"), a man who is aware of his failure ("I have seen...my greatness flicker") and is, finally, uneasy about death ("I was afraid").

In the context of the entire poem, however, these lines expose an outrageous egotist. He is quick to blame the superficiality of his society ("tea and cakes and ices") when clearly he has himself selected that society by his own choice. The question he asks ("Should I...Have the strength...?") implies a choice when in fact he clearly does not have the strength. His description of his efforts to achieve greatness ("wept and fasted, wept and prayed") are such an absurd hyperbole that we cannot believe him. His confession ("I am no prophet") disguises the fact that he is not even a whole man as does the line above ("I have seen my head...") in which he actually compares himself with John the Baptist. And the last phrase ("I was afraid") is the technique of a man who hides terror by confessing to uneasiness.

Notice that this satire is not based simply on one or two exaggerated characteristics. It is developed from the maze of a man's ironic observations about himself.

One can learn a good deal about poetic satire from these three examples. First, the function of irony is to disguise at least partially the poet's satiric intent. It is difficult (though not impossible) to hone a sharp edge without it. Second, the satirist should consider the value of surprise. The "snap" may come at the end of a phrase, a line, or a stanza; but no matter where it is placed, it should jolt the reader. Finally, the primary way to convert simple satire to that which is sophisticated is to broaden the base so that satiric elements are distributed over a wide area and touch on many aspects of the subject.

Is Tension
Always Necessary?   Direct contrasts in theme are found in a great majority of poems. Irony in its various forms is used more sparingly. And satire is the least prevalent. But all are forms of poetic tension.

Must every poem contain some kind of tension? No. Kilmer's "Trees," quoted earlier in this section, contains no tension at all. Nor do the verses written to "Mom," "Dad," and "Dear Sis on Her 16th Birthday" which can be found in any greeting card shop. Works of this genus lie on the page limp as the protozoan which the biologist so calmly and without derision classifies as the least sophisticated form of life.

And it is true too that good poets will sketch out impressions in verse to catch a particular scene or an experience. These may contain no tension, but they usually remain in the poet's journal.

Tension, then, is not essential in verse. But its presence or absence is as radical a distinction as that between one-celled and multicelled organisms.

9

FROM UNITS
TO UNITY

Units of verse including stanzas (recurrent and non-recurrent), typographical divisions, cantos, and refrains; *organizing* these units with narrative, emotional, and logical sequences; *unifying* the poem through a persona (implied or stated), setting and title; *revising* early drafts.

A haiku is so short that even in the act of composition one is not consciously aware of either divisions within the work or its essential unity. Yet it has both. And as a matter of fact, one's effort is apt to be focused on these very aspects.

The separate units in the three-line haiku are the lines themselves. By tradition, the first has five syllables, the second line seven, and the last five. Why? Probably no more reason than there is for the sonata having three movements and the modern play tending to have three acts. There are psychological factors which partially account for these, but the poet's primary concern is for the form as he finds it. The haiku is like a vase which, though it can contain an infinite number of arrangements, lends itself better to some than to others.

Unity in the haiku is usually created by the central image. Often it is a setting such as a river, a grove, or a meadow. The season is frequently stated or implied. Since this usually is the starting point with such a short form, one scarcely thinks of it as being a unifying agent.

Examine the three examples below and notice how the units, the lines of fixed length, focus your attention in such a way that you pause and "read it like a poem" rather than skimming over it like a prose sentence. Notice too how the central image pulls those three lines together.

> On a journey, ill,
>   and over fields all withered, dreams
>   go wandering still.
>
> (Bashō)

> There a beggar goes!
>   Heaven and earth he's wearing
>   for his summer clothes.
>
> (Kikaku)

> Blossoms on the pear—
>   and a woman in the moonlight
>   reads a letter there.
>
> (Buson)

Notice that the five-seven-five syllable pattern is not strictly followed in each of these poems. The translator wanted to convey the original faithfully, and in Japanese haiku, syllabification is not always rigid.

In content, they are surprisingly different. The first, filled with tension, develops a metaphor in which the speaker's "dreams" are seen as a second wanderer. The second poem is lighter in mood and suggests that the beggar has all the universe can offer. The third is perhaps the most evocative. Like Pound's "In a Station of the Metro" (page 10), it presents a single image as if in a photograph. But there are as many implications here as there are in Pound's poem. What color are the blossoms and what might this suggest about the woman? What season is it when a pear tree blossoms, and what might this suggest about the woman's age? What might she be reading at this stage in her life? What follows pear blossoms, and what might the woman look forward to? These speculations are set off by the three separate images, one for each line. But the poem as a whole is unified by the single scene which includes them all.

Structure is important even when working with poems of this length. As one turns to longer forms, one has to be even more consciously aware of both the division of parts and the methods of unity. This is why they are treated together in this chapter.

The Units
of Verse In Chapter 3 I listed the various stanza forms as they applied to rhyme schemes. Stanzas are even more important as a basic organizational unit.

It is possible, of course, to write metered as well as unmetered verse without any stanzaic divisions. Poems of this sort, however, are almost as rare as short stories without paragraphs. Of those included in this text, Robley Wilson's "On a Maine Beach" (p. 112) comes close to being an example, but even in that poem one can detect quatrains through his rhyme scheme. Lack of stanzaic divisions does not always mean a lack of stanzaic organization.

Each stanza length has its own set of advantages and disadvantages. In considering them, remember that the same assets and liabilities apply to the irregular units in free verse.

Couplets, as I pointed out in Chapter 3, are less popular today than they were in the past because the rhymes are so noticeable. They also present problems as units of thought or impressions. Unless one is careful, couplets begin to organize themselves into a series of epigrams.

But this does not mean that they should be ignored entirely. It is important for a poet to experiment with as many forms as possible to keep himself loose. And the disadvantages of the couplet are not insurmountable.

One way to familiarize oneself with a particular form is to "translate" a published poem into it. Here, for example, is the first stanza of Snodgrass's "A Flat One" as he wrote it and next a revised version (printed with apologies to the poet) "translated" into rhyming couplets. Those who are interested in this form might enjoy doing the same to the second and third stanzas.

> Old Fritz, on this rotating bed
> For seven wasted months you lay
> Unfit to move, shrunken, gray,

> No good to yourself or anyone
> But to be babied—changed and bathed and fed.
> At long last, that's all done.

Revised as rhyming couplets:

> Old Fritz, on this rotating bed
> Unfit to move, babied and fed,
>
> For seven wasted months you lay
> Shrunken, haggard, alone and gray.
>
> You did no good for anyone,
> But now at last all that is done.

The triplet offers a larger unit. For this reason it is popular both with metered, rhymed verse as well as with free verse. Review once again Robert Creeley's "The Language" (p. 111) and try to visualize how the poem would be different if it had been written without stanzaic divisions.

Clearly the use of stanzas in that poem has a minimal effect. For some, they may only serve like stop signs on a residential street, forcing the driver to be cautious and observant. But notice that the triplets also serve to build a larger organizational division. There are four stanzas and then a break which is signaled both by the repetition of the phrase "I love you" and by the repeated use of italics. This is related to the theme which is stated once and is then restated with fresh images. Although this division into halves (both in content and structure) could be shown without stanzaic divisions, the stanzas help to suggest it subtly.

The quatrain, often associated with ballads, allows an entire scene to be developed. For this reason it is more popular with narrative poetry than are the shorter forms. It also serves as a "form within a form" in the sonnet, as was described in Chapter 3. My concern there was for the development of sound patterns; but the four-line subdivisions of the sonnet can also serve as units of thought or feeling.

The quatrain is sometimes used in free verse, though the tendency is to make the divisions varied in length. Robert Creeley, for example, often uses quatrains with verse which is in other respects similar to "The Language."

The longer forms—quintet, sestet, septet, and octave—all share the advantage of providing a solid block of writing in which entire sets of images or extended metaphors can be developed within its borders. The variety of rhyme schemes and random rhyme endings in these long stanzas is practically limitless.

Remember, however, that the longer the stanza the more careful one has to be to provide some sort of coherence within that unit. In the final analysis, this is the only limit to the length of a stanza or stanza-like divisions.

It is helpful at this point to make a distinction between *recurrent* and *nonrecurrent stanzas*. Strictly speaking, the term *stanza* applies only to recurrent units. That is, in metered and rhymed verse, the metrical and rhyme schemes of one stanza are repeated in the others. Monotony is avoided by muting the metrical scheme and the sound devices within each stanza rather than changing the system as one moves from one stanza to the next. Snodgrass's "A Flat One" is a good example of this. The stanzas are consistent in form with each other, though variations do occur within each stanza.

Dylan Thomas's "Fern Hill" is written in syllabics, a form of free verse, but his stanzas are also recurrent. As I pointed out in Chapter 5, each stanza repeats with surprising regularity the same syllable count, line by line, as the others. The very definition of syllabics calls for such recurrence—even though the result may appear to be remarkably free.

Adrienne Rich's "Like This Together" seems at first reading to be written in regular stanzas, but the degree of recurrence is actually far less than in "Fern Hill." There are six stanzas, but even the length of these units vary from twelve to fifteen lines. They do resemble each other visually, but they are not matched in meter or rhyme (it is not metered or rhymed) nor do the lines match in numbers of syllables. Her lines seem to be broken more or less into breath units and the stanzas are unified not by form but by a dominant visual image which in all but the third stanza appears in the first couple of lines. When one considers all these factors, it is clear that her stanzas resemble in some respects the nonrecurrent paragraphs of prose. Like paragraphs, her stanzas vary in length and are unified more by content than by form.

It is only one step from this to the loose typographical divisions in the free verse of such poets as E. E. Cummings, Allen Ginsberg, Lawrence Ferlinghetti, and many others. In these cases the word "stanza" is used rather freely to describe any group of lines which are set off by extra spacing. These are truly nonrecurrent in that they, like the prose paragraph, are not intended to echo each other in length or internal structure. They are merely divisions of thought, feeling, tone, or topic.

The *canto* is a longer division which is found in both metered and free verse. It usually consists of several stanzas, and the divisions are often signaled by printing numerals at the head of each. It serves somewhat the same function as the chapter does in fiction. The canto can be very helpful in longer poems to suggest a new setting, a new mood, or a new aspect of the theme. Sometimes it is possible to signal such shifts in the first few lines in the same way that Adrienne Rich does in her stanzas.

The *refrain* is closely associated with lyrics written for singing. All but the simplest stanza forms depend on the written page for their identification, and so do cantos. But the refrain can be detected easily by ear alone.

Refrains in ballads are a simple example. There, a line or two is repeated either after each verse (stanza) or at regular intervals such as every three verses. In contemporary popular music the refrain may dominate the lyrics, taking well over half of the playing time.

In sophisticated verse, the refrain is used sparingly if at all. As a device, it has less of a place in works intended primarily for the written page. The tendency is to use the visually effective division between stanzas and the variety of typographical arrangements available in free verse.

Of the poems printed in this volume, Donald Justice's "Another Song" serves as a good example of the refrain. With "song" in the title and with lines which echo Shakespeare's lyrics intended to be sung in *A Midsummer Night's Dream,* it is altogether appropriate that the last line of each of his three stanzas be a repeated refrain. Review it now (p. 111) and notice how the use of this refrain helps to make it appear like a cheerful, mindless song—this in sharp contrast with the starkly pessimistic theme.

Organizing the
Units of a Poem
There are as many ways to achieve order or coherence in a poem as there are in prose. But often they are more subtle.

The simplest form is the narrative sequence. Telling stories has always been a part of the poetic tradition, and a simple sequence of events serves as well for the length of "Beowulf" as it does for the three stanzas of Anthony Hecht's "Lizards and Snakes."

Old English ballads serve as good examples of the narrative pattern, and they are easy to imitate. Once one begins to "hear" the alternating lines of iambic tetrameter and trimeter, the composition usually comes quickly. All one needs is a protagonist and a challenge followed by a defeat or a victory.

Don't forget, however, that the model is a simple form of verse intended to be sung, often to the accompaniment of instruments. The "literary ballad" such as Coleridge's "The Ancient Mariner" borrows the basic form but adds layers of implication and suggestion.

The tendency today is to avoid the ballad form altogether except for light verse and lyrics intended to be sung. Instead, less regular metrical schemes are used. Of the poems printed in this text, Hecht's "Lizards and Snakes" serves as a fine example of narrative poetry which does not make use of the ballad form.

Narrative organization takes on an even more elaborate form in "A Flat One." The "story" is told in the form of a flashback. In the first stanza the narrator states that Old Fritz was in the hospital for seven months but that now "At long last, that's all done." Fritz is dead. The major portion of the poem then describes those seven months. Only in the last stanza does Snodgrass return to the final day of the patient's life.

Notice that the narrative aspect of the poem is kept to a minimum. The stanzas do not report his progress month by month. Many of them refer to habitual treatment over the course of that period. But the unity of those eighteen stanzas is maintained at least in part by the sequence of events.

A second method of building coherence into a poem is the use of emotional sequences. In the previous chapter I pointed out how often the sonnet establishes a tension between two contrasting feelings or attitudes. But in almost every sonnet there is one emotion or attitude which dominates and thereby unifies the poem as a whole.

The fact that strong emotions tend to unify a poem partly accounts for the prevalence of love in verse. But remember that too much unity can become monotonous just as easily as an excessively repeated theme can ruin a piece of music. The infusion of mixed feelings in a love poem such as we have seen in the works of Rich and Snodgrass helps to combat this danger. A poem can vibrate with ambivalences and still remain essentially unified by love or affection.

When logic is used to organize a poem, one has to be careful not to let it get abstract and theoretical. There is no law against the abstract poem, of course, but there is a risk of boredom.

I have included Frost's "Fire and Ice" partly because it illustrates one form of poetic tension; but also because it is a good example of a poem which appears to pose a theoretical problem to be solved by logic. This is, of course, deceptive, for he is really talking about emotions and he is responding to them subjectively. But the outward appearance of the poem's organizational pattern is that of a logical argument.

Unity by
Person and Place   Sequences of events, feelings, or logical alternatives are highly effective methods of organizing a poem, but some works maintain a sense of unity without any of these. In most cases they are dominated either by a strong persona or by the setting.

Adrienne Rich's "Like This Together" is such a poem. As I pointed out earlier, the stanzas are each unified by a separate visual image, but the overall organization of the poem is not based on an orderly sequence of events. To some degree, the relationship between the two characters in the poem is the unifying factor; but another factor is the dominant presence of the "speaker." It is a highly personal statement, and we never for a moment lose the sense that a speaker is revealing her inner thoughts. Contrast this sense of personal presence with the tone established in Creeley's "The Language." He also is talking about love, but the poem does not read like a personal confession.

What is it, finally, that holds together poems like Robley Wilson's "On a Maine Beach" and Dylan Thomas's "Fern Hill"? The dominant factor in each of these poems is place. True, there are thematic concerns which also provide unity, but what gives us a sense of order in our first reading is in both cases the extended and detailed use of a particular setting. In Wilson's poem, there is no protagonist at all. Someone is speaking, but we can't guess his age or sex as we can in "Fern Hill" or "Like This Together." In spite of this, the poem has coherence. The unity comes from that central image of the rock pool on a beach in Maine.

Notice how frequently a person, place, or object is highlighted in the title. This is one more way a poet can unify his work. "Lizards and Snakes" and "To the Snake" are titles which emphasize the key image in each of these poems. "Like This Together" focuses on a relationship. In Ezra Pound's "In a Station of the Metro," the title stands like an additional line, unifying the poem by providing the only direct statement about the setting.

If the poet refuses to give his work a title, editors will identify each poem with its opening line. This accounts for the title of E. E. Cummings's poem, "Buffalo Bill's." Usually, however, poets prefer to write a title which will highlight some specific aspect of the poem and in that way increase the unity.

Approaches
to Revision

In examining one's own work, it is useful to identify both the units by which the poem is divided and the kind of central unifying agent which is giving the poem coherence. These may have developed without any conscious planning.

If the poem seems somewhat aimless or scattered in its approach, it may be a simple matter to highlight the narrative sequence, the emotional responses, or whatever the unifying factor may be. This is particularly important in longer poems.

Real problems arise when a poet fails to identify the system of organization in his work. There is a tendency, for example, to add an analytical final stanza as a method of clarifying the intent of the poem. Picture, if you will, such an explanation tacked on to Hecht's "Lizards and Snakes." In that case, one would be adding an analytical stanza to a poem which was already unified and clarified through a narrative sequence. If a narrative poem needs greater unity, it is wise to consider making the narrative portion clearer rather than turning to a different method of coherence.

"Like This Together" is a good example. This is more difficult in theme than some of the others included in this text. Miss Rich has chosen to leave some aspects of the poem—particularly toward the end—partially ambiguous. But if she had wanted a more precise statement, one direction would have been to sharpen the system of coherence already in the poem. That is, she could have expanded upon the relationship between the persona and her companion.

Much less frequently, a poem may seem to be too obviously a step-by-step narration or a simple statement of love or a photographic treatment of a place or person. In these cases the problem is not so much excessive coherence as it is a lack of sophistication. The answer is *not* simply making it fuzzy. That would be like correcting a dull photographic composition by placing the subject out of focus.

On the contrary, the most effective approach is to find and develop ambivalences in one's feeling on the subject. Notice how frequently ambivalences or contrasts are involved in the poems already discussed: hate is softened by love in "A Flat One," love is countered by doubts and silence in "Like This Together," joy of living is countered by the omnipresence of death in "Fern Hill," a symbolic suggestion of life teaches us ultimately something about death in "On a Maine Beach."

When a poet consciously knows what system of division he has been using and what his method of coherence is, he has control over his revisions. He is then able to increase the suggestion of his work without loss of clarity.

10

REVISING
A POEM

Conscious revision seen as the route to intuitive revision, not the reverse; *subjective evaluation* seen as of limited value compared with *precise* analysis; the *six critical questions* which help in judging the work of others as well as one's own.

As a general rule, novice poets make very few revisions; developing poets revise with conscious, laborious effort; and accomplished poets revise intuitively, scarcely making any separation in their own mind between revision and the original composition. My intent in this chapter is to encourage that second stage in which each poem is worked over with a conscious, critical eye. When one reaches the third stage, there will be no need for texts on literary composition.

This same three-stage division often applies equally well to creative writing classes and to friends who may be willing to serve as critics. Beginning classes and critics who are not widely read don't know what questions to ask. As a result, they tend to respond subjectively. "I like it," they say. Or, "It doesn't do anything for me." This may help or bruise the poet's ego, but it doesn't tell him anything about his work. The judgment may be based on some completely personal preference—"I never have liked love poetry," or "poems should be happy." Comments like these are of no help to a poet.

The best criticism from a class or an individual is primarily descriptive and only secondarily evaluative. That is, the critic tells the poet what he has done, and it is largely up to the poet to decide whether that is what he wants. "Your images are very imaginative, really fresh," a helpful critic might say, "but the poem doesn't seem to use any sound devices at all." If the poet is lazy or inexperienced, he may use the well-worn defense, "that's just what I intended to do." But any poet who is sincerely concerned with verse as an art form must ask himself whether he is truly satisfied with a poem which does not do more with sound than does prose. In some cases he may wish to do just this; in other cases he may wish to sacrifice some other poetic device such as regular rhythm; but good criticism will help him decide whether he has made these decisions wisely or by accident.

Six

Critical Questions Good writing classes, like individual critics, tend to concern themselves with six central questions. These are important because they are the same questions the poet must learn to ask himself about his own work. Eventually they will become internalized.

Each of these topics has been the subject of at least one chapter, but the order here has been changed. While the discussion of every poem will vary with the work and with the inclinations of the group, it is often helpful to begin by examining those aspects which strike the reader first, postponing those more complex concerns as tension and thematic unity for later.

First, *are the images effective?* In a difficult poem, isolated images may be all that reaches the reader the first time through. These may be vivid visual details used for their own sake, or they may be vehicles for metaphors; but the poet needs to know what has really made an impression on his readers. It is mainly by listening to the reactions of others that he will eventually be able to judge for himself what is a fresh image and what is bland, flat, or even hackneyed.

Second, *is the diction fresh?* Here the critic turns from phrasing to individual words. It is his job to identify not only clichés but familiar phrasing, echoes from song lyrics, and conventional adjectives which provide no overtones. This requires a close reading. The critic must be very specific. It is no help whatever for the poet to hear someone say, "I don't like the words you use." What he needs is comments on individual words and phrases.

Notice that when a poem fails to have effective images and also fails to use fresh, precise diction, the result is usually a lack of poetic compression. Such a poem can be said to be prosaic in so far as its language is close to that of prose. But once again, criticism must be precise. If a reader's general impression is that a poem lacks compression or is prosaic, he owes it to the poet to locate specific samples of dull, wordy, over-modified writing or flat, unimaginative images.

When the poet revises, he must also begin with these two questions. He must question each phrase and each word as if it were being presented to a group of perceptive critics.

Third, *are there sound devices?* True, some poems depend heavily on sharpness of image and do not make use of such techniques as rhyme, assonance, alliteration, consonance, and onomatopoeia. But they are rare. In student-written poems, lack of sound devices is more often a matter of forgetfulness than intention.

Occasionally the problem may be just the reverse: sound devices which are obtrusive. As I pointed out in Chapter 3, rhyming couplets can do this particularly when they are emphasized with regular, end-stopped lines. Contiguous alliteration can also become blatant. Just how much is too much obviously is a matter of individual opinion, but if several readers make the same complaint, the line certainly deserves reconsideration.

Fourth, *does the poem make use of rhythm?* Here again, the critic should be as specific as possible. If the poem is metered, where does the meter become monotonous and where, on the other hand, do the substitutions become so numerous that the flow of reading is interrupted? If it is free verse, what rhythmical systems is the poet using? He needs to know what comes through to the reader.

Just as the use of images and the diction of a poem are closely related, so are the sound devices and the rhythmical effects. Both, in this case, depend ultimately on the ear. It is for this reason that poets often read their own work out loud many times as they revise. The attempt is to hear the work as others will probably hear it. Revisions are partly intuitive, of course, even from the start. But one has to be consciously aware of both rhythm and sound to be sure that one has made the most of each.

Fifth, *does the poem contain some type of tension*? It is rare indeed that a poem achieves any kind of literary sophistication without developing tension in contrasting thematic concerns, tones, moods, attitudes. It may be, of course, that the poet is content to leave his poem fairly simple. But there are times when a poet *thinks* he has created something with genuine sophistication when in fact what comes through to the reader is relatively simple. Such work may be altogether appropriate in one's journal or as occasional verse or, like an artist's sketch, as preparation for a longer or more complex work. A good critic—whether in a class or not—can help a poet to determine the degree of sophistication in a poem by discussing the forms of tension he sees—or fails to see.

Sixth, *just what is the essential unity in the poem*? Frequently this will turn into a discussion of the poem's theme or central concern. As I pointed out in the previous chapter, the unity of a poem may be achieved by a narrative sequence, emotional responses, or a logical structure. And it may be enhanced by a persona or by the setting. Discussing the unity of a poem in these terms helps to avoid over-simplifying the poem's intent. If, on the other hand, the poem really can be summarized by a simple moral truth or "lesson," it is probably a very simple piece—and most likely hackneyed as well.

The unity of a poem, of course, need not be based on a single, clear concern. As we have seen, "Fern Hill" is concerned with youth and vitality and growth; it is also concerned with mortality and death. But they are linked in such a way as to provide an artistic whole. As a poet revises, he usually tries to maintain this whole no matter how complex and varied his concerns may be.

There are occasions when a poem may shift from one mood or suggestion to another in the course of revisions. There is no harm in this, but it is important to make sure that each line and every image in the new version really belongs there. This is particularly important when the poet finds that his emotional attitude toward his subject has changed between, for example, the third and the fourth draft. In more extreme cases, the tenor in an extended metaphor may shift quite unintentionally. The change may be an improvement, but basic revision throughout the work will be necessary to keep the poem consistent.

Look on these six questions not as a check list but as a guide to criticism of poetry—both the works of others and your own efforts. One way to practice criticism is to use them when reviewing the poems which are printed in the following chapter. Most important, however, use them when revising your own work. Eventually they will become internalized, an unconscious set of standards which will direct the course of lengthy revisions. It is at this point that the writing of poetry ceases to be primarily a craft and becomes, instead, a fully developed artistic act.

11

POEMS FOR STUDY

Lizards and Snakes

ANTHONY HECHT

On the summer road that ran by our front porch
    Lizards and snakes came out to sun.
It was hot as a stove out there, enough to scorch
    A buzzard's foot. Still, it was fun
To lie in the dust and spy on them. Near but remote,   5
    They snoozed in the carriage ruts, a smile
In the set of the jaw, a fierce pulse in the throat
Working away like Jack Doyle's after he'd run the mile.

Aunt Martha had an unfair prejudice
    Against them (as well as being cold   10
Toward bats.) She was pretty inflexible in this,
    Being a spinster and all, and old.
So we used to slip them into her knitting box.
    In the evening she'd bring in things to mend
And a nice surprise would slide out from under the socks.   15
It broadened her life, as Joe said. Joe was my friend.

But we never did it again after the day
    Of the big wind when you could hear the trees
Creak like rockingchairs. She was looking away
    Off, and kept saying, "Sweet Jesus, please   20
Don't let him hear me. He's as like as twins.
    He can crack us like lice with his fingernail.
I can see him plain as a pikestaff. Look how he grins
And swinges the scaly horror of his folded tail."

ROBERT CREELEY

> Locate *I*
> *love you* some-
> where in
>
> teeth and
> eyes, bite
> It but
>
> take care not
> to hurt, you
> want so
>
> much so
> little. Words
> say everything,
>
> *I*
> *love you*
> again,
>
> then what
> is emptiness
> for. To
>
> fill, fill.
> I heard words
> and words full
>
> of holes
> aching. Speech
> is a mouth.

5

10

15

20

Another Song

DONALD JUSTICE

Merry the green, the green hill shall be merry.
Hungry, the owlet shall seek out the mouse,
And Jack his Joan, but they shall never marry.

And snows shall fly, the big flakes fat and furry.
Lonely, the traveler shall seek out the house,
And Jack his Joan, but they shall never marry.

5

Weary the soldiers go, and come back weary,
Up a green hill and down the withered hill,
And Jack from Joan, and they shall never marry.

The Sloth

THEODORE ROETHKE

In moving-slow he has no Peer.
You ask him something in his ear;
He thinks about it for a Year;

And then, before he says a Word
There, upside down (unlike a Bird)   5
He will assume that you have Heard—

A most Ex-as-per-at-ing Lug.
But should you call his manner Smug,
He'll sigh and give his Branch a Hug;

Then off again to Sleep he goes,   10
Still swaying gently by his Toes,
And you must know he knows he knows.

On a Maine Beach

ROBLEY WILSON

Look, in these pools, how rocks are like worn change
Keeping the ocean's mint-mark; barnacles
Miser on them; societies of snails
Hunch on their rims and think small thoughts whose strange
Salt logics rust like a mainspring, small dreams   5
Pinwheeling to a point and going dumb,
Small equations whose euphemistic sum
Stands for mortality. A thousand times
Tides swallow up such pools, shellfish and stone
Show green and yellow shade in groves of weed;   10
Rocks shrink, barnacles drink, snails think they bleed
In their trapped world. Here, when the sea is gone,
We find old coins glowing under the sky,
Barnacles counting them, snails spending slow
Round lifetimes half-awake. Beach rhythms flow   15
In circles. Perfections teach us to die.

Pied Beauty

GERARD MANLEY HOPKINS

Glory be to God for dappled things—
  For skies of couple-colour as a brinded cow;
    For rose-moles all in stipple upon trout that swim;
Fresh-firecoal chestnut-falls; finches' wings;
  Landscape plotted and pieced—fold, fallow, and plough;   5
    And all trades, their gear and tackle and trim.

All things counter, original, spare, strange;
  Whatever is fickle, freckled (who knows how?)
    With swift, slow; sweet, sour; adazzle, dim;
He fathers-forth whose beauty is past change: 10
          Praise him.

Like This Together

ADRIENNE RICH

1.
Wind rocks the car.
We sit parked by the river,
silence between our teeth.
Birds scatter across islands
of broken ice. Another time   5
I'd have said "Canada geese",
knowing you love them.
A year, ten years from now,
I'll remember this,
this sitting like drugged birds   10
in a glass case—
not why, only that we
were here like this together.

2.
They're tearing down, tearing up
this city, block by block.   15
Rooms, cut in half,
hang like flayed carcasses,

their old roses in rags,
famous streets have forgotten
where they were going. Only   20
a fact could be so dreamlike.
They're tearing down the houses
we met and lived in,
soon our two bodies will be all
left standing from that era.   25

3.
We have, as they say,
certain things in common.
I mean: a view
from a bathroom window
over slate to stiff pigeons   30
huddled every morning; the way
water tastes from our tap,
which you marvel at, letting
it splash into the glass.
Because of you I notice   35
the taste of water,
a luxury I might
otherwise have missed.

4.
Our words misunderstand us.
Sometimes at night   40
you are my mother:
old detailed griefs
twitch at my dreams, and I
crawl against you, fighting
for shelter, making you   45
my cave. Sometimes
you're the wave of birth
that drowns me in my first
nightmare. I suck the air.
Miscarried knowledge twists us   50
like hot sheets thrown askew.

5.
Dead winter doesn't die.
It wears away, a piece of carrion
picked clean at last,
rained away or burnt dry.   55
Our desiring does this,
make no mistake, I'm speaking
of fact: through mere indifference

we could prevent it.
Only our fierce attention   60
gets hyacinths out of those
hard cerebral lumps,
unwraps the wet buds down
the whole length of a stem.

6.
A severed hand   65
keeps tingling, air still suffers
beyond the stump. But new
life? How do we bear it
(or you, huge tree)
when fresh flames start spurting   70
out through our old sealed skins,
nerve-endings ours and not yet ours?
Susceptibilities we still
can't use, sucking
blind power from our roots—   75
what else to do but
hold fast to the
one thing we know,
grip earth and let burn.

"Dove Sta Amore"

LAWRENCE FERLINGHETTI

> Dove sta amore
> Where lies love
> Dove sta amore
> Here lies love
> The ring dove love   5
> In lyrical delight
> Hear love's hillsong
> Love's true willsong
> Love's low plainsong
> Too sweet painsong   10
> In passages of night
> Dove sta amore
> Here lies love
> The ring dove love
> Dove sta amore   15
> Here lies love

A Flat One

W. D. SNODGRASS

Old Fritz, on this rotating bed
For seven wasted months you lay
Unfit to move, shrunken, gray,
No good to yourself or anyone
But to be babied—changed and bathed and fed.   5
     At long last, that's all done.

Before each meal, twice every night,
We set pads on your bedsores, shut
Your catheter tube off, then brought
The second canvas-and-black-iron   10
Bedframe and clamped you in between them, tight,
     Scared, so we could turn

You over. We washed you, covered you,
Cut up each bite of meat you ate;
We watched your lean jaws masticate   15
As ravenously your useless food
As thieves at hard labor in their chains chew
     Or insects in the wood.

Such pious sacrifice to give
You all you could demand of pain: 20
Receive this haddock's body, slain
For you, old tyrant; take this blood
Of a tomato, shed that you might live.
     You had that costly food.

You seem to be all finished, so   25
We'll plug your old recalcitrant anus
And tie up your discouraged penis
In a great, snow-white bow of gauze.
We wrap you, pin you, and cart you down below,
     Below, below, because   30

Your credit has finally run out.
On our steel table, trussed and carved,
You'll find this world's hardworking, starved
Teeth working in your precious skin.
The earth turns, in the end, by turn about   35
     And opens to take you in.

Seven months gone down the drain; thank God
That's through. Throw out the four-by-fours,
Swabsticks, the thick salve for bedsores,

Throw out the diaper pads and drug   40
Containers, pile the bedclothes in a wad,
   And rinse the cider jug

Half filled with the last urine. Then
Empty out the cotton cans,
Autoclave the bowls and spit pans,   45
Unhook the pumps and all the red
Tubes—catheter, suction, oxygen;
   Next, wash the empty bed.

—All this Dark Age machinery
On which we had tormented you   50
To life. Last, gather up the few
Belongings: snapshots, some odd bills,
Your mail, and half a pack of Luckies we
   Won't light you after meals.

Old man, these seven months you've lain   55
Determined—not that you would live—
Just to not die. No one would give
You one chance you could ever wake
From that first night, much less go well again,
   Much less go home and make   60

Your living; how could you hope to find
A place for yourself in all creation?—
Pain was your only occupation.
And pain that should content and will
A man to give it up, nerved you to grind   65
   Your clenched teeth, breathing, till

Your skin broke down, your calves went flat,
And your legs lost all sensation. Still,
You took enough morphine to kill
A strong man. Finally, nitrogen   70
Mustard: you could last two months after that;
   It would kill you then.

Even then you wouldn't quit.
Old soldier, yet you must have known
Inside the animal had grown   75
Sick of the world, made up its mind
To stop. Your mind ground on its separate
   Way, merciless and blind,

Into these last weeks when the breath
Would only come in fits and starts   80
That puffed out your sections like the parts
Of some enormous, damaged bug.

You waited, not for life, not for your death,
    Just for the deadening drug

That made your life seem bearable.   85
You still whispered you would not die.
Yet in the nights I heard you cry
Like a whipped child; in fierce old age
You whimpered, tears stood on your gun-metal
    Blue cheeks shaking with rage   90

And terror. So much pain would fill
Your room that when I left I'd pray
That if I came back the next day
I'd find you gone. You stayed for me—
Nailed to your own rapacious, stiff self-will.   95
    You've shook loose, finally.

They'd say this was a worthwhile job
Unless they tried it. It is mad
To throw our good lives after bad;
    Waste time, drugs, and our minds, while strong   100
Men starve. How many young men did we rob
    To keep you hanging on?

I can't think we did *you* much good.
Well, when you died, none of us wept.
You killed for us, and so we kept   105
You; because we need to earn *our* pay.
No. We'd still have to help you try. We would
    Have killed for you today.

Fern Hill

DYLAN THOMAS

Now as I was young and easy under the apple boughs
About the lilting house and happy as the grass was green,
    The night above the dingle starry,
        Time let me hail and climb
    Golden in the heydays of his eyes,   5
And honoured among wagons I was prince of the apple towns
And once below a time I lordly had the trees and leaves
        Trail with daisies and barley
    Down the rivers of the windfall light.

And as I was green and carefree, famous among the barns   10
About the happy yard and singing as the farm was home,

In the sun that is young once only,
      Time let me play and be
   Golden in the mercy of his means,
And green and golden I was huntsman and herdsman, the calves   15
Sang to my horn, the foxes on the hills barked clear and cold,
      And the sabbath rang slowly
   In the pebbles of the holy streams.

All the sun long it was running, it was lovely, the hay
Fields high as the house, the tunes from the chimneys, it was air   20
     And playing, lovely and watery
      And fire green as grass.
     And nightly under the simple stars
As I rode to sleep the owls were bearing the farm away,
All the moon long I heard, blessed among stables, the nightjars   25
     Flying with the ricks, and the horses
      Flashing into the dark.

And then to awake, and the farm, like a wanderer white
With the dew, come back, the cock on his shoulder: it was all
     Shining, it was Adam and maiden,   30
      The sky gathered again
     And the sun grew round that very day.
So it must have been after the birth of the simple light
In the first, spinning place, the spellbound horses walking warm
     Out of the whinnying green stable   35
      On to the fields of praise.

And honoured among foxes and pheasants by the gay house
Under the new made clouds and happy as the heart was long
     In the sun born over and over,
      I ran my heedless ways,   40
     My wishes raced through the house-high hay
And nothing I cared, at my sky blue trades, that time allows
In all his tuneful turning so few and such morning songs
     Before the children green and golden
      Follow him out of grace,   45

Nothing I cared, in the lamb white days, that time would take me
Up to the swallow thronged loft by the shadow of my hand,
     In the moon that is always rising,
      Nor that riding to sleep
     I should hear him fly with the high fields   50
And wake to the farm forever fled from the childless land.
Oh as I was young and easy in the mercy of his means,
      Time held me green and dying
     Though I sang in my chains like the sea.

The Still Voice of Harlem

CONRAD KENT RIVERS

Come to me broken dreams and all
  bring me the glory of fruitless souls,
I shall find a place for them in my gardens.

Weep not for the golden sun of California,
  think not of the fertile soil of Alabama...   5
nor your father's eyes, your mother's body twisted
  by the washing board.

I am the hope of your unborn,
  truly, when there is no more of me...
there shall be no more of you....   10

To the Snake

DENISE LEVERTOV

Green Snake, when I hung you round my neck
and stroked your cold, pulsing throat
  as you hissed to me, glinting
arrowy gold scales, and I felt
  the weight of you on my shoulders,   5
and the whispering silver of your dryness
  sounded close at my ears—

Green Snake—I swore to my companions that certainly
  you were harmless! But truly
I had no certainty, and no hope, only desiring   10
  to hold you, for that joy,
        which left

a long wake of pleasure, as the leaves moved
and you faded into the pattern
of grass and shadows, and I returned
smiling and haunted, to a dark morning.   15

Fire and Ice

ROBERT FROST

SOME say the world will end in fire,
Some say in ice.
From what I've tasted of desire
I hold with those who favor fire.

But if it had to perish twice,   5
I think I know enough of hate
To say that for destruction ice
Is also great
And would suffice.

"Buffalo Bill's"

E. E. CUMMINGS

Buffalo Bill's

defunct
            who used to
            ride a watersmooth-silver
                                    stallion   5
and break onetwothreefourfive pigeonsjustlikethat
                                            Jesus

he was a handsome man
                        and what i want to know is

how do you like your blueeyed boy   10
Mister Death

PART TWO * * *

The
Writing
of
Fiction

12

THE SCOPE OF FICTION

The blend of *experience* and *invention;* the *three stances* of fiction; mimetic fiction, premise fiction, and dream fiction; fiction as contrasted with *descriptive writing; simple vs. sophisticated* work as seen in both content and technique; the *motive* of the writer.

Fiction tells an untrue story in prose. This brief statement is a reminder of just how broad the scope of this genre is. It also defines where its limits are: When a story is told in lines of verse, it becomes narrative poetry. When it is intended to be acted out on the stage, it is drama. And when it is intended to be factually true—that is, openly and consistently based on actual characters and events—we call it nonfiction and classify it under headings like biography, autobiography, and historical analysis.

Experience
and Invention Fiction is "untrue" in the sense that it is not dependent on actual people and events. Stories which ask the reader to assume the existence of ghosts, dragons, or unicorns are good examples of just how free the genre is. But it is equally true that fiction is rooted in the actual world—and frequently in the life-

experiences of the author. Fictional characters who "come alive" in a story are often the ones which were based consciously or unconsciously on real people the writer has known. And in the same way, descriptions of places which readers describe as "vivid" are usually close to scenes from the writer's own life.

As a result, fiction is usually an unstable mixture of personal experience and invention. The blend will vary from story to story and with different elements in the same work. One character may be an exact likeness of the author's brother and another an almost complete invention. Or the basic incident may be autobiographical while the setting and characters are devised.

It is, of course, possible to write a good story which is based literally event by event on experience. Life occasionally takes on the pattern of fiction, and that is when one is tempted to report it directly. The danger is that the author may be tempted to include irrelevant material and may hesitate to revise and reshape the pattern of events. Too often, such stories remain like journal entries which are of interest only to the writer.

On the other hand, it is possible to do the reverse: to avoid the personal element either intentionally or from a kind of psychic modesty. Slick fiction, for example, is usually constructed by revising old conventions of plot and situation. More sophisticated, good science fiction stories may concentrate on plot to such a degree that the writer's own life and associates are never used. Sometimes beginning writers are tempted to stick with western scenes, fantasy situations, or conventionalized plots mainly because they are reluctant to reveal aspects of their own lives. It takes time and encouragement to convince such students that their lives and their most inner feelings are the primary resource upon which they can draw. In addition to these personal experiences, of course, there are episodes which the author may have observed or heard about. But even in these cases, the most valuable material will be that which is in some way familiar to the author.

The Three
Stances of Fiction Every story and novel establishes a set of assumptions which become its own "rules" for what can and what cannot be expected to happen. There are three different patterns and these can be thought of as the author's *stance*.

The first of these is *mimetic fiction*. The word *mimetic* means imitative (as in *mimic*), and this type of fiction imitates actual life. The characters in such stories are "realistic" in that they are guided by what we think of as the laws of nature in our daily life. We can assume that they will not turn into animals or have supernatural powers, that the dead will not return to haunt the living, and that neither cats nor horses will talk. Most fiction today is written from the mimetic stance—as are the three samples included in this volume.

The second stance is *premise fiction.* Here the author offers a premise in which the pattern of realism is revised. In the play Hamlet, for example, we are asked to accept the existence of ghosts. In Kafka's story, "Metamorphosis," we must accept the fact that a young man could, one morning, turn into a six-foot cockroach. No scientific explanation is given. It is simply announced at the opening of the story:

> As Gregor Samsa awoke one morning from uneasy dreams he found himself transformed in his bed into a gigantic insect. He was lying on his hard, as it were armor-plated, back and when he lifted his head a little he could see his dome-like brown belly divided into stiff arched segments on top of which the bed quilt could hardly keep in position and was about to slide off completely. His numerous legs, which were pitifully thin compared to the rest of his bulk, waved helplessly before his eyes.
>
> What has happened to me? he thought. It was no dream. His room, a regular human bedroom, only rather too small, lay quiet between the four familiar walls.

Notice that although a single, extraordinary premise is given, we are soon assured that everything else about the story is going to conform to what we might expect in the real world. Indeed, the rest of the family responds just as you might expect they might—assuming that Gregor has indeed turned into a gigantic insect.

Those who have felt alienated from their families will soon see Gregor's transformation as highly symbolic, but it is still necessary to believe the original premise and to take the situation literally. Kafka did not begin the story with the statement that "Gregor awoke feeling *as if* he had been turned into a gigantic insect." He *was* transformed. And readers of fiction are willing to accept such violations of the natural order.

Another frequently anthologized sample of premise fiction is Shirley Jackson's "The Lottery." This story starts with what appears to be a perfectly realistic situation: A small town is preparing for some kind of lottery. It is not until the final page that one discovers with a sense of shock just what the lottery is all about. Unlike Kafka's "The Metamorphosis," this story withholds the brutal premise until the end. Once again, we are asked to believe something which we know doesn't happen literally in real life, but we accept it nonetheless while we are "in the story."

A third stance is *dream fiction*. Instead of limiting the "unreal" element to a single premise, the dream story moves with its own logic just as sleeping dreams do. Sometimes they are light and whimsical as in *Alice in Wonderland*. More often they are dark and ominous as in Kafka's "A Country Doctor" or his novels, *The Castle* and *The Trial*. And almost always they are symbolic as in John Cheever's "The Swimmer."

Dream fiction is the least used of the three forms and the most risky for the beginner because it so easily turns into an aimless rendition of the author's fantasies. When it is an unrevised record of the writer's own inner world, it becomes a kind of descriptive writing—a clinical account which is no more *literary* than a diary or a psychiatrist's transcription of his patient's dreams. In general, this is of interest only to the writer himself.

What makes the works of Lewis Carroll, Kafka, Cheever, and others *literary* is the fact that they utilize the illusion of a dream to achieve a specific thematic concern. That is, the dream is used as a device, not as the final concern itself.

Understanding these three stances of fiction helps to avoid confusions about the term "realism." Critics use this to describe a specific literary movement in the development of the novel starting in the mid-nineteenth century and developing into naturalism toward the end of that century. As such, "realism" is a valuable term. In careless speech, however, the term is often used to describe either mimetic fiction or, still more loosely, any work which is vivid. This leads to long, pointless arguments about whether dream-like stories are "realistic."

For the sake of clarity, it is best to reserve "realism" for its precise historical sense, to describe fiction which is vivid as "vivid," and to identify work which imitates the range of possibilities in our actual world as "mimetic."

**Fiction vs.
Descriptive Writing**   The scope of fiction is enormously broad. As I have pointed out, combining experience with invention

provides an unlimited number of situations and characters with which the author may work. And the range is made still broader by the writer's choice of stance: stories rooted in the actual world, based on some hypothetical premise, or freed to follow the erratic patterns of the dream.

But there are boundaries. There are points at which fiction becomes some form of nonfiction. Locating these boundaries is one way of defining just what the genre of fiction is.

Once again, it is helpful to recall Northrop Frye's distinction between literary writing and descriptive writing, as described in Chapter 1.

Descriptive writing, you will remember, has as its primary function the task of describing or interpreting some aspect of the world about us. Newspaper articles, for example, must answer the questions of *Who? When? What? Where?* and *How?* Each question refers to the incident being reported. We judge the article by how accurate and how insightful it is. The same applies to a doctor's records on a patient or a social worker's report on a client. And even a journal, though a personal document, is essentially descriptive writing, for its function is to record the thoughts and emotions of its author. In each of these cases, the writing is tied to events in the actual world and is judged by how effectively it does this.

Literary writing, as defined by Northrop Frye, is fundamentally different in its approach. Each work is a self-contained world and is judged on that basis, as a painting or a symphony is judged. Poetry and drama as well as fiction are forms of literary writing in this sense; but of the three genres, it is fiction which most frequently is confused with forms of descriptive writing.

When a writer of short stories does not see his work as literary in this sense, he may end up writing journal entries or even segments from a diary. It is a clear indication that a writer is in trouble if he begins to defend an unconvincing story with the excuse, "But that's the way it happened."

True, experience is the raw material. True, the writer of sophisticated fiction depends on it. But almost always it is fashioned, rebuilt, and reworked to create an illusion of reality for the reader. The reordering tends to be a conscious process at first, and during that period a text such as this can be of help. Later, writing becomes more intuitive. At that point, one doesn't depend as much on advice.

It is important to remember that almost every specialized form of fiction has a corresponding form of descriptive writing. Although most short stories use the mimetic stance and are based on a combination of experienced and observed events, this diagram covers the full spectrum of fiction as seen in short stories and novels.

FORMS OF FICTION	NONFICTIONAL FORMS

Mimetic Fiction
  primarily based on :
      personal experience —— autobiographies, journals, & diaries
      observed incidents —— reporting & journalism
      one man's life —————— biographies & case histories
      a historical figure —— historical studies
      allegory ————————— essays (often religious or political)
Premise Fiction ————— speculative scientific articles and social commentary
Dream Fiction ————— clinical records of actual dreams and fantasies

The division is not always clear. Truman Capote's *In Cold Blood*, for example, has been described by the author as "non-fiction fiction" because although it is written like a novel (with dialogue and thoughts included) it is based literally and openly on actual events. Technically, this "novel" is really a vividly written case history. The distinction in this and in all cases is based on whether the work is *primarily* intended to report or record or comment on real events or, in the case of fiction, primarily an artistic creation which is intended to stand on its own.

               Simple vs.

               Sophisticated Fiction This distinction has already been made in the poetry section. It is equally important in fiction. Essentially, sophisticated works "do" more in the sense that they suggest more, imply a greater range of suggestions, develop more subtle shadings of meaning. This text is concerned with sophisticated writing, but this does not mean that such work is "better." It is simply "other" in the sense that the biologically simple jellyfish is different from the far more sophisticated porpoise.

The span between the most simple and relatively sophisticated fiction is enormous. Compare a comic strip about adolescents like *Archie, The Jackson Twins,* or *Gil Thorpe* with a novel about adolescents like Knowles's *A Separate Peace* or Salinger's *Catcher in the Rye*. They are similar in that they are both samples of fiction as I have been defining it—they both tell untrue stories in prose. Further, they both have plot, characters, setting, and themes. And they share certain basic techniques: dialogue, thoughts, action, description, and exposition. They even use the same subject matter: that highly charged period between childhood and adulthood. And before one brands one as "good" and the other as "bad," remember that many intelligent adults read the comics in the morning paper, and *Catcher in the Rye* is still barred from many secondary schools as immoral and unacceptable.

But obviously they are utterly different forms of fiction. Archie as a fictional character is *simple* and so are the stories in which he appears. There are only a limited number of suggestions or implications which can be made from the highly conventional, monotonously repetitive types of situations in which he is placed. On the other hand Holden is a sophisticated character as is the novel in which we come to know him. It is important here to distinguish this literary use of *sophisticated* from its popular use which describes merely personal characteristics. Mark Twain's Huck Finn, for example, is certainly unsophisticated as an individual, but the complexity and intricacy with which the author presents him is unmistakably sophisticated.

Since this text is primarily concerned with writing which is sophisticated, we should examine the term carefully. There are two ways of doing this. First, one can analyze the *content* of a story, the basic elements such as plot, characters, and the like. Second—and equally important to the practicing writer—one can examine the *process* by which the story is presented as seen in the five *narrative modes* available to the writer of fiction: dialogue, thoughts, action, description, and exposition.

Starting with plot, it is obvious that all fiction, whether simple or sophisticated, is developed through a sequence of actions. Simple fiction, however, not only reduces the complexity of the plot, but it usually avoids originality as well. Simple plots tend to be based on well-used conventions known in the magazine field as "formulas." The pleasure some people derive from, say, husband-tempted-by-widow-next-door-but-finally-returns-to-wife is not the excitement of a fresh experience but, rather, the anesthesia of the safely familiar.

Chapter 15 is devoted entirely to structure, from individual scenes to the construction of plot. The point to remember here, however, is that sophistication in plot does not necessarily mean complexity. What one aims for is a situation and a sequence of actions which are fresh and which subtly suggest a great deal to the reader. The determining factor is how much the reader discovers, not how many twists and turns the synopsis may take.

The same is true with characters. In simple fiction, the characters do a lot, but you never get to know much about them. It is possible to read carefully some fifteen separate novels about Doctor Savage and still know less about him as a character than one learns about the doctor who is the protagonist in a four-page short story, "The Use of Force" which appears here as Chapter 16.

All fiction has setting, but in simple fiction it is often all too familiar: New York City pieces make use of Madison Avenue or 42nd Street, San Francisco scenes are "in the shadow of the Golden Gate," and Paris stories have a vista looking out onto the Eiffel Tower. "Originality" frequently takes the form of the exotic: a ski resort high in the Andes, a spy headquarters four hundred feet beneath the House of Parliament, a royal palace constructed entirely in glowing lucite on the planet Octo.

Sophisticated fiction, on the other hand, tends to avoid both the hackneyed and the bizarre. The setting is used as a way of increasing credibility and placing the reader in the center of the story—regardless of whether it is based on an actual place or upon the dreamscape of the author.

Theme is another aspect of fiction which varies with the degree of sophistication. Simple themes suggest truisms which make no more impact on us than the background music in a restaurant. So-called detective magazines and their television counterparts reiterate endlessly, "Crime doesn't pay, but it's exciting to try." Teen magazines and many of television's situation comedies suggest repeatedly that "Nice girls eventually end up with nice boys, but only after being hurt." The fact that we know nice girls who have ended up with rotten boys and nice boys who never got married at all doesn't seem to weaken the popularity of this simple thematic concern. There are others which will be discussed in the next chapter.

Sophisticated fiction tends to have thematic concerns which suggest mixed feelings. Often this takes the form of ambivalence, a blending of love and hate for the same person at the same time. Further complexity is sometimes achieved with irony, a reversal of one's normal expectations.

Every serious reader evaluates the level of sophistication on the basis of elements like these either consciously or unconsciously. The writer, however, is equally concerned with technique—both in his own work and in that of others. For purposes of analysis, it is helpful to see fiction as a genre which is presented in five different ways or *narrative modes*. Every sentence of a story is made up of one or more of these modes: dialogue, thoughts, action, description, or exposition. I will develop the idea of narrative modes further in Chapter 22 because they are a helpful method of looking at a writer's style. I am concerned here, however, mainly with the matter of literary sophistication.

Dialogue and thoughts are two effective ways of suggesting character, and often they are used in tandem so that one sees a contrast between the inner and the outer person. In simple fiction, however, they are often stereotyped—predictable lines for predictable characters.

Action is the dominant mode for simple fiction—particularly adventure stories. But as we will see in the examples included in this text, sophisticated fiction makes significant use of action too. The difference is that as the story begins to gain a greater range of suggestion, the action necessarily must take on a more subtle role of implication. Put another way, action shifts from being an end in itself to being a means of suggestion.

The same is true of description. In a sophisticated story, almost every phrase devoted to describing characters, places, possessions, and the like contributes to the theme or to some aspect of characterization.

The last of these five narrative modes, exposition, is perhaps the most dangerous. In simple fiction it is used to point up the theme as one progresses through the story and, often, to sum it up directly at the end. "Down deep," we are told periodically, "Old Karl had a warm spot in his heart." And in case we missed it, we are given the clincher at the end: "Though his parting words were gruff, there was an undertone of kindness in the old prospector's voice. It was clear that he still knew the meaning of love."

Those who are used to sophisticated fiction, grimace at this because it is a familiar convention. It is also close to the technique of the essay. A sophisticated story may use just as much exposition, but it will rarely label the theme that way. This is not because authors want to be evasive, but because the success of literarily sophisticated fiction depends on the degree to which the reader discovers for himself the various thematic suggestions in a story. This inductive process is similar to the way we make judgments about people and situations in actual life. In short, thematic discovery in fiction of this sort is through vicarious experience rather than through direct statement.

Motives of the Writer

At the beginning of this chapter I rejected the notion that sophisticated writing is "better" than that which is simple. Yet it should be clear by now that my concern both here and throughout this text is for literary sophistication. A writer's decision as to what kind of writing he hopes to create depends on his original motive.

There are, of course, an infinite variety of motives which drive people to write in an infinite number of ways. But they can be grouped into three basic types each of which has a different set of assumptions and result in a different kind of fiction.

First, there is the *private motive*. This is what leads to writing merely for the personal pleasure of the act without any regard for another reader. Often it takes the form of journal entries. Spontaneous and usually unrevised, writing like this is essentially a private act.

Many writers find it helpful to keep a journal regularly or to write from time to time "off the top of one's head." It is for the writer what sketching often is for the painter. But it is a mistake to ask a friend or a writing class to evaluate such work. There is really no way to judge it as "good" or "bad" or even "sophisticated" or "simple." It may be valuable as practice or enjoyable as a release, but it shouldn't be passed off as anything more than that.

Second is the *commercial motive*. In its pure form, commercial writing is the opposite of private writing since it is motivated entirely by outer rather than inner demands. It is writing for others. It is producing a product.

Generally speaking, a commercial writer is one who defines his work as a craft and his primary goal as monetary reward. His product is entertainment. With some exceptions, what sells is "good" and what does not is "bad." He studies the market carefully and invests his time and energies in those areas which seem to have potential profit.

The work of this frequently maligned profession tends to be conservative and conventional mainly because that is what the readers of large-circulation magazines pay for. Like the businessman, his work consists of supplying a demand.

The third is the *literary motive*. A writer in this area is moved in part by what I have called the private motive. But he is not content to leave his work at that stage. Fiction for him involves reaching readers—a highly sophisticated form of communication.

Like the commercial writer, he would also like to be paid for his efforts, but this is not his primary goal. For every nationally known novelist whose works are on the level of Updike, Salinger, or Bellow, there are hundreds who continue to write without a major following. What keeps them going? Like sculptors, painters, and composers, they value the quality of the artistic object being created. Having some kind of audience is obviously important for any literarily inclined writer—an unread manuscript is like an unplayed symphony. But unlike the commercial writer, he does not generally tailor his work to meet the whims of the public. His revisions are largely inner-directed rather than outer-directed.

Because of this, the literary writer often has to be content with a small audience (little magazines are small in payment and circulation as well as in format), and he frequently does something else for his major income. But he has a special satisfaction in knowing that he is reaching readers who will spend time with his work and react to it with some sensitivity. More than that, he is working in one of those few areas where he does not have to compromise. For many, this is very important.

Every literary writer has his own personal drives, and one can see what variety there is from reading *Writers at Work* (Malcolm Cowley, ed.) which contains some of the best interviews conducted by the staff of the *Paris Review*. What I am concerned with here, however, is not the variety but that which is shared: a common respect for literature as something of value in itself. Without this, and without extensive reading to support it, no text can help an individual to create new literature.

The scope of fiction is as wide as the human imagination. The more sophisticated a writer's skills become, the more he can make use of this range of possibilities.

13

THE SOURCES OF FICTION

Sterile sources: the "seven deadly sins"; fruitful sources: *drawing on experience* including family relationships, other interpersonal relationships, and moments of intensity; the technique of *metamorphosis* to sharpen material, to mute thematic patterns, and to gain control over a personal experience.

In a great majority of cases the failure of a story to achieve significance, credibility, or even interest is due primarily to the origin, the source from which the story was developed. These stories are doomed at conception. It is for this reason that I start this chapter with what will be a rather discouraging set of prohibitions.

As I pointed out in the previous chapter, a story is a blend of personal experience and invention. The danger comes when what one thinks of as invention is merely a borrowing from a familiar convention. Like clichés, these overused plot patterns automatically reduce a piece of writing to the simplest level. As soon as the reader recognizes the familiar ruts, he slips into that glazed half-attention with which he watches the average television drama or listens to the monotony of background music at a restaurant.

The following, then, are seven deadly sins of fiction which, because of their sterility, tend to corrupt any attempt at sophisticated writing.

The Shootin' and Killin' Rerun. The source is television. It comes in two forms, the abbreviated Western and the war story. It is extraordinary how many well-read, articulate students revert to these standard plots, somewhat disguised but still complete with their stylized, almost ritualized representations of such virtues as manliness and courage as well as their antonyms, weakness and cowardice. The result is almost always failure.

The frequency and the strength of this temptation is due, I believe, to the fact that there are many intelligent individuals who have, by the time they reach twenty, absorbed more television drama than they have literary works. If, for example, you have watched five television dramas a week for four years, you have absorbed 1,040 separate (but similar) plots, at least 3,120 attempts at characterization, more than 4,160 separate dramatic scenes, and the equivalent of 20,800 pages of dialogue. It is true that not much of this material was studied carefully, but the repetition of plot types, stock characters, and highly formal patterns of diction and syntax are presented in a day-to-day sequence which outdoes the most scientific presentation of programmed learning yet devised by educators.

The danger is not due to the subject matter. Good novels have, after all, used nineteenth-century western United States as a setting, and several great novels have made use of war. The reason these shows prove to be so disastrous as source material is that they have almost nothing to do with the complexity of genuine human experience or even genuine human beings. The script writer himself is not writing from experience. He has as *his* source nothing but a set of stylized conventions involving situations, characters, and the use of language.

Most writers consider themselves beyond or "above" such influence. Many are. But one should always be on guard. When a plot begins to have a familiar sound to it, hunt down the source ruthlessly.

The Adolescent Tragedy. The adolescent period is an excellent one for fiction as long as the author keeps his material genuine and fresh in detail. But there are three dangerous pitfalls: lack of perspective, unconscious borrowing from slick and conventionalized fiction, and sentimentality.

The author's lack of perspective or a sense of proportion stems from the fact that in many cases the experience is too fresh. The author is still *in* the story rather than *above* it; he cannot control it. Thus, what appears to be a true tragedy to the author-protagonist appears to the reader as pallid comedy.

To avoid this, make sure that there is enough time between the event and one's effort to convert it into fiction. The more emotional the experience, the more time it will require to gain some measure of detachment.

Unconscious borrowing from slick fiction is sometimes as difficult to spot as influences from television. But it does happen. Those who do not read stories in the women's magazines may find themselves reaching back to conventionalized plots half-remembered from comics. Whenever one detects the slightest borrowing from such sources, it is important to ask, "Where did the rest of this come from?" Not only the plot but types of characters, lines of dialogue, and even descriptive details may be contaminated.

Sentimentality, the third danger in writing about adolescents, may come from secondary sources like magazines and television or it may just as easily come from the simple desire to move the reader. The difference between the sentimental story and one which is genuinely moving is a matter of sophistication. When a story is simple and rigged to short-circuit the emotions of the reader, we say it is sentimental. These are the stories in which the lonely, misunderstood little boy, the plain little girl with glasses, the cripple, the blind girl, the son of alcoholics are placed in some pitiable situation—any cold street corner will do, but a bombed-out village is better—simply to evoke tears.

The hardest version of sentimentality for a critic to attack is that which is based on a real-life situation. In such cases, the solution may be found in achieving more distance or more control; and it in almost every case calls out for greater sophistication.

In the next chapter I have included John Updike's "Friends from Philadelphia." It has to do with late adolescence. There are a number of details which could have turned to sentimentality, but Updike maintains control with a gentle sense of humor.

This particular story is included in a paperback collection of Updike's work called *Olinger Stories*. They are arranged in order of the age of the protagonist, starting with ten and ending with adulthood. The early stories in that collection serve as excellent examples of how to avoid the pitfalls of adolescent fiction.

The Preadolescent Tragicomedy. For some reason, female writers are more attracted to this dangerous formula than males, but this may only be due to a masculine reluctance to identify himself as writer with the preadolescent, a phenomenon which has more to do with psychology than literary judgment. In any case, the story turns an age which can be truly comic or terrifying or intricate in its perceptions into something which can only be described as "cute."

Once again we must distinguish between what is a rewarding source for fiction, the preadolescent period, and what this particular type of failure is based on, a convention. If the author of a "sweet little story about a girl of five in love with a man of thirteen" honestly looked for the source of the story, the search would end in the pages of women's magazines, not in his or her own life. The mechanics of the situation may be real; it is the author's tone which adds that extra cup of sugar and fulfills the recipe for "cute fiction."

The formula for the preadolescent boy is no less absurd than the one for the adolescent. He has freckles, is preferably a redhead, keeps frogs and snakes in his pocket, proves his virility by fighting, and uses bad grammar to express occasional nuggets of great wisdom. Recently he has been made to represent various ethnic minorities without any visible improvement either of the formula or of the dignity and traditions of the group so graced. He is a stylized Tom Sawyer mummified by writers who are more familiar with Lassie than Mark Twain. He serves no purpose but financial gain for the popular writer and so should be returned to the commercial world from whence he sprang.

Once again, honest analysis of the origin of one's fiction is the best means of separating the sterility of literary formulas from the potency of experience and observation.

The O. Henry Twist. This is, I hope, almost self-explanatory. The formula of the trick ending has been so popular that it is imitated by many who have never read O. Henry. The transmission often comes through television. O. Henry's fiction was never very sophisticated to begin with, and it doesn't improve when converted into a television script.

True, his stories were entertaining. But his method was not that of fiction in the contemporary sense. They were more like charming, well constructed, well told, after-dinner anecdotes. When this technique is imitated, the result is usually a slow moving, unconvincing build-up to a single punch line. It is simple and it is apt to be dull. Student writers who are interested in working with sustained irony do much better by studying contemporary authors like Cheever, Roth, Updike, and Bellow.

Mock Faulkner.   No writer can help being influenced by his favorite modern author, but the attempt to imitate him (either consciously or unconsciously) often results in unintended satire. Hemingway and Salinger are frequently borrowed from, but Faulkner is truly contagious. My favorite example is an early attempt at fiction by a college sophomore who managed to pack into a single story one seduction, one rape, one case of incest, and a suicide—all in 2,000 words. Grim as the subject matter and the author's intention were, the end result was a hilarious burlesque.

The origin of that story was not, of course, Faulkner's work but a corrupted memory of selected passages. There was no awareness of the intricate structure of a Faulknerian novel in which violence, which does often appear, becomes woven into the fabric of the entire work. In *Sanctuary,* for example, the scene which is so frequently branded as objectionable is in fact so obliquely presented that many readers are not aware of just what happened until later in the novel—or even until they have turned to the critics for help.

In addition, the imitative story showed no awareness of the relationship between the length of a story and the degree of violence which it can contain without spilling over into the area of melodrama. If one thinks of violence as electrical voltage, it is easy to see that what is successfully sent through a heavy-gauge woven cable will burn out if sent through a single strand of light wire

By way of specific example, it is worth noting Faulkner's "Dry September" and J. F. Powers's "The Eye." Both stories involve a brutal lynching. Both stories mute the degree of violence by refusing to describe directly the actual lynching scene. Neither author can be accused of literary cowardice. Inclusion of the lynch scenes in these two stories would have overloaded the circuit and the result would have been melodrama; exclusion, in these cases, allows for the maximum possible impact. In the same way, "The Use of Force" by William Carlos Williams (see Chapter 16) handles the theme of sexual violence with a restraint which keeps the story from "blowing apart."

The Gray Flannel Sermon is one of the most common patterns in college writing courses. The protagonist is a hard-driving businessman. He doesn't have time for his wife or children. The story usually begins with a sample of his ruthless drive to the top. The setting is often his luxurious office on the eighty-eighth floor looking out over the twinkling lights of Manhattan or San Francisco Bay. On his desk there are three telephones and a picture of his long-suffering wife. The plot builds toward his realization that Man-does-not-live-by-Success-alone and ends as he puts a bullet through his head. Or sometimes he jumps.

It would be nice to think that these stories were influenced by Dreiser's *American Tragedy* or by the more recent "businessman novels" such as *The Man in the Gray Flannel Suit* and *Sincerely, Willis Wayde*. But usually they are not. The tradition seems to have come through script writers who themselves have been influenced by older script writers who have read Dreiser's *American Tragedy*. How else could these young authors all describe the same mahogany desk with its identical set of three telephones, the same long-suffering wife, and the same "understanding" secretary who in almost every case has the same shade of blond hair?

The Poe Gimmick.   One does not have to abandon one's respect or even admiration for Poe's inventiveness in order to scorn the well-worn and essentially boring imitations of his work. There are three reasons why warmed-over Poe is generally unsuccessful. The first is an historical consideration: Poe was working in a period when the short story as an independent genre was just being born. His tricks were fresh and truly surprised readers who were, in this area, naive. Since then, our expectations have increased. We are no longer content with pure melodrama such as we find in "The Pit and the Pendulum" or "Ms. Found in a Bottle." We now expect fiction to contain more elaborate characterization, more complexity of theme, and greater variety of tone. Even that last bastion of melodrama, the horror film, could make no more use of Poe's material in the film called *The Raven* than to treat it as fodder for the lowest sort of satire.

Another reason for the collapse of the Poe market as a source for good fiction is that most of his gimmicks were one-shot affairs. That is, once the trick has been used, we can no longer be truly surprised by it. And when almost the entire impact of the story is based on the melodramatic elements, the contemporary writer cannot borrow without being obviously imitative.

Essentially, however, the problem is the same as in the other types: the imitation lacks both originality and sophistication. It becomes so far removed from genuine human experience and reactions to that experience that it no longer suggests an insight into anything.

The Free-Flying Fantasy is a kind of "eighth sin." It is not really derivative, but in some respects it is the most deadly of all.

In the 1920s it was called "automatic writing." The author simply typed whatever came into his head for three hours and saved the final fifteen pages as a "story." Occasionally they were published, but no one has republished them. They tended to be rather boring.

This technique of aimless composition is not to be confused with *stream-of-consciousness* writing. The latter, made famous by James Joyce, is designed to give the illusion of entering the mind of a specific character. The subject of concern is a part of the story, not the author's own psyche. No matter how metaphorical automatic writing becomes, it remains a clinical act—either purely descriptive or partly therapeutic.

Recently it has been defended as "literary tripping," an hallucinogenic voyage on paper. But what appears on the page is remarkably similar to the automatic writing of the 20s.

As I pointed out in the previous chapter, such writing is often rewarding for the author in terms of self-discovery or merely as enjoyment. But it is a private act. It is all expression and does not concern itself with communication. It is a kind of descriptive writing— a clinical look at the writer. Fiction may come from it eventually, but it is still raw material. It belongs in the writer's journal.

These, then, are eight of the most common disasters in short story writing. The repetition of "thou shalt not" is highly negative, of course, and for some may seem discouraging. But one of the primary functions of this text is to reduce the agonizing period of trial and error in the creative process so that the writer can as quickly as possible move on to the problems which are more intricate and increasingly individual. There is no greater waste of time for a writer than to spend hours writing and revising a piece which is so rooted in stale conventions or unproductive sources that it can never succeed. When one is able to reject these from the start, one is ready to start examining the true source of fiction: the life experiences of the author himself.

Drawing
on Experience   There are usually two phases in the genesis of a successful story. The first is selecting the experience or some aspect of an experience; the second is a process of reshaping this material in fundamental ways, a technique called *metamorphosis*.

This selection of a significant or meaningful incident may come easily without conscious searching. But often it does not. Even experienced writers have "dry periods" in which their search for material becomes deliberate. Here are some of the areas which they probe.

Family relationships are natural subjects for fiction. Everyone has had either parents or foster parents; everyone has experienced in some proportion that mixture of love and resentment which is a natural part of that relationship. And that instable balance is normally in constant flux. In very general terms, it is apt to be a progression from idealization through disillusionment to a new acceptance usually based on a fairly realistic evaluation. But this is a vast oversimplification, and stories which are based on a simple thematic statement of "The day I discovered my father was no saint" are apt to turn out thin and unconvincing. The writer has to probe deeper in order to discover and dramatize those unique shifts in his own attitude. Often it is some *specific* characteristic of, say, the father that is altered in some slight but significant way which lends itself to good fiction.

In addition to child-parent relationships, there are a variety of other intrafamily attitudes which also shift significantly: brother and sister, a boy and his younger brother, two brothers and their father, two sisters and a maiden aunt, daughter and mother, three brothers or three sisters, or any combination of these and an uncle. All of these relationships keep shifting in real life, and the shifts are remembered because something was done (action) or said (dialogue) or thought in such a way as to dramatize the change. In some cases the writer can draw on such relationships directly, but more frequently he has to metamorphose experience into something related but different—a process which I will explain shortly.

Next, turn from family relationships to those outside the family. The girl-boy relationship is a field which is heavily mined with stereotypes. One false step (like "But darling, we're married in the eyes of heaven," or "Her eyes were like limpid pools") and the story has exploded in your face. In most cases you can find a safe path by asking these two essential questions: What *really* happened? What was there about the action, the thoughts, the dialogue which was truly unique? There are times, however, when what really happened (action and dialogue particularly) would on paper appear so close to a cliché that the author must either turn the piece into a satire or alter the facts to make the fiction credible. When the author gives as an excuse, "But it really happened that way," he is exposing a basic misunderstanding about the nature of fiction. Experience can be an important ingredient in fiction, but it is not a model for the final product.

Some of the best relationships to examine are those which involve an age difference. It is often difficult (though not impossible) for a young writer to enter the lives of characters who are far older. One way to bridge the gap is to make use of those real-life situations which were the first means of gaining insight into the lives of those much older. This includes significant child-adult relationships outside the home.

A third way to stimulate one's memory is to recall moments of intensity. Often these involve some kind of discovery about oneself or another person. Here the author begins not with an analytical understanding of just what the significance is; he begins with the assumption that for this particular detail to have remained fresh and clear there must have been some special meaning in it for him.

Such a memory may be highly fragmentary. Settings like a particular drug store, a specific field or grove where the author used to play, a view from a car window, or a living room seen only once often stand out with extraordinary—and usually significant—sharpness. Characters (not to be confused with "characters" who are "unforgettable" because of their quaint similarity to clichés held dear by the *Reader's Digest*) may remain in the mind only from an overheard conversation or a quick glimpse: a subway attendant, a store clerk, a hitchhiker, or an auto mechanic. And incidents do not even have to be directly connected with the observer. They may involve an argument overheard in a supermarket; the smashing of a window; an automobile accident; or the playful flirtation of a girl and three boys on a beach, a park, or a parking lot.

One of the first things to do with such a memory-fragment is to recall every possible detail: the visual minutiae, the sounds, and the intricacies of one's own feeling. From these one may discover why that particular experience remained in one's memory while so many others drifted beyond recall. The final story may or may not include the author himself, and it will doubtless be far removed from the facts of the experience, but it has the advantage of being rooted in an initial fragment of the author's experience.

Metamorphosis
of Experience Experience, then, is the usual origin of fiction. But only occasionally is the final product unaltered fragments of autobiography. Fiction develops—consciously or unconsciously—through a process of literary metamorphosis. Such shifts in the basic conception of a story idea usually stem from two diametrically opposed needs: to clarify or sharpen the patterns which made the experience memorable in the first place and, conversely, to break patterns and relationships which seem too simple, too obvious or contrived. There is a third justification for metamorphosis which is often ignored: when the experience is still so close to the author that he cannot manipulate it objectively.

Sharpening and clarifying is basic to fiction. It is an oversimplification to say that all literature is the transformation of disordered experience into communicable patterns of events, thematic significance, and character revelation. But like many oversimplifications, it is a part of the truth. Take thematic unity, for example. Suppose the experience consisted of a hot August day on which plans for a family picnic in the country were ruined when the car boiled over in the heart of the city's slums. The thematic elements which have kept the experience itself vivid in the writer's mind may consist of such varied details as the boy's first awareness of his father as a man hopeless in a crisis, a surprising insight into the instability of his parents' relationship, a recognition of a special bond between father and daughter, the beginnings of social consciousness in the face of an economically repressed community, an introduction to racial distinctions, and an ironic contrast between the narrator's sense of high adventure and his parents' sense of disaster.

A good story can echo all of these themes. But the writer will probably want to focus on just one or two. Here is the first stage of the metamorphosis. But with any one of the elements, there will be contradictory details. The primary impression, for example, may have been based on the father's inability to take control of the situation. Yet it is quite possible that in certain areas he was calm and competent. In such a situation the author may have to make extensive modifications to clarify his theme.

More radical, the final story may end with no children involved—this would swing the attention directly to the parents. Or the entire family might be dropped in order to build from some minor sequence of events observed while waiting for the car to be repaired. Occasionally all one retains is the flavor of the setting and a few individual details, such as a man's conversation with his girl leaning out of a fifth floor window or an impatient cab driver waiting for his car to be repaired at the garage.

The first and primary reason for metamorphosing experience, then, is to sharpen the focus and to clarify the literary concerns such as theme, characterization, motivation, tone, and the like.

The second function of literary metamorphosis is the reverse in that occasionally the patterns of experience are too neat, too contrived for fiction. When the theme of a story is blatant, we are acutely aware of an author at work and no longer enter into the story as if it were an extension of experience. It becomes only a trick. And there is nothing to be gained by telling the reader that "it really happened that way." If, for example, the father in the story outlined above really was consistently irascible or without exception dependent on his wife's suggestions, he would become a "flat" character, a cliché of fiction. Variation and further insight would be needed not to clarify characterization but to make it more convincing. Or if the story ended up so obviously in the category of "The day I discovered father was not perfect," the author might be well advised to add other thematic elements so that we no longer have the feeling that it has become an extended anecdote.

The third and final justification for these basic transformations is the experience which has not yet been emotionally digested. In most cases it takes a year or more for an author to look on a personal experience with some objectivity and perspective. True, some experiences turn into fiction without much change. But this is far rarer than most people realize. And when one is still very much involved in an experience, one has little control over it.

In these cases, it is sometimes helpful to break the mold set by the experience itself. This is usually done through an initial metamorphosis of the story. Childhood experiences are sometimes converted in this way by dropping the child and seeing the story through the eyes of an adult; the original setting can be shifted to some completely different place; ages can be changed; even the sex of a character can be shifted (as in the extraordinary source of Proust's Albertine), and, most basic of all, what originally came to mind as a minor or secondary theme can be developed as the primary theme of a story. Through this technique, the author can often re-establish control over a story which might otherwise have been only a journal entry.

All the steps outlined in this chapter can occur quite unconsciously. In such cases, the author is unable to explain where his plot or his characters came from or why he made the initial changes which, from a critic's point of view, seem so basic. And some authors depend more on such unconscious processes than others.

But whenever one finds it difficult to start a story, and whenever the first draft seems to fall short of one's own standard, it is extremely important to follow these steps. First, make sure that the story itself is not rooted in some well-used situation which is far removed not only from your own experience but the experience of the writers who have profited by it. Second, examine all the memorable experiences of your own life, particularly those which seem to shift either your own views or the attitudes of others. Next, consider a number of radical transformations or metamorphoses which might, on the one hand, sharpen both themes and characterization and, on the other hand, keep the story from becoming contrived or artificial.

When one considers the extraordinary variety of experience stored in the mind of an individual and the endless number of "inventive" devices available to anyone who is well read, the matter of linking the two becomes as complex as is the arrangement of chromosomes which make each organism unique. This is the true meaning of *creative* writing.

14

A STORY BY
JOHN UPDIKE

Friends from Philadelphia

In the moment before the door was opened to him, he glimpsed her thigh below the half-drawn shade. Thelma was home, then. She was wearing the Camp Winniwoho T shirt and her quite short shorts.

CHANGE (DIALOGUE)
"Why, my goodness: Janny!" she cried. She always pronounced his name, John, to rhyme with Ann. Earlier that vacation, she had visited in New York City, and tried to talk the way she thought they talked there. "What on earth ever brings you to me at this odd hour?"

"Hello, Thel," he said. "I hope—I guess this is a pretty bad time." She had been plucking her eyebrows again. He wished she wouldn't do that.

Thelma extended her arm and touched her fingers to the base of John's neck. It wasn't a fond gesture, just a hostesslike one. "Now, Janny. You know that I—my mother and I—are always happy to be seeing you. Mother, who do you ever guess is here at this odd hour?"

CHANGE (DIALOGUE)
"Don't keep John Nordholm standing there," Mrs. Lutz said.

148

Thelma's mother was settled in the deep red settee watching television and smoking. A coffee cup being used as an ashtray lay in her lap, and her dress was hitched so her knees showed.

EXTERNAL DETAIL

"Hello, Mrs. Lutz," John said, trying not to look at her broad, pale knees. "I really hate to bother you at this odd hour."

TO INNER THOUGHTS

"I don't see anything odd about it." She took a deep-throated drag on her cigarette and exhaled through her nostrils, the way men do. "Some of the other kids were here earlier this afternoon."

TO

"I would have come in if anybody had told me."

DIALOGUE

Thelma said, "Oh, Janny! Stop trying to make a martyr of yourself. Keep in touch, they say, if you want to keep up."

He felt his face grow hot and knew he was blushing, which made him blush all the more. Mrs. Lutz shook a wrinkled pack of Herbert Tareytons at him. "Smoke?" she said.

"I guess not, thanks a lot."

"You've stopped? It's a bad habit. I wish I had stopped at your age. I'm not sure I even *begun* at your age."

"No, it's just that I have to go home soon, and my mother would smell the smoke on my breath. She can smell it even through chewing gum."

"Why must your go home soon?" Thelma asked.

Mrs. Lutz sniffled. "I have sinus. I can't even smell the flowers in the garden or the food on the table any more. Let the kids smoke if they want, if it makes them feel better. I don't care. My Thelma, she can smoke right in her own home, her own living room, if she wants to. But she doesn't seem to have the taste for it. I'm just as glad, to tell the truth."

John hated interrupting, but it was close to five-thirty. "I have a problem," he said.

"A problem—how gruesome," Thelma said. "And here I thought, Mother, I was being favored with a social call."

"Don't talk like that," Mrs. Lutz said.

"It's sort of complex," John began.

"Talk like what, Mother? Talk like what?"

"Then let me turn this off," Mrs. Lutz said, snapping the right knob on the television set.

"Oh, Mother, and I was listening to it!" Thelma toppled into a chair, her legs flashing. John thought she was delicious when she pouted.

Mrs. Lutz had set herself to give sympathy. Her lap was broadened and her hands were laid palms upward in it.

"It's not much of a problem," John assured her. "But we're having some people up from Philadelphia." He turned to Thelma and added, "If anything is going on tonight, I can't get out."

"Life is just too, too full of disappointments," Thelma said.

"Look—is there?"

"Too, too full," Thelma said.

Mrs. Lutz made fluttery motions out of her lap. "These Philadelphia people."

John said, "Maybe I shouldn't bother you about this." He waited, but she just looked more and more patient, so he went on. "My mother wants to give them wine, and my father isn't home from teaching school yet. He might not get home before the liquor store closes. It's at six, isn't it? My mother's busy cleaning, so I walked in."

"She made you walk the whole mile? Poor thing, can't you drive?" Mrs. Lutz asked.

"*Sure* I can drive. But I'm not sixteen yet."

"You look a lot taller than sixteen."

John looked at Thelma to see how she took that one, but Thelma was pretending to read a rental-library novel wrapped in cellophane.

"I walked all the way in to the liquor store," John told Mrs. Lutz, "but they wouldn't give me anything without written permission. It was a new man."

"Your sorrow has rent me in twain," Thelma said, as if she was reading it from the book.

"Pay no attention, Johnny," Mrs. Lutz said. "Now Frank will be home any time. Why not wait until he comes and let him run down with you for a bottle?"

"That sounds wonderful. Thanks an awful lot, really."

Mrs. Lutz's hand descended upon the television knob. Some smiling man was playing the piano. John didn't know who he was; there wasn't any television at his house. They watched in silence until Mr. Lutz thumped on the porch outside. The empty milk bottles tinkled. "Now don't be surprised if he has a bit of a load on," Mrs. Lutz said.

Actually, he didn't act at all drunk. He was like a happy husband in the movies. He called Thelma his little pookie-pie and kissed her on the forehead; then he called his wife his big pookie-pie and kissed her on the mouth. Then he solemnly shook John's hand and told him how very, very happy he was to see him here and asked after his parents. "Is that goon still on television?" he said finally.

"Daddy, please pay attention to somebody else," Thelma said, turning off the television set. "Janny wants to talk to you."

"And *I* want to talk to *Johnny*," Thelma's father said. He spread his arms suddenly, clenching and unclenching his fists. He was a big man, with shaved gray hair above his tiny ears. John couldn't think of the word to begin.

Mrs. Lutz explained the errand. When she was through, Mr. Lutz said, "People from Philadelphia. I bet their name isn't William L. Trexler, is it?"

"No. I forget their name, but it's not that. The man is an engineer. The woman went to college with my mother."

"Oh. College people. Then we must get them something very, very nice, I should say."

"Daddy," Thelma said. "*Please*. The store will close."

"Tessie, you hear John. People from college. People with diplomas. And it is very nearly closing time, and who isn't on their way?" He took John's shoulder in one hand and Thelma's arm in the other and hustled them through the door. "We'll be back in one minute, Mamma," he said.

"Drive carefully," Mrs. Lutz said from the shadowed porch, where her cigarette showed as an orange star.

Mr. Lutz's huge blue Buick was parked in front of the house. "I never went to college," he said, "yet I buy a new car whenever I want." His tone wasn't nasty, but soft and full of wonder.

"Oh, Daddy, not *this* again," Thelma said, shaking her head at John, so he could understand what all she had to go through. When she looks like that, John thought, I could bite her lip until it bleeds.

"Ever driven this kind of car, John?" Mr. Lutz asked.

"No. The only thing I can drive is my parents' Plymouth, and that not very well."

"What year car is it?"

"I don't know exactly." John knew perfectly well it was a 1940 model. "We got it after the war. It has a gear shift. This is automatic, isn't it?"

"Automatic shift, fluid transmission, directional lights, the works," Mr. Lutz said, "Now, isn't it funny, John? Here is your father, an educated man, with an old Plymouth, yet at the same time I, who never read more than twenty, thirty books in my life...it doesn't seem as if there's justice." He slapped the fender, bent over to get into the car, straightened up abruptly, and said, "Do you want to drive it?"

Thelma said, "Daddy's asking you something."

"I don't know how," John said.

"It's very easy to learn, very easy. You just slide in there—come on, it's getting late." John got in on the driver's side. He peered out of the windshield. It was a wider car than the Plymouth; the hood looked wide as a boat.

Mr. Lutz asked him to grip the little lever behind the steering wheel. "You pull it toward you like *that,* that's it, and fit it into one of these notches. 'P' stands for 'parking'—you start it in that one. 'N,' that's 'neutral,' like on the car you have, 'D' means 'drive'—just put it in there and the car does all the work for you. You are using that one ninety-nine per cent of the time. 'L' is 'low,' for very steep hills, going up or down. And 'R' stands for—what?"

"Reverse," John said.

"Very, very good. Tessie, he's a smart boy. He'll never own a new car. And when you put them all together, you can remember their order by the sentence, Paint No Dimes Light Red. I thought that up when I was teaching my oldest girl how to drive."

"Paint No Dimes Light Red," John said.

"Excellent. Now, let's go."

A bubble was developing in John's stomach. "What gear do you want it in to start?" he asked Mr. Lutz.

Mr. Lutz must not have heard him, because all he said was "Let's go" again, and he drummed on the dashboard with his fingertips. They were thick, square fingers, with fur between the knuckles.

Thelma leaned up from the back seat. Her cheek almost touched John's ear. She whispered, "Put it at 'P.' "

He did, then he looked for the starter. "How does he start it?" he asked Thelma.

"I never watch him," she said. "There was a button in the last car, but I don't see it in this one."

"Push on the pedal," Mr. Lutz sang, staring straight ahead and smiling, "and away we go. And ah, ah, waay we go."

"Just step on the gas," Thelma suggested. John pushed down

firmly, to keep his leg from trembling. The motor roared. "Now 'D'," she said. The car bounded away from the curb. Within a block, though, he could manage the car pretty well.

"It rides like a boat on smooth water," he told his two passengers. The metaphor pleased him.

Mr. Lutz squinted ahead. "Like a what?"

"Like a boat."

"Don't go so fast," Thelma said.

"The motor's so quiet," John explained. "Like a sleeping cat."

Without warning, a truck pulled out of Pearl Street. Mr. Lutz, trying to brake, stamped his foot on the empty floor in front of him. John could hardly keep from laughing. "I see him," he said, easing his speed so that the truck had just enough room to make its turn. "Those trucks think they own the road," he said. He let one hand slide away from the steering wheel. One-handed, he whipped around a bus. "What'll she do on the open road?"

"That's a good question, John," Mr. Lutz said. "And I don't know the answer. Eighty, maybe."

"The speedometer goes up to a hundred and ten." Another pause— nobody seemed to be talking. John said, "Hell. A baby could drive one of these."

"For instance, you," Thelma said.

There were a lot of cars at the liquor store, so John had to double-park the big wide Buick. "That's close enough, close enough," Mr. Lutz said. "Don't get any closer, whoa!" He was out of the car before John could bring it to a complete stop. "You and Tessie wait here," he said. "I'll go in for the liquor."

"Mr. Lutz. Say, Mr. Lutz," John called.

"Daddy!" Thelma shouted.

Mr. Lutz returned. "What is it, boys and girls?" His tone, John noticed, was becoming reedy. He was probably getting hungry.

"Here's the money they gave me." John pulled two wadded dollars from the change pocket of his dungarees. "My mother said to get something inexpensive but nice."

"Inexpensive but nice?" Mr. Lutz repeated.

"She said something about California sherry."

"What did she say about it? To get it? Or not to?"

"I guess to get it."

"You guess." Mr. Lutz shoved himself away from the car and

walked backward toward the store as he talked. "You and Tessie wait in the car. Don't go off somewhere. It's getting late. I'll be only one minute."

John leaned back in his seat and gracefully rested one hand at the top of the steering wheel. "I like your father."

"You don't know how he acts to Mother," Thelma said.

John studied the clean line under his wrist and thumb. He flexed his wrist and watched the neat little muscles move in his forearm. "You know what I need?" he said. "A wristwatch."

"Oh, Jan," Thelma said. "Stop admiring your own hand. It's really disgusting."

A ghost of a smile flickered over his lips, but he let his strong nervous fingers remain as they were. "I'd sell my soul for a drag right now."

"Daddy keeps a pack in the glove compartment," Thelma said. "I'd get them if my fingernails weren't so long."

"*I'll* get it open," John said, and did. They fished one cigarette out of the tired pack of Old Golds they found and took alternate puffs. "Ah," John said, "that first drag of the day, clawing and scraping its way down your throat."

"Be on the lookout for Daddy. They hate my smoking."

"Thelma."

"Yes?" She stared deep into his eyes, her face half hidden in blue shadow.

"Don't pluck your eyebrows."

"I think it looks nice."

"It's like calling me 'Jan.'" There was a silence, not awkward, between them.

"Get rid of the rette, Jan. Daddy just passed the window."

Being in the liquor store had put Mr. Lutz into a soberer mood. "Here you be, John," he said, and in a businesslike way handed John a tall, velvet-red bottle with a neck wrapped in foil. "Better let me drive. You drive like a veteran, but I know the roads."

"I can walk from your house, Mr. Lutz," John said, knowing Mr. Lutz wouldn't make him walk. "Thanks an awful lot for all you've done."

"I'll drive you up. Philadelphians can't be kept waiting. We can't make this young man walk a mile, now can we, Tessie?" The sweeping way the man asked the question kept the young people quiet all the way out of town, although several things were bothering John.

When the car stopped in front of his house, he forced himself to ask, "Say, Mr. Lutz. I wonder if there was any change?"

"What? Oh. I nearly forgot. You'll have your daddy thinking I'm a crook." He reached into his pocket and without looking handed John a dollar, a quarter, and a penny.

"This seems like a lot," John said. The wine must be cheap. His stomach squirmed; maybe he had made a mistake. Maybe he should have let his mother phone his father, like she had wanted to, instead of begging her to let him walk in.

"It's your change," Mr. Lutz said.

"Well, thanks an awful lot."

"Goodbye now," Mr. Lutz said.

"So long." John slammed the door. "Goodbye, Thelma. Don't forget what I told you." He winked.

The car pulled out, and John walked up the path. "Don't forget what I told you," he repeated to himself, winking. The bottle was cool and heavy in his hand. He glanced at the label, which read *Château Mouton-Rothschild 1937*.

15

STRUCTURE :
FROM SCENES TO PLOT

Episodes in experience related to *scenes* in fiction; *plot* described as a succession of scenes; *nonchronological* patterns of plot; *controlling the pace* by revising the plot; building a story toward an epiphany.

Clocks move at a steady rate. And in one sense, so do our lives. Awake or asleep, we progress from birth to death at a steady pace.

But now take a moment to review what you did yesterday from the time you got up to the end of the day.

Notice how naturally that chronology turned into a list of identifiable events or episodes: getting dressed, eating breakfast, and, for students, attending classes, a coffee break with friends in the cafeteria, a conversation in the hall, and lunch. For nonstudents, the events would be different, but the rhythm from one unit of activity to the next is essentially the same. The point is that while the *clock* moves perfectly regularly, our *life* as we look back is seen as a sequence of episodes.

These episodes have certain characteristics which every writer of fiction should consider. First, we often identify them by where they occurred—the setting. Second, we recall who was there—the characters. Third, such episodes remain clear long after we have forgotten what came just before and just afterward. Those unstructured periods of time which merely link one episode with the next (walking, waiting, driving, watching television, sleeping) tend to blend together and blur quickly.

Finally, we don't always remember these events in the order in which they occurred. Students complaining about bad teachers are not necessarily going to start with kindergarten; football fans recalling dramatic games they have watched are not going to begin with the first one they attended; and a man recalling his love for a woman is not necessarily going to begin with the day he met her.

Fiction tends to imitate these patterns. What we call *episodes* in life become *scenes* in fiction. These are the basic units. And their arrangement is what we call *plot*.

The Construction of Plot
in "Friends from Philadelphia"
A scene in a short story is not as clearly defined as in drama, but generally speaking it consists of an episode which is identifiable either because of the setting or the characters involved. The reader usually senses a transition from one scene to the next whenever the author changes the setting or alters the "cast of characters" by having one leave or arrive.

Using these two characteristics as a loose definition, we can see Updike's story as an arrangement of six scenes. This is unusual for a story of this length. The next story, "The Use of Force," has only one. The tendency in works of this length is to have two or three.

The first scene involves just two characters, Thelma and John, standing at the door. It blends quickly into the second which includes Thelma's mother and shifts the setting almost without transition to the living room. This is a longer scene which ends with a lull while they watch an unidentified television show. The third scene begins with Mr. Lutz's arrival and is dominated by him.

The final three scenes are in the car: driving to the liquor store, Thelma and John waiting in the car, and the final brief scene with Mr. Lutz again. It might be helpful to locate and mark these scenes in the text and to study the transitions from one to the next.

In a story of this length, authors sometimes hold the plot in their heads and make no use of outlines. But in other cases, they find it helpful to map out a tentative list of scenes. This is particularly valuable when the decisions such as when to start, how much to include, and where to close become conscious problems.

In this story, for example, Updike could have begun with a conversation between John and his mother. Instead, she is never presented directly at all. We are told that she had wanted to call his father and that John insisted on walking, but no direct quotations are used. We assume that there was a brief argument and we could imagine an entire scene built around the incident, but Updike chose instead to begin with the scene in which Thelma answers the door.

Another alternative would have been to withhold the revelation about the expensive wine which Mr. Lutz bought and used that information to cap a scene with John's father and the friends from Philadelphia. Instead, the author's decision was to keep the story brief and "economical," referring to John's family without actually developing scenes there.

It is generally a mistake to revere a published story to such an extent that one cannot consider any alternative method of construction. In this case, adding scenes at the beginning or at the end would have provided more scope to the story—but at the cost of the sense of economy he achieves in the present version. Another author might have added more information about the relationship between John and Thelma. New scenes could have been added by way of flashbacks, a device I will return to later. But Updike's decision was to keep the story sparse, tight, and brief.

Nonchronological
Patterns of Plot   The three stories included in this volume move chronologically from scene to scene. A majority of stories do—particularly those which are relatively short. But the writer is not bound by the chronology of time.

The single flashback is the simplest method of revising the chronological order of a plot. The term, first used by film writers, describes more than a simple reference to the past given through exposition or dialogue. By definition, it consists of a whole scene which took place previous to the main action of the story and which is presented in dramatic form, complete with setting and usually dialogue.

Take, for example, the reference to past action which occurs toward the end of "Friends from Philadelphia." As I have pointed out, the decision Updike made was to use indirect dialogue in the form of thoughts as follows:

> His stomach squirmed; maybe he had made a mistake. Maybe he should have let his mother phone his father, like she had wanted to, instead of begging her to let him walk in.

This is not a true flashback. It is simply a reference to the past. The story is drawing to a close and the incident is not important enough to risk slowing the pace. But for purposes of comparison, here is one way the material could be presented as a full flashback:

> His stomach squirmed; maybe he had made a mistake. After all, his mother had wanted to call his father instead.
> "Walk all that way?" she had asked him. "As if we didn't even own a car?"
> "I like walking," he said.
> "It won't take a minute to call him," she said, her hand on the phone.
> "You're always calling," he said. She took her hand off the phone.

The setting is clear by implication, and we know roughly when this occurred. Notice that the standard clue to a reader that a flashback is beginning is the use of the past perfect tense, "his mother *had* wanted..." and "she *had* asked him." Once one is into the scene, the simple past tense is more natural. Readers who have not written fiction respond to this subtle shift of tense often without being consciously aware of it.

Sometimes it is necessary to be more specific about where the flashback is located—both in time and geography.

> Two years ago that February he had gone to the same supermarket with his mother. It had been snowing all morning.
> "I'm worried about your father," she said. "He doesn't have snow tires and we've been having trouble with the car. I think I'll call the school."
> "Oh come on," he said. "Dad's not a child."

Multiple flashbacks are sometimes used when the author wants to suggest a complicated set of clues leading to a symbolic or a literal trial. Conrad's *Lord Jim* is in this form and so is Faulkner's well known, "A Rose for Emily." Such an approach tends to fragment the story line, of course, and it may be for this reason that it is usually found in longer works and ones which have a type of mystery or trial which maintains the story's unity and the reader's interest.

The frame story traditionally refers to a tale told by a character appearing in a larger work such as the separate narrations within Chaucer's *The Canterbury Tales.* But by common usage it also refers to any story in which the bulk of the material is presented as a single flashback. Often it begins with a narrator speaking in the first person; he then narrates a story which occurred some time earlier; and at the end the scene shifts to the time and place of the opening.

By way of illustration, Updike's story could be converted simply by shifting to the first person and adding new paragraphs for the opening and the closing. It might begin like this:

> It's been ten years since I've seen Thelma. I understand she married very well—a television executive who's in line for the directorship of CBS or NBC. I don't think about her much these days except on those rare occasions when I'm in a liquor store looking for some inexpensive dinner wine.
>
> That's when I remember standing there at the door and seeing her thigh for a moment below the half-drawn shade.

To make this a complete frame story, the revised version would finally return to this period at the end of the story. The tendency today is to drop that final return since it is apt to be a summary and anti-climactic.

Conrad used the frame story frequently. "Youth" is a particularly interesting example because it is actually a double frame: an unnamed narrator recalls a number of men sitting around a mahogany table and remembers how one of them, Marlow, narrated a lengthy story about his early sailing experiences. At the close of the story Marlow finishes and the original narrator describes the faces of the listeners sitting around the table.

The frame technique is still used today, but, as I have pointed out, it is often modified by deleting that final return to the opening scene. Still more frequently, authors tend to remove both the opening and closing, leaving the story to be told in the first person with no clearly defined listener. The result is no longer a frame story, but it may retain some of the flavor. In this text, both "The Use of Force" and "Sausage and Beer" use such an approach. The author has to weigh carefully whether the manner in which the story is being narrated and the identity of a fictional audience are essential to the work as a whole.

Controlling the Pace
by Revising the Plot
Every reader is aware that some sections in a story "move slowly" or "drag," while others "move quickly." A writer, however, has to know *why* this has happened.

In part, the pace of fiction is controlled by the style. This is discussed in Chapter 22. By far the greatest factor, however, is the *rate of revelation*. That is, a story seems to move rapidly when a great deal is being revealed to the reader; and conversely, it slows down when the author turns to digression, speculation, description, or any type of exposition.

The rate of revelation is high when the plot is progressing rapidly—events occurring in quick succession. Writers of simple fiction such as adventure stories and so-called "true romance" take full advantage of this. Events tumble after each other at a pace which is only surpassed by the simplest of all fiction, the comics. What these stories sacrifice is the richness of suggestion and the range of implication which one finds in sophisticated fiction.

The writer of sophisticated fiction is caught between two dangers: if he relies too heavily on entertaining but nonsuggestive action, he will bore his reader for lack of significance; yet if he becomes philosophically discursive, he will also bore his reader for lack of drama. As a result, in most successfully sophisticated stories, the pace is shifted frequently.

Openings are frequently given a high rate of revelation. This is not done with a paragraph of background information since the story has not really begun until the reader sees a character dealing with a specific situation. Exposition, remember, is like the connective links between episodes of experience—the explanations of how the character got there and what the extenuating circumstances were. The high rate of revelation at the beginning of a story calls for an immediate involvement in a situation already going on. This is why so many stories begin with a character arriving somewhere or responding to some disruption such as a death in the family, a departure, or an argument.

"Friends from Philadelphia" is not a highly dramatic story, but notice that Updike begins with an arrival (as does Williams in "The Use of Force") and a small "crisis" to be solved. He then slows the action after John makes his request and creates a kind of lull before Mr. Lutz returns. This low-keyed paragraph has no dialogue, a minimum of action, and description which is kept vague.

> Mrs. Lutz's hand descended upon the television knob. Some smiling man was playing the piano. John didn't know who he was; there wasn't any television at his house. They watched in silence until Mr. Lutz thumped on the porch outside. The empty milk bottles tinkled.

In longer stories such as my own "Sausage and Beer" (Chapter 18) entire pages may be devoted to scenes which have a reduced rate of revelation. But the writer must be sensitive enough to feel the story lose momentum and to correct it in time. The motion is like a skater in that the length of the glide depends on how strong the original thrust was. Those who have read *Moby Dick* will remember the alternation between dramatic chapters and those which are discursive. This is an extreme example. Short fiction normally moves from scene to scene with rising action coming toward the ends of scenes or at the end of the story. Quieter sections are often used as transitions.

In very short stories it is sometimes best to limit the action to a single scene. "The Use of Force," which is reprinted in the next chapter, is an example of this. In such cases, one usually begins with a relatively mild tone and increases either the intensity of the action or the rate of revelation. After reaching a climax, there is usually a resolution of some sort—often no more than a couple of sentences.

It is important to remember that both in single and multi-scene stories one can lose impact by maintaining high dramatic intensity throughout. Variations in dramatic impact keep the reader from "turning off."

Building

Toward an Epiphany   The primary difference between a journal entry and a finished, sophisticated short story is the fact that the latter usually builds toward what James Joyce called an *epiphany*. In brief, it is a moment of recognition or a discovery. It usually comes in one of two forms: either the reader learns something significant from the events of the story or the reader and the central character share the discovery.

In "Friends from Philadelphia," we come to know a lot that the protagonist, John, doesn't. But the primary discovery comes at the end of the story when we learn that Mr. Lutz has pretended that he paid less than a dollar for a wine like *Château Mouton-Rothschild 1937*. John himself learns nothing from this since he doesn't know one wine from another. The reader may not know much about wines either, but he responds to the fact that the label is French and it specifies a dated vintage. He is also used to having significant material placed at the end of a story.

Armed with these cues, the reader realizes that Mr. Lutz is a far more complex individual than the mildly drunk materialist he ap-

peared to be. In this act of his we see the same combination of kindness and patronizing superiority with which he has treated John
earlier. And behind it we can see how ambivalent some "successful"
men feel about those who have had more education.

In other cases, the epiphany is shared by the protagonist and the
reader. When you read "The Use of Force," notice how the doctor
begins to see the significance of the relationship with his young patient.
As readers, we learn as he learns. The discovery is not abrupt as it
was in "Friends from Philadelphia," but is unfolded in a story which
moves rapidly in a single scene through to its climax.

The building of scenes and their arrangement as plot becomes more
intuitive after writing twenty or thirty stories. But there are ways a
beginning writer can speed this process. First, examine the scene
construction of short stories in print. Mark in the margin where they
begin and end. Study the transitions and the shifts in pace and in
mood.

Second, study and question one's own scene construction. Be on
guard against two problem areas: the scattering of scenes which
cover too broad a spectrum of time for the length of the story and,
on the other hand, those long, talky or highly descriptive scenes which
sag for lack of development.

If the story seems too brief or thin or lacking in development, don't
start "padding" the existing scenes with more explanation and longer
sentences. Carefully consider whether the reader needs to know more
about the characters or the situation through the addition of entire
scenes. Conversely, if the story seems to ramble, don't think that the
only solution is to remove a sentence here and a phrase there. Consider
cutting or combining entire scenes.

Finally, ask yourself just what it is that the reader learns from
going through this experience. This shouldn't be a simple "moral"
which the reader can shrug off as a truism, nor must it be a far-
reaching philosophical or psychological truth. What most authors aim
for is a subtle sense of having achieved some insight either with the
protagonist or independently.

This chapter corresponds roughly to the one entitled "From Units
to Unity" in the section on poetry. The type of unit in fiction is
different from that in verse, and the methods of creating an artistic
whole vary as well. But the story resembles the poem (and the play
as well) in that it is a construction of units; and like all art forms,
the whole is greater than the sum of its parts.

16

A STORY BY
WILLIAM CARLOS WILLIAMS

The Use of Force

They were new patients to me, all I had was the name, Olson. Please come down as soon as you can, my daughter is very sick.

When I arrived I was met by the mother, a big startled looking woman, very clean and apologetic who merely said, Is this the doctor? and let me in. In the back, she added. You must excuse us, doctor, we have her in the kitchen where it is warm. It is very damp here sometimes.

The child was fully dressed and sitting on her father's lap near the kitchen table. He tried to get up, but I motioned for him not to bother, took off my overcoat and started to look things over. I could see that they were all very nervous, eyeing me up and down distrustfully. As often, in such cases, they weren't telling me more than they had to, it was up to me to tell them; that's why they were spending three dollars on me.

The child was fairly eating me up with her cold, steady eyes, and no expression to her face whatever. She did not move and seemed, inwardly, quiet; an unusually attractive little thing, and as strong as a heifer in appearance. But her face was flushed, she was breathing rapidly, and I realized that she had a high fever. She had magnificent blonde hair, in profusion. One of those picture children often reproduced in advertising leaflets and the photogravure sections of the Sunday papers.

She's had a fever for three days, began the father and we don't know what it comes from. My wife has given her things, you know, like people do, but it don't do no good. And there's been a lot of sickness around. So we tho't you'd better look her over and tell us what is the matter.

As doctors often do I took a trial shot at it as a point of departure. Has she had a sore throat?

Both parents answered me together, No...No, she says her throat don't hurt her.

Does your throat hurt you? added the mother to the child. But the little girl's expression didn't change nor did she move her eyes from my face.

Have you looked?

I tried to, said the mother, but I couldn't see.

As it happens we had been having a number of cases of diphtheria in the school to which this child went during that month and we were all, quite apparently, thinking of that, though no one had as yet spoken of the thing.

Well, I said, suppose we take a look at the throat first. I smiled in my best professional manner and asking for the child's first name I said, come on, Mathilda, open your mouth and let's take a look at your throat.

Nothing doing.

Aw, come on, I coaxed, just open your mouth wide and let me take a look. Look, I said opening both hands wide, I haven't anything in my hands. Just open up and let me see.

Such a nice man, put in the mother. Look how kind he is to you. Come on, do what he tells you to. He won't hurt you.

At that I ground my teeth in disgust. If only they wouldn't use the word "hurt" I might be able to get somewhere. But I did not allow myself to be hurried or disturbed but speaking quietly and slowly I approached the child again.

As I moved my chair a little nearer suddenly with one cat-like movement both her hands clawed instinctively for my eyes and she almost reached them too. In fact she knocked my glasses flying and they fell, though unbroken, several feet away from me on the kitchen floor.

Both the mother and father almost turned themselves inside out in embarrassment and apology. You bad girl, said the mother, taking her and shaking her by one arm. Look what you've done. The nice man . . .

For heaven's sake, I broke in. Don't call me a nice man to her. I'm here to look at her throat on the chance that she might have diphtheria and possibly die of it. But that's nothing to her. Look here, I said to the child, we're going to look at your throat. You're old enough to understand what I'm saying. Will you open it now by yourself or shall we have to open it for you?

Not a move. Even her expression hadn't changed. Her breaths however were coming faster and faster. Then the battle began. I had to have a throat culture for her own protection. But first I told the parents that it was entirely up to them. I explained the danger but said that I would not insist on a throat examination so long as they would take the responsibility.

If you don't do what the doctor says you'll have to go to the hospital, the mother admonished her severely.

Oh yeah? I had to smile to myself. After all, I had already fallen in love with the savage brat, the parents were contemptible to me. In the ensuing struggle they grew more and more abject, crushed, exhausted while she surely rose to magnificent heights of insane fury of effort bred of her terror of me.

The father tried his best, and he was a big man but the fact that she was his daughter, his shame at her behavior and his dread of hurting her made him release her just at the critical moment several times when I had almost achieved success, till I wanted to kill him. But his dread also that she might have diphtheria made him tell me to go on, go on though he himself was almost fainting, while the mother moved back and forth behind us raising and lowering her hands in an agony of apprehension.

Put her in front of you on your lap, I ordered, and hold both her wrists.

But as soon as he did the child let out a scream. Don't, you're hurting me. Let go of my hands. Let them go I tell you. Then she shrieked terrifyingly, hysterically. Stop it! Stop it! You're killing me!

Do you think she can stand it, doctor! said the mother.

You get out, said the husband to his wife. Do you want her to die of diphtheria?

Come on now, hold her, I said.

Then I grasped the child's head with my left hand and tried to get the wooden tongue depressor between her teeth. She fought, with clenched teeth, desperately! But now I also had grown furious—at a child. I tried to hold myself down but I couldn't. I know how to expose a throat for inspection. And I did my best. When finally I got the wooden spatula behind the last teeth and just the point of it into the mouth cavity, she opened up for an instant but before I could see anything she came down again and gripping the wooden blade between her molars she reduced it to splinters before I could get it out again.

Aren't you ashamed, the mother yelled at her. Aren't you ashamed to act like that in front of the doctor?

Get me a smooth-handled spoon of some sort, I told the mother. We're going through with this. The child's mouth was already bleeding. Her tongue was cut and she was screaming in wild hysterical shrieks. Perhaps I should have desisted and come back in an hour or more. No doubt it would have been better. But I have seen at least two children lying dead in bed of neglect in such cases, and feeling that I must get a diagnosis now or never I went at it again. But the worst of it was that I too had got beyond reason. I could have torn the child apart in my own fury and enjoyed it. It was a pleasure to attack her. My face was burning with it.

The damned little brat must be protected against her own idiocy, one says to one's self at such times. Others must be protected against her. It is social necessity. And all these things are true. But a blind fury, a feeling of adult shame, bred of a longing for muscular release are the operatives. One goes on to the end.

In a final unreasoning assault I overpowered the child's neck and jaws. I forced the heavy silver spoon back of her teeth and down her throat till she gagged. And there it was—both tonsils covered with membrane. She had fought valiantly to keep me from knowing her secret. She had been hiding that sore throat for three days at least and lying to her parents in order to escape just such an outcome as this.

Now truly she *was* furious. She had been on the defensive before but now she attacked. Tried to get off her father's lap and fly at me while tears of defeat blinded her eyes.

17

VIEWPOINT:
THE MEANS OF PERCEPTION

The *means of perception* defined; *variations* in the means
of perception; *first vs. third person* and the *spectrum*
which they represent; the *focus* of a story; the means of
perception, person, and focus seen as the *three basic
options; reviewing and revising* these options.

**The Means
of Perception**   This term simply refers to the agent through
whose eyes a piece of fiction appears to be presented. For example:
"He looked at his grandfather, wondering if the old man had understood." Here the means of perception is clearly the boy. We know his
thoughts and hopes. We don't know the grandfather's reaction and
will not until he speaks or makes some gesture to the boy. Our view
of the scene, then, is not the author's but the boy's.

The means of perception is often used synonymously with *point of
view,* and *viewpoint* but both these older terms are occasionally confused with *mood* and *tone.* When a critic writes, "The story is told
from the point of view of an embittered and sarcastic old man," he
is saying that the means of perception is the old man; but he may

also be referring to the fact that the mood of the story is bitter and the tone is at least partially ironical. For the sake of clarity, it is helpful to use *viewpoint* as a synonym for the means of perception, and to refer to *tone* and *mood* separately. In this text, both tone and mood are considered as aspects of style in Chapter 23.

Most fiction—particularly the short story—limits the means of perception to a single character, regardless of whether the first or third person is being used. This means that as readers we enter the mind of only one character, we do not know factual material that he doesn't know, and we are not addressed directly by the author. In the example given, for instance, we would be surprised to have the next sentence read, "Actually Grandfather did agree, but he knew that he could never tell the boy." We would be even more surprised to read, "Little did either of them realize that on the very next day Grandfather would take a trip to the hospital." Here we not only moved out of the boy's world, we moved out of the story altogether. We have the sense of the author talking to us which, although possible, is a sharp break in the convention, similar to that when the playwright jumps to the stage and describes the next act.

The primary advantage to limiting the means of perception to a single character is that the reader is more readily drawn into the story. This is partly due to his sense of identification with that character—a feeling which should not be confused with sympathy, respect, or even approval. More important, it is due to that aspect of fiction which is illusion as opposed to factual or assertive writing.

Here, for example, is an objective account such as a reporter might write for a newspaper:

> January 22. A twelfth case of diphtheria was reported by Kurt Jorgenson, Health Officer, last night. Helga Olson, 10, daughter of Mr. and Mrs. Fred Olson of Granite Road, had contracted the disease some three or four days earlier according to the visiting physician, Dr. William Carlos Williams. The child has been sent to Regional Memorial Hospital.

Like most journalistic writing, this is loaded with facts. The goal is to be precise. Unlike Williams's story, it gives a date (the story only implies winter), specific names (the story gives only one), an address (the story suggests a rural setting), and a conclusion to the medical aspect of the case. A police report would do essentially the same, though perhaps with more brevity. A case worker's view might include details about the family's financial status and whether there were relatives who had been exposed. But in each instance, the view remains "objective" in that it is essentially outside the mind of any one character.

In another sense, however, this little news item is highly *im*precise. We have more facts than we really need, but we have no clear picture at all of what went on in the minds of those involved. The reporter might have gone on still further with, "Dr. Williams stated that the girl had resisted medical examination even by her parents, thus delaying the diagnosis." But no matter how many details the newspaper gives, its account will still seem superficial compared with the literary story. The essential difference is that the news reporter simply *tells* about an incident while the successful writer of fiction makes the reader *live* it.

The primary advantage, then, of limiting the means of perception is creating this illusion of taking part in the action. There are also two other advantages. First, it serves as a natural device for withholding information. Notice that the newspaper article followed the rigid journalistic convention of giving the most important fact first: the girl *did* have diphtheria. The story, on the other hand, is limited to the doctor's means of perception and is presented in the same sequence as it occurred to him. As a result, that piece of information is withheld until close to the end. It has also been demoted in importance, overshadowed both by the physical struggle between the two principle characters and by the psychological conflict within the doctor.

Almost every story withholds information. Imagine "Friends from Philadelphia" starting out with, "John would never forget the day Mr. Lutz rather patronizingly bought an expensive bottle of wine for John's family." The story does not depend wholly on this bit of information, but it would be badly damaged if it were given too soon.

The final advantage of limiting the means of perception is that it gives the author the opportunity to provide the reader with incorrect or biased material. A good example of this technique appears in Updike's story at the point where Mr. Lutz enters for the first time:

> "Now don't be surprised if he has a bit of a load on," Mrs. Lutz said.
> Actually, he didn't act at all drunk. He was like a happy husband in the movies. He called Thelma his little pookie-pie and kissed her on the forehead; then he called his wife his big pookie-pie and kissed her on the mouth. Then he solemnly shook John's hand and told him how very, very happy he was to see him. . . .

Although the story is written in the third person, it is sharply limited to John's point of view. At first we may take the statement, "he didn't act at all drunk" as being literally true as if it came from the author. But Mr. Lutz's behavior makes us change our minds. The initial judgment was John's and was naive. As readers we were led to share that naiveté and then take a broader view as well.

Variations in the Means of Perception

Although a majority of short stories limit the means of perception to a single character, there are other approaches.

One variation is the reportorial style in which the author does not enter the mind of any character. Although I have been warning against this as a device for fiction, it is enormously successful in Shirley Jackson's "The Lottery." That story is told objectively as if a feature writer were on the scene. The reason this approach does not usually succeed in student writing (and the reason it is not found at all frequently in published work) is that it eliminates the opportunity of identifying with any one character. The reader is always kept outside the action. It succeeds in Miss Jackson's story partly because the subject of concern is not an individual but an entire community. Another factor is the degree of dramatic impact. With such a strong story, the reportorial style is a method of control.

Another variation—and a more common one—is the use of multiple viewpoints. Since this approach is usually reserved for longer short stories and novels, it is not represented in this text. One of the more famous examples, however, is "The Short Happy Life of Francis Macomber" by Ernest Hemingway. The plot involves a triangle: Mr. and Mrs. Macomber who are on a safari in Africa and their guide, Wilson. Through hunting, Macomber is able to redefine himself; but this discovery also leads to his death.

The bulk of this story is told alternately from the point of view of the husband and Wilson, the guide. A few brief insights are given into the private mental world of Mrs. Macomber, and two solid blocks of thought and feelings are given to the wounded lion.

But this should not be thought of as the "omniscient point of view." The author is quite careful not to skip rapidly from one mind to the other. Long sections of the story are given to first one and then another character. And the wife, an essential character, is seen largely through the eyes of others. Even at the very end where her intention becomes the crucial point of the story, Hemingway refuses to enter her mind.

Student authors often try to write from a truly omniscient point of view. This tendency comes from the fact that in school they wrote many more expository papers than stories. But experienced authors in this century have generally avoided this form. If Hemingway had used a truly omniscient view in his story, there would be much jumping from mind to mind. Worse, he would lose the chance to withhold periodically the reactions of his characters.

Faulkner has experimented a good deal with point of view. One of the most interesting is in the novel *As I Lay Dying*. Here he uses the first person exclusively, but he shifts the means of perception from chapter to chapter. In a sense he shifts the fictional world, leading us to view one situation in several different ways. This, of course, lends itself better to a long work. Each chapter becomes a short story in itself with its own individual style.

Stories and novels such as these should be studied carefully. But there are good reasons why such experiments are only rarely found in print. Most writers feel they need experience in single-perception fiction before trying variations.

First vs.
Third Person
A child's first piece of original fiction is usually a mixture of autobiography and fantasy. Without thinking of technique he selects the first person.

"And I went down behind Mr. Syke's house where the woods are and I saw a little pond and right next that pond lying down was a blue lion and I *ran*."

Everything is here: a setting, a sequence of action, a climax with man pitted against beast (at the age of five, stories are apt to be epic and archetypal), an emotional response, and a resolution. But if you ask him why he used "I" instead of "he," the child can only shrug and say "it happened to me, that's why." This answer has a certain charm at the age of five, but it loses its luster when it is repeated at the age of twenty. And so does the story. When one adopts the techniques of a five-year-old, one must settle for the same limited audience.

Actually it is dangerous to select the first person just because the story is based on personal experience or third person because the incident originally happened to someone else. The decision should be made not on the basis of where the story came from but what the story as a literary work is to become.

One use of the first person, for example, is not to reveal the most personal feelings of the author but to satirize the speaker. When Swift decided to write *Gulliver's Travels* from the point of view of Gulliver speaking in the first person, it was not to reveal Swift's own views directly through his protagonist. Some of the finest satire in that book comes from the author's subtle ridicule of conventional middle-class views as seen in Gulliver's reactions.

Exactly the same technique was used by Sherwood Anderson in the short story "I'm a Fool." Again, we have the first person used by the protagonist. A fine irony is drawn from the fact that this poor boy is a far greater fool than he ever suspects, not because of what he has done but because of the melodramatic way in which he tells it. Here again, the author has not selected the first person to reveal his inner convictions or secret life but to gain a new dimension by allowing the reader to learn more about the character than the character himself knows. In this way the satire is sharpened with irony.

Another use of the first person occurs in stories of reminiscence. Having a mature character look back and report on his earlier experience actually provides a kind of double viewpoint. One of the best and most complex examples of this is in Conrad's long story "Youth." Here the protagonist as an old man tells a story about himself as a youth. The age and attitudes of the teller are made clear both at the beginning and at the end as well as in intervals during the story. The listeners are old and there are old men in the story itself. Thus, attitudes of youth and age are compared and contrasted throughout the work. All the advantages of the single means of perception are preserved, yet a double vision is presented vividly.

In addition, the first person is the best form with which to create the illusion of a storyteller speaking out loud. Almost every author has tried his hand at this form, but it has limited uses. It adds to the irony of Anderson's "I'm a Fool" and to the regional flavor of Faulkner's "Spotted Horses" and to the character revelation in many of Conrad's works. It should be noted, however, that it is a difficult form which depends as much on a good ear for dialogue as music depends on a good ear for tone. There is a tendency among amateurs to stress the dialectic variations excessively and to use the informality of daily speech to excuse a kind of thematic haze which has settled on the work.

The fourth and final advantage of the first person occurs when it is used to place the means of perception outside the protagonist. In Fitzgerald's *The Great Gatsby,* for example, the protagonist, Gatsby, cannot be given the means of perception because so much of the novel depends on the mystery of his past. And it would be awkward giving it to his love, Daisy, because she has never been able to understand Gatsby's values. So the "I" of the story is a secondary character who is related to each of the other two in his value and background. He never views impartially, but he does provide the reader with equal insights into two different worlds.

The advantages of the third person are not as easy to categorize. There are, of course, some very simple considerations: It is the form to use if the story is to have more than one means of perception. It is clearly the form to use if the protagonist dies at the end of the work. And it has a certain advantage if the protagonist is the sort most readers would have difficulty identifying with. But these are not enough to explain the popularity of the third person.

The most persuasive defense for the third person is its flexibility. Whereas the first person sets the author squarely within the mind of a single character, the third person can fluctuate between a kind of neutral style and that which is truly an echo of first-person narration. In the following passage, for example, the means of perception remains with the boy, but there is a shift away from the neutral view toward the boy's own speech.

> He had been kept after school again. It was a simple matter of writing "Good boys do not cheat" fifty times and then cleaning up the classroom, but it took the length of the afternoon. Now he was in a hurry to get home because the shadows were long and it would be dark and scary soon. The short cut was through crazy old Mr. Syke's back lot—"Old Mr. Syke is higher than a kite" they used to chant, though no one had ever seen him actually drunk. He slipped through the hedge, down across the corner of the lawn, and under the trees. The air was still. He walked fast and held his breath. A few more feet and he would be past the pond where.... But there it was again, the enormous blue lion. It lay calmly by the edge of the pond, its paw dangling in the water. "Run" he thought, and he was running.

This is no longer a story written by a child. We have some factual material at the very beginning which, though known by the character (and therefore in harmony with the means of perception), is told in neutral terms. Then the passage begins to echo the phrasing of what might be the boy's own telling. The first hint of this is the word "scary" which is borrowed from his own vocabulary. And we are then prepared to accept Mr. Syke as "crazy." All this leads us to a quick and natural acceptance of the blue lion.

Here the third person borrows some of the objectivity of the clinical report and some of the subjectivity of first-person narration. It avoids the cold detachment of a psychologist's statement which would humorlessly place "crazy old Mr. Syke" and "blue lion" in quotation marks to indicate that these are not the "truth." And it avoids a slavish adherence to a child's vocabulary which, particularly in longer pieces, becomes difficult to maintain.

The popular argument that the first person lends to a story "immediacy" or "realism" which cannot be achieved in the third person is absurd. Of the three stories included in this volume, two are written in the first person and one in the third. It would be pointless to argue that the third-person story would be improved if converted to first. The decision for each story has to be made on the basis of the story's own needs.

How does one decide? One way is to try different versions in rough draft. The decision will be made partly on analysis such as I have suggested above, but also on the "feel" of the story. This is a subtle factor which one can best learn by making conversions from first to third and the reverse. Those who wish to develop this sensitivity should convert one full page from each of the three stories included in this volume, changing the first-person stories to third and then converting "Friends from Philadelphia" into a first-person narration, first from the point of view of John and then of Mr. Lutz. Work like this is often far more effective as a learning process than is abstract critical analysis.

The Spectrum from
First to Third Person
It is helpful to talk about the first and third persons as if it were a simple choice between two alternatives. But it is also a simplification. The fact is that the author

selects a way of presenting his story from a spectrum which has as many shadings as the rainbow has colors. Just as it is easier for the artist to speak of "blue" and "green" as clearly definable entities, it is easy for the writer to speak of "first person" and "third person." But any writer at home with fiction can sense more subtle distinctions.

These gradations run from the most inward, limited, and personal to the most external and impersonal. I list them here as separate entities, but in practice each blends with the next.

1. *Stream of consciousness* is the most subjective form of writing. In a sense it is the purest form of the first person. The writer creates the illusion of listening to a character's thoughts without interruption from the outside world. The result is wandering, disjointed, highly personal. The connections are by association rather than by logic or narrative sequence.

This approach has both assets and liabilities. If done carefully, it is a free-flowing insight into a character. (Don't confuse this with journal writing which is a free-floating insight into the author himself —and usually is so full of private references than it is of value only to himself.) But the liability is that the writer is cut off from such valuable devices as action, dialogue, setting, and even exposition. Because of this limitation, it is rarely used as the sole medium for a story. The most famous example, the last fifty pages of Joyce's *Ulysses,* is only a small portion of that novel. Short stories often limit it to a paragraph or two.

2. *First person as-if-told* allows us to move outside the mind of the narrator insofar as he describes the actions and dialogue of others. But the echoes of everyday speech ("Well now," "Like I said before," "Ain't nothin' to worry about," and so on) may limit the author's vocabulary.

3. *First person in neutral style* avoids the restriction of common speech, though it too has limitations, as noted above.

4. *Third person* is the most flexible approach to fiction, though normally it is limited to a single means of perception.

5. *First person plural* ("we") is a very rare and difficult form to be tried, if at all, only by those who have been writing for some time. One example is seen in Faulkner's "That Evening Sun" which begins in the first person but soon shifts to "we" and remains so. In "A Rose for Emily," he uses "we" throughout. The viewpoint is the townspeople

collectively. And in Conrad's novel, *The Nigger of the Narcissus,* the "we" refers generally to the crew. But in most of these works, there is an implied single viewer behind the collective "we."

6. *Objective reporting* or the *reportorial style* is at the opposite end of the spectrum from stream-of-consciousness writing. Instead of being totally immersed in the mind of a character, the reader remains an outside observer. His view is like that of a reporter.

Normally reportorial writing is nonliterary, a form of descriptive writing as defined in Chapter 12. But occasionally it is borrowed as a literary form when an author wants to create the *illusion* of objective reporting while in fact writing a self-contained piece of fiction. European short story writers have been more inclined to use this approach than British and American authors. But Shirley Jackson's "The Lottery" is as fine an example as can be found anywhere.

**The Focus
of a Story** The focus of a story answers the question, "Whose story is it?" In "The Use of Force," for example, it is obvious that the focus is *not* on the father of the girl. Since the means of perception is not his, we don't know his thoughts, and he neither does enough nor says enough for us to guess. But the focus could be on him. After all, there is a drama going on within a father as he watches a doctor try to force a spoon into the mouth of his treasured daughter.

The focus of the story as written is on the doctor and the girl. The story on one level has to do with the conflict between them. But in a more narrow sense, the focus is on the doctor alone, for the most important conflict in the story is the one which exists between his professional self and his emotionally charged, sexual self.

In this case, as with a majority of stories, the focus is on the character who is also the means of perception. But the two don't have to be the same. In some stories a secondary character is given the means of perception and the focus is on a character about whom we learn by observation. Some of the best examples are found in longer short stories and in novels. One of the more famous is Fitzgerald's *The Great Gatsby* in which the protagonist, Gatsby, cannot be given the means of perception because so much of the novel depends on the mystery of his past. So the "I" of the story is a secondary character who is Gatsby's friend.

Occasionally an aspect of nature or society is made a part of the focus just as if it were a character. In Hemingway's *The Old Man and the Sea,* the sea itself becomes an antagonist, sharing the spotlight with the old man. And in Faulkner's "A Rose for Emily," the focus is not only on Emily but on the townspeople represented as a single antagonist.

The Three
Basic Options

Consciously or unconsciously, every author has to make three basic decisions before he writes the first paragraph of any story. First, through whose eyes am I going to present this (the means of perception)? Second, which person shall I use (first vs. third)? Finally, just whose story is this (focus)? If a new story starts easily and develops rapidly, the writer shouldn't stop to consider how many decisions he has made without conscious effort. But when it doesn't seem quite right from the very start, or when the first draft seems vaguely dissatisfying, it is often helpful to review all the other ways the story could have been written.

In the following passage there are three characters. Clearly the husband, Max, is the means of perception.

> When Max came home his wife was sprawled in their only comfortable chair, sipping a Coke, and watching "The Light of Her Life" on Channel 3. The boy was at the table with arithmetic book and papers before him, but his eyes were on the television show too. Keep calm, Max told himself. Play it cool.
> "Where were you?" he asked, hanging up his cost as if it were a casual question.
> "When?"
> "This afternoon. I called and there was no answer." He wasn't going to tell her he called seven times. A wife, he figured, should never feel she was worth seven calls.
> "I was here," she said. She hadn't once taken her eyes off the shimmering screen. "Phone must be busted."
> She looked up at him and smiled.

The story has begun. We have a setting, three characters, and a tension bound to the mystery as to where she was. But most of all we have a clear means of perception which is going to shape the course of the entire story. No matter what we may think of a man who won't let his wife know that she is worth seven telephone calls, we have identified with him. We are in his mind, see what he sees, and wonder about the very things he is wondering about.

The whole direction, tone, and possibly the theme as well, shifts when we change the means of perception.

> When Celia heard him open the door she tensed. But there was no need for that, she told herself, no need to feel guilty. After a morning of cleaning house, washing clothes, waxing floors—which most husbands offer to do themselves—and making meals for the boy—after all that a woman deserved escape. And why shouldn't she spend the afternoon at a double feature? Yet she knew she would not tell him. Bad enough to be caught watching a show like this on television—Impossible to admit spending the afternoon watching *Red River Rodeo* and *Sioux City Belle.*

While this paragraph is a simple rewriting of the first version, it suggests a totally new story. Whether it will be better or worse than the story suggested by the first opening is up to the author to decide. My point here is that the author should make this decision knowingly.

But there are other approaches possible. In both of these versions the boy has been all but neglected. A third story is suggested by giving him the means of perception.

> For an hour he had fingered the arithmetic book, staring sightlessly at the page headed with "Problems in long division." But ahead of him, beyond the book, just past his mother's left shoulder, was the television set which had drawn him into a doctor's private world. Jim Noble was arguing with his wife who was saying "So what's wrong with split fees, Jim? We've got bills to pay like everyone else." The words made no sense, but the way they talked to each other made his stomach feel like it was filled with marbles. And then he saw his father standing in the doorway looking as if he had just lost his job or something.

Here the problem of marital division is taken from the boy's point of view. Presumably the satiric scene from the medical soap opera and possibly even the reference to "problems in long division" foreshadow an aspect of the theme. The parents are significant only insofar as they affect the boy. It is a third story.

Next, there is the matter of person. Each of these three versions could be told in the first person. This decision, as I have pointed out, has to be made in terms of what the story is to become. It would be quite possible, for example, to present the story from the husband's point of view in the first person, allowing him to defend himself as a fair and reasonable man while showing the reader just how immature he actually is. The same could be done from Celia's point of view. Or the boy could present his parents in what he feels is a kindly light while actually showing how selfish they are. "Every afternoon," he might report quite sincerely, "when I come home from school she's gone to a movie so she won't bother me with housecleaning and stuff when I should be doing my homework. That's why I'm first in my class." In this single statement presented from the boy's point of view in his own words, we the readers make a judgment about Celia which is contrary to the boy's. If this differential between the boy's interpretation of his mother and our evaluation of her continues, we have a story in which the first person has created a sustained irony.

But whose story is it? That is, which character is the protagonist? In the last instance we might assume that it would be the boy's story since he is telling it. But if the mother emerges as the most fully drawn, the most completely analyzed, the story could easily become hers. The boy, then, would be simply the naive reporter, the innocent narrator who thinks he is describing a kindly and considerate mother while in fact he reveals a portrait of adult immaturity. Or the mother, given the means of perception, might present a story which primarily concerns either the boy or her husband.

Seen schematically, those three options can be visualized like this:

A story primarily about	CELIA	MAX	THE BOY
Seen through the eyes of			
CELIA	1, 2	3, 4	5, 6
MAX	7, 8	9, 10	11, 12
THE BOY	13, 14	15, 16	17, 18

Here the odd numbers represent first-person presentations and the even, third person. The total of eighteen versions represent not only eighteen first paragraphs but that number of different stories as well. And if one recalls the fact that the distinction between first person and third is really an entire spectrum of options, the variations become limitless.

No writer, of course, ever goes through all the options. In many cases, all the decisions can be made unconsciously—particularly when the author has read a lot. But it is important to remember just how wide the range of options is whenever a story is not going well.

Reviewing and Revising

It is generally a good idea to consider at least briefly why one has chosen a particular means of perception, person, and focus. Asking these questions early in the formation of a story sometimes can save hours of rewriting later on.

After the first draft is completed, the sections which should be reviewed most carefully are the opening and the closing. And of the two, it is the ending which seems to give the most trouble. There is an apparently overwhelming need on the part of some beginners to add a final paragraph which sums up the theme of the story. At worst it comes out as a moral: "He learned once and for all that . . ." or, "After that, Tom was careful about what he said when the old man was around; and never again did he bring up the touchy business of World War II."

Although good authors occasionally speak for themselves in their fiction, they rarely attempt to summarize an entire story. This reluctance is due in some cases to a conviction that a story ought to explain itself through action and dialogue. More often, it is due to the fact that most sophisticated fiction cannot be summarized in a paragraph. To try would merely reduce complexity to unjustified simplicity. Because of this, an urge to summarize frequently serves as a danger signal indicating either that the story is in fact a simple one or that it did not show what the author hoped it would.

The second most common failure is the summary introduction. "It was a beautiful August day on Lake Placid," an inept writer begins, "and there was little to suggest that before sunset Tom would learn much about the vicissitudes of weather and perhaps a bit about himself as well." The story is now dead. Here again the means of perception is the all-seeing author rather than Tom. Worse, it gives promise of boredom through literary simplicity.

Another common weakness is shifts in the means of perception. As has been pointed out, the most common form for short fiction is the single viewer. This is particularly true of works which are less than 4,000 words long. And in those rare cases where two or more characters *are* used, the shifts are usually kept at a minimum.

It is generally wise to establish the means of perception early. Introductions which give a paragraph of dialogue or description of the scene are apt to seem detached and boring. Psychologically, most stories "start" as soon as the means of perception is established. For this reason it is often a good idea to enter the mind of one character at least briefly before filling in the background. This is particularly important in stories which begin with dialogue.

Finally, one must be on guard against playing with a bizarre point of view merely for its own sake: the adventure story which assures us that the hero will live because it is written in the first person, until we discover at the end that it is a note written in a bottle; the first person poor-little-boy story which turns out, in the last sentence, to be about a happy-little-dog; the father-son story which turns out in the last sentence to concern two creatures from outer space. Such a warning should not be necessary; but it is. The fact that certain authors such as Poe and Kafka have used plots which are clever, even tricky, does not justify a story whose single purpose is to entertain the reader by surprising him. Such singularity of intent reduces the story to the most unsophisticated level.

As I pointed out in earlier chapters, the success of a story is heavily dependent on its source—the raw material—and the formation of plot. But selecting the right viewpoint is just as important. In fact, of the three concerns, this last is the most frequently neglected. Many students who feel free to metamorphose experience and experiment with plot continue to leave the viewpoint unchanged and unquestioned in draft after draft.

The writer of fiction is not in full control of his craft until he can imagine and truly *feel* just what changes he could create in a particular story by altering the means of perception.

18

A STORY BY
STEPHEN MINOT

Sausage and Beer

I kept quiet for most of the trip. It was too cold for talk. The car, a 1929 Dodge, was still fairly new, but it had no heater, and I knew from experience that no matter how carefully I tucked the black bearskin robe about me, the cold would seep through the door cracks and, starting with a dull ache in my ankles, would work up my legs. There was nothing to do but sit still and wonder what Uncle Theodore would be like.

"Is it very far?" I asked at last. My words puffed vapor.

"We're about halfway now," he said.

That was all. Not enough, of course, but I hadn't expected much more. My father kept to his own world, and he didn't invite children to share it. Nor did he impose himself on us. My twin sister and I were allowed to live our own lives, and our parents led theirs, and there was a mutual respect for the border. In fact, when we were younger Tina and I had assumed that we would eventually marry each other, and while those plans were soon revised, the family continued to exist as two distinct couples.

But this particular January day was different, because Tina hadn't been invited—nor had Mother. I was twelve that winter, and I believe it was the first time I had ever gone anywhere alone with my father.

The whole business of visiting Uncle Theodore had come up in the most unconvincingly offhand manner.

"Thought I'd visit your Uncle Theodore," he had said that day after Sunday dinner. "Wondered if you'd like to meet him."

He spoke with his eyes on a crack in the ceiling as if the idea had just popped into his head, but that didn't fool me. It was quite obvious that he had waited until both Tina and my mother were in the kitchen washing the dishes, that he had rehearsed it, and that I wasn't really being given a choice.

"Is Tina going?" I asked.

"No, she isn't feeling well."

I knew what that meant. But I also knew that my father was just using it as an excuse. So I got my coat.

The name Uncle Theodore had a familiar ring, but it was just a name. And I had learned early that you just do not ask about relatives who don't come up in adult conversation naturally. At least, you didn't in my family. You can never tell— Like my Uncle Harry. He was another one of my father's brothers. My parents never said anything about Uncle Harry, but some of my best friends at school told me he'd taken a big nail, a spike really, and driven it into his heart with a ball peen hammer. I didn't believe it, so they took me to the library and we found the article on the front page of the *Herald* for the previous Saturday, so it must have been true.

I thought a lot about that. It seemed to me that a grown-up ought to be able to *shove* it between his ribs. And even if he couldn't, what was the point of the ball peen hammer? I used to put myself to sleep feeling the soft spaces between my ribs and wondering just which one was directly over my heart.

But no one at school told me about Uncle Theodore, because they didn't know he existed. Even I hadn't any real proof until that day. I knew that my father had a brother named Theodore, in the same way I knew the earth was round without anyone ever taking me to the library to prove it. But then, there were many brothers I had never met—like Freddie, who had joined a Theosophist colony somewhere in California and wore robes like a priest, and Uncle Herb, who was once in jail for leading a strike in New York.

We were well out in the New England countryside now, passing dark, snow-patched farm fields and scrubby woodlands where saplings choked and stunted each other. I tried to visualize this Uncle Theodore as a farmer: blue overalls, straw hat, chewing a long stem of alfalfa, and misquoting the Bible. But it was a highly unsatisfactory conjecture. Next I tried to conjure up a mystic living in—didn't St. Francis live in a cave? But it wasn't the sort of question I could ask my father. All I had to go on was what he had told me, which was nothing. And I knew without thinking that he didn't want me to ask him directly.

After a while I indulged in my old trick of fixing my eyes on the big radiator thermometer mounted like a figurehead on the front end of the hood. If you do that long enough the blur of the road just beyond will lull you nicely and pass the time. It had begun to take effect when I felt the car slow down and turn abruptly. Two great gates flashed by, and we were inside a kind of walled city.

Prison, I thought. That's it. That's why they kept him quiet. A murderer, maybe. "My Uncle Theodore," I rehearsed silently, "he's the cop killer."

The place went on forever, row after row of identical buildings, four stories, brick, slate roofs, narrow windows with wire mesh. There wasn't a bright color anywhere. The brick had aged to gray, and so had the snow patches along the road. We passed a group of three old men lethargically shoveling ice and crusted snow into a two-wheeled horse cart; men and horse were the same hue. It was the sort of setting you have in dreams which are not nightmares but still manage to leave a clinging aftertaste. At least, *I* have dreams like that.

"This is a kind of hospital," my father said flatly as we drove between the staring brick fronts. There was a slow whine to second gear which sang harmony to something in me. I had based my courage on the romance of a prison, but even this slim hold on assurance was lost with the word "hospital."

"It's big," I said.

"It's enormous," he said, and then turned his whole attention to studying the numbers over each door. There was something in his tone that suggested that he didn't like the place either, and that did a lot to sustain me.

Uncle Theodore's building was 13-M, but aside from the number, it resembled the others. The door had been painted a dark green for many years, and the layers of paint over chipped and blistered paint gave it a mottled look. We had to wait quite a while before someone responded to the push bell.

A man let us in, not a nurse. And the man was clearly no doctor either. He wore a gray shirt which was clean but unpressed, and dark-green work pants with a huge ring of keys hanging from his belt. But for the keys he might have been a W.P.A. worker.

"Hello there, Mr. Bates," he said in a round Irish voice to match his round face. "You brought the boy?"

"I brought the boy." My father's voice was reedy by comparison. "How's Ted?"

"Same as when you called. A little gloomy, maybe, but calm. Those boils have just about gone."

"Good," my father said.

"Funny about those boils. I don't remember a year but what he's had trouble. Funny."

My father agreed it was funny, and then we went into the visiting room to await Uncle Theodore.

The room was large, and it seemed even larger for the lack of furniture. There were benches around all four walls, and in the middle there was a long table flanked with two more benches. The rest was space. And through that space old men shuffled, younger men wheeled carts of linen, a woman visitor walked slowly up and down with her restless husband—or brother, or uncle. Or was *she* the patient? I couldn't decide which might be the face of madness, his troubled and shifting eyes or her deadened look. Beyond, a bleak couple counseled an ancient patient. I strained to hear, wanting to know the language of the place, but I could only make out mumbles.

The smell was oddly familiar. I cast about; this was no home smell. And then I remembered trips with my mother to a place called the Refuge, where the lucky brought old clothes, old furniture, old magazines, and old kitchenware to be bought by the unlucky. My training in Christian charity was to bring my chipped and dented toys and dump them into a great bin, where they were pored over by dead-faced mothers and children.

"Smells like the Refuge," I said very softly, not wanting to hurt anyone's feelings. My father nodded with an almost smile.

We went over to the corner where the benches met, though there was space to sit almost anywhere. And there we waited.

A couple of times I glanced cautiously at my father's face, hoping for some sort of guide. He could have been waiting for a train or listening to a sermon, and I felt a surge of respect. He had a long face with a nose so straight it looked as if it had been leveled with a rule. I guess he would have been handsome if he hadn't seemed so sad or tired much of the time. He worked for a paint wholesaler which had big, dusty offices in a commercial section of Dorchester. When I was younger I used to think the dirt of that place had rubbed off on him permanently. But later I could see that it wasn't just the job, it was home too. The place had been built in the eighties, the pride of our grandfather. But it was no pride to us. It was a gross Victorian imitation in brick of the square sea captain's house, complete with two iron deer on the lawn. At some point the brick had been painted a mournful gray. It was lucky, our parents kept telling each other, that Grandfather never lived to see what happened to the place. The land was sold off bit by bit, and the city of Dorchester, once a kind of rural cousin to Boston, spread slowly the way tide comes in over mud flats, until it surrounded us with little brick stores—hardware, drug, delicatessen, plumbing—on one side and double-deckers on the other three. Somehow my father had come to feel responsible for all this; it was his nature to take on more responsibility than most people do.

For Tina and me the place had its compensations. We called it the Ark, and we knew every level of that enormous place, from the kitchen with its cook's pantry without a cook and a maid's pantry without a maid up through the four floors to the glass-sided cupola which we called the Bridge and reserved as our private area, just as our parents reserved their bedroom.

We used to arrange the future from up there; I the father and she mother, planning on two children—twins, of course. And we also planned to replace the iron deer with live ones, paint the Ark a shimmering green, and burn down Gemini's Delicatessen across the street—the one with sausages hanging in the window—because Mother had told us that it was just a front for the numbers racket which kept customers streaming through the doors. She detested sausage and resented having the numbers game played "at our very door," so, naturally, in the name of order it had to go.

But waiting for Uncle Theodore in that dream room was worlds away from all that youthful planning. I could see, or thought I saw, in my father's face a kind of resignation which I used to interpret as fatigue but now felt was his true strength.

I began to study the patients with the hope of preparing myself for Uncle Theodore. The old man beside us was stretched out on the bench full length, feet toward us, one arm over his eyes, as if he were lying on the beach, the other resting over his crotch. He had a kind of squeak to his snore. There was nothing in him I could not accept as my Uncle Theodore. Another patient was persistently scratching his back on the dark-varnished door frame. If this were Uncle Theodore, I wondered, would I be expected to scratch his back for him? It wasn't a very rational speculation, but there was nothing about the place that encouraged clear reasoning.

Then my father stood up, and when I did, too, I could see that Uncle Theodore was being led in by a Negro who wore the same kind of key ring at his waist that the Irishman had. The Negro nodded to my father, pointing him out to Uncle Theodore, and then set him free with a little nudge as if he were about to pin the tail on the donkey.

Surprisingly, Uncle Theodore was heavy. I don't mean fat, because he wasn't solid. He was a great, sagging man. His jowls hung loose, his shoulders were massive but rounded like a dome, his hands were attached like brass weights on the ends of swinging pendulums. He wore a clean white shirt open at the neck and blue serge suit pants hung on suspenders which had been patched with a length of twine. It looked as if his pants had once been five sizes too large and that somehow, with the infinite patience of the infirm, he had managed to stretch the lower half of his stomach to fill them.

I would have assumed that he was far older than my father from his stance and his shuffling walk (he wore scuffs, which he slid across the floor without once lifting them), but his face was a baby pink, which made him look adolescent.

"Hello, Ted," my father said. "How have you been?"

Uncle Theodore just said "Hello," without a touch of enthusiasm, or even gratitude for our coming to see him. We stood there, the three of us, for an awkward moment.

Then: "I brought the boy."

"Who?"

"My boy, Will."

Uncle Theodore looked down at me with red-rimmed, blue eyes. Then he looked at my father, puzzled. "But *you're* Will."

"Right, but we've named our boy William too. Tried to call him Billy, but he insists on Will. Very confusing."

Uncle Theodore smiled for the first time. The smile made everything much easier; I relaxed. He was going to be like any other relative on a Sunday afternoon visit.

"Well, now," he said in an almost jovial manner, "there's one on me. I'd forgotten I even *had* a boy."

My face tingled the way it does when you open the furnace door. Somehow he had joined himself with my father as a married couple, and done it with a smile. No instruction could have prepared me for this quiet sound of madness.

But my father had, it seemed, learned how to handle it. He simply asked Uncle Theodore if he had enjoyed the magazines he had brought last time. We subscribed to the old version of *Life,* and my mother used to buy *Judge* on the newsstand fairly regularly. It was the right subject to bring up, because Uncle Theodore promptly forgot about who had produced what child and told us about how all his copies of *Life* had been stolen. He even pointed out the thief.

"The little one with the hook nose there," he said with irritation but no rage. "Stuffs them in his pants to make him look bigger. He's a problem, he is."

"I'll send you more," my father said. "Perhaps the attendant will keep them for you."

"Hennesy? He's a good one. Plays checkers like a pro."

"I'll bet he has a hard time beating you."

"Hasn't yet. Not once."

"I'm not surprised. You were always the winner." And then to me: "We used to play up in the cupola for hours at a stretch."

This jolted me. It hadn't occurred to me that the two of them had spent a childhood together. I even let some of their conversation slip by thinking of how they had grown up in the Ark, had discovered the Bridge before I was born, had perhaps planned the future while sitting up there, looking down on the world, on Gemini's Delicatessen and all the other little stores, had gone to school together, and then at some point— But what point? And how? It was as incomprehensible to me looking back as it must have been for them looking forward.

"So they started banging on their plates," Uncle Theodore was saying, "and shouting for more heat. Those metal plates sure make a racket, I can tell you."

"That's no way to get heat," Father said, sounding paternal.

"Guess not. They put Schwartz and Cooper in the pit. That's what Hennesy said. And there's a bunch of them that's gone to different levels. They send them down when they act like that, you know. The doctors, they take a vote and send the troublemakers down." And then his voice lowered. Instinctively we both bent toward him for some confidence. "And I've found out—God's truth—that one of these nights they're going to shut down the heat *all the way. Freeze us!*"

There was a touch of panic in this which coursed through me. I could feel just how it would be, this great room black as midnight, the whine of wind outside, and then all those hissing radiators turning silent, and the aching cold seeping through the door cracks—

"Nonsense," my father said quietly, and I knew at once that it was nonsense. "They wouldn't do that. Hennesy's a friend of mine. I'll speak to him before I go."

"You do that," Uncle Theodore said with genuine gratitude, putting his hand on my father's knee. "You do that for us. I don't believe there would be a soul of us"—he swept his hand about expansively—"not a soul of us alive if it weren't for your influence."

My father nodded and then turned the conversation to milder topics. He talked about how the sills were rotting under the house, how a neighborhood gang had broken two windows one night, how there was talk of replacing the trolley with a bus line, how Imperial Paint, where my father worked, had laid off fifty percent of its employees, how business was so bad it couldn't get worse. But Uncle Theodore didn't seem very concerned. He was much more bothered about how a man named Altman was losing his eyesight because of the steam heat and how stern and unfair Hennesy was. At one point he moved back in time to describe a fishing trip by canoe through the Rangeley Lakes. It was like opening a great window, flooding the place with light and color and the smells of summer.

"Nothing finer," he said, his eyes half shut, "than frying those trout at the end of the day with the water so still you'd think you could walk on it."

He was interrupted by the sleeper on the bench beside us, who woke, stood, and stared down at us. Uncle Theodore told him to "Go blow," and when he had gone so were the Rangeley Lakes.

"Rangeley?" he asked, when my father tried to open that window again by suggestion. "He must be one of our cousins. Can't keep 'em straight." And we were back to Mr. Altman's deafness and how seriously it hindered him and how the doctors paid no attention.

It was with relief that I smelled sauerkraut. That plus attendants gliding through with carts of food in dented steel containers seemed to suggest supper, and supper promised that the end was near.

"About suppertime," my father said after a particularly long silence.

Uncle Theodore took in a long, deep breath. He held it for a moment. Then he let it go with the slowest, saddest sigh I have ever heard.

"About suppertime," he said at the end of it.

There were mumbled farewells and nods of agreement. We were thanked for copies of *Judge* which we hadn't brought; he was told he was looking fine, just fine.

We were only inches from escape when Uncle Theodore suddenly discovered me again.

"Tell me, son," he said, bending down with a smile which on anyone else would have been friendly, "what d'you think of your Uncle Ted?"

I was overwhelmed. I stood there looking up at him, waiting for my father to save me. But he said nothing.

"It's been very nice meeting you," I said to the frozen pink smile, dredging the phrase up from my sparse catechism of social responses, assuming that what would do for maiden aunts would do for Uncle Theodore.

But it did not. He laughed. It was a loud and bitter laugh, derisive, and perfectly sane. He had seen my statement for the lie it was, had caught sight of himself, of all of us.

"Well," he said when the laugh withered, "say hi to Dad for me. Tell him to drop by."

Father said he would, and we left, grateful that the moment of sanity had been so brief.

It was dark when we got back into the car, and it was just beginning to snow. I nestled into the seat, soothed by the familiar whine of second gear.

We had been on the road about a half hour when my father said quite abruptly, "I could do with a drink." It was so spontaneous, so perfectly confidential that I wanted to reply, to keep some sort of exchange going. But I couldn't suggest a place to go—I couldn't even throw back an easy "So could I."

"It's OK with me," I said, without any of the casual air I tried hard to achieve.

There was a long pause. He flipped the manual windshield wiper. Then he said, "I don't suppose you like sausage."

"I love sausage," I said, though I had never had any at home.

"Well," he said slowly, "there's a place I go—but it might be better to tell your mother we went to a Dutchland Farms for supper."

"Sure," I said, and reached up to flip the windshield wiper for him.

When we got to the city we traveled on roads I had never been on. He finally parked on a dark street and began what turned out to be a three-block hike. It ended at an unlit door, and after some mumbled consultations through an apartment phone we were ushered into a warm, bubbling, sparkling, humming, soothing, exciting bit of cheerful chaos. There was a bar to our right, marble tables ahead, booths beyond, just as I had pictured from the cartoons in *Life* magazine. My father nodded at a waiter and said hi to a group at a table, then headed toward the booths with a sure step.

We hadn't got halfway before a fat man in a double-breasted suit came steaming up to us, furious.

"Whatcha doing," he said even before he reached us, "corruptin' the youth?"

I held my breath. But when the big man reached my father they broke out in easy laughter.

"So this is the boy?" he said. "Will, Junior—right?" We nodded. "Well, there's a good part of you in the boy, I can see that—it's in the eyes. Now, there's a girl too, isn't there? Younger?"

"She's my twin," I said. "Not identical."

The men laughed. Then the fat one said, "Jesus, twins sure run in your family, don't they!"

This surprised me. I knew of no other twins except some cousins from Maine. I looked up at my father, puzzled.

"Me and Ted," he said to me. "We're twins. Nonidentical."

We were ushered to a booth, and the fat man hovered over us, waiting for the order.

"Got sausage tonight?" my father asked.

"Sure. American or some nice hot Italian?"

"Italian."

"Drinks?"

"Well—" My father turned to me. "I guess you rate beer," he said. And then, to the fat man, "Two beers."

The man relayed the order to a passing waiter. Then he asked my father, "Been out to see Ted?"

"You guessed it."

"I figured." He paused, his smile gone. "You too?" he asked me.

"Yes," I said. "It was my first time."

"Oh," he said, with a series of silent nods which assured me that somehow he knew exactly what my afternoon had been like. "Ted was quite a boy. A great tackle. A pleasure to watch him. But no dope either. Used to win meals here playing chess. Never saw him lose. Why, he sat right over there."

He pointed to the corner booth, which had a round table. All three of us looked; a waiter with a tray full of dirty glasses stopped, turned, and also looked at the empty booth as if an apparition had just been sighted.

"And you know why he's locked up?"

"No," I whispered, appalled at the question.

"It's just the number he drew. Simple as that. Your Dad, me, you— any of us could draw the wrong number tomorrow. There's something to think about."

I nodded. All three of us nodded. Then the waiter brought a tray with the order, and the fat man left us with a quick, benedictory smile. We ate and drank quietly, lost in a kind of communion.

19

CHARACTERIZATION

Characterization as *illusion* based on three elements: *consistency* of behavior and attitudes, *complexity,* and *individuality;* techniques of developing these elements including *direct analysis,* the use of significant *action, dialogue, thoughts,* and *physical details; blending* these various techniques.

Characterization, like all aspects of fiction, is illusion. When we as readers say that a fictional character is "convincing," "vivid," or "realistic," it is not because he resembles the person next door, but because we have the illusion of having met and come to know someone new.

It is not necessary, for example, to have been a country doctor in order to appreciate Williams's protagonist in "The Use of Force." And if Uncle Theodore in "Sausage and Beer" comes through vividly for a reader, it is due primarily to elements within the story and is not dependent on having known other patients in mental hospitals.

Consider for a moment the full range of characters you feel that you have "met" through fiction. The list may include such varied types as Faulkner's Snopeses and Tolstoi's aristocratic Anna Karenina. Fiction has induced you to cross the barriers of age, class, sex, race, and national identity. Our sense of credibility is in no way dependent upon having lived in Mississippi or in Russia during the nineteenth century. And our compassion for Gregor in Kafka's "The Metamorphosis" certainly is not dependent on knowing from experience what it is like to wake up one morning as a six-foot cockroach.

Credibility of characterization, then, is not dependent on the reader's experience; it stems from elements within the writing itself. Specifically, there are three: consistency, complexity, and individuality.

In practice, of course, making a character "come alive" on the page is not at all this mechanical. Most writers borrow heavily from people they have known and then metamorphose the details in a variety of ways, both consciously and unconsciously. This is the way they find those hundreds of minute details which go into a finely drawn character. But the reason for this dependence on experience is that it is the most natural way to develop consistency, complexity, and individuality.

Consistency In real life we come to expect a certain consistency in our friends—patterns of behavior, outlook, dress, and the like. In spite of variations, some people tend to be naturally generous or constitutionally sloppy or ambitious.

In addition, these characteristics tend to be interlocked. If a man is an insurance executive, we don't expect him to be politically radical or to have a long black beard or to speak in incomplete sentences prefaced with "like," or to race his Honda on Sunday afternoons. It might be nice if he did, of course; and making such a contradiction plausible could be the start of a story. But that comes under the heading of *complexity*, which I shall turn to shortly. The point here is that consistency of character is one of the basic assumptions we make about people in real life and it is also the fundamental assumption upon which fictional characterization is built.

In simple fiction, consistency is pushed to the point of predictability —and monotony. We know, for example, that Dick Tracy will never under any circumstances take a bribe or punch a sweet little old lady in the nose. It is most unlikely that little orphan Annie will turn junkie. And Tarzan is not going to start wearing a suit. For many readers, these rigid conventions destroy the illusion of credibility; yet for others it is so effective that they send letters and presents to these fictional characters in care of their local paper, utterly confusing art and life.

In sophisticated fiction, the major characters are usually complex.

Pure consistency is limited to minor characters. The parents in "The Use of Force," for example, may have all kinds of conflicting emotions, but what we see is simple, honest concern for their daughter. And the waiter at the end of "Sausage and Beer" is also what E. M. Forster calls a "flat character," one who is all consistency and is merely there to serve a function. Satiric characters and comic figures generally tend to have the same consistency.

Complexity In complex characterization, consistency becomes the springboard for development. That is, certain assumptions are made, then countered, and finally understood as a pattern of the whole character.

Take, for example, the doctor in "The Use of Force." On the simple level, he is an honest, hard-working country doctor who is just getting a start in his profession. He is willing to go out on a house call for three dollars, tending the needs of this poor family with the same professional thoroughness he gives to all his patients. This is consistency on the level of a comic-strip doctor.

But we are not left on that level for long. We begin to pick up warning phrases as soon as he meets his new patient: "The child was fairly eating me up with her cold, steady eyes. . ." and she was "an unusually attractive little thing. . ." and "she had magnificent blonde hair, in profusion." All this before the conflict even begins!

Soon our friendly, hard-working country doctor develops what appears to be an unrelated self: "After all, I had already fallen in love with the savage brat. . .she rose to magnificent heights of insane fury of effort bred of her terror of me." And finally, toward the end, "I could have torn the child apart in my own fury and enjoyed it. It was a pleasure to attack her."

In some respects, this is an extraordinary reversal of our initial assumptions. Why is it that in this story the shift results in complexity of character development whereas in many student efforts we feel that the jump is inconsistent and unconvincing? Much of the answer is found in the author's restraint. There is an *implication* of rape and murder in this story, but what actually happens is still within the bounds of our expectation for a character of this type.

Complexity in "Friends from Philadelphia" takes a more subtle form. The protagonist, John, is seen at first as awkward, sincere, and almost shy. When Mr. Lutz comes in, John can not even think of the words with which to describe why he was there. But once he gets behind the wheel of Mr. Lutz's car, he begins to act with bravado. "One-handed, he whipped around a bus. 'What'll she do on the open road?' " This is not a fundamental change in character, it is a second "side" or aspect of the same boy. And if that side of him developed, he might even grow up to be another Mr. Lutz.

Mr. Lutz himself is complex. At first, he appears to be a simple, slightly drunk, loud-mouthed father. But it soon develops that he feels a combination of respect for and superiority over college graduates. He is quick to point out that he himself did not go to college but that, in spite of it, he is able to buy a car "whenever I want." And we know that this is a repeated pattern when his daughter says, " 'Oh, Daddy, not *this* again...' "

There is further complexity in the contrast between his apparent fond feelings for his family and Thelma's statement, " 'You don't know how he acts to Mother.' " And at the end we are not entirely certain whether he has bought the expensive wine for John's family simply as an extension of his natural (and somewhat alcoholic) generosity, or whether it is an act which, like buying new cars, is motivated mainly by his own ego. It is actually a combination of these.

In "Sausage and Beer," the complexity in Uncle Theodore takes the form of alternation: He appears at first to be quite sane and then reveals himself hopelessly out of contact with the real world. When, at the end of the visit, the boy assumes that a polite lie will do as well for a mad uncle as it does for other relatives, Theodore has an unnerving moment of lucidity.

More basic to the development of the story, however, is the complexity which I hope is apparent in the father. Before the visit, he is austere and distant. He is not the kind of man who confides anything. But visiting the hospital is an ordeal for both of them and after that he reveals a different side of himself. He draws his son (and the reader) into an almost secret world of sociability, and in doing so he reveals his own love for his son.

Complexity, then, involves adding at least one other aspect to a character's original pattern. If the variation is too slight, the character may seem hackneyed and dull or inconsequential. But if the change is too great, the reader will not believe in the character and the story fails. Adjusting the degree and type of complexity often becomes one of the major concerns as one revises.

Individuality Some characters are memorable and some are not. Occasionally we recall a particular character long after the plot has been forgotten. In other cases we have to ask questions like, "Wasn't there a father in the story somewhere?" or, "I remember the fight, but what was it all about?" The characters who stick in our memory are those that have a high degree of individuality.

To some degree, individuality is simply a function of complexity. A many-sided character who remains credible is apt to seem individual or unique. But there is another factor as well and this is the element of the unusual.

In specific terms, it is more difficult to develop sharp, convincing characters when their names are Bill and Frank and they are college roommates than it is to develop an Uncle Theodore living in an insane asylum. The unusual setting, the unlikely occupation, the striking deformity all serve to make a character vivid and memorable.

But these same devices can also be pitfalls. When used as an artificial stimulant to an otherwise dull story, the result is failure. An inconsequential tale about two college roommates is not going to be saved by being metamorphosed into an inconsequential tale about two hunchbacks living in an abandoned fun house.

It is possible, however, to stress the unusual aspects of unusual people one has known. It is helpful to find incidents which dramatize aspects of characters in a fresh way. And it is essential to avoid those standardized, middle-class fathers and mothers and brothers and sisters and dogs which appear with such regularity both in television dramas and in commercials.

Of the three stories in this text, "Friends from Philadelphia" is probably the most directly autobiographical. We know this partly from Updike's own comments in the preface to *Olinger Stories,* and also because the story has the ring of personal experience. If the characters have been altered, it is probably a matter of selection—including what contributes thematically and excluding what does not. It is possible, for example, that the original experience was a scene between John and the two parents; the character of Thelma might have been borrowed from a different family altogether. This is the kind of grafting which goes into even autobiographical stories.

"The Use of Force" may well have been autobiographical too. Williams was, in fact, a doctor. But it is quite possible that the emotions of sexual aggression which dominate the story were in the original experience only a quick flash. Or they may have been recognized only after the event was over. Perhaps in real life there were

thirteen brothers and sisters standing around, but he, as author, eliminated them in order to concentrate on the sick girl. Elimination of
extraneous details is sometimes as important as invention in the
revelation of character.

In the case of "Sausage and Beer," I can be more explicit. Uncle
Theodore is autobiographical and the hospital really exists. But the
physical description of Uncle Theodore is based on a man I once
saw for about ten seconds in a hotel lobby, and the bench in the
waiting room is taken from Grand Central Station, New York, as
is the man lying on it. The father in the story is drawn after an
uncle of mine; the twin sister is fictional; and the house in Dorchester
with the cupola is actually in Cambridge but, because I have never
been in it, the interior is taken from a place in Chicago.

The story had its origin in actual visits to my uncle and these were
chosen mainly because they seemed to have "fictional potential"—an
almost unconscious feeling for what is memorable. The many visits
were reduced to one and treated as a kind of initiation. The final
sharing or "communion" with the father is fictional, unfortunately.
And so is the historical period. In an early draft, the final scene took
place in a restaurant; but by moving the time back to the end of the
Prohibition days, I could let father and son share a quietly illegal
pastime, eating and drinking in a speakeasy. Since the ending needed
a slight increase in voltage to compete with the asylum scene, and
because I wanted to dramatize the almost religious sharing of food
and drink (the sausage and beer), the speakeasy helped to individualize
both the father and the final scene itself.

Direct Analysis

of Character Consistency, complexity, and individuality
are the goals one works for in creating fictional characters. The
techniques which one uses to achieve these goals are more numerous.
In addition to direct exposition, one can use a character's action,
dialogue, thoughts, and physical details. Each of these deserves a close
look.

The direct approach often seems like the easiest. The writer wants
to present aspects of personality and biographical background and
so is tempted to do it in a single paragraph. The result is pure exposition such as in the following sample:

> At fifty-two John Carrington was a failure. His marriage had ended
> in divorce, his shoe store had been leveled for the new Interstate 95, what
> the state had paid him was now "loaned" to a collection of cousins and

friends who thought him a fool for his generosity, and his battle against obesity had collapsed utterly when the rusting scales hit 200.

Yet for all this, Carrington was happy for the first time in his life. Somehow it was easier to deal stoically with failure than it had been to face the harassment of his wife, his business, his friends, and calories. Besides, as custodian of the town hall he could give somber and sage advice to whoever would listen—from the young things seeking marriage licenses to the Mayor himself.

These two paragraphs provide a fund of information which the author may draw on later. We have from the very start a block of biographical notes, a general appraisal, an apparent contradiction to this appraisal, and at least one significant physical detail about his appearance.

The direct approach, then, is fairly easy to write, is honest, is easy for the reader to follow, has some literary precedent, and appears to free the writer for the really serious matter of developing plot.

But these "advantages" should be qualified: It is not really an easy task when one realizes that characterization is almost always a continuing process which runs through the entire piece. What one reveals in the opening block of analysis—or any such paragraph—is not the whole story. One must decide just what should be given to the reader and what should be withheld.

Maintaining the pace can also be a problem. Exposition of any kind slows or even stops the flow of a story, and direct description of a character or his feelings is no exception. If such a passage is used as an introduction, it simply delays the start of the story.

If one examines the three stories included in this volume and marks those sections which analyze character or background explicitly, it becomes dramatically clear just how sparingly most authors use this device. In general, the longer the work, the more an author can afford to analyze directly. Novels, for example, are often more discursive. In the short story, however, where pace is particularly important, direct analysis of character is usually held to single sentences or mere phrases. "But the worst of it," Williams writes in a rare bit of direct analysis, "was that I too had got beyond reason." The story soon returns to the dramatic action which is revealing this very point.

Direct, analytical statements are not always used to present the truth. Sometimes they are ironic, leading the reader astray by giving false or superficial information. The reader discovers the real truth indirectly as the story unfolds. A brief example of this is seen in

"Friends from Philadelphia." Mr. Lutz enters and we are told, "Actually, he didn't act at all drunk." But then as he calls his wife his "big pookie-pie" and tells John how "very, very happy he was to see him here," we as readers realize that he has indeed put away two or three cocktails.

In some cases the entire story is presented from the point of view of a naive protagonist and thus *all* the exposition is inaccurate. Sherwood Anderson's "I'm a Fool," for example, is told in the first person by a young man who really doesn't understand just how much of a fool he really is. And Peter Taylor's frequently anthologized "A Spinster's Tale" is a brilliant analysis of how a girl can grow up to be a spinster, and it is told through first-person narration by the spinster who hasn't the slightest idea of what she is revealing about herself.

The Use of
Significant Action

Some novice writers tend to avoid action. Their stories turn inward on the character, stressing thoughts and long, moody descriptions. This is partly a reaction against the simple plots of television and the comics. The point to remember is that it is not action alone which makes a story simple, it is the absence of any significance to the action.

"The Use of Force" is a good example. There is a lot of action there. Essentially the same plot could appear in *True Confessions* under the title, "My Daughter Was Molested by an M.D." What makes the story a sophisticated piece of fiction is not any lack of action but the development of subtle significances within the action. There is the balance between the perfectly reasonable doctor who has seen children die of diphtheria for lack of diagnosis and the man who at the height of his emotion "could have torn the child apart...and enjoyed it." Notice that these conflicting attitudes are not separated in psychotic fashion or like the double life of Dr. Jekyll; they occur simultaneously and are treated so in a single paragraph (the third from the last). It is ambivalences like this which do not appear in simple fiction.

"Friends from Philadelphia" is a less highly charged story, and it may seem at first that Updike has relied almost exclusively on dialogue to develop his characters. But if one examines the story closely, it becomes clear that action is equally important. The reader comes to know these four characters in much the same way as he learns about new acquaintances in daily life: by observing little, apparently insignificant actions and almost unconsciously making judgments.

Thelma, for example. When John first arrives she "extended her arm and touched her fingers to the base of John's neck. It wasn't a fond gesture, just a hostesslike one." Later she pouts when the television was turned off and *pretends* to read a book, and we learn that she has been plucking her eyebrows. Then, in the car, she lets him open the glove compartment because her fingernails are too long. These are all little details and are scattered across a story, but added to the dialogue, they produce a portrait of a superficial, affected young girl who is decidedly self-centered. All this in spite of the fact that the story is being told from the point of view of a young man who thinks she is just wonderful.

In the case of John, we would have only a superficial view if we were limited to his shy and apologetic dialogue in the first half of the story. It is not until we see the way he drives that we understand another aspect of him. In that instant he takes on the bravado of Mr. Lutz himself. Notice also that although he refused a cigarette from Mrs. Lutz, pointing out that his mother would smell it, he later says to Thelma, " 'I'd sell my soul for a drag right now!' " This is the same sort of adolescent "sophistication" with which he earlier "whipped around a bus" with only one hand on the wheel.

In selecting significant action, don't forget that an extremely minor detail can make a major contribution to a story if it is repeated or reinforced by details which are similar. If, for example, a wife of a chain-smoking husband empties an ashtray during a conversation, the reader learns nothing. The action serves no purpose. But if she does this three times during a single scene, the reader will consciously or even unconsciously make a judgment about her. One can achieve the same result if she interrupts the conversation at various points by picking a piece of lint off his jacket, straightening the pillows beside her on the couch, putting away the magazine he has dropped next to his chair, rubbing her finger over the coffee table to test for dust, *and* emptying that ashtray.

In addition, there are those little details which do not have to be repeated because they are somewhat startling in themselves. The reader reacts in very specific ways when a character picks his nose, probes his ear with his finger, cleans his nails with a mother-of-pearl penknife, gnaws at a fingernail, cracks his knuckles, picks at a pimple, or yawns so widely that tears come to his eyes.

Mature readers respond readily to such cues. It is not usually necessary to label them with explanatory phrases like, "Always meticulous, she..." and "Disgustingly, he...." Remember that drawing conclusions from the actions we see is exactly the technique which we use in daily life to analyze those about us. We say that a person is mature because we have seen him remain calm in a moment of crisis; or that he is a hypocrite because, while lauding the Boy Scouts, he won't let them use woods for camping; or that she is still a child at forty because she collects dolls and reads bedtime stories to them. These are the specific examples of action from which we draw inductive conclusions. Judging character and attitude in fiction, as in life, moves from the specific to the general and abstract.

The Use of
Dialogue and Thoughts
The most obvious use of dialogue is as an unfolder of plot. A character comes to the door and says he needs help in order to buy a bottle of wine and he is told that the husband will soon return. The plot in this case has moved more by dialogue than it has by action or thoughts. But a writer hasn't really begun to develop his art until he sees every line of dialogue as an opportunity to develop character as well.

"Friends from Philadelphia" is a particularly good example of this because Updike relies heavily on dialogue. (This is generally true of both his short stories and his novels.) At the very opening of the story it is Thelma's pronunciation of the name "John" and her self-consciously sophisticated phrasing (" 'what on earth ever brings you to me at this odd hour?' ") which gives us an immediate clue as to her personality. And in sharp contrast there is the hesitant dialogue of John: " 'Hello, Thel,' he said. 'I hope—I guess this is a pretty bad time.' "

Thoughts are merely internalized lines of dialogue. Normally they are presented without quotation marks. Quite often they are linked to dialogue either as a reaction to what that character has said or a response to some other character. Here is one of the few samples from the Updike story:

"Oh, Daddy, not *this* again," Thelma said, shaking her head at John, so he could understand what all she had to go through. When she looks like that, John thought, I could bite her lip until it bleeds.

Often it is possible to provide some insight into character by having the thoughts take a turn one might not expect. In "Sausage and Beer," for example, one might expect the boy to become depressed or anxious when he first saw the hospital grounds. But it is his sense of drama which takes over:

> ...Two great gates flashed by, and we were inside a kind of walled city.
>   Prison, I thought. That's it. That's why they kept him quiet. A murderer, maybe. "My Uncle Theodore," I rehearsed silently, "he's the cop killer."

There are, incidentally, four conventions connected with dialogue which readers respond to unconsciously. The first is the use of quotation marks for spoken sections. "The Use of Force" is a rare exception. Its departure may be partially justified by the fact that there is relatively little dialogue in the story, but even here it is confusing for some readers. Second, most writers do not use quotation marks for thoughts. This allows a writer to differentiate between what a character stated out loud and what went on in his mind—often a significant distinction.

Third, most writers indent the first line of each new speaker. This may appear to waste paper, but readers are used to it both in fiction and in drama. In exchanges between two characters, the reader does not have to be told each time which one spoke. It is a convenient signal.

Fourth, "he said" is used more like a punctuation mark than a phrase, and for this reason it is repeated frequently. The prohibition against redundancy just doesn't apply to it. And trying to find substitutions like "he retorted," "she sneered," "he questioned," "she hissed" are worse than obtrusive, they sound amateurish.

Of course, one can find stories which ignore one or more of these conventions. But not many. Most writers find that by using these familiar signals they can concentrate on more sophisticated problems like character development.

In addition to the direct use of dialogue and thoughts, there is also the indirect use of each. A fine example of indirect discourse appears in the opening of J. D. Salinger's "Uncle Wiggily in Connecticut." He begins with a one-sentence statement about the situation and then moves directly into an echo of their conversation.

> It was almost three o'clock when Mary Jane finally found Eloise's house. She explained to Eloise, who had come out of the driveway to meet

her, that everything had been absolutely *perfect,* that she had remembered the way *exactly,* until she had turned off the Merrick Parkway. Eloise said, *"Merritt* Parkway, baby," and reminded Mary Jane that she had found the house twice before, but Mary Jane just wailed something ambiguous, something about her box of Kleenex, and rushed back to her convertible.

Notice how the sound of their speech is simulated both by the choice of words and by the stress which he achieves through italics (indicated in a typed manuscript by underlining). The story then moves into a conventional pattern, but with heavy use of dialogue. This opening section could also have been presented as dialogue directly quoted, of course, but his treatment has given the scene a kind of breathless quality.

A more common form of indirect dialogue consists of reporting on the conversation without attempting to echo the speech pattern. In "The Use of Force," for example, Williams refers to conversation this way:

> ...But first I told the parents it was entirely up to them. I explained the danger but said that I would not insist on a throat examination so long as they would take the responsibility.

This is not, of course, as vivid as direct quotations. And it doesn't add to our perception of the character. But it does allow the writer to skip over spoken sections rapidly. It is a useful device to cover arrivals and departures, and to suggest the passage of time.

One way to study how different types of dialogue can aid in characterization is to select a story which depends heavily on the device ("Friends from Philadelphia" is a good choice), underline the quoted passages, and then mark in the margin what aspect of the speaker is being revealed. Take, for example, the scene in which Mr. Lutz first appears. Updike starts with indirect discourse, then provides action, and soon moves into dialogue directly quoted, and in less than a page we learn that (1) Mr. Lutz probably does drink a good deal; (2) he is an outgoing, expansive man who (3) is proud of his social and financial achievements, but (4) defensive about his education.

The Use of
Physical Details

There are two types of physical details which can contribute either directly or indirectly to characterization. The first is the character himself: what he looks like. This may not be conclusive evidence of anything (big men can be passive, little men can be aggressive, beautiful women can be attractive or unattractive); but it can add to and sharpen other judgments we make about a character. The girl in "The Use of Force" has "magnificent blonde hair, in profusion." She is described as "One of those picture children often reproduced in advertising leaflets and photogravure sections of the Sunday papers." This, of course, is no indication of the "savage brat" she becomes; but it does provide a vivid contrast between her external appearance and her inner emotions and in this way it dramatizes her character.

In "Friends from Philadelphia" Mr. Lutz is described as "a big man, with shaved gray hair above his tiny ears." Why the "tiny ears"? Perhaps the original model looked like that. Or Updike may have decided that this was a way of both individualizing his character and adding to the vividness of his physical size. In either case, it is a little detail which we use in visualizing this extroverted, restless character.

In "Sausage and Beer," Uncle Theodore is described as heavy but not fat:

> He was a great, sagging man. His jowls hung loose, his shoulders were massive but rounded like a dome, his hands were attached like brass weights on the ends of swinging pendulums.

The real uncle was actually tall, lean, and rather distinguished looking. But the father in the story had been described in essentially those terms, and it was important to have these twins strikingly dissimilar in appearance as they were in their fates. The physical description of Uncle Theodore was for that reason developed from the memory of a perfect stranger, someone I had seen only for an instant.

The other category of descriptive details includes everything a character owns: his house, car, clothes, cigarette lighter, ring—every possession from the largest to the smallest. Remember that each one represents a decision, and every decision is an aspect of a man's character.

The first view we get of Thelma Lutz is her "Camp Winniwoho T shirt and her quite short shorts." And when we first see her mother, she is using a coffee cup as an ashtray in her lap "and her dress was hitched so her knees showed." Her husband is dramatically revealed through his much-adored new Buick. In the case of Uncle Theodore in "Sausage and Beer," his suspenders had been patched with a length of twine and he shuffled in scuffs "which he slid across the floor without once lifting them." The ruin of the man's life is echoed in these small details of dress.

Blending
the Techniques

For the sake of analysis, I have divided the various methods of developing characterization into five general headings: direct analysis (exposition), action, dialogue, thoughts, and the description of physical details. These actually represent all of the *narrative modes* available to the writer of fiction. That is, not only are these techniques of presenting character, they are the five basic methods by which every element of a story is presented. I will return to the concept of *narrative modes* as they apply to style in Chapter 22.

Although it is convenient to analyze these five techniques separately, one actually uses them interchangeably. Many paragraphs will employ four or all five modes. Authors may stress one or another to develop their characters, but fiction as a genre is a blending of the different narrative modes.

Updike, as noted before, relies more heavily on dialogue than the other authors represented in this text. But notice that even in his story the speeches are constantly being interrupted with descriptive details, action, or thoughts. It is very unusual (though not unheard of) for an author to limit his technique of character development to speech alone. Both Salinger and Hemingway occasionally moved in this direction. But stressing one mode excessively means neglecting the others, and most authors enjoy using all the devices available.

Character development can be worked out fairly consciously, even deliberately, at the time of writing the first draft. It is worth asking oneself just what aspects of a character are going to be developed and through which scenes (actions, dialogue, physical details) they are going to be dramatized. It is best to hold back on abstract analysis until all the other methods have been considered. Once again, the goal is to *show* more than one has to *tell*.

In stories based fairly directly on personal experience and on living people, the development of character may come naturally and without conscious plan. But even in these cases, it is important to look over that first draft from the point of view of an objective reader and to determine just what and how much is being revealed. The great danger in such stories is that the writer may fill in gaps by recalling the original model, forgetting that other readers are limited to what they see on the page.

In revising, there are four questions one can ask about character development. First, does the opening give a solid block of analytical material which could be revealed more subtly in the body of the story? In "Sausage and Beer," for example, two entire pages were cut from the original opening. Second, does the final paragraph sum up all the character development which should have been going on in the story? In some cases, simple cutting is the solution. But in others, that summary paragraph is a warning that the story itself did not reveal as much about character as it should have.

Third, are there long, solid blocks of any one device? If, for example, there are page-long runs of dialogue, it may be helpful to add thoughts, gestures, or other types of action to increase our insight into the characters. This is also true of those page-long descriptions of characters. Remember that allowing descriptive detail to take over that much of a four-page short story is like having a novel turn descriptive for one hundred consecutive pages. Quite often such passages are motivated mainly by a reluctance to try dialogue. The best cure for this is to read a lot of Salinger, Updike, or Hemingway and then return to the story with dialogue ringing in one's ears.

Finally, it is important for the writer to ask himself whether his protagonist is sufficiently complex. Does he have more than one aspect? As I have already pointed out, the doctor in "The Use of Force" is both a restrained, conscientious physician and at the same time an unrestrained male who found it "a pleasure" to attack his young patient. Even the little girl is a contrast between the picture-book blonde and the "savage brat." In Updike's story, John is both the uncertain, shy adolescent and the young sophisticate who drives a little too fast—and one-handed at that. Mr. Lutz is both a self-assured success and a product of nagging insecurities. In "Sausage and Beer" the father is on the one hand distant and removed from his son, yet he is also capable of reaching out to establish a close camaraderie with his boy at the end.

In many respects, the degree of literary sophistication in a story has more to do with characterization than it does with complexity of plot. Good science fiction stories, for example, often develop enormously complex plots; but what keeps them relatively *simple* in the literary sense is that less attention is paid to the intricacies of character and ambivalences of attitude. Developing characters with consistency, complexity, and individuality is not something one masters and then ignores; it is the continuing effort of any writer.

20

NARRATIVE TENSION

Dramatic conflict as a general term describing man
pitted against *man,* some aspect of *himself, society,* or
nature, and as an *alienated individual; narrative devices*
as a second general category including the use of *curiosity, suspense, irony, paradox, satire,* and *shock.*

They were new patients to me, all I had was the name, Olson. "Please
come down as soon as you can, my daughter is sick."

So I went to them and after some difficulty got a look at the girl's
throat. Both tonsils were covered with membrane. She was our latest case
of diphtheria.

Technically, that is a story. It is a prose narration which involves
characters and a sequence of action. It even has a plot structure: a
beginning, a development, and a consequence. But what makes it
dull even as a conversational anecdote is a total lack of narrative
tension.

There are many ways of achieving tension, but it is helpful to
think of them in two main categories. The first, dramatic conflict,
involves a confrontation between the protagonist and some other force
such as an antagonist, an aspect of himself, a group, and the like.
Sometimes this confrontation takes the form of alienation: the character walled off from an individual or a group and trying to establish
contact or membership.

The second approach is to use narrative devices. That is, the writer presents his material in such a way as to arouse the reader's curiosity or give a sense of suspense. The use of curiosity, suspense, irony, paradox, satire, and shock all come under this heading.

For the sake of clarity, I shall treat these separately. But if one examines the stories included in this text, it is clear that each uses several forms of narrative tension at the same time. The same is true for most stories, novels, plays, and even narrative poems. The fact is that story-telling in all of its forms depends on various types of tension for its vitality.

Important as tension is, one shouldn't think of it as a starting point for a story. Rarely, if ever, does an author sit down to his typewriter saying, "I am going to write about man against society" or "I am going to develop high irony somehow." The stage at which one should examine the tensions in a story is directly after completing the first draft.

In some cases, a particular scene will seem dull, flat, or simply boring. In worse cases, the whole story will drag. This is one area in which a writer should listen very carefully to the response of several readers. The solution may be simply to develop what tensions have already been suggested in the story. In more serious situations, basic revisions such as adding another character or metamorphosing the plot may be necessary. To do this, a writer must know what kinds of dramatic conflicts and narrative devices are available to him.

Dramatic
Conflict Conflict is a basic source of vitality in all narrative forms. We have come to call it "dramatic" partly because of the historical connection with tragedy, but primarily because the term suggests direct confrontation between major forces—"dramatic" in its nonliterary sense.

On its simplest level, dramatic conflict is the mainspring of simple fiction. Work of this type is often reduced to the point where there is almost nothing but simple conflict. Man against man, for example, is the core of almost every Western. The struggle between the hero and the antagonist is formalized in dress (color of hats), in ethics (clean vs. dirty fighting), and ritualized in action (a physical fight in which many bottles, two chairs, and at least one mirror will be shattered).

The same applies to other forms of dramatic conflict. Man against an aspect of himself is repeated over and over in juvenile fiction (usually a boy's conscience against the temptation to cheat or lie—an essentially moralistic pattern). Man against the group is a pattern in adventure fiction (the detective tangling with the Mafia, "Chaos" agents, spy rings; the American hero pitted against the Oriental foe-of-the-year—"Japs," Koreans, Chinese, Vietnamese). Man against nature brings to mind Tarzan and his eyeball-to-eyeball confrontations with giant spiders and short-tempered crocodiles. And even that most modern type of inverted conflict, alienation, is seen in fiction for the very young: the little switch engine who was sneered at by all the locomotives, the little reindeer who was laughed at by those on Santa's regular team, the ugly duckling who was actually a beautiful swan, and the archetypal Cinderella—duckling to swan again.

With associations like these, it is no wonder that some novice writers unconsciously avoid conflict almost entirely and allow their characters to wander wide-eyed and passive through a series of non-events. The moment of decision in such stories usually passes unnoticed, and the non-climax becomes the decision *not* to get drunk, get stoned, or hire that motel room.

Non-happenings like these could be avoided if the writer understood that sophistication is achieved not by eliminating conflict but by making the conflict itself subtle, suggestive, and integrated into the story as a whole. Put more directly, sophistication requires using, not ignoring, the basic elements of fiction. And dramatic conflict is certainly basic.

"The Use of Force" is an excellent example. Although it is a relatively short work, it combines two different forms of dramatic conflict. The first and most obvious is the struggle between the doctor and the girl. This begins as a professional necessity; but it quickly transforms itself into a symbolic assault, man against woman. The complexities involved in this conflict already have raised the story to the level of literary sophistication.

In addition, there is the inner struggle, man against an aspect of himself. He is very much aware of this internal conflict. On the one hand, he can assure himself that he has seen "at least two children lying dead in bed of neglect in such cases." This is his professional justification. Yet on the other hand, he is aware that he has "already fallen in love with the savage brat" and that she "rose to magnificent heights of insane fury of effort bred of her terror of me."

In a much milder way, both types of dramatic conflict appear in

"Friends from Philadelphia." The division within John which makes him on the one hand shy and awkward and on the other an adolescent braggart has already been described in the chapter on characterization. But the little antagonisms between characters is equally important in this story.

Notice that from the start Thelma is sniping at John. He misses her sarcasm, but the reader doesn't. Then there is an implied tension between Mr. and Mrs. Lutz when she says to John, "Now don't be surprised if he has a bit of a load on." And this is reinforced later in the story when Thelma is speaking to John about her father. "You don't know how he acts to Mother," she says, and we are left with the dark hint of real strife in the family. There is also an implied contrast between the two fathers—John's being academic and under-paid and Thelma's being financially well off but insecure about his education. This suggests a fundamental contrast between the two families as well.

The third type of dramatic conflict, man against society, is not illustrated in the three stories included here, but it is a familiar pattern which is found in many well-anthologized works. In Shirley Jackson's "The Lottery," for example, the individual who is finally selected as the town's scapegoat faces the entire community in an almost archetypal confrontation. In Clark's "The Ox-Bow Incident," three innocent men face the wrath of a mob and on the basis of circum-stantial evidence are hanged. This has become the basis of an endless series of simple imitations, but the story still maintains some degree of literary sophistication. Another example is seen in Faulkner's "Dry September." This also deals with a lynching, but the story is primarily concerned with a sexually charged bigot and his motivation.

One has to be careful in stories like this to avoid stereotypes. As I have pointed out before, western scenes—particularly if set in the nineteenth century—are risky at best. Racial conflicts are charged with tension, but the writer has to have lived through that situation per-sonally if he is to recall and use those precise details which will make the scene convincing.

One also has to guard against melodrama. Too much voltage for a particular story will simply turn the reader off even if the incident was drawn from experience itself. In "The Lottery," restraint is shown in withholding the brutality until the very end. In "Dry September," the climax of the story is not the lynching itself but the return of the protagonist to his wife after having committed the crime. In this final scene, we come to realize just how sexual the sadistic act of violence has been. It is this insight and not the lynching itself which becomes the epiphany or moment of discovery.

Man against society takes many forms since almost any kind of group can represent the whole society. Racial barriers, for example, wall off blacks and other minorities from the white society; national prejudices work against the foreign born; snobberies of various sorts are exercised by social classes against the individual. "Society" may be as simple a group as a fifth-grade class seen through the eyes of the unfortunate student who has been selected as the scapegoat.

A fourth type of dramatic conflict is man against nature. The stories in this text do not make extensive use of it, but those who are familiar with Conrad's works will remember how sophisticated this conflict becomes in such works as "Youth" and *Typhoon*. Hemingway's *The Old Man and the Sea* and Faulkner's "The Bear" both make extensive use of conflict with animals and the forces of nature generally.

It is significant that each of these major works has built an aspect of nature into a symbol. In "Youth," for example, the sea is repeatedly associated with time. This is developed when the old ship, the *Judea* (from the Old Testament, complete with a steward named Abraham), is eventually consumed by the sea and the young hero sets forth in one of the three small boats heading for the "mysterious East" where they are saved.

It is not always necessary to have such elaborate symbolic systems, but they do serve particularly well in works which use aspects of nature. Without symbolic suggestions, these stories tend to revert to rather simple exploits.

Remember, too, that an aspect of nature does not have to be the primary "antagonist" of a story. It may serve in some minor capacity to amplify or highlight some aspect. This is done in "Sausage and Beer." Although these descriptive details might easily be missed, the story opens with the protagonist struggling against the cold of winter, touches on this pattern again at the hospital, and then turns to warmth at the end when the father and son are finally joined in a kind of communion. The phrasing was intentional. The opening paragraph starts off with silence and cold:

I kept quiet for most of the trip. It was too cold for talk. The car...
had no heater, and I knew from experience that no matter how carefully
I tucked the black bearskin robe about me, the cold would seep through
the door cracks and, starting with a dull ache in my ankles, would work
up my legs.

Then at the hospital itself, Uncle Theodore tells about his night-
marish theory:

"And I've found out—God's truth—that one of these nights they're
going to shut down the heat *all the way. Freeze us!*"
There was a touch of panic in this which coursed through me. I could
feel just how it would be, this great room black as midnight, the whine
of wind outside, and then all those hissing radiators turning silent, and
the aching cold seeping through the door cracks—

It is not until the end of the story that this pattern of silence and
cold is broken. When father and son enter the speakeasy together,
this is the description:

...We were ushered into a warm, bubbling, sparkling, humming, soothing,
exciting bit of cheerful chaos.

In this particular case, a peripheral use of man against nature
leads us to the fifth and final form of dramatic conflict: alienation
and isolation. This is different from the other four in that it is not
as clearly a confrontation. Instead, individuals are walled off from
each other. Often the alienated couple consists of a man and woman
or a parent and a child. The conflict often takes the form of hostility
or misunderstanding.

Returning to "Sausage and Beer," the first two quoted passages
set up a conflict between an individual and the chill of winter. But
in each case this is used to amplify the sense of alienation between
individuals—first between son and father, then between an insane man
and the entire outside world. The resolution of the story comes after
both father and son have passed through the trying experience together
(a harsh reminder of how brutally our lives are affected by pure
chance) and the alienation is ended in a kind of communion between
them.

The theme of alienation and isolation is one which is also found
in Saul Bellow's work. It appears in short stories like "Mr. Green"
(where, incidentally, white man is walled off from the black community), in the short novel, *Dangling Man,* and in two longer novels,
The Rainmaker and *Herzog.* In all of these, he avoids what could

have become melodramatic by using irony and paradox, two devices which I shall examine later in this chapter.

Narrative Devices
to Develop Tension

The varieties of dramatic conflict I have described so far involve *what* goes into a story to provide tension; now I turn to *how* one tells a story to increase that tension.

We hear and use these devices on a simple level every day in casual conversation. "I had a hair-raising experience today," a speaker says, attracting attention by arousing curiosity. "I was on Interstate 91 doing about seventy and suddenly I saw this truck bearing down on me right in my own lane." At this point he is holding his listeners with suspense.

"It's situations like that," a second speaker says, "which make driving on superhighways such a pleasure." He is threatening to take over with sarcasm, a simple form of irony.

"The more terrifying interstate highways get, the more popular they become," adds another, rejecting the ironic voice and offering a paradox.

"The solution is to use highway deaths as a regular topic of conversation," the ironist says, building toward satire. "All we have to do is to keep talking and keep being witty, and in that way we just won't notice the body count."

"You all think you're hilarious," the first speaker says, trying to seize the stage again. "But have you ever seen a truck driver decapitated right before your eyes?" There is a hush. He has stopped them dead with shock.

In forty-three seconds of casual conversation, this group has employed six narrative devices. But they have used them on a simple level and they probably don't recognize what they have done in narrative terms. The writer can often compose dialogue in the same intuitive fashion, but when it comes to evaluating his first draft, he should be able to analyze just what narrative devices he has used and whether others are needed to maintain the necessary tension in his work.

Curiosity, the first of these six devices, is like all forms of tension in that it consists of two elements, one pulling against the other. In this case, the reader's desire to know strains against an author's withholding of information. The author must give enough so that the reader really does want to find out.

For example, a story might begin with: "Robley Wilson stood there calmly surveying his guests who were much too absorbed in conversations and their drinks to notice him." There is nothing wrong with this opening, but it doesn't have the voltage of: "Dripping wet, Robley Wilson stood there..." or "Bleeding profusely from the head, Robley Wilson...." The first opening is factual and may have withheld some of the same information which the other two did; the second and third also withhold information, but enough is given so that the reader is determined to find out what happened just before the opening scene.

Curiosity is not limited to opening paragraphs, of course, nor does it have to be as blatant as in these illustrations. Take, for example its use in "Friends from Philadelphia." At the opening Thelma asks, "'What on earth ever brings you to me at this odd hour?'" and as readers we ask, What *did* bring him there at that odd hour? And the question is heightened as he announces to Mrs. Lutz that he has "a problem." True, it is a simple problem, but look how far it carries the reader into the story. Next, we meet Mr. Lutz and begin to wonder what sort of man he is. There is some evidence that he is self-centered and materialistic, but John likes him. What is he really like? These major questions are presented against minor ones such as the real relationship between the Lutzes and between them and their daughter. Here, of course, hints about dramatic conflict arouse curiosity, blending the two aspects of narrative tension.

In "Sausage and Beer," there is the initial question, Where are they going? which is soon followed or absorbed by the larger question, Who is Uncle Theodore? In the last third of the story, there is once again the question, Where are they going?

This particular story is a good example of a common problem in creating tension. The original intent was to focus on the relationship between the father and son. But as often happens, a secondary character began to take over the early drafts. The scenes with Uncle Theodore were so strong that it was difficult to keep the story from "running downhill" (a lack of tension) once they left the hospital. It was partially to correct this that the story was moved back a decade so that what was a restaurant in the early drafts could become a speakeasy and the originally bland final scene could be dramatized a bit by arousing the reader's curiosity.

There are, of course, dangers in arousing curiosity with details which clearly serve no other purpose. Because this is a common technique in mystery fiction and in a great deal of television drama, its use tends to make a serious piece of fiction seem simple and contrived. To avoid this, most authors try to find material which serves other purposes as well.

If the speakeasy is justified in "Sausage and Beer," it is because in addition to arousing the reader's curiosity it also provides a sharper insight into the father's private world (the boy is not to tell his mother), and in addition highlights the boy's passage, through trial, into the adult world (ending with his first "communion").

Suspense is a heightened form of curiosity. Usually that which is withheld is the outcome of the story itself. Once again, the author's problem is what to hold back and how long to hold it. In a simple detective story or murder mystery, the convention is to withhold the identity of the guilty party until the end. This is logical enough when "Who did it?" is the only question posed in the story. In more sophisticated works, however, merely identifying the killer may be of secondary importance. In the novels *Crime and Punishment* and, more recently, *In Cold Blood,* the question of who committed the crime is revealed within the first third of the book, reserving the major portion of the work for the questions about what the killers' motives were and how they then react to their crimes. Exactly this same pattern—though in miniature—is revealed in a grim story by Joyce Carol Oates, "Boys at a Picnic." Once again, an apparently senseless murder is used not as an end in itself but as a means for developing the twisted character of the killer. A close study of any two of these works can provide real insights into the sophisticated use of suspense.

Of the three stories in this volume, only "The Use of Force" makes extensive use of suspense. Brief as that story is, we become deeply concerned with the problem of whether the doctor or the girl will be victorious. In fact, it is important that we as readers share some of the doctor's emotions and in this way share some of his guilt. This story is a good illustration of the fact that a dramatic use of suspense need not make a story hackneyed. The question the author should ask himself is whether his use of suspense is merely an end in itself or whether it is being used to highlight or dramatize some other sophisticated thematic concern.

Irony in fiction can take three forms. First there is the statement, either by a character or by the author himself, in which the literal meaning is the opposite of the intended meaning. This is *verbal irony* in that it always takes the form of words, but it might also be called conscious irony because it is usually used knowingly by a character or directly by the author. Frequently this verbal irony is merely an extension of understatement. If during a hurricane, for example, a character says "Quite a blow," we take the comment not as inaccurate but as a commonplace use of understatement. But if he says, while watching his house and property destroyed by the pounding surf, "Great day for sailing!" the understatement has been pushed to the point where it is exactly the opposite of the intended meaning and we have verbal irony. If he is bitter, as well he might be, we may also say he is sarcastic.

Verbal irony can be used in brief flashes or it can be a sustained tone throughout an entire work. As an example of the former, we have Nelson Algren's description of Lefty's knife in "A Bottle of Milk for Mother": "His own double-edged double-jointed spring-blade cuts-all genuine Filipino twisty-handled all-American gutripper." On the first level, this is a description of praise; all but the last hyphenated modifier are taken from advertisements in (ironically) comic magazines. But the very excess of praise and the final modifier are enough to assure us that the author's view of the weapon is exactly the opposite.

Another example of the same type of irony can be found in Joseph Heller's *Catch-22,* a novel which is permeated with both irony and paradox. "He was a militant idealist who crusaded against racial bigotry by growing faint in its presence." Note how "militant" is not only nullified but reversed by the final phrase. Or: "He knew everything about literature except how to enjoy it." Or: "The case against Clevinger was open and shut. The only thing missing was something to charge him with."

When verbal irony is sustained throughout an entire work, it is usually a vehicle for satire. That is, the author continually reverses his actual feeling in order to make the ridiculed more ridiculous. In nonfiction, Swift's "A Modest Proposal" is perhaps the best-known example. His proposal to solve the overpopulation problem in starving Ireland by eating small children is presented with such restraint, such logic, such modesty that every year a small number of literate freshmen read it straight, turning Swift from an ironic humanitarian into a sadistic cannibal.

In fiction, Anderson's "I'm a Fool" is a good example. Less subtle is Sinclair Lewis's "I'm a Stranger Here Myself" and *Babbitt,* in which the author takes no stand against his characters but allows them to damn themselves.

Dramatic irony is not limited to plays; the term refers to the fact that the final reversal turns on action. The classic example is in Sophocles' *Oedipus Rex.* When the messenger comes on stage saying "Good news!" those in the audience who know the story wince with the realization that the news will actually be catastrophic. For the others, the impact of the irony will be delayed until later in the play, as it will be for the characters themselves. Note that the reversal here turns on outcome. If, by way of contrast, the messenger had already given information known by him and the others to be disastrous and then added with bitter sarcasm, "Now *there's* a piece of good news," we would have verbal irony.

Dramatic irony could be called unconscious irony insofar as the characters are not aware of its presence. The playwright, of course, knows what he is doing, but the presentation is far more oblique than the direct statements quoted from the fiction of Algren and Heller.

Because contemporary writers rarely work with known plots, the hidden information must be made known to the reader in the course of the novel or story itself. This is achieved in Peter Taylor's "A Spinster's Tale" by the title itself. Because we know that this girl will grow into a spinster, much of her self-analysis which is naive on one level becomes highly charged and significant on another. Exactly the same technique is used in Frank O'Connor's "My Oedipus Complex" which, though with a much lighter tone, allows the "innocent" actions of a boy to take on significance which he does not realize.

The third type of irony is sometimes called *cosmic* or the *irony of fate,* though it may take the form of a very minor event. In general terms, it is any outcome which turns out the opposite of normal expectations. It is, however, more complicated than a simple reversal. It is not enough to have a normally brave man turn cowardly. The characteristic must be firmly identified with the agent, and the reversal must be a clear denial. For a man who has spent a lifetime being a fireman to die from smoking in bed, for example, is ironic enough for a news item—though it would make rather clumsy fiction. Good fictional examples from works already discussed can be seen in the conversion of the doctor in Williams's "The Use of Force" into a kind of metaphorical rapist, or the conversion of the mildest of all mild clerks in Thurber's "The Catbird Seat" into a man who masterminds the utter defeat of a fearfully dominant antagonist. Or, beyond the level of characterization, there is irony in Conrad's "Youth" where the scene in which the crew works desperately to save the sinking ship by pumping the water out is followed directly by one in which they try to extinguish the fire in the hold by pumping the water back in.

Verbal, dramatic, and cosmic irony are in some respects quite different from each other, and each form can be developed in an infinite number of ways; but they all establish a tension by playing expectations or assumptions against actual outcome. In verbal irony the assumption is that authors and characters mean what they say, but the reality denies this. In dramatic irony the assumption is that characters cannot know what they have not yet learned, but the fact is that they sometimes stumble very close to the truth either by direct statement or a reversal. In cosmic irony the assumption is that there is order in the universe, and we are jolted when this "logic of life" is reversed.

The analysis of irony can become an entertaining game for the critic in all of us, but one cannot use it successfully until one has read enough fiction to know the "feel" of it. Few literary devices are more elusive. In this respect, it comes close to wit, which can be analyzed to death in lectures and texts but which comes to the writer, if at all, primarily by reading *it* rather than *about it*.

Elusive as it is, irony is none the less important. It serves as a means of salvaging the story or novel which is too close to the author by providing a significant distance between fiction and experience. It can be made to provide the needed tartness in a story which has touched on the sentimental. And it can easily be used to add a kind of comic relief to a story which has begun to approach melodrama. In general—and including all three of these cases—the use of irony is the best antidote for the story which in any way has begun to "take itself too seriously," a particularly common ailment. This odd descriptive phrase in no way suggests that a story should not be serious; it does suggest that the tone of high seriousness is not always appropriate. When one has weighed down a simple story with deadly seriousness, the result may be absurd; the solution in some cases is to increase the magnitude of the story itself; but just as frequently the introduction of irony will be a wiser course.

Paradox is closely related to irony, but it differs in that the tension is created by upsetting only one type of assumption: logic. In brief, we assume that logic will result in the truth, but the paradox arrives at a conclusion which refutes logic. Some of the best examples are found in Joseph Heller's *Catch-22*. "The Texan," he writes, "turned out to be good-natured, generous, and likable. In three days no one could stand him." This is a perfectly balanced paradox. First we are given the material for a logical conclusion; then we are tripped by a reversal which is illogical but immediately acceptable as "true." The same "one-two punch" is seen repeated in his description of a modern farmer: "He advocated thrift and hard work and disapproved of loose women who turned him down. His speciality was alfalfa, and he made a good thing out of not growing any."

Sometimes paradox can be extended as plot. In the same novel, Yossarian, a bombardier, is called before his superiors for missing the target and requiring a second bombing run. The colonel is furious, shouting, "How am I going to cover up something like this in the report?" Yossarian says "Why don't you give me a medal?" After much argument, what began as a possible court-martial hearing ends with a citation for heroism, "For going around twice." This entire scene is the development of an absurd paradox just as any of the examples given in the paragraph above could have been developed.

Satire creates tension by playing an exaggerated view of characters, places, or institutions against the "true" or "reasonable" view. The distortion may be slight and the resulting "light satire" mildly chiding, as in the works of J. P. Marquand; they may be heavy but essentially comic, as with Peter DeVries's novels; or they may be bitter and corrosive, as with much of Mary McCarthy and sections of Heller's *Catch-22*. But in spite of the variety, all satire has some measure of exaggeration devised to ridicule the subject.

Irony and paradox are natural ingredients in satire as many of the examples given above show. But these three forms of tension should not be thought of as inseparable. Certainly the dramatic irony of *Oedipus Rex* is not accompanied by satire, nor is the cosmic irony in Williams's "The Use of Force." It is difficult to find samples of good satire free from irony, but Mary McCarthy's savagely comic "Cruel and Barbarous Treatment" comes close.

There are two dangers in the use of satire which often damage early attempts. The first is a lack of focus. That is, the author has not decided just what the butt of his satire is and the resulting story

is often diffuse and scattered. It is well worth examining the first
draft of any satiric work with a cold, unsmiling critic's stare (which
is particularly difficult when intoxicated with one's own hilarious wit).
After one isolates the target of the satire—usually a type of person,
a place, or an institution or some combination—one can peel off that
which has been added at the time only because it seemed clever. This
process often results in far sharper, more accurate ridicule.

The other danger is one of simple excess. I use this phrase quite
consciously, for satire which has become excessive is almost always
simple. Rather than giving lengthy examples here I recommend first
reading one entire issue of *Mad,* an excellent primer of blunt satire,
and then reading a complex and sophisticated sample of satire such
as McCarthy's "Cruel and Barbarous Treatment" or Heller's *Catch-22.*

Satire is often avoided on the unfounded assumption that a story
must be either wholly satiric or strictly literal. This is unfortunate.
Frequently a story can be intensified or enlivened by turning the
satiric ridicule on a secondary character, an aspect of the society, or
some institution involved in the plot. If the level of satire is kept light,
there is not apt to be any damaging break in the tone of an otherwise
nonsatiric story.

Shock is the last method of creating tension in fiction and is one
of the most frequently misused. I have described it as the incredible
made credible, and in most cases of failure the author simply has
not made it credible. Occasionally such authors rely on a kind of
blackmail which, were it stated directly, would come out as, "If you
don't like it, you're square." But a reader's yawn in the face of
unconvincing violence is neither square nor beat, it is roundly damning.

There is a moment of shock for most readers of "Sausage and
Beer" when Uncle Theodore turns sane for a moment and reacts to
the boy with "a loud and bitter laugh." The shock here is coupled
with irony because of the fact that he appears most threatening in
that one moment of lucidity.

In "The Use of Force," the shock comes more gradually as the
reader begins to understand just how violent and how sexually charged
the doctor's inner emotions have become. In fact, it is this sense of
shock which provides the dramatic voltage of that story.

A more violent and yet chillingly successful example of shock
appears in *Catch-22.* An idyllic day at the beach is shattered when
a flyer named McWatt buzzes a soldier standing on a raft. Some

"arbitrary gust of wind or minor miscalculation of McWatt's senses dropped the speeding plane down just low enough for a propeller to slice him half away." The following description of the body and the general panic on the beach converts this moment of shock into a nightmare.

At first glance, this may appear to be a *deus ex machina*—an agent brought into the plot arbitrarily the way Greek playwrights lowered their gods by ropes. But when one recovers from the shock, it is worth examining how carefully this scene has been prepared for. Two hundred pages earlier Heller began to give us a clear picture of McWatt and his method of flying. From countless different scenes we came to know him as one who took chances calmly, buzzing tents, buildings, and people as if the risk taken in regular bombing raids were not enough for him. The moment of shock is brutally effective, not just because the body of a man has been sprayed over a group of swimmers, but because while on the one hand we are jolted with something utterly unpredicted, on the other there is a part of us muttering "It was bound to happen."

Here, of course, we have returned to the principle of making events both unexpected and yet entirely credible. The need for internal logic continues no matter what the type of fiction. The only difference in Heller's work is that the voltage of the unexpected has been increased.

These, then, are six methods of creating tension in fiction. It is not a complete list, but it provides a wide range of diagnostic vocabulary with which to analyze ailing fiction, and it should serve to stimulate inventiveness which is so acutely needed when rewriting.

The varieties of tension are like the types of conflict discussed earlier in this chapter in that they are such a basic part of fiction that they are often taken for granted. Frequently they appear in the first draft without conscious planning. There is no danger in this except for those who confuse first drafts with finished work. A close critical analysis of both conflict and the forms of tension in a first draft is an essential step toward effective revision and rewriting.

21

ORIENTATION :
PLACE AND TIME

The importance of *setting* as seen in specific examples; *geographic* setting—a sense of place; *historical* setting— time as history; the use of *season; time of the day;* methods of *revision*—metamorphosing, heightening, and muting of details.

Orientation is the sense of being somewhere specific. This includes not only an awareness of what country one is in, but what kind of city or town and what sort of house or room. In terms of time, it may involve the historical period, the season, or the time of day.

Stories vary in the degree to which they stress orientation and in which aspects are emphasized, but even the most dreamlike fantasies provide, as do dreams themselves, material which helps the reader to place himself. Without this illusion of being present, a reader will remain outside the work just as if it were an essay.

The following examples give an idea of how much difference geographic and temporal setting can make. The action and dialogue remain constant, but the orientation in each is significantly different from the other two.

It had snowed all Sunday, ruining his day of rest with the howling, rattling demands of his Eazy-All Sno-Blower. And that night the storm must have kept at it because by morning the walks were drifted over as if no one had touched them. He called the bank and told them he couldn't make it and went back to blasting the snow into his neighbor's yard. Normally he wouldn't have bothered—he hated the Eazy-All almost as much as snow itself—but the letter was bound to come that Monday and the postman wouldn't come to the door unless it was cleared and sanded. All this, then, for the sake of the letter. And when the postman finally did come, he still had to hand it over the last drift.

He had only to read the first line. Mildred must have seen the postman coming and was now standing in the open door in her bathrobe, shivering.

"Well?" she asked.

"Nothing," he said. Then he crumpled the sheet and threw it into the spinning blades of the machine which sent the shreds flashing into the street like snowflakes.

He didn't know until well into July why no one in his right mind spends summer months in Madrid. And since the leather exporters with whom he was supposed to be doing business were, apparently, all in their right minds, there was really nothing to do but drink warm wine and wait for the letter. In fact, for three days he hadn't even bothered to pick up his mail at American Express. But on Monday he made a special effort, moving through the deserted streets like a slug crawling over a hot rock. It was there, and for a moment he thought the hike might have been worth it. He must have smiled when he opened it, for the American clerk said, "Good news?"

He read the first line. That was enough. "Nada" he said to the American clerk, hoping that would end the conversation. Annoyingly it did, so he threw the crumpled note in the basket and set out once again through the shimmering, breathtaking streets.

It had rained for twenty-eight consecutive days. The bean sprouts had rotted in the ground, the fodder was so moldy the cows refused it, and the road up West Hill to town was so gutted he couldn't even get the buckboard over it. They were still living on salt pork left from the winter's supply, but if he couldn't get the buckboard to town in another week, they would be out of kerosene for the lamps. They wouldn't starve, but he'd have to do the morning milking in the dark, which was a sloppy damn business. And after a solitary winter mostly snowed in, he needed some voice to listen to other than Mildred's. So it was an occasion for him and the woman when Harry Miles rode up on his aging mare with a letter.

"A letter," Harry said, handing it down. Harry never was one for clever talk. He just sat there dripping in the rain waiting for the letter to be opened.

"Well?" he said. "Got some good news maybe?"

"Nothing."

The three of them watched the yellowed notepaper being crumpled into a small ball and then dropped into the clay-brown water which ran down the ruts.

The setting is important in all three of these passages, but in quite different ways. In the first, the "Sno-Blower" scene, the geographic setting is vague. We know it must be in America because nowhere else in the world do bankers operate equipment like that to clear their sidewalks, but beyond that we cannot place the town. It might be any American suburban community north of the Mason-Dixon Line. Temporal setting, however, is very exact: We know the decade since machines of that sort are fairly recent; we know the season of the year, the day of the week, and approximately the hour of the day. We also know a good deal about the social setting both from the sort of work he does and from the kind of equipment he can afford.

The second, the Madrid scene, swings the emphasis from temporal setting to geographic setting. Whatever happens in that story, the city of Madrid will play a significant part. The very fact that I found it natural to label it "the Madrid scene" even though the name of the city is used only once shows how vividly a specific, highly individualized city can flavor even a short fictional passage. The season is also important, but one tends to think of this as a *Madrid* summer, returning once again to geographic setting. Social setting is almost nonexistent, partly because the character is uprooted from his own world, but partly, we might assume, because the author considers it unimportant in this particular story. We know that he is not a bum because he has a job of sorts; and we know he is not a *Dolce Vita* aristocrat for the same reason. But there are many grades between, and this story, so far, makes no attempt to differentiate them. Compare this with the social emphasis in the opening paragraph of Fitzgerald's "Winter Dreams"—or with almost anything by Fitzgerald for that matter.

The third selection, the farm scene, makes little use of specific geography—the farm could be almost anywhere. But it is packed with rural details, so in this respect geographic setting is important. The real emphasis, however, is on social setting: the salt pork, the kerosene, the moldy fodder are partly a matter of the period—this appears to be nineteenth century—but they are also clues to the standard of living, which is primarily a social concern.

The Sense of
Geographic Setting   "Where am I?" is the stereotyped response for those who are regaining consciousness. It is also an instinctive question on the part of a reader who has begun a new story.

One of the most common questions concerning geographic location is whether to use and label cities and towns from real life or to create one's own area. But there is a fallacy in the question itself. Since all fiction is only an illusion of reality and, as Frye puts it, "hypothetical," an author does not have a choice of a "real" area versus one of his own creation. All fictional settings are imaginary, and the difference between Henry Miller's "New York" in *Tropic of Cancer* and the unspecified city in Kafka's *The Trial* is only the difference between the creative imaginations of the two authors.

The author's choice is not, then, "Shall I set this story in a real city?" but "Shall I use the name and certain characteristics of a real city in the exercise of my imagination?"

There are two good arguments for drawing on a known city. First, it can serve as a kind of geographic shorthand for the reader. There is a certain familiarity with our larger cities like New York, San Francisco, and Chicago which is shared even by those who do not live there. In addition, using a real-life city is a convenience for the author. It saves him the trouble of making up his own map.

But there are two major dangers involved as well. First, unless the writer is really familiar with the city he is using, he may begin to depend on scenes and details he has unconsciously absorbed from other stories and from television. Students who have never been to New York, for example, regularly fall back on such standard conventions as a rainy night on Forty-Second Street, poodles on Park Avenue, hysteria on Madison Avenue, rumbles on either the lower East Side or the upper West Side, and general perversion in the Village.

The same is true for Paris. If in blind ignorance the author spices his story with shots of the Eiffel Tower, cancan dancers, and prostitutes with hearts of gold, the fiction is bound to reflect the television programs and musical comedies from which this material was taken.

One should also be aware of the fact that binding oneself to the physical facts of a specific geographic area may stifle the process of metamorphosis as outlined in Chapter 13. The work may never be weaned from experience. This is particularly true of stories set in the town or city where they are being written, and it is more dangerous still when they are based on recent experience.

Perhaps for this reason, the great majority of published stories are set in towns or cities which are linked to but not identified directly with real-life locations. John Updike describes this in his foreword to *Olinger Stories* in which "Friends from Philadelphia" was included:

> The name Olinger is audibly a shadow of "Shillington," the real name of my home town, yet the two towns, however similar, are not at all the same. Shillington is a place on the map and belongs to the world; Olinger is a state of mind, of my mind, and belongs entirely to me.

In this spirit, John Updike has used Olinger, Pennsylvania, in eleven short stories. The names and ages of the protagonists vary, but essentially they are the same boy. The approach is similar to that of Sherwood Anderson's in *Winesburg, Ohio*. On a broader scale, Faulkner blended historical and fictional elements this way in his stories and novels set in his imaginary Yoknapatawpha County, Mississippi.

William Carlos Williams's "The Use of Force" makes scant use of geographic details. From what few hints he provides, one might imagine the scene to be a midwest farming community. In actual fact, Williams was a practicing physician in New Jersey, and this story probably came from that area. Notice that while the outer landscape has not been filled in, one does have a vivid sense of being in an old-fashioned kitchen "where it is warm."

Interiors are stressed in "Sausage and Beer" as well. The locale is identified as New England, and the home in which they live is in Dorchester, a real city outside of Boston. But a greater emphasis is placed on the two interiors, the visiting room at the asylum and the speakeasy. Notice that both smells and sounds are used. The reader's question of "Where am I?" calls for more than a factual reply.

There are two extremes in the handling of setting which a writer should guard against. One is the story which so ignores the surroundings that it becomes detached and difficult to visualize. As I have pointed out before, even dreams usually provide an environment, and readers need at least that in order to enter the story psychologically.

The other extreme is emphasizing the locale at the expense of plot, theme, or characterization. At best, this turns into what is known as local color writing. Bret Harte, Mark Twain, and Sarah Orne Jewett were all in this tradition, each working with a different section of America. But too often, stories which become too concerned with the regional surroundings merely become dull. Worst of all, they can appear to be patronizing. This happens when the author has tried to depict a culture or society which he has seen only from the outside. A tourist spending some time in New Mexico may be informed enough to write a story about tourists in New Mexico, but that does not mean that he is ready to try a story about what life is for a Navaho living on the reservation.

Time as

History Orientation involves more than place. The reader also wants to know about time. The historical period, the season, and the hour of day are all aspects of this concern, and it is entirely up to the author whether any of these should be emphasized in a particular story.

Most stories are set in the same historical period in which they are written. It is simply easier and more natural that way. The author is using settings, customs, speech patterns, and incidents which are familiar to him. It requires a great deal of reading to be sufficiently familiar with an earlier period to use it as a fictional base.

There is an even more compelling reason for novice writers to avoid earlier periods. The tendency is to move back to the nineteenth century, borrowing not from real events but from that great backlog of televised dramas and historical novels which themselves, on the whole, were rooted in the convention rather than in life. It is essential that the writer ask himself, Where did I get that idea? On what am I basing that scene? What made me name that character "Lulubelle" and put her in that saloon?

There are, I think, two justifications for trying an historical period other than one's own. First, some writers have a special interest in some period of history and have been reading material about it over the course of many years. This concern may be a part of one's cultural or racial tradition. Even in these cases, of course, the writer has to be careful to avoid those over-used scenes and situations which will reduce his work to the hackneyed.

The second justification is in the case of those who are old enough so that their childhood has become "history." Occasionally it is possible to push back a decade or so to avoid that "dead period" which editors object to on nonliterary grounds. Their prejudice springs from the fact that a story which takes place noticeably in the historical past but less than twenty years before the time of the writing looks like a manuscript which has been circulating a long time.

As I have explained, "Sausage and Beer" was moved back from the early 40s to the early 30s primarily for the dramatic effect of the speakeasy. But having made the decision, I was then able to draw on other details from that period—the incredible cold of cars before there were heaters, the titles of such magazines as the old *Life* and *Judge,* and the W. P. A. But the story is also an example of how careful a writer has to be when he moves even slightly out of his experience: old-car experts were quick to point out that 1929 Dodges did not have those round radiator thermometers "mounted like a figurehead on the front end of the hood."

Time of
the Year

Seasons can help a writer. They can also turn into clichés. Of the three stories in this volume, the first, "Friends from Philadelphia," does not refer to the time of year at all. We can only guess that it was spring or summer, judging by the fact that no one bothered with coats when arriving or leaving.

"Sausage and Beer," on the other hand, makes a distinct use of season. As I have already pointed out, the cold of winter is described at the opening, later in the drive, and again at the hospital to stress the sense of chilled estrangement between father and son as well as between the two brothers.

Season can also be used as a method of metamorphosing a personal experience into something which is manageable. An episode which occurred in the heat of midsummer can sometimes be shifted to January merely to remove it from the confines of experience. Or an event which happened to take place in autumn might lend itself to spring and at the same time give the writer some sense of freshness and objectivity over his material. One must, of course, be on guard constantly against the clichés of season. A first love which ends with a paragraph about the spring buds on the apple tree is as thorough a failure as a story about an old couple which ends with the falling leaves of November. Seasons can be enormously valuable—but only when they are used with some subtlety and originality.

The Time
of Day
There is the danger of clichés in the hour of the day as well. A surprising number of stories begin with waking and wondering where one is. Fewer—but still too many—use the stock film ending: hand in hand in the sunset, "looking forward to another day."

In spite of these problems, the time of the day can often serve to orient the reader and to provide for the writer a system of organizing his material. "Friends from Philadelphia" is an excellent example of both.

In this story, Thelma introduces the element of time when she says to her mother, " 'who do you ever guess is here at this odd hour?' " John awkwardly echoes this when he apologizes: " 'I really hate to bother you at this odd hour.' " We soon learn that it is late afternoon, and the plot then turns on the need to get to the liquor store before 6:00 o'clock. Time is not used symbolically here, but it does serve to orient the reader and to provide a structure for the plot.

One rather common weakness in novice stories is a failure to allow for the passage of time in a specific scene. Characters meet, sit down in the living room, deliver dialogue which may last some two minutes, and then leave saying, "It's been great to be able to talk this over with you." The solution is simply to provide some reference to a period of conversation or silence which is not presented in direct form. As I have already pointed out, there is a lull in the conversation in "Friends from Philadelphia" when they watch television. And in "Sausage and Beer" there are statements like, "...the conversation turned to milder topics." Without them, the visit with Uncle Theodore would appear to last no more than three minutes at the most.

There are, then, two questions to ask oneself about the time of day in a story: first, would it help the reader to have an idea of just what hour a scene is taking place? And, second, does the story allow for the passage of minutes or hours in a particular scene?

Revising
the Orientation
Most often, revising aspects of place and time comes early in the development of a story. It may, as I have

pointed out, take the form of fundamental metamorphosing of the original experience. As the story develops, however, such sweeping changes become more and more difficult. A basic sense of geographic and seasonal setting tends to permeate a story so that revisions become much more elaborate than, say, changing a Nebraska farmhouse into a Chicago apartment or replacing the references to a winter scene with details about summer. If one has used place and season prominently, they become a part of the "feel" of the story. For this reason, it is best to make sure that the place and the season of a story are right before one has invested many hours of work.

There is, however, a great deal of heightening and muting of these details which go on through successive drafts. Heightening often is the result of chance. One selects a season, perhaps, because that is when the experience took place; and then various implications and suggestions come from the material and demand development. The use of cold as a vehicle to suggest separation and isolation in "Sausage and Beer" evolved in just this way.

In more serious cases, sharpening the visual details of a story is demanded because the action has gone on in a non-place. A surprising number of unsuccessful stories are placed in some ill-defined urban area which conveniently allows the protagonist to dodge city traffic one minute and, when the plot demands it, to find himself wandering "in the outskirts of town" the next. In such cases it is well worth shifting the story to a specific town or city which the author knows well, whether or not the name is used.

Muting aspects of setting is necessary when one has stumbled into a hackneyed use of place or season. I have already touched on the kinds of clichés which damage fiction, but I should stress here that it is easy even for experienced writers to borrow from overworked conventions. Sometimes it is due to the fact that the experience has, infuriatingly, echoed a fictional cliché. There is no cosmic law which forbids life from imitating the worst in fiction. Occasionally a beautiful girl falls in love with a handsome boy while strolling by the Eiffel Tower in Paris on a lovely spring day. They may live happily ever after—but any story which uses those details is dead before it begins. If the author really has lived through an experience like that, it will be easy to find some other day to highlight. And he may well wish to mute those seasonal and geographic details which resemble the song-lyric version of that city.

More often, the borrowing is from a literary convention. Stories about migrant workers tend to sound like Steinbeck; hitchhiking stories often pick up the smells and sounds of Kerouac's *On the Road* or the many motorcycle films which have been produced in the past ten years; scenes involving city gangs often use the standard details including switch blades and leather jackets. One often has to mute these details and stress ones which the reader will see as if for the first time. Once again, the writer must never assume that details from life experience will necessarily be convincing as fiction. If he presents a setting which the reader will associate with another author or a film or song lyrics or cigarette ads or musical comedies, his work will be corrupted by the association. Muting those details and highlighting others will be necessary, and these revisions can be made without cracking the original conception.

It is important to understand that a sense of place, historical period, season, and time of day are not adornments to a story. They are what the author sees and feels as he writes. They are also the primary means by which the reader psychologically enters the story and experiences it as if he were physically present. It is this phenomenon—not just a matter of logic—which we call credibility in fiction.

22

LITERARY CONCERNS:
THEME, TONE,
SYMBOL, AND STYLE

Theme described as the *central concern* of a story; *tone* seen as a variable regardless of the subject matter; *suggestive* and *symbolic* details presented as methods of increasing the "resonance" of fiction; *style* analyzed as a product of *diction, syntax, narrative mode,* and *pace.*

In a broad sense, of course, this entire text deals with literature. But the title of this chapter refers to four abstract concepts which are at the heart of literary composition.

On a simple level, each of these is used quite unconsciously. All fiction except the freest sort of journal entry has a theme of some sort. And it is always written with some kind of tone—usually reflecting the emotion of the writer at the time of the experience or shortly thereafter. Symbolic details can be stumbled upon accidentally, and style is present in every line of writing whether the author is aware of it or not.

On a more sophisticated level, however, these are four concerns

with which experienced writers grapple for the length of their productive lives. They are not concepts to be learned, they are continuing
concerns.

The
Theme

As I pointed out in the poetry section, theme is
stressed out of all proportion by some secondary school teachers.
Well-read and sensitive students begin to suspect and eventually to
resent the implication that any poem or story can be summed up in a
single, complete statement. And rightfully so. No literary work can be
broken down to a single aspect any more than a highly complex
alloy can be reduced to a single element.

Themes are, nonetheless, an essential aspect of most stories. They
are not always the most important element (some stories are primarily
studies in character or mood pieces), but they are what keeps fiction
from being an aimless journal entry or a pointless fantasy. Without
some kind of thematic unity readers are apt to respond with questions
like, "But what's the point?" or "What or you getting at?"

There are usually several themes, one of which can be called
primary. Because of this, some critics prefer the *central concern,* a term
which I will use interchangeably with *theme. Central concern* serves
as a reminder that we are not dealing with something as logically
specific as a thesis or as ethically concerned as a moral. It is also a
reminder of why some type of theme is nonetheless important. After
all, what is a story which has no concern at all?

Like almost every other aspect of literature, the theme can be
simple or highly sophisticated. Fiction for the very young repeats with
tireless regularity such themes as "It's terrible being the littlest (ugliest,
weakest, stupidest), but with luck you can be the hero of the day."
This is no more demanding than the themes which still appear with
fair regularity in women's magazines and on television: "Nice girls
win out eventually," "Crotchety old grandfathers are sometimes just
lonely old men," and "Newly marrieds face problems which we mature
readers solved two and three years ago."

Since sophisticated fiction usually deals with a number of concerns,
it is sometimes difficult to decide just what the central one is. This is
true of the three stories we have been working with. In "Friends from
Philadelphia," for example, Updike is concerned in part with patterns
of deceit—Mrs. Lutz is not honest when she says her daughter is free

to smoke, and both John and Thelma are deceitful to their respective parents about smoking, and Mr. Lutz does his best to cover up his own drinking habits. The author is also concerned with attitudes toward material possessions—Mr. Lutz and his car specifically. And certainly the story deals in part with what it is like to be the son of an underpaid teacher. All of these are concerns or themes. But none is really the *central* concern or *the* theme.

There is a wide latitude of approaches here, but probably they should all include both Mr. Lutz and John in some way. The thematic unity of the story stems from the suggestion that material success can be both a pleasure and a source of frustration as well. Mr. Lutz seems to take real pleasure in buying a new car every year, but he is pathetically insecure when it comes to dealing with college graduates. Or, if one wants to phrase the theme in a way which emphasizes John more, one can describe it as suggesting that people who don't emphasize material wealth are both fascinated and in some ways dependent on those who do. We can support this from the way that John is attracted to Thelma in spite of his complaints about her affectations, and also from the way he is attracted and transformed by that car.

These are two ways of describing the theme, and there are certainly others as well. It depends on where one places the emphasis. The point to remember is that this story which *appears* to be a simple anecdote is actually arranged to present a thematic statement. One can see how important that theme is by trying to add two more paragraphs beyond the published version. It is almost impossible. The story has ended because the thematic suggestion has been made.

The same is true in "The Use of Force." The thematic unity of the story comes from the suggestion that force which is exerted for professional and socially approved reasons can easily become a kind of rape. Or one can get at the same idea by stating that rational man is never more than moments away from bestial man. And as soon as that statement is dramatically completed, the story is finished. This is not to say that all that action and dialogue are adornments and the theme *is* the story. But theme is a significant element and obviously the author has tinkered with experience to highlight that particular element.

Turning now to "Sausage and Beer," I should point out that an author is not necessarily the best judge of his own work. (Faulkner's analysis of his own novel, *Sanctuary*, for example, is absurd.) But it is sometimes helpful for writers to learn what was in the mind of fellow writers as they wrote. The first thematic concern of "Sausage and Beer" was the suggestion that when one discovers just how much of life is run by pure chance, one is initiated into adulthood. Thus, the boy and his twin sister could think of themselves as a couple, but they would never be able to marry each other. They had no control over this. In the same way, the boy's father and Uncle Theodore were born twins, but by chance their lives took utterly different routes. The waiter at the end of the story highlights this aspect of the story.

But in the development of the story, a second major concern began to grow and may have to some degree taken over as the central concern. This might be described as the need to reach others and the difficulty we all have in this effort. In the case of Uncle Theodore, contact with the real world is sporadic—like a light with a bad electrical connection. In the case of father and son, however, the progression is from polite distance to a kind of communion. For some, this has taken over as the central concern of the story.

Many times the theme of a story requires sharpening. Outside readers—whether in a writing class or not—can be very helpful to a writer in his effort to judge just how clear he has been. Clarification occasionally takes the form of more exposition. More often it is done through dialogue (like the waiter in "Sausage and Beer" and Mr. Lutz's comments about college graduates in Updike's story) or through thoughts (like the doctor's in "The Use of Force"). More subtle highlighting can be achieved by adding incidents which keep the reader's attention focused on the thematic concern.

Just as frequently, however, the theme of a story may appear too obvious. The most productive kind of revisions in these cases is not designed simply to "fuzz it up" but to amplify and broaden the thematic suggestion. It may be possible, for example, to have a second or third character demonstrate other aspects of the same theme.

The point to remember is that any sophisticated story generates a number of concerns. The writer's task is to develop one of them without becoming blatant. This is often the "fine tuning" which goes on in those final drafts when one keeps thinking that the story has taken far too much time already.

Tone We remember experiences with the coloring of the emotion we felt at the time. We remain embarrassed at awkward moments which occurred years before; we continue to smile at comic events, and we remain bitter toward those who hurt us. The tendency is to write with a tone which reflects our own reactions.

But the writer who is not too close to his material can control his tone. Sometimes he can make much more out of a situation by rejecting or at least amending the emotion he feels.

The fact is that almost any experience can be presented with almost any tone. Take, for example, the famous story of Oedipus which Sophocles treated in what Northrop Frye calls "high mimetic" or heroic terms. The tragic case of a man who accidentally kills his own father and marries his mother seems to demand that kind of "heavy" treatment. Yet Frank O'Connor proves otherwise in a story called "My Oedipus Complex." Here the protagonist is a young boy who shares his mother's bed while his father serves in the First World War. At the war's end, there is a conflict between father and son which is both comic and potentially murderous. It is not a satire of the Oedipus story. O'Connor's young Oedipus has a most convincing love for his mother and an intense hatred for his father. But the tone is light, and in the end, instead of disaster, we have a resolution—the birth of a second child which suddenly throws the father and son together for the first time.

During the past two decades there has been a special interest in treating a variety of previously revered subjects in absurdly comic fashion. Authors like James Purdy, Joseph Heller, Bruce Jay Friedman, and Roald Dahl have turned death, despair, sadism, and even rape into comic subjects. The result is referred to as *black humor* (not to be confused with *black literature*) and usually leaves the reader caught between shock and laughter. The movement is identified with the 50s and 60s, but it has its roots in Nathanael West's *Miss Lonelyhearts* (1933). A still earlier example of black humor is seen in a play in which two gravediggers joke about suicide and the gallows and then are joined by the protagonist who jests with the diggers while they sing a comic song and toss skulls up, one of which turns out to be the remains of a dear old friend, himself a comic. This hilariously grotesque scene (Act V, Scene 1 of *Hamlet*) is sometimes ignored by teachers who feel, perhaps, that it is too contemporary for contemporary readers.

It is best not to try black humor unless one has read at least three or four novels and a dozen stories in this vein. But it provides for all

of us the strong reminder that any subject can be treated with whatever tone the author wishes—assuming that the author is far enough
from the experience to have some kind of objectivity.

In practical terms, this realization helps one to lighten stories which
have become too heavy, too close to melodrama. There is a tendency
among many male college students to push fictional situations to their
ultimate. Given the plot in "Friends from Philadelphia," their instinct
is to add one more scene where John is humiliated at the discovery
of Mr. Lutz's patronizing "gift" and ends by considering suicide.
Given "The Use of Force," the story turns into a literal rape and
murder.

The question to ask of a story which has taken on the dimensions
of high tragedy in five typed pages is: Can this relatively delicate
wire take a heavy surge of voltage without burning out? By "burning
out" I simply mean appearing ridiculous. There is nothing more
heartrending in a creative writing class than to hear the students
respond to a climactic, tragic scene with chuckles and such critical
responses as "Oh, come on now!"

One achieves a lightness of tone first by backing off from the
protagonist a bit. This may mean shifting to the third person. But
first or third, it also requires that the author occasionally smile at
his protagonist. This is the key to *distance,* that sense of separation
between the author (or narrator) and the protagonist.

Updike achieves this by occasionally having his character make
ludicrously inaccurate judgments ("Actually, he didn't act at all
drunk"). Williams, writing in the first person, allows the more mature,
controlled aspect of his character to speak to his visceral self ("The
damned little brat must be protected against her own idiocy. . . . Others
must be protected against her. . . . But in a blind fury. . . . In a final
unreasoning assault. . . .").

In my own story, there was a conscious effort to keep the asylum
scene from turning excessively dark by working in some of the simple,
humdrum complaints which the mad share with anyone living within
an institution. Uncle Theodore's little worries about fellow patients
were invented for this purpose. This is one of those cases in which
the actual experience had to be softened to keep the scene from
becoming melodramatic.

Occasionally, the needed tonal shift is just the opposite: from light
to dark or from superficial to penetrating. In these cases, the author

must pick out what the implications are in his own early draft and expand them. Characters who were treated superficially (or as stock types) have to be given action and dialogue which will reveal them fully. The author may have to make conjectures about the real people who have served as models.

Finally, there is the matter of intentional shifts in tone within a work. Why is it that in some cases this is treated as a literary sin while in others it is considered the mark of mastery? The answer, I think, is due to one factor: preparation. When a shift in tone is planned, the reader must be prepared for it early in the story.

Since none of the stories in this volume are long enough to sustain real shifts in tone, I shall have to refer to three stories which are widely anthologized. The first, James Joyce's "The Dead," is dominated by a gay, superficial party which appears to be the lightest sort of social satire. But the story ends on a note of despair as one discovers that all the characters are metaphorically dead and, ironically, the only "live" figure is in fact nothing more than a memory of one long since gone. The reason this shift in tone is successful is that the reader is prepared first by the title itself and then, quite unconsciously, by the fact that all the conversation at that party has been, despite the laughter, extraordinarily morbid.

In a more recent example, J. D. Salinger's "Uncle Wiggily in Connecticut," begins with pure froth and ends with a desperate cry for reassurance by the protagonist. It succeeds largely because patterns of deceit, cruelty, separation, and death have been subtly woven into the early scenes. It is remarkably similar in this respect to Albee's play *Who's Afraid of Virginia Woolf?* in which the hilarious first act involves a series of jokes each of which is keyed to the themes of deceit and impotence which dominate the highly serious final act.

The third example is quite different. In Shirley Jackson's frequently anthologized story, "The Lottery," the initial tone is calm, low-keyed, and warmhearted. The story continues in this mood until the very end which suddenly becomes a nightmare of violence and senseless death. How does she achieve it? She too has prepared the reader.

But while the other two stories offer a set of clues to the reader, hinting about the change in tone to come, this one employs only an ominous suspense. The reader is very quickly made aware that something extraordinary is about to happen in this town, but that "something" is withheld until the end of the story. The effect is like the warning in the calm before a summer storm.

The use of suspense is risky, as I pointed out in the chapter on narrative tension. It can easily make a story into a mere trick or, worse, a literary cliché. It is partly for this reason that the more common method of handling tonal shifts is to insert significant material early in the story such as was done in Joyce's "The Dead" and Salinger's "Uncle Wiggily."

Suggestive and
Symbolic Details   A symbol, as defined in the poetry section of this text, is any detail, such as an object, action, or state, which takes on a range of meaning beyond and larger than itself. Most frequently it is a visual image. I use the term "suggestive detail" to refer to items which don't have the impact of true symbols but which do have overtones and implications.

To be specific, the car in "Friends from Philadelphia" is clearly a symbol (and a rather conventional one) of material success. It suggests an attitude (Mr. Lutz's philosophy of life) and a goal (the acquisition of material objects) both of which go way beyond the object itself.

Thelma's costume, on the other hand—"the Camp Winniwoho T shirt and her quite short shorts"—is not a true symbol but it certainly suggests a lot about her. It is an effective combination of her adult sexual allure (which John responds to) and her childishness, which the readers see more clearly than he does. Some might be willing to refer to her costume as a symbol of adolescent sexuality, but that gives this minor detail an apparently major significance. For this reason it seems more appropriate to refer to it as merely a suggestive detail.

Short-story titles themselves are often symbolic details. The title, "Friends from Philadelphia," for example, places special emphasis on characters who never appear in the story at all. Thematically, however, these dinner guests are most important because of Mr. Lutz's attitude toward them. " 'Oh. College people,' " he says. " 'Then we must get them something very, very nice. . . .' " These characters represent everything that Mr. Lutz admires and resents, a central symbol for the story.

"Sausage and Beer" is an even more directly symbolic title. For many readers, it may merely highlight the end of the story when father and son share food and drink. On this level, the title simply adds to the thematic unity. But for others, the waiter who brings the tray and leaves them with a "benedictory smile" and the final phrase stating that father and son were then "lost in a kind of communion" suggest that the sausage and beer are like the wafer and wine used in certain Christian services. Recognizing this central symbol is not essential to an understanding of the story, but it should add another range of overtones or *resonance*.

Occasionally even the plot of a story becomes symbolic. "The Use of Force" is an excellent example. The fact that the patient is a young girl, "an unusually attractive little thing," who is described initially as "fairly eating me up with her cold, steady eyes" charges the story with sensuality from the very start. This plus the nature of the examination and the descriptive terms which are used to describe the battle give the episode the overtones of a rape. In this way, the entire plot turns into a single symbol.

This is not to be confused with *allegory* in which the characters become nothing more than vehicles for abstract concerns or institutions. No matter how symbolic the action in "The Use of Force" becomes, we still are concerned with the doctor as an individual. In Swift's *Gulliver's Travels,* however, or Orwell's *Animal Farm,* the concern of the author (and our concern as readers) shifts from the character to what he represents. It is helpful to think of the allegory as halfway between fiction and the essay or, in the terminology with which I began this text, midway between literary writing and descriptive writing. We don't mind if Christian and Evangelist in Bunyan's *Pilgrim's Progress* do not behave like real people; we're much more interested in the concepts which they are designed to illustrate.

It is perhaps because of the wooden, contrived quality of allegorical figures that the technique is used so rarely in contemporary fiction. The same applies to extensive or heavy use of symbol. When the tenor, the abstract quality being described, begins to dominate the work, some of the fictional quality is sacrificed. Put more bluntly, the idea begins to erode the illusion.

Symbolic and suggestive details are enormously valuable if a story is to achieve that aspect of sophistication I have called *resonance*. Without it, fiction sometimes sounds like a piano melody played with one finger. The goal, however, is to have it serve the story, not dominate it.

Style All fiction has style. You can't compose without it any more than you can write script without revealing—for better or for worse—your handwriting. The writer's task is to examine just what his style is and then to judge whether it is what he wants for a particular work.

Essentially, there are four factors which determine a writer's fictional style: diction, syntax, narrative mode, and pace.

Diction refers to the type of words a writer uses. This is a more significant factor in English than most other languages because there is such a radical difference in sound and tone between those words which came to us from the Norse and Anglo-Saxon and those which are from the Greek or Latin. To cite an extreme example, contrast your reactions to these two samples:

> Edgar got in the boat and gripped the seat, sweating like an ox. He hated the sea.

> Julius entered the vessel and embraced the cushions, perspiring profusely. He detested the ocean.

In the first, the nouns and verbs are without exception of Anglo-Saxon or Old Norse origin. In the second, every noun and verb is of Latin origin. Except for the articles and the conjunctions, these could be two different languages, each with its distinctive sound, and each with its own tone. Past generations were taught that words of Latin and Greek derivations were "elegant" and "refined," and some of that prejudice remains. For a writer who wants to make the most of this enormously varied language, however, the free choice of diction becomes one of the basic methods of affecting his style.

Needless to say, no writer looks up the derivation of every word he uses. But we all have a built-in awareness of the distinction between these two verbal heritages: one dominated by short, abrupt sounds which imply simplicity, roughness, and in some cases obscenity; the other characterized by longer words, smoother sounds, and imbued with a sense of elegance or even pomposity.

Aside from derivations, there are the subtle distinctions between short words and long ones, harsh ones and smooth ones, crude ones and those which sound elegant. Some of these distinctions are biases we have learned from derivations. *Car* is not Anglo-Saxon, for example, but we react to it as if it were when it is placed next to *automobile*. This is only one of many factors which affect our unconscious reactions to words.

Fiction is not written word by word, however. When it is going well it flows sentence by sentence or even by whole scenes. Choices between synonyms are made unconsciously. The time to examine the diction is when reading over the completed first draft. In some cases it may seem stiff or formal. This is frequently a problem in dialogue, in those overworked opening paragraphs, and in stories presented in the as-if-spoken style. Less often, the problem may be a certain bluntness or coarseness which unintentionally slides into the colloquial. In either case, word choice has to be reviewed carefully.

Syntax is the second factor which determines style. Long, elaborate constructions have a distinct effect not only on the feel of the passage but even on the pace at which one's eye moves over the page. Read the following two passages quickly and try to identify your differing reactions:

> When Nick opened the door and went into the room he saw Ole Anderson, a former heavyweight prizefighter, lying on the bed with all his clothes on. He was too long for the bed and lay without looking at Nick, his head on two pillows.

> Nick opened the door and went into the room. Ole Anderson was lying on the bed with all his clothes on. He had been a heavyweight prizefighter and he was too long for the bed. He lay with his head on two pillows. He did not look at Nick.

The first has two sentences. The second has five. The first might be criticized by some as containing a run-on sentence and the second for having what is often called "baby sentences." But writers of fiction, fortunately, have more latitude than students in their weekly themes, and in this case Ernest Hemingway chose the second as his highly individualistic style. The selection is from "The Killers."

At the opposite end of the stylistic scale are authors like Marcel Proust, Henry James, Thomas Wolfe, and William Faulkner. These highly varied novelists were all fascinated with the long sentence, and each of them occasionally strung one out for almost the length of an entire page.

But length is not the only variable. The construction itself can be simple or complex; the punctuation can be strict or loose; the phrasing can be rhythmic or nonrythmic. Whenever one of these variables is pushed to an extreme, the author is a pronounced stylist.

Being a conscious worker of style, however, is not everyone's goal. Notice that none of the three stories included in this text uses extreme syntactical patterns—nor does the great majority of published fiction.

This is mainly because extremes in style—particularly syntactical variations—can become obtrusive. There is a fine line between sentence structure which is effectively complex and that which is just tricky and distracting.

There is one aspect of syntax, however, which every writer of fiction should consider carefully no matter what he intends to do with the matter of style: Don't be monotonous. Regardless of whether one tends toward Hemingway's brief units or toward Henry James's lengthy, heavily qualified sentences, perfect regularity will put any reader to sleep. In short, vary the length. Remember that just as the long, complex line in free verse slows the reader as he works out the rhythms, the syntactical relationships, and the nuances of the various independent clauses, so also the long, heavily qualified, rambling sentence like this one when found in fiction, whether as description or exposition, even if it is appropriate to the sense, slowly drags the paragraph to a creaking halt. Make the next one short.

The third of these major elements in the style of fiction is *narrative mode*. I am using *mode* here in a special sense to designate the five methods of presentation available to the writer of fiction: dialogue, thoughts, action, description, and exposition.

The first two, dialogue and thoughts, are closely related in that they quote either directly or indirectly the words of a character. The last three are in a sense external to the character and in fiction require a means of perception.

Needless to say, any one sentence may involve more than one mode. A statement like "I hate the way you use that green eyeshadow" is basically dialogue, but it also implies the speaker's thoughts, a description of the girl, and exposition about her habits. In spite of these various functions, one mode is usually basic in each sentence. Take, for example, the opening of "Friends from Philadelphia." I have added analysis of each sentence in brackets.

> In the moment before the door was opened to him, he glimpsed her thigh below the half-drawn shade. [Action, as determined by the verb, and implied description] Thelma was home, then. [Exposition] She was wearing the Camp Winniwoho T shirt and her quite short shorts. [Description]
> "Why, my goodness: Janny!" she cried [Dialogue] She always pronounced his name, John, to rhyme with Ann. [Exposition].

A writer normally makes decisions like these quite unconsciously. One narrative mode may take over for a paragraph or so, but the work as a whole maintains a kind of overall balance. When a writer emphasizes one narrative mode throughout, however, he has made a significant stylistic decision. A novel like J. D. Salinger's *Franny and Zooey* and stories like Hemingway's "A Clean, Well Lighted Room" rely heavily on dialogue. They give few stage directions and almost no thoughts. This has an entirely different stylistic effect from stories like Stephen Crane's "The Open Boat" which stresses action and description and Dostoevsky's "Notes from the Underground" which is heavily introspective.

In reviewing the stylistic effect in a particular story, it is helpful to remember that stressing one particular mode nudges a work of fiction toward another genre or subgenre. Emphasis on dialogue, for example, moves the work toward drama (though often rather static drama for lack of action). Exposition or introspection by a narrator can make a story resemble an essay. Too much description and action with little penetration into thoughts begins to make the work read like journalism or a clinical report.

The reason most stories maintain a rough balance between the five narrative modes is not due to any kind of rule or even precedent. It is simply a desire on the part of writers to use what is available. Recognizing this, it is still possible to adjust the overall stylistic effect by highlighting a neglected mode (dialogue is often avoided when one first writes fiction) or by reducing one which has been allowed to take over.

Pace is the last of these four major factors in the development of style. As I have pointed out before, pace is simply the rate at which a story reveals information. This information is often in the form of events—the development of plot. But it can also be dramatic revelation of character.

Slow pace is often the mark of unsuccessful fiction, but not always. Marcel Proust in *Remembrance of Things Past* slowed his plot development to the point where he was able to spend a hundred-odd pages on a single dinner party. Some readers find Proust intolerable for this reason. Others find that the rate of revelation is maintained in character development and in the unfolding of social and philosophical implications.

An even slower narrative pace is found in Dostoevsky's *Notes from the Underground*. The first third of this novel has no plot whatever and is technically an informal essay. It holds the perceptive reader the way an essay does: by the ingenuity with which a variety of complex ideas are presented.

Fast pace is often associated with such varieties of simple fiction as Westerns, adventure stories, and the like. It certainly is true that work of this type rushes through plot at a high rate. Every page has something happening. Exposition, introspection, and description are cut to absolute minimums in order to maintain a helter-skelter pace.

But before one brands rapid pace as necessarily associated with simple fiction, read the stories from the Old Testament. The complex tale of Jacob and how with the aid of his mother he tricked his father into giving him the blessing which by rights should have gone to Esau, the first born—this certainly has enough plot to fill a long contemporary story. Yet it is told in the equivalent of four and a half printed pages. And the story of Noah with all its implications of alienation from the society and, while on board, enormous strife within the family certainly contains enough raw drama for a full-length novel. Yet this is compressed into the equivalent of six printed pages. This extraordinary compression is found in the *Book of Ruth, Job,* and virtually every other narrative sequence. And it is maintained in the *New Testament* as well.

It should be remembered, however, that Biblical stories are like Greek myths in that normally the reader is already familiar with the material. True, there is a first reading or first hearing for each individual, but the work soon becomes absorbed as cultural heritage. In a sense, they are outlines of stories in which the reader (and poets, artists, and subsequent writers) fills in details such as just what doubts Noah might have had on that cloudless, August day when he first laid the keel in his dusty backyard.

Determining the pace which is appropriate for a particular story or novel is similar to making decisions about the other three stylistic elements, diction, syntax, and the balance of narrative modes. In each case, there are extremes both in simple and sophisticated works. Between the two poles there is a wide latitude from which to choose. There are no absolute rules, but this is the best advice one can give: Trust your literary instinct in the first draft and let the story itself suggest the style; then trust your intellect as you review your work, and be willing to make stylistic revisions.

23

REVISING FICTION

The *value of revision;* the *mechanics* of revising; the *six critical questions* concerning vividness of *characterization,* the construction of *plot,* the building of *tensions,* the development of *theme,* the use of *setting,* and appropriateness of the *tone;* the value of *group discussions* of one's work.

When one examines the working habits of established writers as reported in *Writers at Work* (Malcolm Cowley, ed.) and elsewhere, it is extraordinary how few common characteristics there are. But there is one clear and significant point: The proportion of time spent on revisions compared with the time spent on the first draft is about three times higher for the professional than the beginner. As a general rule, both those taking college courses in creative writing and those struggling on their own spend far too little time rewriting.

One factor may be the nature of courses in writing. A college term is relatively short, and the effectiveness of the course demands a fairly high output of new material. Rewriting cannot in most cases be given as much credit as new writing, and credit is a fearfully important commodity for both undergraduates and graduate students. But the tendency to underrate extensive revisions is also found in those hundreds of informal writing groups and clubs which are made up largely of adults not driven by the academic struggle.

Another factor is a rather persistent belief that the writing of fiction is a great game of chance, with the roulette wheel spun either by the muses or the subconscious. This view was proposed by Plato, was pushed to its logical extreme by the Dadaists of the 20s, and is still supported by a few remnants of this school.

More significant, however, is the fact that many writers simply do not know what to do with a first draft. Criticism from friends, teachers, and associates varies considerably, and the bewildered writer is apt to be left with the feeling that whatever worth there might be in the first draft would be damaged or lost if it were tinkered with. One of the functions of this text is to provide a way of looking at one's own work which will suggest a multitude of possible revisions.

After one has asked the right questions and answered them honestly, there are certain mechanical considerations in the task of revising a manuscript. Retyping stories takes time and as a purely mechanical act is to be avoided as much as possible. The best way to cut down time wasted is to use scissors and rubber cement. Changes in diction and syntax can be made in pencil until the paragraph can no longer be read easily. Then is the time to retype the paragraph and paste it over the old. When an entirely new paragraph is to be added, cut the page in two and splice the new material into the middle of the page. New pages may be incorporated into the original numbering scheme by adding letters, for example, 13, 13a, 13b, 14, and so on. Delete paragraphs with a clear line through the first and last sentences and an X through the material. Cut individual words and sentences with a heavy, soft-lead pencil. Sketchy, hesitant, and vague deletions and additions only postpone the final decision and make the working manuscript look hopeless.

For some reason, many beginners resist with emotional intensity any use of scissors and paste. Perhaps these tools remind them of primary-school activities, but for a writer to waste time copying entire pages unnecessarily is far more childish. The goal is to spend as little time as possible in the mechanical task of arranging words on the page, reserving as much time as possible for the creative process itself. The technique of scissors and paste seems clumsy at first—as does the typewriter itself when one is learning; but when mastered, it becomes a natural and expedient part of writing.

Six

Critical Questions   As in the case of poetry, discussions about a story or novel tend to cover six general areas. This is true whether the critic is acting as an individual reader or as a member of a class.

I list them here in the order in which they frequently are raised. There is a tendency, for example, to discuss characters and scene construction before the theme because they are in some respects more visible, more immediately available. Setting and tone, on the other hand, are often brought up toward the end of a discussion since they depend on what the thematic concerns are.

But it would be a great mistake to insist on any particular order. A good discussion is in a sense an organic development: It should move in whatever direction appears productive. The point of this list is not to restrict or direct discussion but to encourage as broad a range of analysis as possible.

First, *are the primary characters vivid or convincing?* I use the word *or* here because in the case of satire a character may stand out sharply the way a cartoon figure does without being *convincing* the way a fully-drawn character should be. In either case, successful characters can be described as *vivid*. (It is important to recall here the warning against the word *realistic* as a sloppy synonym for *vivid*.)

Secondary characters, of course, don't have to meet the same standards. We don't insist on getting to know the father in "The Use of Force" or the waiter in "Sausage and Beer" as well as the primary characters. But even in these cases, they have to be presented in such a way as to appear as a natural part of the story. If the reader feels that a character has been added needlessly or, worse, blatantly for a specific purpose, then the story is in need of revision.

In analyzing characters, don't rely entirely on general impressions. Look closely at those narrative modes which have been used. Is his dialogue convincing? Do we get into his inner world of thoughts? Do we see him *doing* enough so we can judge him from his actions? Can we see him physically? Finally, has the author relied too heavily on exposition for details which could have been shown more subtly?

Second, *is the story constructed successfully?* It is often helpful to analyze just how many scenes there are before beginning to evaluate how they are handled. Once this is done, it is natural enough to discuss which seem to be the most successful ones. Some may be too brief to provide a sense of being present; others may seem to drag. Frequently, a scattering of scenes may be combined to give the story a more solid base.

After discussing the scenes individually, it is important to discuss the order: Is this the most effective sequence? If the opening is slow, for example, it might be worth starting with a livelier scene and returning to the original situation at a later point in the story. If the order is complicated with a story-teller or with numerous flash-backs, one should discuss whether the advantage of such a sequence is worth the risk of confusion and distraction. Keep in mind that while there is no "right" way for any one story, every approach has both advantages and disadvantages—and in different proportions. The critic's job is not to make pronouncements like, "You can't write a story that way," but, rather, to describe what seems to be successful from the reader's point of view and what is confusing or dull. Frequently, such reactions stem from the handling of the plot.

Third, *does the story contain the type of tensions which keeps fiction alive and interesting?* It is, of course, easy to say that a story is "flat" or that "it's just plain dull." But a critic who is helpful moves directly to the problem of determining what kinds of tensions might be established. In some cases this may be a matter of creating a conflict between the protagonist and another character or some other force. This could mean basic revisions in plot. In other cases it might require developing some literary device such as curiosity or irony (covered in Chapter 20.)

Fourth, *what is the theme and is it sophisticated enough to be fresh and evocative?* There is sometimes a tendency to move right in on this question from the start. There is no real harm in this, but the discussion is apt to stay there as if *theme* is all there is to fiction. Starting a critical discussion with some of the more manageable topics at least makes sure that they are covered. And they sometimes can fill the prolonged silence which often follows the reading of a story.

The critic should have a chance to describe what he feels the central concern is and what the minor threads might be before the author says a word. This is the only way a writer can tell just how much has reached his readers. Sometimes the most helpful comments in this area are not evaluative at all but merely descriptive. The critic describes what has reached him as a reader accepting some interpretations and rejecting others on the basis of textual evidence.

It doesn't take long for the author to discover where he has succeeded and where he has failed.

Fifth, *is the setting vivid and does it contribute to the theme?* If one discusses the setting before being sure about the theme, the subject is only partially covered. As I pointed out in Chapter 21, it helps if the setting is convincing enough to orient the reader and to draw him into the story. But in some cases, setting may also contribute to the development of the theme. It is possible, of course, for a story to be successful without use of setting. This is the case in "The Use of Force." Or it may make extensive use of setting such as the symbolic contrasts between the asylum and the speakeasy in "Sausage and Beer."

Regardless of how fully it is used, it is important that the setting is not in any way a cliché. Occasionally it is necessary to tell a writer that what he thought was an accurate use of his own home is hackneyed. The problem in these cases, of course, is not the home itself but the kinds of details the author has used to present it. Freshness is a basic demand in any setting.

Finally, *is the tone of the story effective?* In many cases this may involve questioning the near-tragic tone of a story which might be told with greater control or even a light touch. Occasionally it may involve finding ways to treat the subject with greater seriousness.

It is difficult to be specific about the tone without analyzing the style as well. If the critic is going to be specific and helpful, he will have to pick out specific examples of diction and syntax to support his reactions. Criticism such as "It seems melodramatic" is not really valuable until it is linked to a certain paragraph or, better yet, specific phrases.

The great value of a group discussion—whether a class or an informal gathering of writers—is that it gives a fairly wide range of responses. Every critical comment is tinged with the personal preferences of the speaker; but when a number of readers touch on the same point, the writer can be sure that something has gone wrong.

Although some novice writers are reluctant to subject their work to such criticism, they are usually the ones who need it the most. Others accept critical comments with elaborate defenses. "I really wanted to leave it baffling"; "I think a theme should mean anything a reader wants it to mean"; "I don't care whether my characters are convincing or not"; "But that's just the way it happened"; "But that's the way I dreamed it." They are also refusing criticism. And in doing so, they are rejecting the possibility of growth.

In the early stages, critical reaction is essential for a writer's development. After a number of years, he begins to serve as his own critic. But this is because he has internalized so much reaction to his work that he is able to judge fairly well what is going to reach his readers and what is not. He has reached the point where he reads his own work with a kind of controlled schizophrenia—part author and part a reader who is meeting these characters and this situation for the very first time.

PART THREE * * *

The
Writing
of
Drama

24

THEATER:
A LIVE PERFORMANCE

Drama seen as essentially a "live" performance; drama's six basic characteristics: dramatic impact, visual elements, auditory quality, the fact that it is physically produced, is a continuous art, and is a spectator art; the origins of a play; and the natural boundaries of the genre.

A play is a "live" performance. It is produced physically in front of an audience and is performed by actors. This is drama's greatest asset. It is also a key to understanding the genre.

Ever since the advent of the "talking movie," critics have prophesied the end of legitimate theater. Television and, more recently, the renewed interest in cinema as a sophisticated art form have been seen by some as further threats. But the fact is that there is a constant growth of new little theaters many of which have been converted from ballrooms, movie houses, and even warehouses. Many middle-sized cities have resident companies which have been formed within the past ten years. And this is augmented by the construction of university theaters which often contain the finest equipment available. It is clear from this growth of theaters that there is a genuine need for performances given by actors on a stage.

Obviously film and drama each have certain assets and liabilities. Since a play's greatest strength is the psychological impact of actors on the stage, contemporary playwrights have stressed this aspect of their genre. Some, for example, prefer theaters which have given up the proscenium arch and seat the audience on three sides of the stage. Others prefer theater in the round and write their plays to utilize such a design. Pushing further, some playwrights have their characters mingle with the audience. In William Carlos Williams's *Many Loves,* for example, the "director" and the "playwright" are in the audience and frequently stop the play to argue about its direction and purpose, moving freely between the world of the spectators and that of actors acting as actors in a series of plays. The effect for the audience is like dreaming that one has repeatedly awakened.

But whether a play is experimental or, like Arthur Miller's *The Price,* utterly conservative, the fact that it is a live performance is what differentiates it fundamentally not only from film but from poetry and from fiction as well.

Six Basic
Characteristics of Drama   Like the other two genres, drama has its own distinguishing characteristics. Each of them is a natural development of the fact that the genre is a live performance.

Plays can be found which do not contain one or two of these just as some poems can be found which make little use of rhythm and some stories are written without dialogue. Clearly these are not rules; they are merely recurring characteristics. Most playwrights consider them the assets of the genre.

First, drama is by definition a *dramatic art.* That is, it generally has an emotional impact or force. In the case of comedy, we call it vitality. This is not just a tradition; it is a natural aspect of an art form which requires an audience to give its undivided attention for two and a half to three hours.

This impact is often established early in a play with a *dramatic question* which seizes the attention of the audience long before the theme becomes evident. Dramatic questions are usually blunt and simple: Is this stranger a threat? Whom are they waiting for? Why do these characters hate each other? In most cases, these initial questions develop into specific conflicts. Although the need for tension like this is not as strong in very short plays and in comedies, it is usually greater in drama than in either fiction or poetry.

As in fiction, irony and satire often add to the dramatic aspect of a play. And still another device is the use of shock. Unusual or violent situations can explode where the audience least expects them.

Dramatic impact is hard to sustain, however. For this reason, most plays work up to a series of peaks, allowing the emotions of the audience to rest in between. This system of rising and falling action does not follow any prescribed pattern and is often intuitive on the part of the playwright—just as it is in the writing of short stories. But without some such structure, a play risks failure no matter how significant the themes may be.

Second, drama is a *visual art*. Action on the stage is usually a significant and an organic part of the whole production. It is not enough in the twentieth century to have characters simply walk back and forth reciting poetry as they did in the highly stylized tradition of Greek theater. In most cases, the movement of characters on the stage is as important as the lines themselves.

And the visual concern extends beyond the characters. The set itself is often another important part of the production. Sophisticated lighting boards can convert the set from a static backdrop to a dynamic factor in developing the moods of each scene. And the addition of projected images and movie sequences—experiments in mixed media—is one more appeal to the visual aspect of theater.

Third, drama is an *auditory art*. Here, unlike in fiction, words are thought of primarily as speech. In some respects, this brings the playwright closer to the poet than to the novelist. Like the poet, the playwright is apt to read his lines out loud, listening to the composition rather than studying it on the page.

For some, this concern leads to writing drama in verse. For others, dramatic dialogue becomes a method of creating a dreamlike experience which depends on impressions rather than a logically developed plot. This is one of the characteristics associated with theater of the absurd. Still others use special effects like electronic music, humming, or recorded chanting. Not only are sounds important, but the space between lines can be significant. In Harold Pinter's work, for example, the pauses become almost as important as the lines themselves.

Fourth, drama is a *physically produced art*. Beginning playwrights are apt to think of this as primarily a limitation: Sets have to be constructed with wood and nails, and the script cannot ignore totally the task of the set designer and the stage crew.

But as already indicated, the physical aspect of a stage production is a fundamental asset. When a play is realistically presented, it has a kind of intense credibility. And when it is expressionistic, it opens the imagination to what is suggestive and symbolic. And there is an array of techniques which mix actors with audience and audience with the illusion of the play, techniques which are simply not available in any other genre, including cinema.

Fifth, drama is a *continuous art*. Members of the audience, unlike readers of fiction or poetry, must receive the play at whatever pace the playwright sets. They cannot linger on a sage observation or a moving episode. They cannot turn back a page or review an earlier scene.

Again, this characteristic does not make the genre "better" or "worse" than others. But it is an aspect which one can utilize. Just as the poet often depends on the reader's willingness to go over a work many times, the playwright can utilize the rapid sweep of his genre, relying on the fact that his work will be taken in at a single sitting and at exactly the pace he himself determines. With practice, he can make one portion of a scene move rapidly or another move slowly. He can drop hints which a novelist, working in a more leisurely genre, would have to repeat several times. He has his audience trapped in their seats, and he has full control over how rapidly this "experience" will occur and exactly which aspects will be highlighted.

Finally, and closely connected, is the fact that drama is a *spectator art*. Even more than spectator sports, audience reaction is important. Poets are relatively far removed from such concerns. It is rare indeed when a poet is willing to change a line of his verse because of a critical review or a poor public response. Novelists are slightly more susceptible. Their potential audience is larger than a poet's and they tend to be aware of this. Many novelists will make fairly extensive revisions on the basis of their editor's suggestions. Thomas Wolfe, for example, trusted his editor, Maxwell Perkins, to make substantial changes in the form of cutting. An extreme case is F. Scott Fitzgerald who rewrote his novel, *Tender is the Night,* years after its original publication, struggling to overcome the negative response of the public.

Playwrights are even more sensitive to the reaction of the public.

The brooding, nervous individual in the back of the theater on opening night is apt to be the playwright. He listens for those awful moments when the audience laughs at the wrong moment or collectively
squirms with boredom. He eavesdrops on comments made during
intermission, and he relies heavily—perhaps too heavily—on the reviews the next day.

This does not mean that a serious dramatist is a slave to the dic-
tates of the critics and the audience. In most cases he has a basic
conception of the work which remains unalterable. The point is that
because he is dealing with a "live" performance and with an audience
going through a collective experience, he is legitimately concerned
with how his spectators respond.

Origins
of a Play
The genesis of each artistic work is unique.
But there are patterns which characterize each genre. As I have
pointed out, poems often begin with an image—a specific visual detail,
a vehicle which seems to be searching for a tenor. In the case of fiction, the genesis is more often a sequence of events which the author
has experienced either directly or vicariously and which seems to
radiate aspects of character. When one begins to work with a good
story idea, it is exciting because of this developing sense of discovery.

The origin of a play is apt to be more explosive, more "theatrical"
in the best sense. Rather than a subtle sequence of events which unfold
aspects of character, the original concept often comes as a situation:
dramatic, vivid, and evocative. This is particularly true of short plays
in which the initial impact—the set and the situation—must seize the
imagination of the audience much more rapidly than does the opening
of a story or novel.

Often this opening situation is the one which hit the playwright
first and served as the genesis of the play. In most cases we can only
speculate, but both the plays included in this volume are of the type
which might well have begun that way. In *Hello Out There* the
immediate situation involves a man in a jail cell trying to make contact with the outside world, calling "Hello out there!" And this basic
theme is repeated by a girl who, we soon learn, is trapped in this small
town in much the same way that he is locked in his cell. We cannot
tell whether Mr. Saroyan's initial concept was the sensation of being
trapped in a jail cell (which he saw as being dramatically similar to

being trapped by circumstances in a small town), or whether it began with the remembrance of what it was like to be isolated in a small town. Or perhaps it sprang from the loneliness we all feel as adolescents. In any case, the dramatic situation of a character trapped and calling out for contact with others serves as that initial impact—and quite probably as the genesis of the play.

In Edward Albee's *The Sandbox,* the treatment is not realistic but expressionistic. That is, the play is presented with the kind of distortion we associate with dream fiction. But even though the technique of the play is quite different, the basic situation is a highly charged, dramatic set of tensions just as it is in *Hello Out There*. A grandmother is being disposed of like an unwanted child by her daughter and passive son-in-law. She is placed in a sandbox and left there, we soon discover, to die.

Dreamlike as this play is, it exposes common attitudes toward the young (the grandmother is treated like a child), toward the old, and toward dying. The play, written in memory or Albee's own grandmother, is clearly derived, not from abstract concerns, but from human strengths and weaknesses and on dramatic conflicts within the family.

Finding material for a play is in other respects similar to the process in fiction. One has to have characters who are interesting, a set of tensions which will reveal them, and some kind of development or discovery which will draw the work to a close. Like stories, plays may spring from personal experience or, more often, from events the playwright has heard about. The big difference lies in the dramatist's search for dramatic impact.

The Natural Boundaries of Drama

There is no sharp line between genres. As we have seen, poems which rely heavily on nonlyrical, denotative language become more like prose, stories which stress exposition begin to resemble essays, and those which rely heavily on dialogue move in the direction of drama. It would appear that the boundaries of any genre are set not so much tradition as by effectiveness. As one approaches another genre, certain liabilities occur which should be accounted for by the writer. But one way to understand the full potential of a genre is to explore each of its outer limits.

It is possible, for example, to bring drama close to poetry. Greek plays were written in verse and so was classical French drama of the seventeenth century. Shakespeare took a mid-course, keeping his blank verse very free and slipping into prose for his comic and low-life characters. Twentieth-century American writers like Maxwell Anderson and Robert Lowell revived the use of verse drama, while at the same time dealing with highly contemporary situations. It is clear from these examples that the use of verse in drama does not reduce either the impact or the pace.

The liability of verse drama occurs when the lines begin to approach the verbal sophistication which we associate with poetry itself. Because drama is a continuous art form, the audience cannot linger over lines and savor a complex metaphor. The fact that drama is a production makes the use of sophisticated verse a liability rather than an asset. Drama, then, can move in the direction of a poem, but it should not be confused with poetry itself.

In the same way, drama has elements of the essay. Characters are often given lines which in fiction would seem highly didactic. The playwright can get away with this up to a point partly because the genre does not contain pure exposition such as is used in fiction and also because the pace of drama is more rapid than a novel. A good play has a certain momentum which will sweep the audience through essay-like soliloquies if they are not too long.

Some plays make extensive use of political, social, religious, or moral issues. "Guerrilla theater" and the full range of protest drama of the past decade, the proletarian drama of the 1930s (Clifford Odets's *Waiting for Lefty,* for example), and the morality plays of the Middle Ages are all *thetic drama* in that each is dominated by a strong thesis. And most of them were compelling dramatic experiences for the audiences of their time.

They also tend to be literarily simple. They depend heavily on specific political or moral issues of the day. Once these causes become past history, the play usually becomes a period piece. Skelton's *Magnificence,* for example, was enormously successful with those who were alarmed at the extravagance of Henry VIII just as Barbara Garson's *MacBird* delighted those critical of President Johnson in 1966. But both plays depend on the social issues and the personalities which they attack.

It is time-consuming to argue whether a play should have immediate social relevance and be dominated by a thesis the way an essay is or whether it should concern itself with broad themes. The two approaches have different advantages and serve different functions. One has the power to influence the immediate society in specific ways, serving as a weapon of reform, while the other has durability and relevance which may cut across cultures and centuries.

As in the case of poetic drama, there is a point of reduced effectiveness. When a play is made to resemble the essay or the broadside too closely, it loses the dramatic illusion which allows the audience to enter into and "experience" the action. Instead, the spectator remains outside the work just as if he were listening to a speech. At this point the work has neither the evocative power of drama nor the didactic capacity of exposition. The playwright, then, can move in the direction of the essay, but he shouldn't confuse his genre with the essay form itself.

Finally, although drama in some respects resembles fiction, it begins to lose effectiveness if it is allowed to wander too far in this direction also. Fictional plots often lack the kind of dramatic unity which lends itself to stage productions and they are apt to have a number of shifts in time and setting. Drama, on the other hand, tends to be more unified. There are many exceptions, but both the mechanical limitations of a set and the psychological appeal of coherence encourage the playwright to keep his plot moving chronologically and without shifts in place.

Another characteristic of fiction is the use of thoughts. This can be done in drama by having characters speak to themselves or, occasionally, by using one of a number of special techniques such as addressing the audience directly, using a chorus, or playing a recorded voice. In general, though, plays rely on the special assets of the genre: action and dialogue. The audience can gather a great deal about a character's thoughts by what he does and says. Simulated thoughts tend to slow the pace of a play and are used far less than in fiction.

There are exceptions to every one of these "boundaries" of drama. There is more experimentation going on today than at any previous point in history. There are plays which move freely back and forth in time like the loosest sort of novel (Arthur Miller's *After the Fall,* for example), plays which do not make use of the visual aspect (Jules Feiffer's *The Unexpurgated Memoirs of Bernard Mergendeiler* is played in total darkness), and even plays which do not have actors (Picasso's *Desire* contains one entire scene which consists of a "dance" between two undulating mobiles).

The fact remains that live performances presented on a stage have certain assets not found in any other genre. Most playwrights are concerned with developing these assets rather than imitating other genres. The point of this chapter and those which follow is not to describe "rules," but to explore the range of opportunities which is inherent in the genre of drama.

25

A PLAY BY
WILLIAM SAROYAN

Hello Out There

For George Bernard Shaw

Characters:

A YOUNG MAN
A GIRL
A MAN
TWO OTHER MEN
A WOMAN

Scene: There is a fellow in a small-town prison cell, tapping slowly on the floor with a spoon. After tapping half a minute, as if he were trying to telegraph words, he gets up and begins walking around the cell. At last he stops, stands at the center of the cell, and doesn't move for a long time. He feels his head, as if it were wounded. Then he looks around. Then he calls out dramatically, kidding the world.

YOUNG MAN: Hello—out there! (*Pause.*) Hello—out there! Hello—out there! (*Long pause.*) Nobody out there. (*Still more dramatically, but more comically, too.*) Hello—out there! Hello—out there!

A GIRL'S VOICE *is heard, very sweet and soft.*

THE VOICE: Hello.

YOUNG MAN: Hello—out there.

THE VOICE: Hello.

YOUNG MAN: Is that you, Katey?

THE VOICE: No—this here is Emily.

YOUNG MAN: Who? (*Swiftly.*) Hello out there.

THE VOICE: Emily.

YOUNG MAN: Emily who? I don't know anybody named Emily. Are you that girl I met at Sam's in Salinas about three years ago?

THE VOICE: No—I'm the girl who cooks here. I'm the cook. I've never been in Salinas. I don't even know where it is.

YOUNG MAN: Hello out there. You say you cook here?

THE VOICE: Yes.

YOUNG MAN: Well, why don't you study up and learn to cook? How come I don't get no jello or anything good?

THE VOICE: I just cook what they tell me to. (*Pause.*) You lonesome?

YOUNG MAN: Lonesome as a coyote. Hear me hollering? Hello out there!

THE VOICE: Who you hollering to?

YOUNG MAN: Well—nobody, I guess. I been trying to think of somebody to write a letter to, but I can't think of anybody.

THE VOICE: What about Katey?

YOUNG MAN: I don't know anybody named Katey.

THE VOICE: Then why did you say, Is that you, Katey?

YOUNG MAN: Katey's a good name. I always did like a name like Katey. I never *knew* anybody named Katey, though.

THE VOICE: *I* did.

YOUNG MAN: Yeah? What was she like? Tall girl, or little one?

THE VOICE: Kind of medium.

YOUNG MAN: Hello out there. What sort of a looking girl are *you?*

THE VOICE: Oh, I don't know.

YOUNG MAN: Didn't anybody ever tell you? Didn't anybody ever talk to you that way?

THE VOICE: What way?

YOUNG MAN: You know. Didn't they?

THE VOICE: No, they didn't.

YOUNG MAN: Ah, the fools—they should have. I can tell from your voice you're O.K.

THE VOICE: Maybe I am and maybe I ain't.

YOUNG MAN: I never missed yet.

THE VOICE: Yeah, I know. That's why you're in jail.

YOUNG MAN: The whole thing was a mistake.

THE VOICE: They claim it was rape.

YOUNG MAN: No—it wasn't.

THE VOICE: That's what they claim it was.

YOUNG MAN: They're a lot of fools.

THE VOICE: Well, you sure are in trouble. Are you scared?

YOUNG MAN: Scared to death. (*Suddenly.*) Hello out there!

THE VOICE: What do you keep saying that for all the time?

YOUNG MAN: I'm lonesome. I'm as lonesome as a coyote. (*A long one.*) Hello—out there!

THE GIRL *appears, over to one side. She is a plain girl in plain clothes.*

THE GIRL: I'm kind of lonesome, too.

YOUNG MAN (*turning and looking at her*): Hey—No fooling? Are you?

THE GIRL: Yeah—I'm almost as lonesome as a coyote myself.

YOUNG MAN: Who *you* lonesome for?

THE GIRL: I don't know.

YOUNG MAN: It's the same with me. The minute they put you in a place like this you remember all the girls you ever knew, and all the girls you didn't get to know, and it sure gets lonesome.

THE GIRL: I bet it does.

YOUNG MAN: Ah, it's awful. (*Pause.*) You're a pretty kid, you know that?

THE GIRL: You're just talking.

YOUNG MAN: No, I'm not just talking—you *are* pretty. Any fool could see that. You're just about the prettiest kid in the whole world.

THE GIRL: I'm not—and you know it.

YOUNG MAN: No—you are. I never saw anyone prettier in all my born days, in all my travels. I knew Texas would bring me luck.

THE GIRL: Luck? You're in jail, aren't you? You've got a whole gang of people all worked up, haven't you?

YOUNG MAN: Ah, that's nothing. I'll get out of this.

THE GIRL: Maybe.

YOUNG MAN: No, I'll be all right—*now.*

THE GIRL: What do you mean—now?

YOUNG MAN: I mean after seeing you. I got something now. You know for a while there I didn't care one way or another. Tired. (*Pause.*) Tired of trying for the best all the time and never getting it. (*Suddenly.*) Hello out there!

THE GIRL: Who you calling now?

YOUNG MAN: You.

THE GIRL: Why, I'm right here.

YOUNG MAN: I know. (*Calling.*) Hello out there!

THE GIRL: Hello.

YOUNG MAN: Ah, you're sweet. (*Pause.*) I'm going to marry *you.* I'm going away with *you.* I'm going to take you so San Francisco or some place like that. I *am,* now. I'm going to win myself some real money, too. I'm going to study 'em real careful and pick myself some winners, and we're going to have a lot of money.

THE GIRL: Yeah?

YOUNG MAN: Yeah. Tell me your name and all that stuff.

THE GIRL: Emily.

YOUNG MAN: I know that. What's the rest of it? Where were you born? Come on, tell me the whole thing.

THE GIRL: Emily Smith.

YOUNG MAN: Honest to God?

THE GIRL: Honest. That's my name—Emily Smith.

YOUNG MAN: Ah, you're the sweetest girl in the whole world.

THE GIRL: Why?

YOUNG MAN: I don't know why, but you are, that's all. Where were you born?

THE GIRL: Matador, Texas.

YOUNG MAN: Where's that?

THE GIRL: Right here.

YOUNG MAN: Is this Matador, Texas?

THE GIRL: Yeah, it's Matador. They brought you here from Wheeling.

YOUNG MAN: Is that where I was—Wheeling?

THE GIRL: Didn't you even know town you were in?

YOUNG MAN: All towns are alike. You don't go up and ask somebody what town you're in. It doesn't make any difference. How far away is Wheeling?

THE GIRL: Sixteen or seventeen miles. Didn't you know they moved you?

YOUNG MAN: How could I know, when I was out—cold? Somebody hit me over the head with a lead pipe or something. What'd they hit me for?

THE GIRL: Rape—that's what they *said*.

YOUNG MAN: Ah, that's a lie. (*Amazed, almost to himself.*) She wanted me to give her money.

THE GIRL: Money?

YOUNG MAN: Yeah, if I'd have known she was a woman like that —well, by God, I'd have gone on down the street and stretched out in a park somewhere and gone to sleep.

THE GIRL: Is that what she wanted—money?

YOUNG MAN: Yeah. A fellow like me hopping freights all over the country, trying to break his bad luck, going from one poor little town to another, trying to get in on something good somewhere, and she asks for money. I thought she was lonesome. She *said* she was.

THE GIRL: Maybe she was.

YOUNG MAN: She was *something*.

THE GIRL: I guess I'd never see you, if it didn't happen, though.

YOUNG MAN: Oh, I don't know—maybe I'd just mosey along this way and see you in this town somewhere. I'd recognize you, too.

THE GIRL: Recognize me?

YOUNG MAN: Sure, I'd recognize you the minute I laid eyes on you.

THE GIRL: Well, who would I be?

YOUNG MAN: Mine, that's who.

THE GIRL: Honest?

YOUNG MAN: Honest to God.

THE GIRL: You just say that because you're in jail.

YOUNG MAN: No, I mean it. You just pack up and wait for me. We'll high-roll the hell out of here to Frisco.

THE GIRL: You're just lonesome.

YOUNG MAN: I been lonesome all my life—there's no cure for that—but you and me—we can have a lot of fun hanging around together. You'll bring me luck. I know it.

THE GIRL: What are you looking for luck for all the time?

YOUNG MAN: I'm a gambler. I don't work. I've *got* to have luck, or I'm a bum. I haven't had any decent luck in years. Two whole years now—one place to another. Bad luck all the time. That's why I got in trouble back there in Wheeling, too. That was no accident. That was my bad luck following me around. So here I am, with my head half busted. I guess it was her old man that did it.

THE GIRL: You mean her father?

YOUNG MAN: No, her husband. If I had an old lady like that, I'd throw her out.

THE GIRL: Do you think you'll have better luck, if I go with you?

YOUNG MAN: It's a cinch. I'm a good handicapper. All I need is somebody good like you with me. It's no good always walking around in the streets for anything that might be there at the time. You got to have somebody staying with you all the time—through winters when it's cold, and springtime when it's pretty, and summertime when it's nice and hot and you can go swimming—through *all* the times—rain and snow and all the different kinds of weather a man's got to go through before he dies. You got to have somebody who's right. Somebody who knows you, from away back. You got to have somebody who even knows you're wrong but likes you just the same. I know I'm wrong, but I just don't want anything the hard way, working like a dog, or the *easy* way, working like a dog—working's the hard way and the easy way both. All I got to do is beat the price, always—and then I don't feel lousy and don't hate anybody. If you go along with me, I'll be the finest guy anybody ever saw. I won't be wrong any more. You know when you get enough of that money, you *can't* be wrong any more—you're right because the money says so. I'll have a lot of money and you'll be just about the prettiest, most wonderful kid in the whole world. I'll be proud walking around Frisco with you on my arm and people turning around to look at us.

THE GIRL: Do you think they will?

YOUNG MAN: Sure they will. When I get back in some decent clothes, and you're on my arm—well, Katey, they'll turn around and look, and they'll see something, too.

THE GIRL: Katey?

YOUNG MAN: Yeah—that's your name from now on. You're the first girl I ever called Katey. I've been saving it for you. O.K.?

THE GIRL: O.K.

YOUNG MAN: How long have I been here?

THE GIRL: Since last night. You didn't wake up until late this morning, though.

YOUNG MAN: What time is it now? About nine?

THE GIRL: About ten.

YOUNG MAN: Have you got the key to this lousy cell?

THE GIRL: No. They don't let me fool with any keys.

YOUNG MAN: Well, can you get it?

THE GIRL: No.

YOUNG MAN: Can you *try?*

THE GIRL: They wouldn't let me get near any keys. I cook for this jail, when they've got somebody in it. I clean up and things like that.

YOUNG MAN: Well, I want to get out of here. Don't you know the guy that runs this joint?

THE GIRL: I know him, but he wouldn't let you out. They were talking of taking you to another jail in another town.

YOUNG MAN: Yeah? Why?

THE GIRL: Because they're afraid.

YOUNG MAN: What are they afraid of?

THE GIRL: They're afraid these people from Wheeling will come over in the middle of the night and break in.

YOUNG MAN: Yeah? What do they want to do that for?

THE GIRL: Don't *you* know what they want to do it for?

YOUNG MAN: Yeah, I know all right.

THE GIRL: Are you scared?

YOUNG MAN: Sure I'm scared. Nothing scares a man more than ignorance. You can argue with people who ain't fools, but you can't argue with fools—they just go to work and do what they're set on doing. Get me out of here.

THE GIRL: How?

YOUNG MAN: Well, go get the guy with the key, and let me talk to him.

THE GIRL: He's gone home. Everybody's gone home.

YOUNG MAN: You mean I'm in this little jail all alone?

THE GIRL: Well—yeah—except me.

YOUNG MAN: Well, what's the big idea—doesn't anybody stay here all the time?

THE GIRL: No, they go home every night. I clean up and then I go, too. I hung around tonight.

YOUNG MAN: What made you do that?

THE GIRL: I wanted to talk to you.

YOUNG MAN: Honest? What did you want to talk about?

THE GIRL: Oh, I don't know. I took care of you last night. You were talking in your sleep. You liked me, too. I didn't think you'd like me when you woke up, though.

YOUNG MAN: Yeah? Why not?

THE GIRL: I don't know.

YOUNG MAN: Yeah? Well, you're wonderful, see?

THE GIRL: Nobody ever talked to me that way. All the fellows in town—(*Pause.*)

YOUNG MAN: What about 'em? (*Pause.*) Well, what about 'em? Come on—tell me.

THE GIRL: They laugh at me.

YOUNG MAN: Laugh at *you?* They're fools. What do they know about anything? You go get your things and come back here. I'll take you with me to Frisco. How old are you?

THE GIRL: Oh, I'm of age.

YOUNG MAN: How old are you?—Don't lie to me! Sixteen?

THE GIRL: I'm seventeen.

YOUNG MAN: Well, bring your father and mother. We'll get married before we go.

THE GIRL: They wouldn't let me go.

YOUNG MAN: Why not?

THE GIRL: I don't know, but they wouldn't. I know they wouldn't.

YOUNG MAN: You go tell your father not to be a fool, see? What is he, a farmer?

THE GIRL: No—nothing. He gets a little relief from the government because he's supposed to be hurt or something—his side hurts, he says. I don't know what it is.

YOUNG MAN: Ah, he's a liar. Well, I'm taking you with me, see?

THE GIRL: He takes the money I earn, too.

YOUNG MAN: He's got no right to do that.

THE GIRL: I know it, but he does it.

YOUNG MAN (*almost to himself*): This world stinks. You shouldn't have been born in this town, anyway, and you shouldn't have had a man like that for a father, either.

THE GIRL: Sometimes I feel sorry for him.

YOUNG MAN: Never mind feeling sorry for him. (*Pointing a finger.*) I'm going to talk to your father some day. I've got a few things to tell that guy.

THE GIRL: I know you have.

YOUNG MAN (*suddenly*): Hello—out there! See if you can get that fellow with the keys to come down and let me out.

THE GIRL: Oh, I couldn't.

YOUNG MAN: Why not?

THE GIRL: I'm nobody here—they give me fifty cents every day I work.

YOUNG MAN: How much?

THE GIRL: Fifty cents.

YOUNG MAN (*to the world*): You see? They ought to pay money to *look* at you. To breathe the *air* you breathe. I don't know. Sometimes I figure it never is going to make sense. Hello—out there! I'm scared. You try to get me out of here. I'm scared them fools are going to come here from Wheeling and go crazy, thinking they're heroes. Get me out of here, Katey.

THE GIRL: I don't know what to do. Maybe I could break the door down.

YOUNG MAN: No, you couldn't do that. Is there a hammer out there or anything?

THE GIRL: Only a broom. Maybe they've locked the broom up, too.

YOUNG MAN: Go see if you can find anything.

THE GIRL: All right. (*She goes.*)

YOUNG MAN: Hello—out there! Hello—out there! (*Pause.*) Hello —out there! Hello—out there! (*Pause.*) Putting me in jail. (*With contempt.*) Rape! Rape? *They* rape everything good that was ever born. His side hurts. They laugh at her. Fifty cents a day. Little punk people. Hurting the only good thing that ever came their way. (*Suddenly.*) Hello—out there!

THE GIRL (*returning*): There isn't a thing out there. They've locked everything up for the night.

YOUNG MAN: Any cigarettes?

THE GIRL: Everything's locked up—all the drawers of the desk, all the closet doors—everything.

YOUNG MAN: I ought to have a cigarette.

THE GIRL: I could get you a package maybe, somewhere. I guess the drug store's open. It's about a mile.

YOUNG MAN: A mile? I don't want to be alone that long.

THE GIRL: I could run all the way, and all the way back.

YOUNG MAN: You're the sweetest girl that ever lived.

THE GIRL: What kind do you want?

YOUNG MAN: Oh, any kind—Chesterfields or Camels or Lucky Strikes —any kind at all.

THE GIRL: I'll go get a package. (*She turns to go.*)

YOUNG MAN: What about the money?

THE GIRL: I've got some money. I've got a quarter I been saving. I'll run all the way. (*She is about to go.*)

YOUNG MAN: Come here.

THE GIRL (*going to him*): What?

YOUNG MAN: Give me your hand. (*He takes her hand and looks at it, smiling. He lifts it and kisses it.*) I'm scared to death.

THE GIRL: I am, too.

YOUNG MAN: I'm not lying—I don't care what happens to me, but I'm scared nobody will ever come out here to this Godforsaken broken-down town and find you. I'm scared you'll get used to it and not mind. I'm scared you'll never get to Frisco and have 'em all turning around to look at you. Listen—go get me a gun, because if they come, I'll kill 'em! They don't understand. Get me a gun!

THE GIRL: I could get my father's gun. I know where he hides it.

YOUNG MAN: Go get it. Never mind the cigarettes. Run all the way. (*Pause, smiling but seriously.*) Hello, Katey.

THE GIRL: Hello. What's *your* name?

YOUNG MAN: Photo-Finish is what they *call* me. My races are always photo-finish races. You don't know what that means, but it means they're very close. So close the only way they can tell which horse wins is to look at a photograph after the race is over. Well, every race I bet turns out to be a photo-finish race, and my horse never wins. It's my bad luck, all the time. That's why they call me Photo-Finish. Say it before you go.

THE GIRL: Photo-Finish.

YOUNG MAN: Come here. (THE GIRL *moves close and he kisses her.*) Now, hurry. Run all the way.

THE GIRL: I'll run. (THE GIRL *turns and runs. The* YOUNG MAN *stands at the center of the cell a long time.* THE GIRL *comes running back in. Almost crying.*) I'm afraid. I'm afraid I won't see you again. If I come back and you're not here, I—

YOUNG MAN: Hello—out there!

THE GIRL: It's so lonely in this town. Nothing here but the lonesome wind all the time, lifting the dirt and blowing out to the prairie. I'll stay *here*. I won't *let* them take you away.

YOUNG MAN: Listen, Katey. Do what I tell you. Go get that gun and come back. Maybe they won't come tonight. Maybe they won't come at all. I'll hide the gun and when they let me out you can take it back and put it where you found it. And then we'll go away. But if they come, I'll kill 'em! Now, hurry—

THE GIRL: All right. (*Pause.*) I want to tell you something.

YOUNG MAN: O.K.

THE GIRL (*very softly*): If you're not here when I come back, well, I'll have the gun and I'll know what to do with it.

YOUNG MAN: You know how to handle a gun?

THE GIRL: I know how.

YOUNG MAN: Don't be a fool. (*Takes off his shoe, brings out some currency.*) Don't be a fool, see? Here's some money. Eighty dollars. Take it and go to Frisco. Look around and find somebody. Find somebody alive and halfway human, see? Promise me—if I'm not here when you come back, just throw the gun away and get the hell to Frisco. Look around and find somebody.

THE GIRL: I don't *want* to find anybody.

YOUNG MAN (*swiftly, desperately*): Listen, if I'm not here when you come back, how do you know I haven't gotten away? Now, do what I tell you. I'll meet you in Frisco. I've got a couple of dollars in my other shoe. I'll see you in San Francisco.

THE GIRL (*with wonder*): San Francisco?

YOUNG MAN: That's right—San Francisco. That's where you and me belong.

THE GIRL: I've always wanted to go to *some* place like San Francisco —but how could I go alone?

YOUNG MAN: Well, you're not alone any more, see?

THE GIRL: Tell me a little what it's like.

YOUNG MAN (*very swiftly, almost impatiently at first, but gradually slower and with remembrance, smiling, and* THE GIRL *moving closer to him as he speaks*): Well, it's on the Pacific to begin with—ocean water all around. Cool fog and seagulls. Ships from all over the world. It's got seven hills. The little streets go up and down, around and all over. Every night the fog-horns bawl. But they won't be bawling for you and me.

THE GIRL: What else?

YOUNG MAN: That's about all, I guess.

THE GIRL: Are people different in San Francisco?

YOUNG MAN: People are the same everywhere. They're different only when they love somebody. That's the only thing that makes 'em different. More people in Frisco love somebody, that's all.

THE GIRL: Nobody anywhere loves anybody as much as I love you.

YOUNG MAN (*shouting, as if to the world*): You see? Hearing you say that, a man could die and still be ahead of the game. Now, hurry. And don't forget, if I'm not here when you come back, get the hell to San Francisco where you'll have a chance. Do you hear me?

THE GIRL *stands a moment looking at him, then backs away, turns and runs. The* YOUNG MAN *stares after her, troubled and smiling. Then he turns away from the image of her and walks about like a lion in a cage. After a while he sits down suddenly and buries his head in his hands. From a distance the sound of several automobiles approaching is heard. He listens a moment, then ignores the implications of the sound, whatever they may be. Several automobile doors are slammed. He ignores this also. A wooden door is opened with a key and closed, and footsteps are heard in a hall. Walking easily, almost casually and yet arrogantly, a* MAN *comes in.*

YOUNG MAN (*jumps up suddenly and shouts at* THE MAN, *almost scaring him*): What the hell kind of a jailkeeper are you, anyway? Why don't you attend to your business? You get paid for it, don't you? Now, get me out of here.

THE MAN: But I'm not the jailkeeper.

YOUNG MAN: Yeah? Well, who are you, then?

THE MAN: I'm the husband.

YOUNG MAN: What husband you talking about?

THE MAN: You know what husband.

YOUNG MAN: Hey! (*Pause, looking at* THE MAN.) Are you the guy that hit me over the head last night?

THE MAN: I am.

YOUNG MAN (*with righteous indignation*): What do you mean going around hitting people over the head?

THE MAN: Oh, I don't know. What do you *mean* going around—the way you do?

YOUNG MAN (*rubbing his head*): You hurt my head. You got no right to hit anybody over the head.

THE MAN (*suddenly angry, shouting*): Answer my question! What do you mean?

YOUNG MAN: Listen, you—don't be hollering at me just because I'm locked up.

THE MAN (*with contempt, slowly*): You're a dog!

YOUNG MAN: Yeah, well, let me tell you something. You *think* you're the husband. You're the husband of nothing. (*Slowly.*) What's more, your wife—if you want to call her that—is a tramp. Why don't you throw her out in the street where she belongs?

THE MAN (*draws a pistol*): Shut up!

YOUNG MAN: Yeah? Go head, shoot—(*Softly.*) and spoil the fun. What'll your pals think? They'll be disappointed, won't they. What's the fun hanging a man who's already dead? (THE MAN *puts the gun away.*) That's right, because now you can have some fun yourself, telling me what you're going to do. That's what you came here for, isn't it? Well, you don't need to tell me. I *know* what you're going to do. I've read the papers and I know. They have fun. A mob of 'em fall on one man and beat him, don't they? They tear off his clothes and kick him, don't they? And women and little children stand around watching, don't they? Well, before you go on *this* picnic, I'm going to tell you a few things. Not that that's going to send you home with your pals—the other heroes. No. You've been outraged. A stranger has come to town and violated your women. Your pure, innocent, virtuous women. You fellows have got to set this thing right. You're men, not mice. You're home-makers, and you beat your children. (*Suddenly.*) Listen, you—I didn't know she was your wife. I didn't know she was anybody's wife.

THE MAN: You're a liar!

YOUNG MAN: Sometimes—when it'll do somebody some good—but not this time. Do you want to hear about it? (THE MAN *doesn't answer.*) All right, I'll tell you. I met her at a lunch counter. She came in and sat next to me. There was plenty of room, but she sat next to me. Somebody had put a nickel in the phonograph and a fellow was singing *New San Antonio Rose*. Well, she got to talking about the song. I thought she was talking to the waiter, but *he* didn't answer her, so after a while *I* answered her. That's how I met her. I didn't think anything of it. We left the place together and started walking. The first thing I knew she said, This is where I live.

THE MAN: You're a dirty liar!

YOUNG MAN: Do you want to hear it? Or not? (THE MAN *does not answer.*) O.K. She asked me to come in. Maybe she had something in mind, maybe she didn't. Didn't make any difference to me, one way or the other. If she was lonely, all right. If not, all right.

THE MAN: You're telling a lot of dirty lies!

YOUNG MAN: I'm telling the truth. Maybe your wife's out there with your pals. Well, call her in. I got nothing against her, or you—or any of you. Call her in, and ask her a few questions. Are you in love with her? (THE MAN *doesn't answer.*) Well, that's too bad.

THE MAN: What do you mean, too bad?

YOUNG MAN: I mean this may not be the first time something like this has happened.

THE MAN (*swiftly*): Shut up!

YOUNG MAN: Oh, you know it. You've always known it. You're afraid of your pals, that's all. She asked me for money. That's all she wanted. I wouldn't be here now if I had given her the money.

THE MAN (*slowly*): How much did she ask for?

YOUNG MAN: I didn't ask her how much. I told her I'd made a mistake. She said she would make trouble if I didn't give her money. Well, I don't like bargaining, and I don't like being threatened, either. I told her to get the hell away from me. The next thing I knew she'd run out of the house and was hollering. (*Pause.*) Now, why don't you go out there and tell 'em they took me to another jail—go home and pack up and leave her. You're a pretty good guy, you're just afraid of your pals.

THE MAN *draws his gun again. He is very frightened. He moves a step toward the* YOUNG MAN, *then fires three times. The* YOUNG MAN *falls to his knees.* THE MAN *turns and runs, horrified.*

YOUNG MAN: Hello—out there! (*He is bent forward.*)

THE GIRL *comes running in, and halts suddenly, looking at him.*

THE GIRL: There were some people in the street, men and women and kids—so I came in through the back, through a window. I couldn't find the gun. I looked all over but I couldn't find it. What's the matter?

YOUNG MAN: Nothing—nothing. Everything's all right. Listen. Listen, kid. Get the hell out of here. Go out the same way you came in and run—run like hell—run all night. Get to another town and get on a train. Do you hear me?

THE GIRL: What's happened?

YOUNG MAN: Get away—just get away from here. Take any train that's going—you can get to Frisco later.

THE GIRL (*almost sobbing*): I don't want to go any place without you.

YOUNG MAN: I can't go. Something's happened. (*He looks at her.*) But I'll be with you always—God damn it. Always!

He falls forward. THE GIRL *stands near him, then begins to sob softly, walking away. She stands over to one side, stops sobbing, and stares out. The excitement of the mob outside increases.* THE MAN, *with two of his pals, comes running in.* THE GIRL *watches, unseen.*

THE MAN: Here's the son of a bitch!

ANOTHER MAN: O.K. Open the cell, Harry.

The THIRD MAN *goes to the cell door, unlocks it, and swings it open. A* WOMAN *comes running in.*

THE WOMAN: Where is he? I want to see him. Is he dead? (*Looking down at him, as the* MEN *pick him up.*) There he is. (*Pause.*) Yeah, that's him.

Her husband looks at her with contempt, then at the dead man.

THE MAN (*trying to laugh*): All right—let's get it over with.

THIRD MAN: Right you are, George. Give me a hand, Harry.

They lift the body.

THE GIRL (*suddenly, fiercely*): Put him down!

THE MAN: What's this?

SECOND MAN: What are you doing here? Why aren't you out in the street?

THE GIRL: Put him down and go away.

She runs toward the MEN.

THE WOMAN *grabs her.*

THE WOMAN: Here—where do you think *you're* going?

THE GIRL: Let me go. You've no right to take him away.

THE WOMAN: Well, listen to her, will you? (*She slaps* THE GIRL *and pushes her to the floor.*) Listen to the little slut, will you?

They all go, carrying the YOUNG MAN'S *body.* THE GIRL *gets up slowly, no longer sobbing. She looks around at everything, then looks straight out, and whispers.*

THE GIRL: Hello—out—there! Hello—out there!

CURTAIN

26

DRAMATIC IMPACT

Establishing a *dramatic question,* building this into *conflict* between characters; the use of *irony* and *satire;* uses and misuses of *shock;* controlling the dramatic tension through *scene construction.*

The statement that drama should be dramatic sounds like a mere redundancy, but it is actually an important reminder for the playwright. From a purely practical point of view he should remember that he is asking an audience to sit in speechless, motionless attention for the length of an evening. And from a more positive, artistic point of view he should keep in mind that each genre has its own special assets. Plays, partly because of the physical presence of actors, are highly effective methods of arousing strong emotions.

There are five different approaches to creating dramatic impact, and even short plays like *Hello Out There* are apt to use all five. The first two, the dramatic question and conflict, are closely related. The second two, irony and shock, are similar to what I described in the fiction section under the general heading of *tension.* The final approach is the use of separate scenes to build a series of dramatic climaxes through the length of a play. Although the general subject of scene construction deserves a chapter by itself (Chapter 31), I shall deal with it here insofar as it is a playwright's primary method of sustaining his dramatic effect.

Establishing a
Dramatic Question
The dramatic question is the "hook" which holds the attention of the audience long before the theme or thesis becomes clear. It is the question unsophisticated theater-goers ask during the first intermission; it is the unuttered question in the minds of the others; it is the question which draws them all back to the second act; it is the source of such critical clichés as "exciting," "provocative," "compelling," and "suspenseful." It is the core of that which is dramatic.

Students of drama often ignore the dramatic question because it tends to be simple, direct, and beneath their artistic sensibilities. It is what children see in a play which thematically is beyond them. It is one of those base elements which serious drama holds in common with melodrama, the adventure story, the detective story, and pulp fiction. Yet for all this, it is an ingredient which playwrights from Sophocles to Ionesco and Albee have respected and used. It may be a "low" concern in the sense of being unrefined, but it is also "low" in that it is the very foundation of a dramatic performance.

Saroyan's *Hello Out There* is a good example. It begins with a man in jail. How did he get there? What did he do? Should we sympathize with him? These question occur at the very outset. Through the girl we begin to get answers to these, but at the same time a new cluster of dramatic questions is forming: Will she help him? And if she does, will they succeed? Toward the end of the play, we have a sense of foreboding: It is not likely that the ending will turn out to be happy. But as in all tragedies, we still concern ourselves with the survival of the protagonist. There is for most members of the audience a lingering hope that this man whose nickname is Photo-Finish will somehow talk his way out of what looks like impending death.

These concerns, of course, are not the theme. Saroyan's thematic concern is with the loneliness of individuals, comparing life in a small and hostile town with being in jail. The word *lonesome* is repeated as a motif just as the phrase, "hello out there" is, and they are applied not only to the two central characters but to the wife as well. I will return to this in the chapter on suggestion and statement, but it is important here to distinguish the dramatic questions from the themes of the play.

Obviously both are important. Without a theme, a play would be literally pointless. This is often true of musical reviews, but they are outside the scope of drama. On the other hand, a play which fails to develop one or more dramatic questions will probably be a bore no matter how sophisticated its other elements are. The first problem, lack of theme, is an artistic failure, while the second is a dramatic failure. One is as damaging as the other.

The dramatic question is present in almost all drama in the western tradition, regardless of the historical period. Take Sophocles' *Antigone*, for example. In this play a girl has taken it upon herself to bury her brother in spite of the fact that there has been a decree that the slain man must remain untouched. She has acted in defiance of the law with the conviction that her first duty is to a higher level of moral law. This poses two highly contemporary issues: whether the state has the right to demand absolute obedience and whether the individual citizen has a right or the duty to act on conscience even when this violates the law of the land. Discussions of this play quickly focus on these highly charged and relevant questions.

But the writer who wants to be more than a critic should take a close look at what actually happens in the first five minutes of playing time: A woman has knowingly committed a crime; will she get away with it? From the days when Greek audiences sat on stone amphitheater seats and watched drama cycles from sunrise to sundown, to the present, over a span of two thousand years, audiences have asked, "Will she get away with it?"

Looking at the full range of drama from Sophocles to our own decade, there are certain dramatic questions which recur frequently. This does not make the plays redundant; one hardly notices the similarity. But their widespread use does suggest just how important the dramatic question is.

1. *Will he come?* Shakespeare charged the first act of *Hamlet* with this question, applying it to the ghost. More recently, it has been broadened to cover the full length of plays. Odets's *Waiting for Lefty*, written in the 30s, Beckett's *Waiting for Godot* and Pinter's *The Dumb Waiter* all rely heavily on anticipation of a character who never appears. And to some degree, the question is a factor in *Hello Out There* as soon as the threat of a lynching is raised. The range of plays

here is enormous: Elizabethan, 1930s protest drama, theater of the absurd, and contemporary realism. Yet they share a dramatic question.

2. *Who did it?* This is, of course, the literary version of "Whodunit?" We find it running the full length of drama from *Oedipus Rex* to Williams's *Suddenly Last Summer.* The trial scenes in *The Caine Mutiny Trial* and, in a loose sense, *Tea and Sympathy* and *The Crucible* are simply variations of this. In many cases, of course, the audience knows who is guilty; the dramatic question arises out of the attempt on the part of the *characters* to determine guilt. It is a highly variable device, though the trial scene, when portrayed literally, has become overused.

3. *Will he succeed?* This is, cumulatively, the most used of all dramatic questions. It lent itself admirably to the classical tradition of great men performing great tasks, and it applies equally to characters whom we take to be largely noble (from Antigone to Halvard Solness in *The Master Builder*) and those who are evil (Macbeth, Richard III, and Caligula). It has been used less during the twentieth century, partly because of our increasing tendency to view the hero as victim of such forces as society, the economic system, and his own neuroses. Yet we do find it in Edward Albee's *Who's Afraid of Virginia Woolf?* in which a husband struggles to strip from his marriage the layers of deceit which he and his wife have allowed to develop. And in the absurdist tradition, Ionesco's *The Chairs* tells a dreamlike story of an old couple whose greatest ambition is to tell their "message" to the world.

4. *Will he discover what we know?* As we have seen, this is the dramatic core of *Oedipus Rex,* particularly toward the end. It is even clearer in *Othello,* where the truth is revealed to the audience almost from the start. It is easily adapted to our own concern for psychological self-discovery in such diverse plays as *Tea and Sympathy* and *Death of a Salesman.*

5. *Will a compromise be found?* Such a question appears to be lacking in dramatic voltage, but as I have already pointed out it is one of the more compelling questions in *Antigone.* It was repeated with almost wooden fidelity in Galsworthy's *Strife.* We see the same pattern much more subtly developed in Tennessee Williams's *Streetcar Named Desire* where the remains of the old order (Blanche) are pitted against the brutality of the new order (Stanley) ; or in less social

terms, excessive sensitivity is met with blunt insensitivity. It is worth noting that in all three of these examples the dramatic questions encroach on the theme itself—a far different relationship than is seen in the other four types.

6. *Will this end in violence?* This, together with the one which follows, is a highly contemporary concern. We know that there will be violence in a Greek or Elizabethan tragedy, and this assumption keeps it from being the central question. We make no such assumption in contemporary drama. As a result, playwrights such as Williams, Albee, Ionesco, and Saroyan have employed it as the initial and often central dramatic question. The threat of a lynching, for example, holds our attention in Williams's *Orpheus Descending* and Saroyan's *Hello Out There.* The ominous stranger is the initial chill in Albee's *Zoo Story* and Ionesco's *The Killer.*

7. *What's happening?* This is the question most frequently asked of plays in the absurdist tradition. Like dream fiction, these works plunge the audience into a confusing, often inexplicable environment. Playwrights like Pinter, Beckett, Ionesco, and occasionally Albee utilize ambiguity as a dramatic question.

This is, however, a risky device for the novice. Like free verse, it seems easy at first but often slides into meaninglessness. Frequently it requires wit or ingenuity of thematic suggestion to keep the play alive. In short, a dull play is not improved by making it an obscurely dull play.

Conflict

Between Characters   Drama uses every type of conflict— man against the group, against nature, against some aspect of himself. The form which is most generally used to create dramatic impact, however, is simple and direct: man against man.

In *Hello Out There,* for example, the initial suggestion of conflict seems to be between the protagonist and the girl. She is shy and naive, and he appears to be using her for his escape. When he tells her that she is "just about the prettiest kid in the whole world," we are not convinced that he means it. But soon we begin to have faith in him. Our respect for him is strongly supported by the brief monologue which he delivers when Emily first leaves. Since there is no one there to hear him, we must assume that these are his honest thoughts. It is at this point (if not before) that the lines of conflict shift so that they as a couple are pitted against the townspeople—the society at large.

But notice that even when the "enemy" is the whole town, Saroyan represents it in the form of one outraged husband. The climax of the play is reached with the protagonist facing his antagonist. Dramatists often reduce larger conflicts to single confrontations this way in order to increase the dramatic impact.

There are other, more subtle lines of conflict implied in that last scene as well. The outraged husband does not fully trust his wife (he is half-willing to listen to the truth); and in addition, he is being driven to act by his fear of the townspeople.

In Edward Albee's *The Sandbox,* which appears as the next chapter, the lines of conflict are less brutal and more complex. The situation—a kind of fantasy—involves a middle-aged couple and the wife's aging mother. The wife, Mommy, is so dominant over her husband, Daddy, that there is no open combat. But there is a highly subtle conflict between her and her mother, Grandma, the real protagonist of the play. On the one hand she is dominated the way the very old and the very young often are. But in return, she shows a beautiful defiance of spirit which ultimately triumphs—even in death. Albee manages to satirize the worst sort of husband-wife relationship in almost cartoon form while at the same time developing the tensions between parents and children in what is ultimately a serious treatment.

In full-length plays, the conflict between major characters is often echoed in the relationship between secondary characters as well. This is true even in comedies. The fact is that antagonism between characters creates dramatic voltage, and characters which are treated with bland indifference by the others are apt to be a drain rather than an addition to the production.

Irony
and Satire The term *dramatic irony* in its strict sense refers only to those actions or speeches which are unwittingly significant. As I pointed out in the fiction section (Chapter 20), it can be thought of as unconscious irony in that the characters are not aware of it. The most famous example is from *Oedipus Rex* when the messenger comes on stage saying "Good news!" The audience, familiar with the story, knows that the news is terrible. This is only one small sample. Actually the entire play becomes a study of dramatic irony. Since the audience knows that Oedipus is guilty of killing his father,

every act he takes to seek out the murderer and many of the lines he speaks become ironic. For example, when he points out that he is in danger because whoever the killer is might "turn a hand against me," the audience knows full well that he, as murderer, will eventually gouge out his own eyes.

Contemporary drama can use the same device whenever the playwright has based his work on a myth which is familiar to the audience. The other alternative is to use information which has already been revealed in the course of the play. This is what Saroyan does in the very last scene. We have already learned that the wife who brought the charges against Photo-Finish is in fact a slut. So there is a harsh bit of dramatic irony in her final lines:

Well, listen to her, will you?...Listen to the little slut, will you?

Verbal irony, which plays such an important part of determining the tone of fiction, is reflected on the stage mainly in the form of sarcasm. In Albee's *The Sandbox,* for example, Grandma meets a handsome, muscular young man from California. When she asks his name, he says he doesn't know. "Bright, too!" she says to the audience. It is through small touches of verbal irony like this that Albee is able to keep Grandma an enormously appealing character in spite of the strange, dreamlike quality of the play itself.

Cosmic irony or the irony of fate often plays a strong part in contemporary drama. Here, the course of events themselves is the reverse of the pattern one would expect. In *Hello Out There,* for example, the girl who is first seen as on "the outside" ends up in the final scene being in the jail, looking out, giving the same cry of "hello out there" that she had responded to at the beginning of the play.

In *The Sandbox,* there is an effective ironic jolt when one discovers that the young man who appeared to be the innocuous (and not too bright) male model turns out to be in fact the Angel of Death. There is a symbolic logic to this—death certainly does not appear to make decisions with any degree of intelligence and it is forever "flexing its muscles"—but there is still an ironic reversal in this character's identity.

Satire is a form of criticism, but it is a special form in which an exaggerated view of characters or institutions is presented in a comic way. *Hello Out There* is clearly critical of how men live in fear and suspicion and how they dispense "justice," but it is not satiric. Albee's play, on the other hand, uses satire to criticize specific types such as the dominant wife, the passive husband, and attitudes toward the aged, the dying, and the dead. It does this in spite of the fact that the core of the play involves a genuine, nonsatiric tribute to old women such as Grandma.

It is possible to make a play almost entirely satiric. If the target of the satire is clear, and if the treatment is fresh, such plays can be highly entertaining. But it is significant that pure satire is more frequently associated with reviews and skits than with full-length plays. This is partly due to the fact that it is hard to sustain satire (or any form of comedy) without some nonsatiric moments. In addition, pure satire tends to be a fairly simple form of drama. Playwrights often feel that comic criticism simply isn't enough. The blending of satire and serious suggestion such as is found in *The Sandbox* and longer plays like *Who's Afraid of Virginia Woolf?* is a sophisticated solution.

The Use of Shock

There has been a long tradition of violence on the stage. It was pushed to an extreme by the Roman playwright, Seneca, and some of Shakespeare's worst plays were heavily influenced by these works. In *Titus Andronicus,* for example, one poor character is not only raped five times but has both hands cut off and her tongue removed. Elizabethan productions were fairly realistic— even to the extent of using a small slice of raw liver to simulate the girl's severed tongue.

Our own century has seen a series of movements which have stressed various aspects of dramatic shock: Grand Guignol, the Dadaists, theater of cruelty, theater of shock, and the broader group known as theater of the absurd (described more fully in Chapter 29). All of these "new" developments have roots in former dramatic traditions which have risen and fallen in popularity over the course of more than 2,000 years. In most cases, the techniques of shock have taken the forms of physical violence, obscene language, nudity, and unusual visual effects.

Violence is perhaps the most common device. Although the Greeks kept it off stage, the Romans used it extensively, and we have come to associate it with the final act of any tragedy. Although *Hello Out There* is a short play, it follows this pattern closely. The protagonist is struck down in the final scene, and in the tradition of Elizabethan tragedies this is done on stage to provide dramatic impact.

There is a point, however, where physical violence no longer provides impact. Audiences have a "turn-off point," and once that is passed, what was intended as shock will result in laughter. It is not just the degree of violence or the frequency, it is also the kind of preparation which is provided. Violence which appears to be used for its own sake or to revive an otherwise banal play tends to reduce the work to the simplest level.

Profanity, obscenity, and nudity have been used as "new" devices periodically since the time of Aristophanes in 415 b.c.—and even he was working with an established tradition. The degree of shock value depends on what the audience is used to, and this may well be why these devices run in cycles. From the 1870s to the present we have seen drama pull itself out of the suffocating restrictions of Victorian restraint to almost total freedom. In the course of this struggle, a number of otherwise inconsequential plays have been lauded because they helped to win new liberties. The question which faces contemporary playwrights is not how to win the right to perform what one wants, but how to use the freedom already won.

One area which makes use of this new freedom and also shows great promise of variety and even subtlety is the use of unusual visual effects. This will be the subject of Chapter 32, but it should be noted here that the setting, lighting, choreography, and the variety of mixed media all can be employed to create the kind of shock which increases the dramatic impact of a play.

Controlling the Tension
Through Scene Construction
Dramatic impact is not a steady state; it is a surge of energy. If the playwright doesn't provide periodic relief, the audience will create it in the form of "turning off" —at the wrong moments.

Providing short comic scenes ("comic relief") and periods of low intensity (sometimes by soliloquies or pantomimes) are popular methods of lowering the dramatic tension in preparation for another surge of energy. But underlying these techniques is the concept of scene construction.

Building a play scene by scene is the subject of Chapter 31, but it is important to consider it here as a method of maintaining tension. Technically, a scene is any unit of action which is begun and ended by the entrance or exit of a character. This shift in who is on stage creates a psychological effect which may be as dramatic as the end of a chapter in fiction or as subtle as the end of a paragraph.

Think in terms of rising and falling action. The old formulas and diagrams with which students in past generations analyzed Elizabethan drama do not lend themselves to many contemporary plays, but it is almost always possible to describe subjectively a series of emotional peaks with which all but the simplest skits are composed. The playwright is in this sense like a long-distance runner who must plan his bursts of speed carefully, reserving the greatest thrust for the very end of the race.

Dramatic impact clearly involves a great variety of techniques. Providing a dramatic question is only a beginning. Conflict between characters is a development. Using irony and satire can help to keep a work taut, and the use of shock helps to hold the audience. The development of scenes can intensify any one of these techniques.

Obviously a play is not written by consciously juggling all these techniques. They are concerns which direct an experienced playwright quite unconsciously from the original inception through to those frenzied opening-night revisions. For the novice, the process is often a little more deliberate. It helps to judge an outline for a new play on the basis of whether it has the potential for dramatic impact. And it is important to analyze the completed first draft from this standpoint as well. Only in this way can a playwright be sure that his work will hold the attention of an audience.

27

A PLAY BY

EDWARD ALBEE

The Sandbox

*A Brief Play, in Memory of My
Grandmother (1876–1959)*

The Players:

THE YOUNG MAN .... 25.	A good-looking, well-built boy in a bathing suit.
MOMMY .... 55.	A well-dressed, imposing woman.
DADDY .... 60.	A small man; gray, thin.
GRANDMA .... 86.	A tiny, wizened woman with bright eyes.
THE MUSICIAN	No particular age, but young would be nice.

*Note: When, in the course of the play, MOMMY and DADDY call each
other by these names, there should be no suggestion of regionalism.
These names are of empty affection and point up the pre-senility
and vacuity of their characters.*

The Scene: A bare stage, with only the following: Near the foot-lights, far stage-right, two simple chairs set side by side, facing the audience; near the footlights, far stage-left, a chair facing stage-right with a music stand before it; farther back, and stage-center, slightly elevated and raked, a large child's sandbox with a toy pail and shovel; the background is the sky, which alters from brightest day to deepest night.

At the beginning, it is brightest day; the YOUNG MAN *is alone on stage, to the rear of the sandbox, and to one side. He is doing calisthenics; he does calisthenics until quite at the very end of the play. These calisthenics, employing the arms only, should suggest the beating and fluttering of wings. The* YOUNG MAN *is, after all, the Angel of Death.*

MOMMY *and* DADDY *enter from stage-left,* MOMMY *first.*

MOMMY: (*Motioning to* DADDY) Well, here we are; this is the beach.

DADDY: (*Whining*) I'm cold.

MOMMY: (*Dismissing him with a little laugh*) Don't be silly; it's as warm as toast. Look at that nice young man over there: *he* doesn't think it's cold. (*Waves to the* YOUNG MAN) Hello.

YOUNG MAN: (*With an endearing smile*) Hi!

MOMMY: (*Looking about*) This will do perfectly...don't you think so, Daddy? There's sand there...and the water beyond. What do you think, Daddy?

DADDY: (*Vaguely*) Whatever you say, Mommy.

MOMMY: (*With the same little laugh*) Well, of course...whatever I say. Then, it's settled, is it?

DADDY: (*Shrugs*) She's *your* mother, not mine.

MOMMY: *I* know she's my mother. What do you take me for? (*A pause*) All right, now; let's get on with it. (*She shouts into the wings, stage-left*) You! Out there! You can come in now.

(*The* MUSICIAN *enters, seats himself in the chair, stage-left, places music on the music stand, is ready to play.* MOMMY *nods approvingly*)

MOMMY: Very nice; very nice. Are you ready, Daddy? Let's go get Grandma.

DADDY: Whatever you say, Mommy.

MOMMY: (*Leading the way out, stage-left*) Of course, whatever I say. (*To the* MUSICIAN) You can begin now.

(*The* MUSICIAN *begins playing;* MOMMY *and* DADDY *exit; the* MUSICIAN, *all the while playing, nods to the* YOUNG MAN)

YOUNG MAN: (*With the same endearing smile*) Hi!

(*After a moment,* MOMMY *and* DADDY *re-enter, carrying* GRANDMA. *She is borne in by their hands under her armpits; she is quite rigid; her legs are drawn up; her feet do not touch the ground; the expression on her ancient face is that of puzzlement and fear*)

DADDY: Where do we put her?

MOMMY: (*The same little laugh*) Wherever I say, of course. Let me see...well...all right, over there...in the sandbox. (*Pause*) Well, what are you waiting for, Daddy?... The sandbox!

(*Together they carry* GRANDMA *over to the sandbox and more or less dump her in*)

GRANDMA: (*Righting herself to a sitting position; her voice a cross between a baby's laugh and cry*) Ahhhhhh! Graaaaa!

DADDY: (*Dusting himself*) What do we do now?

MOMMY: (*To the* MUSICIAN) You can stop now.

(*The* MUSICIAN *stops*)

(*Back to* DADDY) What do you mean, what do we do now? We go over there and sit down, of course. (*To the* YOUNG MAN) Hello there.

YOUNG MAN: (*Again smiling*) Hi!

(MOMMY *and* DADDY *move to the chairs, stage-right, and sit down. A pause*)

GRANDMA: (*Same as before*) Ahhhhhh! Ah-aaaaaa! Graaaaaa!

DADDY: Do you think...do you think she's...comfortable?

MOMMY: (*Impatiently*) How would I know?

DADDY: (*Pause*) What do we do now?

MOMMY: (*As if remembering*) We...wait. We...sit here...and we wait...that's what we do.

DADDY: (*After a pause*) Shall we talk to each other?

MOMMY: (*With that little laugh; picking something off her dress*) Well, *you* can talk, if you want to...if you can think of anything to *say*... if you can think of anything *new*.

DADDY: (*Thinks*) No...suppose not.

MOMMY: (*With a triumphant laugh*) Of course not!

GRANDMA: (*Banging the toy shovel against the pail*) Haaaaaa! Ah-haaaaaa!

MOMMY: (*Out over the audience*) Be quiet, Grandma...just be quiet, and wait.

(GRANDMA *throws a shovelful of sand at* MOMMY)

MOMMY: (*Still out over the audience*) She's throwing sand at me! You stop that, Grandma; you stop throwing sand at Mommy! (*To* DADDY) She's throwing sand at me.

(DADDY *looks around at* GRANDMA, *who screams at him*)

GRANDMA: GRAAAAA!

MOMMY: Don't look at her. Just...sit here...be very still...and wait. (*To the* MUSICIAN) You...uh...you go ahead and do whatever it is you do.

(*The* MUSICIAN *plays*)
(MOMMY *and* DADDY *are fixed, staring out beyond the audience.* GRANDMA *looks at them, looks at the* MUSICIAN, *looks at the sandbox, throws down the shovel*)

GRANDMA: Ah-haaaaaa! Graaaaaa! (*Looks for reaction; gets none. Now...directly to the audience*) Honestly! What a way to treat an old woman! Drag her out of the house...stick her in a car... bring her out here from the city...dump her in a pile of sand ...and leave her here to set. I'm eighty-six years old! I was married when I was seventeen. To a farmer. He died when I was thirty. (*To the* MUSICIAN) Will you stop that, please?
(*The* MUSICIAN *stops playing*)

I'm a feeble old woman...how do you expect anybody to hear me over that peep! peep! peep! (*To herself*) There's no respect around here. (*To the* YOUNG MAN) There's no respect around here!

YOUNG MAN: (*Same smile*) Hi!

GRANDMA: (*After a pause, a mild double-take, continues, to the audience*) My husband died when I was thirty (*indicates* MOMMY), and I had to raise that big cow over there all by my lonesome. You can imagine what *that was like*. Lordy! (*To the* YOUNG MAN) Where'd they get *you?*

YOUNG MAN: Oh...I've been around for a while.

GRANDMA: I'll bet you have! Heh, heh, heh. Will you look at you!

YOUNG MAN: (*Flexing his muscles*) Isn't that something? (*Continues his calisthenics*)

GRANDMA: Boy, oh boy; I'll say. Pretty good.

YOUNG MAN: (*Sweetly*) I'll say.

GRANDMA: Where ya from?

YOUNG MAN: Southern California.

GRANDMA: (*Nodding*) Figgers; figgers. What's your name, honey?

YOUNG MAN: I don't know. . . .

GRANDMA: (*To the audience*) Bright, too!

YOUNG MAN: I mean...I mean, they haven't given me one yet...the studio...

GRANDMA: (*Giving him the once-over*) You don't say...you don't say. Well...uh, I've got to talk some more...don't you go 'way.

YOUNG MAN: Oh, no.

GRANDMA: (*Turning her attention back to the audience*) Fine; fine. (*Then, once more, back to the* YOUNG MAN) You're...you're an actor, hunh?

YOUNG MAN: (*Beaming*) Yes. I am.

GRANDMA: (*To the audience again; shrugs*) I'm smart that way. *Anyhow,* I had to raise...*that* over there all by my lonesome; and what's next to her there...that's what she married. Rich? I tell you...money, money, money. They took me off the *farm*...which was real decent of them...and they moved me into the big town house with *them*...fixed a nice place for me under the stove... gave me an army blanket...and my own dish...my very own dish! So, what have I got to complain about? Nothing, of course. I'm not complaining. (*She looks up at the sky, shouts to someone off stage*) Shouldn't it be getting dark now, dear?

(*The lights dim; night comes on. The* MUSICIAN *begins to play; it becomes deepest night. There are spots on all the players, including the* YOUNG MAN, *who is, of course, continuing his calisthenics*)

DADDY: (*Stirring*) It's nighttime.

MOMMY: Shhhh. Be still...wait.

DADDY: (*Whining*) It's so hot.

MOMMY: Shhhhhh. Be still...wait.

GRANDMA: (*To herself*) That's better. Night. (*To the* MUSICIAN)
Honey, do you play all through this part?
(*The* MUSICIAN *nods*)
Well, keep it nice and soft; that's a good boy.
(*The* MUSICIAN *nods again; plays softly*)
That's nice.
(*There is an off-stage rumble*)

DADDY: (*Starting*) What was that?

MOMMY: (*Beginning to weep*) It was nothing.

DADDY: It was...it was...thunder...or a wave breaking...or something.

MOMMY: (*Whispering, through her tears*) It was an off-stage rumble
...and you know what *that* means....

DADDY: I forget....

MOMMY: (*Barely able to talk*) It means the time has come for poor
Grandma...and I can't bear it!

DADDY: (*Vacantly*) I...I suppose you've got to be brave.

GRANDMA: (*Mocking*) That's right, kid; be brave. You'll bear up;
you'll get over it.

(*Another off-stage rumble...louder*)

MOMMY: Ohhhhhhhhhh...poor Grandma...poor Grandma....

GRANDMA: (*To* MOMMY) I'm fine! I'm all right! It hasn't happened
yet!
(*A violent off-stage rumble. All the lights go out, save the spot on
the* YOUNG MAN; *the* MUSICIAN *stops playing*)

MOMMY: Ohhhhhhhhhh....Ohhhhhhhhhh....

(*Silence*)

GRANDMA: Don't put the lights up yet...I'm not ready; I'm not quite
ready. (*Silence*) All right, dear...I'm about done.
(*The lights come up again, to brightest day; the* MUSICIAN *begins
to play.* GRANDMA *is discovered, still in the sandbox, lying on her*

side, propped up on an elbow, half covered, busily shoveling sand over herself)

GRANDMA: *(Muttering)* I don't know how I'm supposed to do anything with this goddam toy shovel. . . .

DADDY: Mommy! It's daylight!

MOMMY: *(Brightly)* So it is! Well! Our long night is over. We must put away our tears, take off our mourning. . .and face the future. It's our duty.

GRANDMA: *(Still shoveling; mimicking)* . . .take off our mourning. . . face the future. . . . Lordy!

(MOMMY *and* DADDY *rise, stretch.* MOMMY *waves to the* YOUNG MAN)

YOUNG MAN: *(With that smile)* Hi!

(GRANDMA *plays dead.* (!) MOMMY *and* DADDY *go over to look at her; she is a little more than half buried in the sand; the toy shovel is in her hands, which are crossed on her breast)*

MOMMY: *(Before the sandbox; shaking her head)* Lovely! It's. . .it's hard to be sad. . .she looks. . .so happy. *(With pride and conviction)* It pays to do things well. *(To the* MUSICIAN*)* All right, you can stop now, if you want to. I mean, stay around for a swim, or something; it's all right with us. *(She sighs heavily)* Well, Daddy . . .off we go.

DADDY: Brave Mommy!

MOMMY: Brave Daddy!

(They exit, stage-left)

GRANDMA: *(After they leave; lying quite still)* It pays to do things well. . . . Boy, oh boy! *(She tries to sit up)* . . .well, kids. . .*(but she finds she can't)* . . .I. . .I can't get up. I. . .I can't move. . . .

(The YOUNG MAN *stops his calisthenics, nods to the* MUSICIAN, *walks over to* GRANDMA, *kneels down by the sandbox)*

GRANDMA: I. . .can't move. . . .

YOUNG MAN: Shhhhh. . .be very still. . . .

GRANDMA: I. . .I can't move. . . .

YOUNG MAN: Uh. . .ma'am; I. . .I have a line here.

GRANDMA: Oh, I'm sorry, sweetie; you go right ahead.

YOUNG MAN: I am...uh...

GRANDMA: Take your time, dear.

YOUNG MAN: (*Prepares, delivers the line like a real amateur*) I am the Angel of Death. I am...uh...I am come for you.

GRANDMA: What...wha...(*Then, with resignation*)...ohhhh... ohhhh, I see.

(*The* YOUNG MAN *bends over, kisses* GRANDMA *gently on the forehead*)

GRANDMA: (*Her eyes closed, her hands folded on her breast again, the shovel between her hands, a sweet smile on her face*) Well... that was very nice, dear....

YOUNG MAN: (*Still kneeling*) Shhhhhh...be still....

GRANDMA: What I meant was... you did that very well, dear....

YOUNG MAN: (*Blushing*)...oh...

GRANDMA: No; I mean it. You've got that...you've got a quality.

YOUNG MAN: (*With his endearing smile*) Oh...thank you; thank you very much...ma'am.

GRANDMA: (*Slowly; softly—as the* YOUNG MAN *puts his hands on top of* GRANDMA'S) You're...you're welcome...dear.

(*Tableau. The* MUSICIAN *continues to play as the curtain slowly comes down*)

CURTAIN

28

SUGGESTION AND
STATEMENT

Thematic plays contrasted with *thesis plays;* thematic
suggestion seen in *Hello Out There;* symbolic characters in *The Sandbox;* building on a *thematic core;*
themes of *black identity; direct statement* seen in types
of thetic drama.

Most plays make suggestions, not pronouncements. That
is, they imply more than they state directly. Like fiction, they explore
a general area of concern, working through an as-if-real experience
rather than presenting ideas directly through exposition. The playwright is, of course, concerned with creating a dramatic impact, but
he usually does not give dogmatic or even precise answers to the
questions he raises. *Hamlet,* after all, doesn't tell you how to deal
with stepfathers nor does *The Sandbox* preach about love for one's
parents.

There is, on the other hand, a significant minority of plays which
do in fact make unequivocal statements. At present, such plays are
being used to present racial issues and political causes. They are often

found in black theater and almost always in guerrilla theater—two movements which I will come to later in this chapter.

Plays which raise questions and explore a general theme by implication and suggestion—as do the two in this volume—are said to be *thematic*. Those which present one side of an issue and are primarily intended to persuade through direct statement are *thesis plays* and referred to as *thetic*. Although the demarcation between the two is not always precise, they do represent two distinct attitudes toward the genre, each with its own assets and problems. It is helpful to examine them separately.

Thematic Suggestion in "Hello Out There"

We have examined this play for its dramatic impact. If it had nothing more to offer than that, it would be a melodrama. The terror of an individual facing a lynch mob has been repeated endlessly in television dramas. What elevates the play above the level of a simple thriller is its development of thematic suggestion.

Even a rapid reading of the play suggests that the theme deals with the loneliness of individuals and the need to reach out in friendship or love. The protagonist is held in jail and the girl is trapped in a small town which seems to be no better than a jail. It appears that they might escape together; but in the end his luck runs out and so, apparently, has hers.

Perhaps that is all the casual reader will ever know about the play. But a writer has to examine the technique more closely. Saroyan has used three devices in this play which dramatize his thematic concerns to the point where they are unmistakable: repetition of certain key words throughout the length of the play like refrains, reiteration of the same words in "runs" or clusters, and the use of symbolic names.

The most pronounced use of the refrain is "hello out there." No one could miss the fact that this key phrase is used in the title, at the opening, and again at the closing of the play. More significant, however, is the fact that it is repeated a total of twenty-five times!

This is no accident. If you check the first twelve uses (all of which occur before the girl appears on stage), you will see how Saroyan has established the refrain early with a "run" or cluster of three and then spaced them increasingly farther apart. After the girl appears, they occur only occasionally. The next "run" occurs when the man is left alone in the cell again. He repeats it five times in the course of one short monologue. Once again the phrase is used sparingly until the very end when the girl, trapped and alone, repeats it twice as the curtain descends.

A second series is made up of the two words "scared" and "afraid." They are used interchangeably. They are repeated sixteen times and are used to apply not only to the young couple but to the men in the town and to the husband who eventually kills Photo-Finish. Notice the redundancy in the following "run":

> THE GIRL: ...They were talking of taking you to another jail in another town.
> YOUNG MAN: Yeah? Why?
> THE GIRL: Because they're afraid.
> YOUNG MAN: What are they afraid of?
> THE GIRL: They're afraid these people from Wheeling will come over in the middle of the night and break in.
> YOUNG MAN: Yeah? What do they want to do that for?
> THE GIRL: Don't *you* know what they want to do it for?
> YOUNG MAN: Yeah, I know all right.
> THE GIRL: Are you scared?
> YOUNG MAN: Sure I'm scared. Nothing scares a man more than ignorance.

First he uses "afraid" in a string of three successive lines, and then he uses "scared" three times in an almost poetic sequence.

There are two other refrains in this play which, though they are not as pronounced, still serve to dramatize the thematic concerns. One is "lonesome." It is used a total of twelve times, six of which occur in a "run" just before and just after the girl appears for the first time. Finally, there is "luck" which turns up ten times, six of which are in a cluster in about as many consecutive lines.

These, then, are five phrases or words which are repeated throughout the play and also bunched in clusters: "hello out there," "scared/ afraid," "lonesome," and "luck." They also lie at the heart of what the playwright is working with: the loneliness and fear that we all experience, the reaching out, and the element of luck with which we must always deal.

But how does he get away with so much redundancy? He has, after all, violated a basic "rule" which is still generally honored in the writing of exposition. This shows how far the technique of playwriting is from the essay. He is also using a device which is rarely found in fiction. There are, though, a few examples such as the

refrain of "Pass the bottle" which is repeated by the narrator through
the course of Conrad's "Youth" and a longer refrain which Stephen
Crane uses in "The Open Boat." These are rare samples.

Saroyan's approach here is actually far closer to that of free verse.
The use of repeated words and phrases either scattered or in clusters
is, as I pointed out in Chapter 5, one of the characteristics found
in the Bible, in the works of Walt Whitman and more recently in
Allen Ginsberg's poetry.

A second device found in *Hello Out There* is the rather direct use
of symbolic names. The town where the protagonist is about to meet
his death is called "Matador." And the town from which the free-
wheeling, irresponsible men come is "Wheeling." Saroyan makes sure
that the audience does not miss these names by repeating each one
twice—a recognition of the fact that drama is a "continuous art form"
which does not permit any hesitation.

He puts the same care into the young man's nickname, "Photo-
Finish." Through the character's own dialogue we learn exactly what
it means and how it is linked with the central theme of luck.

More subtle than the name is the symbolic action. The play begins
with an isolated, frightened individual crying out for contact with
someone—anyone. It turns out that this same longing for companion-
ship was what got him into this spot in the first place. Ironically, it is
fear rather than rage which leads the husband to commit murder.
And in the end, the girl has taken the role of the isolated, frightened
individual crying out for contact with someone—anyone.

When one looks closely at these devices of repetition and symbolic
details, they appear extraordinarily blatant. This is often true of
drama. Remember that what one is analyzing here line by line is the
written version of a performance which will slide through the consciousness of an audience in about twenty-eight uninterrupted minutes.
For this reason, playwrights often repeat key phrases; and when they
develop a symbol, they return to it at least once and often frequently.
Drama, more than any other genre, thrives on reiteration.

Symbolic Characters
in "The Sandbox"
Edward Albee's approach to drama
is closer to what was described earlier as dream fiction. We don't
literally dump grandmothers in sandboxes nor do musicians appear
from nowhere nor do muscular young men turn out to be in fact

angels of death—except in dreams. Technically, this is a form of expressionism, an approach I will explore in the next chapter. The point here is that the dreamlike quality lends itself to symbolic suggestion and that it is through symbol that we draw meaning from the play.

On the simplest level, Daddy represents the passive American male who is forever being satirized in drama, fiction, and even the comics. He is not a fully drawn character; he is a cartoon. His first line, however, is more suggestive than are most cartoons. "I'm cold," he says, and in that complaint is both the little boy aspect of him which is sustained throughout the play as well as a symbolic suggestion of the sterile adult, spiritually and sexually "cold." The line by itself does not carry those implications, but in the context of the material which follows, it takes on more special significance—just as the opening line of *Hello Out There* did.

Notice also the use of repetition in his lines, "What do we do now?" In a more realistic play, such lines might not take on much significance. But here they seem to question their whole reason for existing.

Mommy is also more of a symbol than a fully drawn character. Our first impression of her is simply as another cartoon—this one as the dominant wife. But a complication begins to arise after Daddy asks for the second time what they should do. She says:

> We...wait. We...sit here...and we wait...that's what we do.

For what? Because the play is detached in time and place, a phrase like "we wait" takes on broader implication. Recalling plays like *Waiting for Godot,* we wonder if Mommy and Daddy aren't waiting for death.

As it turns out, they are waiting for Grandma's death. Since even the most callous individuals don't dump old parents on the sand and wait patiently for them to die, the act of waiting itself becomes suggestive of what some grown children do over a period of years. In this way, not only the characters but their action becomes symbolic.

In a broader sense, they are also waiting for their own deaths. "Shall we talk to each other?" Daddy asks, and Mommy says he can *if* he "can think of anything to *say*...anything *new*." Of course Daddy can't. They must wait out their lives without touching each other in any meaningful way.

Grandma is the most fully drawn character. We get to know her background on the farm and how she raised her daughter alone and finally had to move in with her daughter and her wealthy husband. Grandma has some of the childlike characteristics and crotchety attitudes one often associates with older people ("There's no respect around here."). But she also has a kind of rural-bred honesty and a dignity and strength with which she faces death. By contrast, she makes her daughter and son-in-law look shallow and hypocritical.

There are, however, two partially comic suggestions which go beyond realistic suggestion. The first occurs in her description of how she was taken in by her daughter and son-in-law:

> They took me off the *farm*...and moved me into the big town house with *them*...fixed a nice place for me under the stove...gave me an army blanket...and my own dish...my very own dish!

Grandma here is reduced to the level of a cat. She is only one step removed from the parents in Beckett's play, *End Game,* who reside permanently in two ashcans.

The other symbolic suggestion is parallel but pushed further. The sandbox itself makes Grandma childish, and her use of it—throwing sand and banging the toy shovel against the pail—makes us think of her even more clearly and literally as a child. We all recognize the fact that senility is in some ways like being very young, but what Albee has done is to suggest this symbolically. And by extension, what the play suggests about the way some adults treat their parents can also be applied to the way they treat their children as well.

The character who is the most clearly symbolic in this highly suggestive play is the Young Man. He is described by the playwright in the description of the scene as the Angel of Death. He is not *like* an angel, he *is* the Angel of Death. Were he the only nonmimetic element in the play, he would be a "premise" in much the same way the black angel is in Bernard Malamud's story "Angel Levine." But Albee has used many dreamlike elements.

Albee makes a number of oblique suggestions about the nature of death through this extraordinary character. In the opening scene he says "Hi!" to Mommy and Daddy twice, but they see nothing ominous about him. They are not yet close to death. He is muscular; death is powerful. His name is still uncertain; we tend to use euphemisms. He has "been around for a while"; from the beginning. He is an actor;

death comes in many guises. And in the end, he gives comfort, as death itself might do for the very old. Most subtle of all, however, is the way Grandma is elevated in stature in that final scene through her treatment of Death. He is not viewed as an enemy to be outsmarted (as in Donne's poem, "Death Be Not Proud") or as an ominous killer (as in Ionesco's *The Killer*), but as an actor who has a line to speak. Grandma, who has passed through an understandable moment of panic, is at the end able to treat Death (and by implication, *death*) with courtesy and with dignity. It is he who says "thank you" and her last line is "you're welcome...dear."

Building on
a Thematic Core
The idea for a new play often comes in the form of an incident or a dramatic situation—a gambler's final bid for freedom, a neglected old woman facing death, and the like. But from there on, the playwright must concentrate on unfolding the theme, first one way and then another.

We have seen how Saroyan used both refrains and symbolic detail to weave together the themes of loneliness, fear, and luck. Albee also uses repetition (the Angel of Death repeatedly greets the living with "Hi!" and an "endearing smile") but he makes much greater use of highly symbolic material. Because both these plays are short, the techniques are easily identified. It is important, however, to study the great variety of thematic suggestion in longer plays as well.

Where should a playwright look? Fortunately for him, drama is an older genre than fiction and some of our earliest samples—Greek tragedies—have astonishingly contemporary themes. Oedipus, for example, is determined to find the truth and this search destroys him. The theme is unfolded through a kind of detective story—except that the hero is unwittingly the criminal he seeks. Behind the theme of self-discovery (which in a contemporary setting we might place in a psychiatrist's office) there is the study of a man throwing himself against the absolute authority of the fates (which today we often see as the social or economic system).

Antigone is frequently thought of as a thesis-play, arguing for the rights of the individual over the state. Antigone insists on burying her brother in spite of the edict against this symbolic act. The question is raised whether she should act on conscience or obey the law of the land. We tend to side with Antigone, but such a reading misses the full complexity of the theme. One shouldn't ignore the fact that Creon, the king, is presented as the reasonable spokesman for civil law, and he defends the state as the only alternative to anarchy and chaos. He is seen, at the beginning of the play, as a reasonable man defending the law on rational grounds. What develops is not wrong pitted against right, but the rigid interpretation of governmental law pitted against an equally rigid interpretation of a higher law. Sophocles' tragedy is not about the individual's death at the hands of the fascist, but the destruction of both individualist and legalist when they find themselves unwilling to compromise.

There is some evidence for the argument that Sophocles admired Antigone more than Creon. But we are not justified in treating the play as an early version of Thoreau's "Civil Disobedience." Sophocles makes it quite clear that a nation of Antigones would be no nation at all; it would be chaos. Nor does the play propose the thesis that compromise is the "best" behavior for man. The vehicle of compromise, Ismene, is not presented as the heroine or even as a highly admirable character. In short, there is no thesis. But the themes are strong: the necessity for the state and for individual conscience and the agony when the two conflict.

Some students carry with them a smoldering hatred of Shakespeare because of their first exposure to him as someone to be revered. It helps to recognize that some of his early plays were extraordinarily bad. He too had to learn. With this in mind, one can then go back over the major tragedies not with blind reverence but with an analytical eye, tracing just how he developed his thematic suggestions. The patterns of suspicion and mistrust in *Othello,* for example; in *Hamlet,* the agony of indecision played against surprising decisiveness; the unfolding of guilt in *Macbeth*—in all of these are extraordinarily intricate developments of theme. The length of these plays allows greater latitude in technique, but the basic devices of reiteration of words, phrases, and images and the development of symbolic suggestion are found in each.

Contemporary themes are closer to those of both the Elizabethan and classical periods than they are to the nineteenth century. Concern about the class structure which preoccupied Pinero and Galsworthy have been replaced with questions about self-deception (Albee's *Who's Afraid of Virginia Woolf?* and Ionesco's *The Chairs* approach this in entirely different ways), addiction to drink, drugs, or homosexuality (from the hard impact of *The Connection* to the gentler treatment of

Boys in the Band), the threat of death (contrast *The Sandbox* with Ionesco's *The Killer* and *Exit The King*) and the huge, compelling array of themes involving black America which I will return to later in this chapter.

There are two basic "rules" in the selection of thematic material for a play, one negative and the other positive. First, watch out for thematic clichés. Moralistic plays exposing prejudice through stock characters and situations, for example, do little either for race relations or for the future of drama. Even more common among one-act plays of late is the bomb shelter situation. The characters in these plays are trapped in a room, or at the bottom of a mine shaft or in a rocket heading for some distant point and they usually discover that their lives have been meaningless, empty, and without value. Too often, the plays are also. The extraordinary persistence of this basic situation (sometimes two or three in a writing class) makes it almost impossible to be fresh.

The other "rule" is simply the opposite side of the same coin: If possible, deal with a theme which is personally important. This is the best way to avoid being swept up by what amounts to thematic fads. Even if the presentation is expressionistic as it is in *The Sandbox,* the theme will be more convincing and will have more resonance if it is a topic which is both meaningful and familiar to the playwright.

Themes of
Black Identity

Black theater is one of the strongest contemporary movements. Black awareness and black identity lend themselves to all genres, but most explosively to drama.

The development of black theater is surprisingly recent. With a few rare exceptions, theater was a white art form until well into the 1960s. Black playwrights like Langston Hughes, Ossie Davis, and Lorraine Hansberry are known to most for one successful play each, but few white theatergoers can name the others they wrote. Langston Hughes alone turned out more than twenty plays. As a result, black playwrights as well as black directors and actors have been deprived of audiences and of the training which comes from regular production. This backlog of artistic frustration amplifies a deep sense of social injustice, to produce themes of bitter denunciation.

The harshest of these are written consciously and directly to a white audience. Plays like LeRoi Jones's *The Toilet* are intentionally designed to shock white, middle-class theatergoers. Rather than themes, these plays present theses—an approach I will examine in more detail shortly.

Paul Carter Harrison's *Tabernacle* is another fine example. The play, described in his subtitle as "A Black Experience in Total Theater," is a conglomerate of, in his words, "role playing, dance movement, choral chants, animism of masks, pregnancy of light and silence—integrated in such a manner as to create concrete images of a unique quality of Black expression."

The plot is based on a trial which took place after the Harlem riots of 1964. For all the varied techniques used in this play, it too is aimed primarily at a white audience. This is clear from the start when a preacher addresses the audience directly telling them that they are about to "witness all the infernal ashes of Cain poured down on our souls." And at the end of this extraordinarily powerful and biting play this same preacher lambastes the audience for sitting in stunned silence. By convention, theatergoers withhold their applause until after the action of the play is over; Harrison has utilized this convention as what he describes as a "pregnant silence," turning it into a metaphor for the political inaction on the part of whites and many middle-class Negroes. Like LeRoi Jones, Harrison deals with strong arguments, and he thrusts them directly at a particular audience.

Conscious appeal to a white audience is also found in plays which are thematic and less accusatory. In Charles Gordone's *No Place to Be Somebody,* for example, the plot of the play is stopped twice for lengthy monologues which are delivered like prose poems from the center of the stage. One of these is formally titled "There's More to Being Black than Meets the Eye." The other is a verse narrative of what it is like for a Negro to try living like white suburbanites, suffering the scorn of both urban blacks and white neighbors.

Other plays address themselves more specifically to black audiences. The seven plays selected originally by the Free Southern Theater group for their pilot program are good examples: *Purlie Victorious* by Ossie Davis, *Do You Want to Be Free?* by Langston Hughes, *Lower Than the Angels* by John O. Killens, *Day of Absence* and *Happy Ending* by Douglas Turner, *Great Gettin' Up Morning* by Ann Flagg, and a modern adaptation of *Antigone.* To this list should be added Martin Duberman's *In White America* which was actually their first production.

To some degree, of course, any good play speaks to all types of audiences. But one particular function of these plays is seen in the goals of the Free Southern Theater. Starting in 1964, the FST has put on plays throughout Mississippi and also in the four neighboring southern states. Some of their audiences were in southern black colleges and some in cities; but a great number were in rural counties where few if any residents had ever seen a play. One of the conscious aims of the FST players has been to define and develop the sense of black identity.

Group identity is not a new function of drama. Shakespeare was concerned with a new national consciousness when he wrote his history plays. The Irish Renaissance of the late nineteenth century was a dramatic attempt in both senses to define and unify Irish identity. And to some degree the proletarian drama of the 1930s worked for class awareness and solidarity.

But none of these is a true parallel to what is happening in black theater today. One way to understand the vitality of this movement is to read *The Free Southern Theater by the Free Southern Theater*—a collection of letters, journal entries, poetry, and drama collected by Thomas C. Dent and others. Some of the plays they put on are included in *New Black Playwrights* (William Couch, Jr., ed.). I mention these volumes here because they represent a significant aspect of what is going on in drama today.

Only a few plays in the black theater movement are unmistakably written for white audiences. A larger proportion are concerned with black awareness and black identity. But perhaps a majority of plays deal with themes which are significant to all audiences. They tend to be thematic rather than thetic.

Goin'a Buffalo by Ed Bullins and *Ceremonies in Dark Old Men* by Lonne Elder III, are two excellent examples. Both involve the problems of black identity, economic survival, and moral corruption in urban life. Both are unmistakably about aspects of the black experience. But neither proposes solutions. They do not present theses; instead, they develop a tragic view of man caught in a highly destructive society.

Direct

Dramatic Statement Except for the works of Jones and Harrison, I have been dealing with plays of suggestion, not statement. Their themes are matters of concern to be examined and reexamined.

Thesis plays, on the other hand, deliver their messages much more directly—often as statement.

Historically, thetic drama has taken two somewhat separate routes, satire and morality plays. Although this text is not intended as a historical review, it is important to trace these roots at least briefly. It is no accident that Harrison's *Tabernacle* is dominated by a satiric character in Judge Tawkin and a serious preacher in Rev. And it is all too easy to shrug off the less sophisticated plays of guerrilla theater if one does not see them in the context of a 3,000-year old tradition.

Most satire is at the heart a moral statement, and Greek satire of the fourth century B.C. was no exception. Aristophanes' *Lysistrata*, for example, although rejected by most secondary schools and some libraries as obscene, is rooted in three highly moral propositions. First, it suggests that war is absurd and can do nothing but make men ridiculous. Second, it quite blatantly suggests that both men and women become grotesque when they give in to sexual passions. And finally it attacks the egotism of both males and females who believe that they can manage perfectly well without the opposite sex. In purely ethical terms we are urged to reject war, control our passions, and recognize our need for the opposite sex. Thematically, if not in treatment, it is a morality play.

And in varying degrees, plays of satire have continued to be didactic. The satiric and nonreligious portion of *The Second Shepherds' Play* is, in essence, a mild jab at deceit and fraud. Jonson's *Volpone* is a sophisticated elaboration of the same ethical position. He broadens the ethical base by adding love of power to love of possessions, and he compounds the pattern of deceit by making the victims as despicable as the villains, and he keeps his audience laughing; but the thesis is clear enough.

Moving to the nineteenth century we can see a further development of the thesis-play in the works of Ibsen. It is a mistake to sum up plays like *Ghosts* and *The Wild Duck* with a simple thesis-statement without qualification and elaboration, but the thesis is there none the less. There are moral ambiguities similar to those in *Antigone,* but the final position of the play remains assertive.

The same is true of Shaw's work. Occasionally, as in *Heartbreak House,* he develops his thesis through allegory. In this play Captain Shotover is the head of a household which represents England as a whole. Hesione Hushabye suggests England's home scene or domesticity; and Addie Utterword, England abroad or the empire itself. The blatant use of abstractions for the names of characters has gone, but the link is made through comic associations and puns which are apparent even from this brief description.

More often, however, Shaw presents his thesis through plots which are not allegorical. His theses are based not only on moral convictions but on social, political, and economic beliefs as well.

During our own century, the thesis-play is often more serious in treatment. Clifford Odets used it to preach political liberalism in *Waiting for Lefty,* and Bertold Brecht blasted at the broader problems of social injustice and the horror of war in plays like *The Caucasian Chalk Circle* and *Mother Courage.* These last two are particularly worth study because of the fact that they so purposely and blatantly defy the conventions of so-called realistic drama. As with early morality plays, the message is not hinted at but shouted out; and the use of ironic wit is not intended to soften the didactic function of the play but to intensify it.

Guerrilla theater of the 1960s and 70s is by definition politically militant. The root of *guerrilla* is the Spanish word *guerrilla,* little war, and has nothing to do with gorilla. Like the morality plays, they are often presented informally to demonstrate specific contemporary political and social issues. One specific example is a sequence of plays given by and to striking grape pickers of California to dramatize their cause and to ridicule their opponents. In some of these, the characters wear cardboard labels to identify them as "striker," "capitalist," "scab," and the like. Notice how close this becomes to the political cartoon—even its function is similar.

In Chapter 24 I suggested that one of the "boundaries" of drama was the essay. That is, as one shifts from theme to thesis and reaches the outskirts of the genre, one begins to take on the techniques of descriptive writing. Direct dramatic statement can be satiric or straight; it can concern itself with issues which are religious, moral, political, or social. But in all cases it stresses the *idea* or *argument* first. The reason it is literally *simple* as I have been using the term is that characterization, plot, and setting are by design subservient to the message. There is a clear parallel here with painting: As it becomes more socially conscious and finally political, it moves closer and closer to the cartoon.

In drama as well as in art, it is futile to argue which approach is "better." If one were asked which was better, a sculpture or a truck, the only possible answer would be, "Better for what?" The same is true of plays. The mainstream of drama from the classical period to the present has been thematic. The themes are turned over and over, examined and dramatized, and the audiences live through the experience; but no single course of action is prescribed. The history of thetic drama is equally long but not as broad. Many of them, like the morality plays, survive mainly as historical interest. When they are rooted in political issues, they often depend heavily on the events of the decade—or even of the year. They do, however, serve a special and valuable function for the age in which they are written.

29

REALISM AND EXPRESSIONISM

Realism in drama compared with mimetic fiction; *expressionism* described as including all types of dramatic distortion; *realism* seen as also rooted in *illusion; expressionism* analyzed through distortions of the set, dialogue, and basic assumptions about what is possible; *theater of the absurd* described as a development of expressionism; *advantages* and *dangers* in each approach.

In the section on fiction I made the distinction between *mimetic* work and that written from the stance of a *premise* or a *dream.* In drama, the terms *realism* and *expressionism* have traditionally served the same purpose. *Expressionism* is used to describe all types of distortion—both the single premise and the dreamlike fantasy.

In spite of their importance, these terms are frequently misunderstood. Realism in drama is not "real" nor is expressionism "unreal."

They are both forms of dramatic illusion. But the techniques of establishing this illusion—the conventions used—are significantly different, and no playwright can afford to confuse the two.

Dramatic realism in its simplest sense means the technique of presenting the various aspects of the play, such as the set, the action, and the dialogue, so that they seem to reflect or mimic what we might see and hear in real life. We don't have to have known characters like those in *Hello Out There* to have the feeling that the play is *realistic*. Expressionism, on the other hand, is essentially the use of purposeful and overt distortion. *The Sandbox* serves as an excellent example. Each approach deserves close examination.

Dramatic
Realism   The convention of realism applies to the set, the costumes, the dialogue, and to all of the action. To be specific, when a playwright presents to his audience a jail cell and corridor, he is signaling the fact that the play will probably be realistic. On this basis, the audience expects the costumes to be familiar. Further, it makes certain assumptions about the dialogue and action. People may be surprised at what a character says or does, but they assume that it will all "make sense" and will echo patterns of personality before the final curtain.

More basic than this, the audience expects a realistic play to follow what are assumed to be the natural laws of the universe. Imagine a final scene in *Hello Out There* in which Photo-Finish and his girl depart in a chariot drawn by three purple dragons. Our taboo against a *deus ex machina*—a forced invention of any sort—is nothing more than a generally accepted convention.

I am using the word *realism* here as a purely descriptive term—not historical. It is in this sense that the distinction between the two poles, realism and expressionism, is so important to the practicing playwright. There are, however, two other uses of the term which should be mentioned here merely for the sake of clarity. The first refers to a school in fiction, and the second to a short-lived historical development in drama. The following diagram is designed to clarify this frequently misunderstood term and to show the relationship between the two traditional uses (numbers 1 and 2) and the definition which I am using in this text (number 3).

1. "Realism" as used in fiction is both an historical and descriptive term:

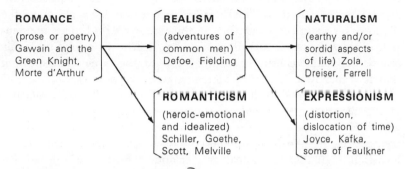

ROMANCE

(prose or poetry)
Gawain and the
Green Knight,
Morte d'Arthur

REALISM

(adventures of
common men)
Defoe, Fielding

NATURALISM

(earthy and/or
sordid aspects
of life) Zola,
Dreiser, Farrell

ROMANTICISM

(heroic-emotional
and idealized)
Schiller, Goethe,
Scott, Melville

EXPRESSIONISM

(distortion,
dislocation of time)
Joyce, Kafka,
some of Faulkner

2. "Realism" as used in drama has also been used in both an historical and descriptive sense:

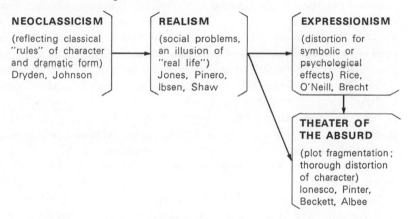

NEOCLASSICISM

(reflecting classical
"rules" of character
and dramatic form)
Dryden, Johnson

REALISM

(social problems,
an illusion of
"real life")
Jones, Pinero,
Ibsen, Shaw

EXPRESSIONISM

(distortion for
symbolic or
psychological
effects) Rice,
O'Neill, Brecht

**THEATER OF
THE ABSURD**

(plot fragmentation;
thorough distortion
of character)
Ionesco, Pinter,
Beckett, Albee

3. "Realism" as applied to drama in this text is a purely descriptive term which simply refers to characteristics which are the antithesis of expressionism:

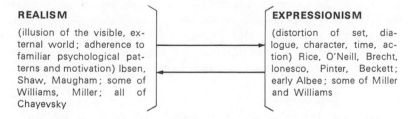

REALISM

(illusion of the visible, external world; adherence to
familiar psychological patterns and motivation) Ibsen,
Shaw, Maugham; some of
Williams, Miller; all of
Chayevsky

EXPRESSIONISM

(distortion of set, dia-
logue, character, time, action) Rice, O'Neill, Brecht,
Ionesco, Pinter, Beckett;
early Albee; some of Miller
and Williams

The "realistic" living-room set which is used in so many plays contains only three walls. Such a room in actual life would be grotesque; we accept it as "real" only because we have accepted the illusion as a valid representation of the familiar world. This is essentially the same psychological process by which we accept a highly representational (realistic) painting while at the same time knowing that it is merely a display of pigments on a flat surface.

Dialogue is discussed in more detail in Chapter 30, but it is worth noting here that it too is only an illusion of reality. Just as the volume and clarity of the actor's words is a clear departure from normal behavior in the home, so the speech patterns and the subject matter create only an illusion of real conversations. By way of specific example, notice our willingness to accept the "stage whisper" as if it were a real whisper in spite of the fact that it can be heard even by those at the rear of the second balcony. Or contrast the clarity of syntax in the speeches of such supposedly inarticulate characters as Willy Loman or Stanley Kowalski with the verbal confusion which is so evident in the transcripts of presidential press conferences. Or contrast the thematic unity in the dialogue during, say the supper scene in Miller's *A View from the Bridge,* with the chaos of themes at any ordinary meal.

And even more than in the case of sets or dialogue, realistic action is only an illusion of what happens in the great jumble of activity we call life. In most plays, the exits and entrances, movement around the stage, and even simple mannerisms and gestures must be carefully contrived to provide certain clues about character and theme while at the same time appearing to be as natural as actions in actual life.

Take *Hello Out There* as an example. The division into secondary scenes, the entrances and exits, and the symbolic placement of Photo-Finish as solitary figure on the stage at the beginning to be matched at the end with the girl placed in the same position—all these details are consciously arranged. Yet the play is clearly realistic. We accept the action as well as the stylized dialogue as suggesting characters and events from our waking world, not some dream.

Realism, then, is a set of illusions; but like mimetic fiction it mimics or echoes patterns which we are used to in our daily lives.

Expressionism

in Drama   Applied to drama, this refers to the kind of distortion we have already seen in premise and dream fiction. It differs from the type of distortion used in realistic drama in that instead of being hidden it is open and often blatant. The audience recognizes these departures from actual-life patterns and quickly casts about for a new system of logic.

Often it is the stage set which first indicates to an audience that a play is going to be expressionistic. Albee's bare stage with the sandbox could, of course, be used in a realistic play. But it prepares the audience to expect almost anything. The "young man" doing calisthenics and then the musician who appears from nowhere add to this sense of fantasy. When Albee finally has the "young man" announce himself as the Angel of Death, the audience is prepared to accept the statement literally. By way of contrast, if a character in *Hello Out There* made the same statement once the realistic stance of the play had been established, the audience would probably assume that he was either drunk or insane, for these would be logical explanations in real life.

If Albee used a completely arbitrary pattern of action and dialogue, the confusion would be irritating and ultimately boring. But he gives the audience enough clues to perceive what I have referred to as a new system of logic. Once one sees the young man as a symbolic representation of death, then it is clear why those who are middle-aged are only vaguely aware of his existence and why those who are old talk with him more readily. Notice that Grandma shifts from casual interest through a moment of panic to final resignation—symbolic changes in attitude toward death itself.

The dialogue in these sections would be baffling if the play were presented as realistic drama. But because the playwright has first made it clear that a nonrealistic system of logic is being used, the audience waits for clues. And once the system of symbols emerges, the play becomes perfectly "logical."

The same applies to plays which are only partially expressionistic. Arthur Miller's *Death of a Salesman,* for example, is fundamentally a realistic play about an aging salesman who lives in what is described as "the New York . . . of today." But there are a number of expressionistic details in the play including a dreamlike character known as Uncle Ben, a kind of family myth who is reputed to have made a fortune in Africa or Alaska. He appears as if from nowhere, speaks lines, and disappears just as mysteriously. When he comes on stage we are not being asked to believe in ghosts nor are we forced to consider Willy insane. These are the only alternatives if we insist that the play literally follow the logic of "real life." But it is also "real life" for sane people to think of themselves as talking with a figment of their imagination, and it is only mildly odd for us to allow this talk to become audible. When we see Uncle Ben actually standing there, we accept the premise that we are in Willy Loman's mind, viewing the scene as he does. Ben's portion of the dialogue is merely the dramatic version of the metaphor we use when we say "He argued with himself." Unconsciously we have begun with the simile, "He thought *as if* he were two people," and then translated the concept into a metaphor. Ben is this metaphor made visible and audible.

The same technique is extended and made the central device in Ionesco's *The Chairs.* Here the imaginary characters far outnumber the two visible characters on stage. Were this play realistic, we would have to take it as a psychological study of two utterly insane people. But the logic of the play insists that we take this symbolically; their castle in the middle of the sea is the sort of isolation many sane people feel their lives to be, and their "friends" are reflections of their needs and hopes and illusions.

These examples of expressionistic dialogue necessarily include expressionistic action. Willy Loman is not seen sleeping in a chair when Uncle Ben comes on stage because this is not a literal suggestion of a dream; he walks over to Uncle Ben and has his boys run out to meet him as well simply because it is not a dream. It is "real" in the sense that the old couple's desire to please their "guests" in *The Chair* is real.

From a writer's point of view, then, expressionism is not a literary period to be studied as an extinct phase of drama. It is one of two poles which present the playwright with a wide variety of techniques. On the one hand, we may rely primarily on the illusion of life as we perceive it, complete with certain expectations in motivation, character, and visual relationships. Or, on the other hand, we may employ some other system of logic, such as metaphors or purely symbolic relationships. Thus, realism and expressionism are as far apart as are a waking experience and a dream experience. In artistic terms, they are as removed from each other as the paintings of Hopper and Wyeth are from those of Picasso and Chagall.

Distinct as they are, it is a mistake to consider them mutually exclusive. The entrance of Uncle Ben in *Death of a Salesman* is an expressionistic device, yet whole scenes of that play are rendered as realistically as are the plays of Ibsen or Chekhov. And playwrights vary their approach from play to play. In the case of Miller, *After the Fall* was highly expressionistic, but he later wrote *The Price* as an absolutely realistic work without the slightest trace of distortion. The practicing playwright should not think of these differing techniques as mere historical schools. Each is well represented on the stage today. Recognizing the worth of both gives a playwright a broad range of options.

Theater of the Absurd

Within the expressionistic tradition, there have been a number of "schools." Most of these, like Dadaism, surrealism, and theater of shock, are of interest only from a historical point of view. But one of them has had such an enormous impact on the contemporary scene that no practicing playwright can ignore it. This is theater of the absurd.

Although the movement borrows heavily from the Dadaists who were breaking the old tradition of the well-made play before, during, and after World War I, theater of the absurd in its strict sense began in the 1950s and continues to the present.

There are some fifteen to twenty playwrights who have been associated directly with the movement, the most famous of whom are Eugene Ionesco, Samuel Beckett, Harold Pinter, and Edward Albee. Jean Genêt and Arthur Adamov are in some ways in a class by themselves, but they must also be included in the absurdist tradition.

The movement can most easily be defined as consisting of two philosophical convictions and three dramatic techniques which are used to present these beliefs. To a surprising degree, these five characteristics are found in all absurdist plays.

First, there is the conviction that life is absurd in the sense of being without ultimate purpose or meaning. The concept of the absurd is at the heart of such existential writers as Sartre and Camus and has had a greater impact on drama than it has on either fiction or poetry. It is more than a simple atheism since it also rules out belief in progress, human dignity, humanism, or historical development. Life becomes *absurd* in this special sense when there are no patterns whatever to guide or direct one's actions.

Why not commit suicide under such circumstances? Camus wrestled with this very question in his essay, "The Myth of Sisyphus." And in various ways each of the playwrights within the tradition of theater of the absurd has done it in dramatic terms. The plays do not offer solutions. They are thematic and merely explore the phenomenon of trying to live in an ultimately meaningless world. Usually this is done through a central metaphor. In Ionesco's *The Chairs,* life is like living in a castle in the middle of the sea with only the hope of creating a "message" for the world as a reason for living. In Beckett's *Endgame* the metaphor is a cellar room with an unclear view of the world through little windows; and in *Waiting for Godot* life is an endless and futile hope for someone's arrival. Harold Pinter in *The Dumb Waiter* uses the basement room of *Endgame* and the waiting motif from *Waiting for Godot* and adds a baffling (meaningless— absurd) bit of violence at the end. Each of these is an effort to create in dreamlike, poetic terms the agony and also the wry humor of living without the assurance of absolute values or meaning.

A second characteristic which affects the philosophical attitudes of these playwrights is an underriding anti-intellectualism. Reason is not going to solve anything. And attempts at reason are seen as self-delusion. Faith in rational thought which so dominated the nineteenth century has been rejected, and with it the hope for social progress. The great gods of Darwin and Freud are dead. Learning is pointless in a world with no future. The past becomes only a faded copy of the present in a prediction of what the future will be.

It is no wonder, then, that we see characters like the teacher in Ionesco's *The Lesson* turn out to be a cold-blooded murderer. And the Orator in *The Chairs,* a man who is about to deliver to the world the great message of truth, turns out to be an idiot whose language is unintelligible nonsense. And in *Endgame,* parents live out their lives in ashcans. In a world without meaning, teachers, parents, churchmen, and the aged are the greatest fools of all.

Turning from philosophical attitude to technique, we see first a heavy reliance on the expressionistic approach. Almost every play considered to be absurdist is a fantasy. In fact, as I have pointed out above, the tendency is to find a dream scene which will serve as the basic metaphor for the play's thematic suggestion. Not only is the set usually detached from time and place, the action is illogical and the dialogue is filled with nonsequiturs.

A second characteristic of technique is the use of dark humor— *dark* in that topics like cruelty, murder, and suicide are often made into the comic element. In Ionesco's *The Chairs,* for example, the old couple at the end of their lives commit suicide by jumping from the windows of their castle. About half the audience is moved to compassion while the other half responds with laughter. The action is simultaneously tragic and absurdly comic.

In other instances the humor comes from the inability of individuals to communicate clearly. Harold Pinter and Ionesco both use non-sequiturs in which a character seems to be answering a different question from the one which was asked. They also have their characters repeat lines meaninglessly. They exploit the entire problem of human communication—our failures to listen properly, speak accurately, or perceive the emotions of others.

Humor serves occasionally as satire. Ionesco's *The Bald Soprano* is really no more than a loose collection of skits some of which satirize middle-class attitudes and, more specifically, British middle-class formalities. The most successful of these is the sequence in which a couple, making polite conversation, discover that they are from the same town, the same street, the same house—and, finally, that they are man and wife.

Albee's satire of Mommy and Daddy in *The Sandbox* is even more pronounced in *The American Dream* where the clichés of middle-class existence are exaggerated into dreamlike distortions in a technique which is close to Ionesco. Harold Pinter's satire is more diffuse. The audience recognizes certain personality types and social situations which, through distortion, are strangely comic; but his work is not intended primarily as satire.

Not all absurdist plays are comic. But the fact that a majority are to some degree funny—at least in a distorted way—points up a particular problem in this type of play. The lack of dramatic structure which characterizes so many of them requires some alternative technique to maintain the commitment of the audience. Humor is one natural solution.

Martin Esslin in *The Theatre of the Absurd* traces this element back to the mime of medieval drama and the nonverbal entertainments of jugglers, acrobats, and clowns. He sees further influences from recent sources such as music hall routines, vaudeville, and silent film routines. These are particularly apparent in plays like *Waiting for Godot* where the playwright must entertain his audience for some two and a half hours without a plot.

The third characteristic is their static quality. That is, rather than developing a dramatic sequence of events which work toward a climax, these plays tend to study and restudy a basic condition. In Ionesco's *The Chairs,* for example, the playwright limits himself to two characters living in their castle in the middle of the sea. But he then explores what an old couple would be like under those circumstances. He presents them first as pompous, then as childlike, then modest, then boastful, and finally filled with pathetic optimism in the face of futility. The play is like a series of poetic stanzas dealing with the problem of human existence.

It may be for this reason that so many plays which are either in this tradition or have been influenced by it turn to grotesque humor or such devices of shock as violence and nudity. Depriving drama of its plot removes one of the most basic techniques of emotional impact, and the playwright is hard pressed to replace it.

Theater of the absurd has had an enormous influence on contemporary drama, but it has not taken over the scene entirely. Black theater, for one, rarely takes an absurdist approach; there is meaning and conviction in protest. And many of the younger white playwrights like Lanford Wilson find strength in the grotesque yet highly realistic and dramatic plots—life twisted so we can see it afresh. Even some of the founders of the absurdist tradition have departed on occasion. Edward Albee is slightly outside the pattern with *The Sandbox* in that he has constructed a plot (leading to a heroic death in the old tradition) and a moving, credible character whom we come to respect. He is entirely outside theater of the absurd in plays like *The Death of Bessie Smith* which is a highly dramatic rendering of an historical event: the night the famous blues singer died because a white hospital would not accept her.

Even Eugene Ionesco departed from the static format in *Exit the King,* a dramatic allegory of a man's introduction to mortality. Although the setting is an expressionistic fantasy, the king and his court go through a sequence of events which is as structured as an Elizabethan tragedy.

Assets
and Liabilities

Realism continues to exist in the contemporary stage because it has many advantages. It catches and holds the imagination of an audience. If constructed with skill, its plot will provide dramatic impact in a series of climaxes through the evening. And it lends itself to social and moral concerns of the day.

The greatest liability for the beginning writer is making use of stock characters, hackneyed dialogue, and conventional situations. Many of the clichés which I warned against in the section on fiction appear in drama as well.

Expressionism of any type—and theater of the absurd in particular —has some of the same advantages and difficulties of free verse. It provides a kind of liberty which every artist wants. But it also eliminates the structure which every artist needs. The question is whether one can provide a new impetus which will keep the work moving and alive.

Satire, wit, comedy—these form one cluster of solutions. But they take skill. Somewhat easier is violence and obscenity. Or it *seems* easier. But the great risk is that it will turn into dramatic graffiti. Worse, *un*dramatic graffiti. It takes more than spontaneity. Martin Esslin puts it this way in *The Theatre of the Absurd:*

> Mere combinations of incongruities produce mere banality. Anyone attempting to work in this medium simply by writing down what comes into his mind will find that the supposed flights of spontaneous invention have never left the ground, that they consist of incoherent fragments of reality that have not been transposed into a valid imaginative whole.

He suggests, further, that it works only when the play

> ...springs from deep layers of profoundly experienced emotion...real obsessions, dreams, and valid images in the subconscious mind.

Much depends on the initial vision of the playwright. But not all. He must also provide the type of cues which will help the audience to share that vision. This takes work. A personal, private dream put on the stage is no closer to an artistic creation than is a journal entry. Absurdist drama succeeds when the audience is swept into a dream and held there. To achieve this requires just as much talent and practice as does success with realistic drama.

30

DRAMATIC DIALOGUE

The *multiple purposes* of dialogue in a play: revelation
of *character,* a method of providing *peripheral information,* a technique of presenting *thematic elements,* a
means of setting the *pace,* and a method of establishing
tone.

A dramatist depends heavily on dialogue. He uses it in
some of the same ways a writer of fiction does, but because he normally
works without the benefit of expository passages, what the characters
say to each other becomes his central device.

It is possible, of course, to have a scene which is acted silently or
danced or sung. But as soon as the work is dominated by any one of
these nonverbal methods, we no longer consider it drama. A performance which is entirely silent is a pantomime or mime; full choreography becomes ballet or dance; dependence on singing becomes
opera or a musical. Spoken dialogue remains at the heart of drama.

Dialogue serves a number of different functions in a play. One of
the most important is the revelation of character. It also serves as a
valuable method of providing peripheral information—events which
have occurred either previous to or separate from the main action
of the play. Next, it can be used to develop thematic elements. Fourth,

it is a means of controlling the pace. And finally, it is the primary method of establishing the tone of any one scene.

The experienced playwright can keep these concerns in mind without being fully aware of them in much the same way that any competent writer uses grammatical patterns quite unconsciously as he constructs a sentence. But regardless of experience, every playwright must make fully conscious use of them when attempting to diagnose a play which has gone wrong.

Revealing
Character
Of the five functions of dramatic dialogue, this one is probably the closest to fictional dialogue. The playwright would do well to review Chapter 19 on characterization and apply those points to the problem of creating a convincing character on the stage through appropriate dialogue.

First, remember that dialogue appears to be "convincing," not because it duplicates the speech patterns of the audience, but because, like the character it is developing, the dialogue is consistent and designed to reveal a complex set of attitudes.

By consistent I do not mean that it should maintain one level of emotion or even usage. On the contrary, it is impossible to understand a character on the stage unless he has shown a variety of responses to differing circumstances. If he is a placid character, for example, it helps if he is thrust into some situation which will drive him to rage or indignation; conversely, if he is generally hot-tempered, the audience will not really come to "know" him until it is able to see some circumstance under which he can be tender, cool-headed, or even passive.

The consistency comes when the audience is given a *pattern* of behavior by which to judge the character. Once this has been established, there is some measure of predictability. If, for example, a section of dialogue reflecting panic is planned for a crisis at the end of the play, some minor pre-echo would help to prepare the audience.

Preparation like this is important even in relatively brief plays such as the two included in this text. In *Hello Out There,* for example, Saroyan is careful to build Photo-Finish into a character who is both immature and yet capable of courage and compassion. This is a sizable task. He does it by providing the audience with enough background (through his dialogue entirely) to give the picture of a drifter, a small-time gambler, and a near-loser. The other side is revealed in his two very brief soliloquies, each expressing his faith in good people and his disgust with hypocrisy. The audience is in this way prepared for that final scene in which he speaks the truth to the man with a gun and, as his last act, urges Emily to escape while she can. Notice how much of this complex presentation of character is done through words alone.

The technique in Albee's *The Sandbox* is in some ways strikingly similar. Because the play is so short, he also must limit himself to only one fully-developed character. But through her dialogue he is able to express a surprising range of qualities. Grandma is sufficiently old and senile to be childlike—almost literally on occasions. But she has had a hard life (described through dialogue) and has apparently done as much with it as anyone could. She has her old person's prejudices ("There's no respect around here"), but she has a strong sense of values (she sees through Mommy). In the end she is seized with panic at the moment of death ("I...can't move...I...I can't move"), but in her final resignation she rises above death, treating it (him) as only a bit actor playing a part ("you did that very well, dear") and somehow impressive ("you've got a quality").

In longer plays, it is possible to develop two and sometimes even four characters with this kind of sophistication. And again, the technique depends heavily on dialogue. Albee's *Who's Afraid of Virginia Woolf?* is a good example.

The first act of this play appears to be pure comedy and was written off by some critics as pointlessly vulgar and mere "boob-appeal," but a second reading reveals the fact that every line contributes to an extraordinarily complex presentation of character. The reason these two characters are so fascinating is that although they each have the ability to be extremely ruthless, each also has areas of fearful vulnerability. The opening scene is comic on one level, and the audience laughs as readily as it would have had the comic lines been given for their own sake; but the comedy is also the means by which husband and wife defend themselves against each other. This opening "battle of the sexes" carefully defines the methods of attack and the points of vulnerability which are to become the very foundation of their characters.

After reading the play once—or seeing it—one should go back over this scene to analyze each line. There are four different types of information given through this bit of hilarious dialogue: those which expose the brutality of the wife, Martha; those which expose her pathetic childishness; those which reveal the strength in the husband, George; and those which dramatize his self-doubts, fear, and emotional impotency. One cannot predict from these lines whether one member of this anguished team will "win" or whether they will destroy each other or whether they will end in a draw. The last act of the play is a surprise to the most sophisticated theatergoer—perhaps *particularly* to him. But having seen the limits of each character through dialogue, the ending is credible.

These two characters are accepted as "real" not because they speak lines we have all heard but because what they say begins to take on a highly complex pattern as if we had listened to them over a period of years.

I do not mean to suggest here that one should doggedly assign certain lines to certain aspects of character or specific attitudes. Imagination is liquid, not mechanical; a character well conceived should be allowed to write many of his own lines. What I do mean, however, is that the playwright must constantly ask himself: "What does this line suggest about this character?" and "Is she really *that* sweet?" and "Can't he relax for a minute?" These are the questions which keep characters from becoming flat.

Providing
Peripheral Information
There are two types of peripheral information which must be presented by dialogue: significant events which occurred previous to the action of the play and any action which must for various reasons be kept off stage. Both are outside the audience's vision even though they may be dramatically important.

The first usually involves the opening of the play. This is a real danger point for the novice. It is extraordinary how frequently the opening scene is destroyed with lines like these:

MOTHER: You see, son, your father was a poor carpenter and left many debts.
SON: It's been hard on you, Mother, over these fifteen years.
MOTHER: Yes. At first I took in washing. Then I turned to sewing. Now I run my own little dress shop.
SON: And I got a paper route four years ago. Last year you gave me a bicycle. Then I could take on two routes.

Such openers are intended to introduce the audience to the characters, but too often they only introduce the characters to each other. The plain fact of the matter is that neither mother and son nor any other set of characters who have known each other for a long time are apt to sit down and review the facts of their lives.

Absurd as this little example is, it represents a problem which every dramatist has faced. And there is a wide variety of solutions. Occasionally, playwrights use the tradition of the chorus in the form of a single commentator such as in Thorton Wilder's *Our Town* and Arthur Miller's *A View from the Bridge*. Or they may have their characters address the audience directly as do Shakespeare's Richard III, Beckett's Krapp, and Albee's Grandma.

But by far the most common method of presenting such material is to use a character who is slightly outside the main action of the play. For Sophocles and Shakespeare this frequently took the form of servants talking about past events. More recently, the tendency is to have close friends or relatives ask questions about the situation. It may be a visitor (Albee's *The American Dream,* Ionesco's *The Chairs*), or a stranger (Pinter's *A Slight Ache,* Pirandello's *The Man With the Flower in His Mouth,* Miller's *The Price*), or a married couple may be paired with a second couple (Tennessee Williams's *Period of Adjustment* and Albee's *Who's Afraid of Virginia Woolf?*). It is surprising how many plays provide at least one character who is sufficiently uninformed so as to serve as the recipient of background information.

The other type of peripheral information which may have to be presented through dialogue is that which occurs at about the same time as the major action of the play. Sometimes this is a matter of sex. The stage is about as free as it has ever been, but now that the playwright has won his freedom, he must decide how he will use it. Entirely aside from morality, there is the aesthetic question of proportion and balance. Adding a highly charged, sexual scene to an otherwise moderate play may be as inappropriate as placing two flashing electric bulbs in the eyes of a Rembrandt portrait.

Another type of action which is sometimes better handled through descriptive dialogue is that which is too complex to stage. Tennessee Williams is no coward, but he is dramatist enough to know that there are problems involved in having a pack of dogs tear a man apart on the stage (*Orpheus Descending*). And although the film version of

Suddenly Last Summer suggested (without directly showing) the hero being devoured by a mob of wild urchins, the stage version most effectively presents this scene through dialogue. T. S. Eliot took the same approach when Celia (in *The Cocktail Party*) was "crucified/ Very near an ant-hill."

The third situation which calls for narrating peripheral information is more general. It is a matter of unity. If the play seems to have too many scene shifts, or if its direction seems to wander aimlessly, the fault may be that too much is happening on stage. Writers who have moved from fiction to drama are apt to be most guilty of this. The fluidity of a novel does not lend itself to a play; the playwright must be highly selective. A scene in drama which serves no purpose but to fill in some minor part of the plot has no place on the stage. In many cases, such scenes can be summed up through references in the dialogue.

This is particularly true in short plays. There would be no advantage, for example, for Saroyan to have included the scene in which Photo-Finish meets the woman who later accused him of rape. What the play would have gained in dramatic detail would have been lost in the lack of unity. In a longer play like *Death of a Salesman,* that is just the type of scene which lends itself to a complete flashback. The decision must be made on the basis of the play as a whole.

Presenting
Thematic Elements
This is generally the most dangerous use of dialogue. It frequently takes the form of a final monologue in which a character is given the task of analyzing what the playwright really wanted to say. Actors hate this role for the simple reason that they must step out of character and become social critics or even drama critics.

The need for such summaries was once formalized in the convention of the epilogue, and some contemporary playwrights have devised modified versions of this technique. The final scenes of *Death of a Salesman, Our Town,* and *Mother Courage* are all good examples.

More generally, however, contemporary drama leaves the summary to the audience. It is the total effect of the action and dialogue which makes the statement, not a chorus or an analytical spokesman.

In Chapter 28, "Suggestion and Statement," I pointed out the various ways in which thematic concerns were developed in the two plays included in this text. The use of the refrain, symbolic names, and symbolic action were all included. Each of these is either presented by or echoed with dialogue.

How, for example, does Albee manage to suggest so much about the ways in which people react to death? Partly it is done with satire through the dialogue of Mommy and Daddy ("Brave Mommy!" "Brave Daddy!"). But primarily it is developed more seriously through Grandma's dialogue with the Angel of Death. When one first reads or sees the play, these lines do not seem as fully charged with suggestion as they in fact are. The implication is oblique, but it is there. No lines are wasted.

In writing a play, try to avoid two extremes in the development of theme through dialogue. On the one hand, guard against those lines which serve no function but fill empty space. When a friend arrives at the door in fiction, the author can skip over the mechanics with a sentence of exposition—"They greeted each other warmly." But the playwright has to write out all those warm greetings. It takes skill to make even these conventional situations add to the total thematic statement of the play.

The other danger is having lines which are too obviously thematic. As I have pointed out before, drama tends to be much more direct in its pronouncements than is fiction, but there are limits. Lines which begin with "Life is..." and "What the world needs is..." are danger signals. Read them over in context. Make sure that it is still the character talking and not the playwright coming through undisguised.

Controlling

Pace   The pace of a play is all-important. Occasionally it moves too rapidly. This is rare and the fault usually lies in the action, not the dialogue. Much more frequently, plays fail because of a pace which is too slow. It seems ponderous; specific scenes seem to sag. Here again the solution may be found in adding dramatic impact such as was described in Chapter 26, or it may be a matter of finding more striking visual effects such as are analyzed in the next two chapters. But often the fault may lie in the dialogue.

In such cases, it is wise to examine the diction, the syntax, and the length of individual speeches. If all these appear satisfactory, one should review the degree to which dialogue has been blended with action and, finally, the amount of new information which is given through the dialogue.

Diction is often "heavy" in plays by writers who have a misguided admiration for Greek and Elizabethan drama. By "misguided" I mean a misunderstanding about the language used in those plays. Translations of classical drama vary tremendously, but many of them adopt a formal, Latinate style which a century ago was considered appropriate for "great" works. They miss the point that most Greek dramatists used a fairly simple style, echoing the speech of literate contemporaries and, particularly in the comedies, the dialects of illiterates as well.

The same is true of Shakespeare's dialogue. It appears formal and even elegant to us largely because so many words and phrases then in common use are no longer heard. Even the so-called great speeches are constructed mainly with simple, concrete nouns and active verbs.

Heavy diction, whether adopted for these reasons or others, consists of long words, Latinate roots, and excess modification. Certain types of characters are best shown through language like this, but they are rare. The best way of judging whether the diction of a particular character is natural and true to his nature is to read his lines aloud. A tape recorder is helpful. And the advice of actors is invaluable.

Heavy diction does reduce the pace of a speech and, in turn, the scene. The same is true of complex and involuted syntax. Such a style may be justified by the character himself, but even in those cases the playwright must remember that no matter how "real" it may sound, the scene is going to be slowed by it.

Large, unbroken blocks of speech are perhaps the major cause of tedium in dialogue. It is here that the Major Statements of Theme and Significance are apt to appear. But even when those have been eliminated, the lines are likely to drag the scene down. What many playwrights forget is that when one character speaks at length, all the other characters on the stage are static. At worst, they have left the play altogether and joined the audience as listeners; at best, they are merely useless.

One way to solve this is to break such speeches with action or with a shift in the number of characters on the stage. Review how Saroyan does this in *Hello Out There*—in effect dividing his play into eight secondary scenes. There is no break in time or in place, but each exit or entrance provides a kind of psychological renewal of

interest. They are a subtle but effective method of keeping the dialogue from becoming heavy and unbroken.

For all this, there are some plays which ignore most of this advice
by giving extraordinarily lengthy speeches and yet still maintain a
fairly rapid pace. O'Neill's *Long Day's Journey Into Night* is one
example. It should be remembered that this play was written at the
end of a long career in drama; as such it serves as a rather dangerous
model for the novice. But some explanation should be given concerning why plays like this maintain enough pace to be lauded by a good
number of critics.

Part of the explanation is due to the poetic quality of the language
itself. Shakespeare was able to roll out long speeches which hold the
attention of at least the trained portion of the audience through
exactly the same qualities which capture those at a good poetry
reading. Some critics, but not all, feel that O'Neill achieved this.

, More to the point, however, is the amount and degree of information which is presented through such lines. An audience will be bored
with a thirty-line speech if it fails to reveal much about character or
the dramatic question; the same audience will be fascinated with a
hundred-line monologue if there are a series of revelations about the
speaker or the situation.

Pace, then, is not merely a matter of diction, syntax, and length
of speeches; it also depends on content. In Chapter 26 I suggested
that the play as a whole must have some sort of dramatic question
to keep the audience alert and committed to the play; the same is true
of long speeches. To test the dramatic voltage of a single speech—
particularly a long one—the playwright must determine just how
many new insights are offered through this dialogue. I do not include
vague and general statements about Life and Beauty and Death as
insights; I am referring to those all-important discoveries about the
inner nature of the speaker and the real significance of the situation.

Determining

Tone   Tone is created both through action and through
dialogue. But of the two, dialogue is a more basic factor. The action of *Arsenic and Old Lace* is essentially serious, but the tone is
kept delightfully light through the dialogue. Within limits, it is not
so much what happens that determines tone but the attitude of those
to whom it happens as revealed by what they say.

Traditionally, light tone and serious tone were given separate scenes, the former often coming in the form of "comic relief." This is still followed by many playwrights. The comic relief is used mainly to keep the audience from emotional exhaustion and occasionally to echo the major theme. An easy way of handling this is to add a comic or a "light" minor character (an echo of Shakespeare's clowns) whose function is to provide relief through either witty or cynical dialogue.

One of the most significant trends in this half of our own century, however, is the linking of light and serious tones in the same scene. One can trace this development in fiction from Nathanial West through Joseph Heller. The same pattern can be seen in drama by studying Brecht's *Threepenny Opera,* Ionesco's *The Chairs,* and Albee's *Zoo Story* and *Who's Afraid of Virginia Woolf?* It was Ionesco who coined the phrase "tragic farce," and although some of these works are closer to farcical tragedies, the term should be accepted as meaningful and significant.

In the case of black theater, wry humor in the dialogue often serves as a way of taking the pressure off what is usually a highly compelling thematic statement. In plays like *Ceremonies in Dark Old Men* by Lonne Elder III and *No Place to Be Somebody* by Charles Gordone there are many genuinely funny lines, but the audience never loses sight of the fact that the issues being dealt with are deadly serious. By controlling the tone this way, these playwrights avoid melodrama; and in this way the dramatic impact at the end reaches the audience with full force.

Regardless of what approach one takes, it is important to remember that dialogue is the primary means of determining tone—not only light versus serious, but calm versus tense, sentimental versus bitter or ironical, and the like. The playwright who wishes to maintain control over the tone of his work must necessarily be master of his dialogue.

These, then, are the five primary functions of dialogue in a play. As a basic rule, no line should serve only one function and many should reflect all five. Obviously one cannot check each line in a script against this list. But if one uses it frequently to analyze individual scenes, the principles will eventually be internalized. At this point one is able to use dialogue with true facility.

31

VISUAL EFFECTS : ACTION

Dramatic action analyzed in its four forms: *exits and entrances* which set off secondary scenes and provide dramatic structure, *relocation* of characters on the stage, *"business"* as solitary but significant activity, and *physical contact* between characters; the *need* for action in drama.

Action is embodied in our very conception of drama. "I *saw* a good play" we say, whereas for its sister art we are more apt to say "I *went* to the opera."

Before turning to the reasons for this, we should examine just what is meant by action. There are four general types: exits and entrances, relocation of characters, "business," and physical contact. These are, of course, all related. But since each serves a somewhat distinct function, it is helpful to consider them separately.

Exits and

Entrances The first, exits and entrances, is the most important form of action for the dramatist. It is as basic a device as chapter divisions are for the novelist and in a sense serves the same function: It is the primary means of finishing one scene and beginning the next.

The word *scene* is deceptive. On the theater program it refers only to those formal subdivisions of an act which are separated unmistakably either by a brief lowering of the curtain or dimming of lights. These are also marked on the script and are minor acts within an act. I shall refer to these as *primary scenes*.

For the dramatist (and the actor), however, a scene also refers to each unit of action which begins with an entrance or an exit and ends with the next shift of characters on the stage. Those whose introduction to drama has been wholly literary are apt to miss the significance of these *secondary scenes*. But anyone who has had any experience in the production of a play knows how important they are both to the actor and to the playwright himself.

Occasionally, a secondary scene may have a strong dramatic unity. That is, it may build to a climax which is dramatically punctuated by the departure of one or more characters. Often, the unity is more subtle. It establishes the almost unnoticed rise and fall of action which distinguishes the play which is "interesting" from the play which appears to be "flat" or "dull."

Hello Out There is an excellent example. It is a one-act play presented in one primary scene. There is one stage set and one apparently uninterrupted flow of action. But from a playwright's point of view, the work is divided into eight secondary scenes. Each of these is marked by an exit or entrance and each has an influence on the rise and fall of dramatic impact.

The play opens with a long sequence of dialogue between the man and the girl. But notice how Saroyan maintains interest by keeping the girl off stage for a while. Her arrival marks the beginning of the second secondary scene. The impact of this may be somewhat muted for the reader, but for the audience it is visually a new situation. And Saroyan highlights this in the dialogue itself: "You're a pretty kid, you know that?" and so forth.

The third scene is a very brief one. She goes out to look for tools, and he is left on the stage alone. But it is important because it allows him to lash out vehemently against what he sees as injustices. And as I have pointed out earlier, the fact that he is alone on the stage is a clear indication that he is speaking his inner convictions. Were it not for this little scene, we might feel that he was cynically lying to the girl simply to save himself.

The fourth scene is one in which Emily and Photo-Finish make the pact to meet in San Francisco. Notice that their relationship has grown with surprising speed. In a story, one might be tempted to spread the action out over the course of a day or so; but Saroyan's dramatic sense leads him to keep the action continuous.

The girl leaves, ending the fourth scene, and there is only a moment of sound effects before a new character suddenly appears on stage. The tension mounts as we learn that this is the angered husband.

The scene builds to new levels when the husband draws his gun, and culminates with three shots. This is the natural termination of the scene, and it is highlighted by the return of the girl.

In the sixth scene, the hero and heroine are alone on the stage. If this were opera, it would be the point where the final duet is sung. As realistic drama, it is a brief, terse, yet at the same time tender moment.

But a problem arises here. How is the playwright going to maintain dramatic interest in that brief yet important section which follows the death of the protagonist? Once again, a new secondary scene is prepared for—the seventh. First the audience hears activity building off stage. Saroyan is careful to include this in his stage directions: "The excitement of the mob outside increases." And then the husband, the wife, and another man all burst in on stage, running. Visually, this is explosive enough to cap even the shooting scene. And it is here that Emily demands that they put the body down—what we can assume is the first dramatically assertive act of her life. And she is slapped to the floor.

The last of these secondary scenes is so brief that it consists of only one line. But to understand just how powerful the device is, imagine the girl delivering that last line with the other characters still on stage, struggling to drag the body off. Emily would be literally upstaged. In addition, her line would be a mere continuation of the preceding dialogue. Having her alone on the stage, probably with a single beam of light on her, isolates the final words. Her plight—now matching that of Photo-Finish at the very beginning of the play—becomes the focal point of the play.

When one first reads a play like this, it is easy to assume that it is one continual flow of action from beginning to end. Such an approach would, of course, be possible. But it would be far more difficult to hold the audience's emotional involvement for that length of time. Exits and entrances in this play provide the basic organizational structure with which the dramatic impact is heightened and lowered and then heightened again in regular succession, holding the audience from beginning to end.

Don't confuse what I am referring to here as secondary scenes with those primary scenes which are designated in the script and which often involve a change in time or locale. Movies, of course, make many rapid shifts like this; but drama on the stage tends to be less fragmentary. This is partly due to the physical difficulty of changing sets. But more than this, there is significant loss of impact every time the continuity is broken. A play cannot flick instantly to a new setting. Even if there is no curtain to drop, there must be a lowering of lights and a pause in the action. The members of the audience shift in their seats and make comments to their friends. Attention has been broken. The device is so much more pronounced than a shift in films that it is used sparingly.

This is particularly true of short plays. Notice that both of the plays included here use a single set and a single sequence of action—though each one divides that action into a number of secondary scenes.

Scene Construction
in "The Sandbox"
Albee's play uses the same device of secondary scenes. Although the action moves as if without a break, there are actually five divisions. In the first, the audience sees Mommy, Daddy, and the Young Man. Mommy is quickly established as the manager, and then the Musician is called on stage—by Mommy of course. The third scene is a brief one in which Mommy and Daddy go off to get Grandma, and the Musician and the Young Man are alone on the stage. There is a little musical interlude here. Although the audience doesn't realize it at this point, these characters both represent aspects of death.

The fourth scene begins when Mommy and Daddy return with Grandma. It is the longest. If you read it over carefully, you can see how it is divided into four sections, shifting the audience's attention from Mommy and Daddy to Grandma and the Young Man and back again. In a recent television version, each of these was treated as a separate "take" and so became like a secondary scene. But on the stage it is merely a shift in emphasis based on who is doing the talking.

In the final scene, Mommy and Daddy leave the stage and

Grandma becomes the primary character. She and the Young Man who is now known as the Angel of Death hold the attention of the audience while the Musician, like fate, plays softly in the background.

Notice that the technique of giving Grandma the emphasis at the end of this play is similar to Saroyan's treatment of Emily at the end of *Hello Out There*. It would have been possible to keep Mommy and Daddy on stage at this point just as Emily could have shared the spots with the others; but in both cases, dramatic highlighting was given to the key character by giving her a single, short scene at the very end.

The two plays are in most respects strikingly different—one realistic and the other highly expressionistic. But each playwright has constructed the action from sequence of secondary scenes. Why? There is no absolute rule, and there certainly are many exceptions; but it is far more difficult to hold the audience's unwavering attention without providing this type of variation in the visual aspect of the play.

Entrances and exits are not, obviously, the first consideration of the playwright. No one begins with the premise, "I am going to write a play with three acts each of which is divided into two primary scenes each of which is subdivided into four secondary scenes." Plays are usually conceived from two or more characters in a particular dramatic situation. And in the first draft of writing, scenes are apt to begin and end as the development of plot demands that they do— the way one determines the length of a sentence in first-draft writing.

But with revisions, a thorough understanding of scene construction is not only a practical skill but a necessary one. If, for example, the play seems to "sag" in the middle, the problem may be lack of a dramatic question; it may be a character who has taken to preaching the theme of the play; or it may be that the rhythm of action has been made monotonous by a lack of secondary-scene construction.

And the diagnosis is only the first step. Equally important is the prescription. It is not enough to get a character off stage simply to answer the telephone, to take a nap, or to mix a drink. The exit must be a part of the dramatic fabric. It must be natural enough (that is, credible) so that the playwright's intention does not show through. Sometimes this effect is created simply through preparation: A telephone call is expected, fatigue and need for rest has been shown, thirst or nervous exhaustion has been established. More often, an overall plan is needed. The ebb and flow of characters is most natural when it appears to be demanded by the plot itself.

Just as the artifically motivated exit is weak, so is the excessively dramatic exit. The exit lines with which Ibsen concluded most of his acts are the sort which we now associate with Hollywood films: We can almost hear that swelling, electronically vibrating chord from the organ. The secondary scene in drama is usually as subtle as the shift from the octave to the sestet in a sonnet or the end of a chapter in a contemporary novel. Once again one must return to the essential fact that art (the work as a whole) should conceal art (the craftsmanship). A good play should be able to convert at least momentarily the best drama critic into an absorbed theatergoer.

Relocation
of Characters   The second form of dramatic action is the relocation of characters on the stage. Often this is left to the actor or director. Long speeches are broken with a moment of silent pacing; a manic speech (such as in *Richard II*) is dramatized by a leap onto a table; a father's speech about infant care is punctuated by removing a sopping diaper and silently wringing it dry out the window. The emergence of the director as a collaborator (lamented by such playwrights as Somerset Maugham) allows for all kinds of fundamental revisions simply through action on the stage.

It is important for the playwright to imagine himself as director, for only in this way can he be sure that he has given enough opportunity for movement on the stage. Saroyan, for example, provides only brief directions to his actors and those only during periods when there is no dialogue ("...he turns away from the image of her and walks about like a lion in a cage"). But one can visualize the action in each scene—moving to the bars of the jail, backing off, turning to shout "Hello out there," drawing together again.

In *The Sandbox* there is less opportunity for moving about on the stage. But Albee has compensated for this with entrances and exits and with a third type of action, *stage business,* which I will turn to shortly.

Historically, movement of characters in drama has had some radical changes. The Greeks, who associated drama with a religious service, formalized and stylized almost all movement. The chorus chanted the strophe while progressing across the stage in one direction, and recited the antistrophe while returning to their original position. Even major characters probably held specific positions, as was the case in grand opera before the reforms of Rudolph Bing and others.

Although the reawakening of drama in England and Europe with the miracle plays was also church connected, there was no link between action and religious ritual itself. Action was as free and natural as it was later in Elizabethan drama, but stage directions were nonexistent.

Only since the advent of play scripts which were intended to be read as well as performed have natural movements of the characters been carefully described by the playwright. What was once left largely to the actor has now been taken over by both the playwright and the director.

The main use of such movement is somewhat similar to exits and entrances. It provides even more subtle divisions of the plot. Long speeches—particularly those which are philosophical and abstract in nature—are deadly if not relieved by some form of action. The same is true of dialogue which on at least one level can be interpreted as idle chatter. The dinner party conversations which Proust strung out with such brilliance for upward to fifty pages in fiction would be hopeless on the stage. The same cleverness, the same insights into character, the same ironies which are used in *Remembrance of Things Past* are simply not enough to hold an audience's attention. The fault does not lie in the audience; the real cause is seen in the fact that one reads fiction two or three times faster than one can speak it, one is free to rest whenever one wants to, and one's favorite reading chair is far more comfortable than a theater seat. All the reasons for including a dramatic question in a play also argue for movement on the stage.

But if this were the sole reason for having characters move about, it would be perfectly acceptable to have random activity, such as endless lighting of cigarettes, going for drinks, or pacing. This is not acceptable simply because meaningless activity is as boring and nondramatic as no activity.

The other function of mobility, then, is statement. That is, the good playwright utilizes action in the same ways he uses dialogue: to further plot, to develop theme, to highlight the dramatic question, and to define character. Each of these deserves a quick examination.

Plot is not thought. It is not intention. It is essentially action. The poetry of Hamlet moves us, but it is his sword thrust through the arras and the poisoned drink drunk and the final duel fought that moves the plot. The monologues of Willy Loman bring us understanding, but it is the theft of a desk pen, the playing of a tape recorder, and the desperate planting of seeds that drives the plot to its culmination. Even in a play as plotless as Beckett's *End Game,* it is the ritualized moving of a stepladder to first one window and then the next that makes up for the lack of coherence in dialogue.

Each of these samples of action on the stage serves equally well to develop both the theme and the dramatic question. Fiction can substitute solid blocks of description, thoughts, and even author's reflection for action; drama cannot use these. When action is lacking, the theme and the dramatic question are left almost wholly to dialogue. There are, of course, subtle and indirect ways of having dialogue develop both these aspects, but the tendency for the novice is to force his characters to become philosophers, spouting the significance of life in the most implausible fashion. Action which *implies* aspects of theme and the dramatic question (as does every example given above) is the best safeguard against the "talky" play.

But it is with characterization that action takes on its most subtle role. Lady Macbeth's handwashing is a favorite example, involving both movement on the stage and individual "business," but almost every contemporary play requires either explicitly or implicitly that characters move in a way which reflects both their mood and their character generally.

Sometimes it is enough for the playwright simply to state that this character is "nervous and high-strung," or that one is "phlegmatic." A competent actor can take it from there. But a good playwright visualizes his character speaking each line, and it becomes natural for him to add such directions as "jumps to his feet and throws the book on the table" or "slumps in the chair as if exhausted" or "remains on the couch, feet up, arm dangling throughout the entire scene."

Stage

Business This term is sometimes used to describe all types of action including moving about on the stage. Technically, however, it refers to activity which does not involve relocation of a character. The motion of the Angel of Death in *The Sandbox* is a beautiful example.

Albee specifies at the outset that this character should be in con-

stant motion throughout the play. It takes the form of slow calisthenics which "should suggest the beating and fluttering of wings."
The action is symbolic of the character's identity. But in addition, it
serves as one of those details which keeps the play visually alive.

But more often, stage business is both less dramatic and less continuous. Grandma's throwing of sand, for example, is a minor but
helpful detail. In other plays it takes the form of sewing, rearranging
hair, biting fingernails, picking one's nose, scratching an ear, examining a shoe, blowing a bugle, worrying a pimple, buttoning and
unbuttoning a blouse, adjusting machinery, taunting a caged mouse,
ironing shirts, looking for a lost purse, fingering a bottle, holding one's
breath, or building a motorized toothpick Ferris wheel.

It is an extraordinary fact that a great majority of plays written
by college students are wholly devoid of fresh and original stage
business. So much time and energy has gone into the theme, the
significance of the whole statement, that no imagination is left for
those little bits of action which can make a character come alive
or save a long scene from sinking with its own weight. So marked
is this lack that students who *do* concern themselves with such
details find themselves praised for works which in other respects are
quite inferior.

Before filling one's script with trivia, however, one should watch
out for a number of dangers. *It is very easy to let business become a
cliché:* the executive practicing golf swings in his office, the teenager curling around a telephone, the major slapping his riding boots
with his riding crop (borrowed, by the way, from Hollywood, not
life), or the Italian mother stirring spaghetti. All of these are but one
step from the villain curling his mustache. It is much wiser to have
the executive showing off his new wire recorder as in *Death of a
Salesman,* or the teenager sweeping out a jail as in *Hello Out There,*
or the military leader showing off his one-shelf "library" as in *Arms
and the Man.* I leave the Italian mother to you.

Stage business often becomes detached from the play itself. This
is particularly common in weak scripts which have been doctored with
bits of action. Business may be thought of as dramatic seasoning, but
it is a poor cook that adds garlic to the ice cream or fudge sauce to
the salad. This does not mean that a playwright must be bland. By
"detached" I mean unrelated, not unusual. To have Hamlet fondle

the skull of a man he once knew is a bizarre bit of stage business, but it is not detached or unrelated to the lines he is speaking, the mood of the scene, or the thematic patterns of the play. He is, after all, discussing mortality and the scene is a light pre-echo of the heavily dramatic grave scene which is to follow. And it is as true a reflection of Hamlet's deep but controlled melancholy as Nora Helmer's dance scene in *A Doll's House* is a reflection of her wily naiveté.

Excessive repetition of the same mannerism is also a danger. Students of literature rarely err in this fashion, but students of television often do. Alfred Hitchcock, for example, frequently uses stage business for its entertainment value alone—not for the development of character but for its simplification. To have a brutal and ruthless character seen clipping and filing his nails periodically might be, in a serious drama, an insight into an ironic aspect of character. But if he engages in this bit of business *every* time he appears, the action no longer suggests character, it *becomes* character. We leave the theater saying "remember the man with the nail clippers?" We remember him not as a man but as a cartoon. Here the technique is no longer a means to an end but an end in itself. Art has not concealed art and we respect the production as great entertainment, which is a compliment to a craftsman but not to a dramatist.

If one avoids these three dangers, there is no limit to the kind of business one can use on the stage. It may serve all the functions discussed under the general heading of relocation of characters, but the primary one is the development of character.

Physical

Contact   Physical contact between characters is the fourth and final type of action on the stage. It is not, of course, a wholly separate classification. Characters must move about on the stage to prepare for a fight or a kiss. But the contact itself has a dramatic impact which has become a kind of convention in itself. And like all conventions, it has its assets and its dangers.

In most cases, physical contact in drama suggests the ultimate degree of a human relationship. Aggressiveness is pushed, finally, to a fight; hatred culminates in murder; love on the stage must, for cultural reasons, be symbolically consummated with a kiss. These are the fundamental types, and they are seen throughout the entire history of drama. The same human relationships are also treated in poetry and fiction; but it is drama which has most consistently translated them into these visible and often almost stylized forms of physical contact.

Variations in cultural attitudes and the direct insistences of audiences have had, of course, a profound influence on the way drama employs this convention. The Greeks, because they were acting on holy ground, kept violence off stage. And kissing with masks is short of effective. But what they lost in dueling scenes, fist fights, and love scenes they made up for with off-stage combat and reports of lovemaking.

The Romans and the Elizabethans wanted their physical contact on stage and got it—in ways which appall modern audiences. It is not enough to say simply that Shakespeare's conception of tragedy insisted on the death of a great man. Elizabethan plays are filled with an endless array of physical combat—particularly duelling, stabbing, and choking.

Love was expressed more in terms of language and self-sacrifice partly because the women were played by boys but more significantly because drama was not such an intimate affair as it is for us. Picture, for example, Hamlet's bedroom scene played without a bed or other props under the glare of the afternoon sun. It was not until the theater moved inside, the props were made essential, and the audience was plunged into darkness that the silent embrace and climactic kiss became a really effective bit of dramatic action.

Contemporary drama uses physical contact to express a great variety of emotions—not only aggressiveness and hatred but love and sexual attraction as well. The problem for the playwright is to determine when he has missed a chance of using the technique and when he has overused it.

A fist fight, for example, is a natural climax for an antagonism which has been building up for a number of scenes. Such varied playwrights as Williams, Miller, and Albee have used them for just this purpose. But they tend to be brief skirmishes, sometimes a single blow. They are not to be confused with the long and elaborate barroom fights which occur with such regularity in Westerns. Sophisticated drama avoids these gymnastic rituals because they provide only the simplest sort of dramatic impact, adding little if any insight into character or theme. Most dramatists find that a single, well-motivated jab to the chin or stomach provides all that is needed without the risk of becoming melodramatic.

The same applies to the love scene. The miles of celluloid Hollywood has contributed to recording the kiss were never intended to provide much insight into the human condition.

Hello Out There deals with both love and aggression. And it is a short play. One question which the playwright faced at the very outset was whether either of these emotions should be translated into some type of physical contact. A playwright's instinct often leads him to dramatize as much as possible; yet a short play is like a short story in that it can take only a certain voltage before burning out.

Saroyan's solution—which may have come consciously or subconsciously—was to mute the expression of love and to dramatize the display of aggression in the strongest possible way. Notice that while the couple clearly love each other, they kiss only once and then briefly. The entire relationship is developed through dialogue, and as a result it is surprisingly restrained.

Fear and hatred on the part of the husband and the mob could have been muted slightly by having Photo-Finish struck down (as the girl is moments later) or dragged off the stage still alive. His fate might ultimately be the same, but the play would have been made somewhat softer. Saroyan could have muted it still further if he had allowed the hero to escape with his girl. But his decision was to make the play a tragedy and to emphasize the hero's ultimate defeat through a dramatic death.

He did not, on the other hand, use all the physical violence available in that situation. He could have had the girl killed as well. This would have been harmonious with his theme. But a double slaughter in a play of this length runs the risk of turning it into a melodrama. So Saroyan caps the violence with a soft and plaintive note of understatement in that last, brief scene.

Diagnosing
Dramatic Action It is very helpful to analyze how other playwrights have used the various types of dramatic action and to speculate on the decisions they made. But ultimately the practicing writer must be able to evaluate his own work. It is important for him

to *see* his play even before he has begun to write a line of dialogue. Here, for example, is an outline of a student play which should never have been written.

> *A college setting:* the protagonist is inwardly worried about his academic work but puts on the guise of sophisticated unconcern. The antagonist, on the other hand, has no desire to be at college, has no internal drive for excellence, but has adopted the guise of the "grind." *The situation:* an all-night study-session in which the "grind" keeps up the pretense by chattering about how much he has to do and by asking questions; the protagonist must adopt the casual approach, but he reveals through telephone conversations home and a few monologues that he is scared and frustrated almost to the point of hysteria. Finally he takes down an ornamental M-1 rifle from the wall and pretends to clean it while his roommate watches. The final, "accidental" blast provides the dramatic climax.

Now there are a number of reasons why this play will probably fail. First, the playwright, if he is a college student himself, is too close to the situation. He has no perspective. Also, although the play suggests some complexity of character, it does not present a naturally dramatic situation. It might have a better chance as a short story than a play. And the final murder, a mechanical version of the fight, is probably more than the play can take; that is, it runs the risk of being melodramatic. True, such murders do occasionally take place in real life, but we are talking about the construction of a one-act play, not case histories.

The most obvious indication that this play will not succeed, however, comes from analyzing the visual effects. First, there are no exits and entrances and thus no chance to build secondary scenes. It is one long block of dialogue. Second, there is little opportunity for characters to move about on stage. It is visually static. A good actor may try to make up for this with stage business, but he doesn't have much help from the playwright.

Finally, the physical violence at the end does not lead naturally from the earlier action of the play. Saroyan, by way of contrast, builds continually toward the physical violence at the end of his play, working the words "scared" and "afraid" into the script as refrains. Although the turn of events at the end jolts the audience, it is a natural culmination of the tension which has been building.

The action of a play, then, is clearly not just "what happens." As exits and entrances, it becomes the basic structure of the play through secondary scenes; as movement on the stage, it becomes intimately connected with plot, theme, the dramatic question, and characterization; as individual business, it becomes a particular form of character insight; and as physical contact it becomes a method of establishing emphasis.

One should be aware of all this while writing the first draft of a play. But the time for a really thorough evaluation of the demands and the potentials of dramatic action is during the rewriting. This is the time for comparing the nature of the work as written with the intention and the ideal. These are questions which will continue to be important even after actual production.

It is possible to write a play with almost no action. It is also possible to produce a painting with only two shades of white. Action is an essential part of the play not simply because tradition has decreed it. The genre demands it. "I *saw* a good play," we say, and quite unconsciously we state that visual effects are fundamental in this art form.

32

VISUAL EFFECTS:
SET AND COSTUME

The *set defined;* various *types* including expressionistic, combination set, and the bare stage; types of *theater designs;* varieties of *costuming* including realistic and symbolic; *lighting* effects; the use of *mixed media;* the playwright's *visual imagination.*

The term *set* is used here to include everything the audience sees excluding the actors themselves. Its greatest impact comes at the very beginning of the play: The house lights dim, the curtain rises, and the audience is plunged into a wholly new world. In this instant, even before the first line is spoken, the audience is preparing itself on the basis of what it sees for high tragedy, for comedy, for a realistic social problem, or for the mystery of a dream sequence.

As the play develops, action, dialogue, and the impact of the plot take over the audience's major interest. But the set—combined with lighting and costume—continues to influence the tone and the mood of the play.

There are three main approaches to set designing: realism, expressionism, and bare staging. Although there are no precise lines dividing these three, each has its own unique characteristics. More important, each has separate advantages and disadvantages. If the playwright does not decide fairly early which vehicle is most appropriate for the particular play he is engaged in, he will not be able to visualize his scenes as he writes. Worse, he cannot develop the full potential of any one approach.

Realistic

Sets The realistic set is so common today that we tend to think of it as the traditional approach. But it is interesting to note that if the 2,500-year history of drama were seen as a week, the length of time dramatists have even considered the realistic set would come to an insignificant half-hour. And already many dramatists have dropped it as too limited.

If we look at the realistic set with some historical perspective, we can see that, although it is not the only approach, it has offered and continues to offer the dramatist a valuable vehicle for his work.

When Ibsen's plays were first introduced to England in the late nineteenth century, the audiences gasped with amazement at the sight of a perfectly reproduced living-room scene, complete with real books in bookcases, real portraits on the walls, and doors that opened and shut. Soon the stage directions for the plays of Barrie and Shaw began to reflect this new realism by including the most minute descriptions—even to the title of a book left "carelessly" on a coffee table.

But the contemporary playwright cannot hope to impress the audience with such a device. This is, after all, an age when television can produce the Atlantic Ocean complete with gulls and a luxury liner for a two-minute drama which is designed simply to suggest that a certain aftershave lotion has the power to attract beautiful women.

Clearly no set designer can hope to make his stage look more realistic than a film shot of the real thing. It is naive to try. Nor should he compete by using tricks. Opera never became more realistic by bringing live horses and even elephants on the stage. A play called *The Kidders* was not made more realistic by having the protagonist shoot a bottle of whiskey from its perch on the newel. (For three successive nights the pin in the post, which was to crack the bottle as the gun fired a blank, failed to operate. On the fourth night the play itself failed.)

But the realistic set has not been abandoned. When it is used with skill and imagination it can establish the tone and even add to the thematic content of a play. Here are five examples of plays which have made creative use of a strictly realistic set.

T. S. Eliot's *The Cocktail Party* concerns characters who are members of the British upper-class society. Although the theme of the play is in no way limited to this group, our understanding of their attitudes, their values, their humor, and their immediate problems depend on recognizing this. The set could consist of an unimaginatively designed living room with the usual indications of affluence. In the New York production, however, a side table with silver tray, glasses, ice bucket, and liquor bottles became a glittering focal point. And the last bottle, the one nearest the audience, was Vat 69, the only good Scotch on the market with a label large enough to be read from the balcony.

Part of this was suggested in the original script. Further, the side table is used repeatedly in stage directions. The set designer made full use of the directions by selecting objects which glittered and caught the eye. This is "realism" in that nothing has been blatantly distorted from what we might expect to see in an actual living room of this sort. But it is a creative and imaginative use of realism.

Tennessee Williams makes use of the same sort of focal point in his play *Period of Adjustment*. Here the characters clearly represent the middle class. The focal object is a television set. Because it is often on, it is placed with its back to the audience, upstage center. This way the characters can watch it, can comment on it while speaking toward the audience.

But the creative and imaginative use of the traditional set is not limited to selecting a significant focal point. In Robert Anderson's play, *Tea and Sympathy,* the mood of a boarding school master's living room is caught with a clutter of significant details, from dark woodwork to the furnishings themselves. And the playwright included at stage left a stairway whose primary function was to allow students to run up and down on their way from classes to their dormitory. This periodic thundering of feet was extraordinarily effective in suggesting a kind of restless energy among the students which was directly, though subtly, connected with the theme of the play.

In the adaptation of James's *The Aspern Papers,* the audience applauded the set before the first line was spoken. This response was not wonder at its "realism," but at the degree to which the set caught the decaying elegance of a Venetian living room. Here again it was the sum total of details like tall windows, peeling green wall paint, and faded tiles that created the mood.

In *Hello Out There* Saroyan gives the set designer a fairly free hand. He specifies only that the scene is "a small-town prison cell." And it is clear from the script that there must be equal space in the room outside the cell since much of the action takes place there too. So one is free to use those familiar details which one associates with such a scene—the sheriff's rolltop desk, the cracked-plaster wall, and the like. The only limitation is the fact that the set should be fairly simple. Plays of this length are usually presented with others on the same evening, and the audience shouldn't have to wait thirty minutes between fifteen-minute productions.

Each of the five realistic sets I have described could, of course, be vividly reproduced in film. And the camera would have added the further dimension of exterior setting. But the roving eye of the camera loses one advantage that the stage offers: concentration on a single set of objects. The side table in *The Cocktail Party* would appear in any filmed version of that play, but it would be seen only momentarily in the great collection of scenes. Because the play is usually limited to one or two sets, each physical detail the playwright or the set designer decides to use becomes magnified in the minds of the audience. It is this concentration of attention in the stage play that makes even the realistic set a creative challenge and an opportunity.

Expressionistic

Sets   The two fundamental characteristics of the expressionistic set are distortion and symbolic suggestion. Instead of trying to mimic the world about us, the scene takes on the visual quality of dreams. It may seem baffling at first, but eventually it provides elements which suggest or symbolize significant aspects of the protagonist's life.

An early example of this approach is Elmer Rice's *The Adding Machine*. Written in 1932, this play deals with a pathetic cipher of a man named Mr. Zero whose world is dominated by the endless clutter of figures from his job as bookkeeper. The first scene, his bedroom, could be presented by means of a realistic set. We all know the kind of details which would suggest such a man. But Rice's expressionistic set calls for a room wallpapered with a vast collection of numbers ready for addition, subtraction, or division. In a sense, Rice is shifting the objective means of perception which is traditional in drama to Zero's own view. We see the room as he imagines it. Rice's sadly comic distortion presents a significant symbolic statement even before the first line is spoken.

Edward Albee, writing over thirty years later, uses the same type of visual distortion and symbolic suggestion. Although the audience cannot guess at the outset how the sandbox is going to be used, it is soon asked to imagine a beach. Mommy says, "There's sand there... and the water beyond." Midway in the play it is clear that they are waiting out their lives in the same vacuous way with which people sit for hours on the beach. The simple set then becomes a symbol which has a wide range of implications about the type of life Mommy and Daddy lead.

But this turns out to be only one of two symbolic suggestions. Grandma is dumped in the sandbox and her first utterance is described by Albee as "a cross between a baby's laugh and cry." She repeats this and later throws sand at Mommy. The sandbox here has to be taken literally as a children's play-place. Grandma has been reduced to the level of a child—partly by age and perhaps equally by the way she is treated.

Albee's set, then, has served as a vehicle just like a dominant image in a poem. And it is used to suggest two different but related tenors— one commenting on the lives of Mommy and Daddy and the other describing an aspect of Grandma's plight.

Expressionistic sets can, of course, be used in plays which were not written for them. Shakespearean tragedies, for example, lend themselves to experimental set designing particularly well because the playwright was never limited by the demands of visual realism. In 1955 in a London production of *King Lear*, the sculptor Noguchi made dramatic use of the symbolic set: The stage was bare except for a number of multisided triangular and rectangular forms some thirty feet in height. Each side was a different color so that by rearranging the forms for each scene, they were made to suggest a palace scene, a forest scene, or "another part of the forest" in a matter of seconds. And because of the varied colors, the mood of a scene could be changed simply by revolving the forms.

The dangers of the expressionistic set are similar to those inherent in expressionism itself. If used carelessly, it can add obscurity to an already clouded play. In this respect, it is like free verse. The very freedom often leads to pure expression (as opposed to communication), which no matter how interesting or original, is something less than art. The other danger is that the technique itself can become so emphasized that the audience cannot accept the production as anything more than a technician's stunt. There will always be musicians who insist on playing the "Flight of the Bumblebee" on a trumpet, poets who will write poems without the letter "e," and playwrights whose expressionistic devices serve only to dramatize a private nightmare; but the experiments we remember, like Rice, Strindberg, O'Neill, and more recently, Beckett, Ionesco, Pinter, and Noguchi, use technique as a means of developing the artistic creation as a whole.

Combination

Sets   I am using the word *combination* in two senses here. First, it combines two or more scenes on the stage at the same time— usually two or more rooms of a house or an interior and an exterior portion of a home. Second, it combines aspects of the realistic set with those of the expressionistic set.

In *Death of a Salesman,* for example, we are shown an upstairs room, two rooms downstairs, and a portion of the yard outside. It is realistic in that the rooms themselves are fairly accurate representations of what we would expect in real life. Yet it is expressionistic in the sense that the audience must use its imagination in separating what is outside from what is inside. An *actor* in the kitchen can obviously see what another actor is doing outside; but it is soon made clear that a *character* must come to the "door" in order to see. This is not as complicated as it seems when one remembers that children at the beach can work the same magic with a "house" which consists only of lines drawn in the sand.

A more extreme use of the split stage is seen in William Ritman's set designed for Harold Pinter's *The Collection.* Working closely with the director, Alan Schneider, and the playwright, Ritman managed to present the illusion of three entirely separate scenes on the relatively small stage of the Cherry Lane Theatre in New York. I have included illustrations (drawn by Richard Tuttle) because it is such an excellent example of what can be done with an imaginative combination of realistic and expressionistic techniques.

The Collection, showing emphasis on the modern apartment, with other areas dark.

The Collection, showing emphasis on the telephone booth, which is, in the play, some distance from either home.

The Collection, showing emphasis on the ornate apartment, with the other areas dark.

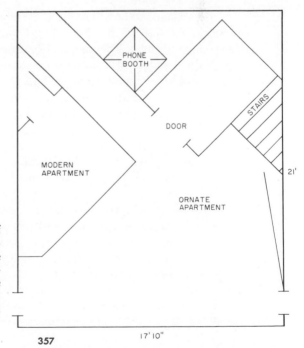

The Collection: a diagram of the stage, showing the technique of representing three entirely different scenes simply by shifts in lighting. Note how the unusual angles add both variety and depth even on a small stage.

When the lighting emphasizes what to the audience is the left side of the stage, we are in a sparse, modern living room. Simply by shifting the lights, however, we are moved to an elegant living room which, because the furnishings are so different, suggests an entirely different style of life. There is no question in the mind of the audience that these two portions of the stage represent two entirely different homes. Beyond this, there is a third area represented: an outside scene with a telephone booth which is, in our imagination, separated spatially from either home. When this is lit, the audience moves to a third scene as easily as if the curtain had been lowered and the stage crew had worked for a frantic fifteen minutes to break down one set and build a new one.

This is more than a trick. It represents the combined imagination of playwright, director, and set designer working together, pooling their experience. With skill, what is sometimes called "the limitations of the stage" becomes an asset, suggesting new ingenuities and fresh visual experiences.

The Bare

Stage When Thornton Wilder's *Our Town* was first produced, the use of the bare stage was greeted as a fairly new approach in theater. The use of two stepladders and a board connecting them suggested a house even to an audience not used to this kind of symbolic representation. And it added to the mood of a simple, small American town in ways an elaborate set could not.

But like so many experiments in theater, it was based on a very old tradition. The Elizabethan audience was perfectly prepared to use its imagination to visualize the rapid succession of scenes in Shakespearean plays. What Wilder did was simply to force the audience to use its "inner eye" in somewhat the same way as did writers of radio drama.

Picasso's extraordinary play, *Desire,* did equally well with a stage containing only a bench. In the off-Broadway production of this play, the director did not even use a curtain for a backdrop, preferring instead the brick wall of the theater itself.

The advantage of the bare stage is that it directs the whole attention of the audience to the actors themselves and to the lines spoken. This concentration of attention is particularly desirable in plays like Shakespeare's in which the language itself is often complex, filled with verbal nuances and, particularly in his comedies, a variety of puns. In the case of *Desire,* the language was important for an immediate and political reason: It was an anti-Nazi play made sufficiently complex so that the French audience of occupied Paris could catch the wit, laughing and applauding, while the German officials sat in bewildered and infuriated silence.

More recently, *Waiting for Godot* is a play which lends itself to a bare stage. Its open landscape is best constructed in the mind's eye.

In spite of these examples, the technique has been used only sparingly in this century. There is so much that can be done with sets either realistically or symbolically that the bare stage is apt to be a limitation rather than an addition. It is a bit like writing free verse without the use of assonance.

The playwright who is considering the bare stage as a set should make sure that he is not doing it simply to be different. If he can analyze exactly how his play will be a fuller, richer performance by the lack of visual effects, then he is well justified in selecting this approach.

Types of

Theater Design The playwright normally has no choice about the type of theater in which his work will be presented. Having a play produced at all is enough to hope for. But if one is a student at a college or university, it is worth examining the type of stage which may be used. It can influence the way one constructs the visual elements of a play.

A *conventional stage* is one in which there is a clear division between the audience and the actors marked by a proscenium arch. This arch used to include columns up each side and some kind of ornamentation across the top. But even when it is minimized as it often is today, it forms a kind of frame—usually with the edge of the curtain on either side and one at the top. The edge of the raised stage completes the frame at the bottom.

The advantage of such a design is that it facilitates the closing of curtains which, in turn, makes it easier to change sets. An elaborate development of that is the revolving stage in which three different scenes can be turned alternately toward the audience.

At the opposite extreme is *theater in the round.* In such an arrangement, the audience encircles the actors as it does in a circus tent.

Instead of a raised stage, there is merely a playing area—usually on the same level as the first ring of seats.

In this way, most of the audience is sitting close to the action, and the division between them and the actors is sharply reduced. Many playwrights enjoy the type of fluidity which occurs when there is no "stage left" or "stage right." Instead of watching a play as if through a distant window, the audience has the sense of being almost a part of the action.

There are two problems with theater in the round. First, the actors must enter and exit by the aisles, reducing the illusion somewhat. Worse, the actors must always deliver lines with half the audience behind them. But proponents of this type of stage argue that the feeling of intimacy far outweighs any disadvantage.

Many campus and community theaters have used a variety of compromises between these two which arrange the seating like a wide wedge of pie. The stage is usually set well into the seating area so that the audience is on three sides. Such designs are like theater in the round in that no one is far from the actors and everyone has a sense of being a part of the action of the play. But it also allows the actors to enter realistically through doors onto the stage and it eliminates the problem of having them speak with their backs to half the audience.

When a playwright thinks in terms of a stage like this, he relies less heavily on backdrops and the "picture in a frame" effect of the traditional stage. He is more apt to rely on that sense of presence which, hopefully, the audience will feel throughout the production. Notice that the complex stage set in *The Collection* (see page 356) would lend itself either to a conventional stage or to the type of compromise I am describing here; but it would be difficult to place that telephone booth in any circular stage without blocking the view for one segment of the audience. The same is true of the split-level set for *Death of a Salesman*.

When a playwright has some conception of what the opportunities and problems are with different types of stages, he will give to any designer a greater range of options. This is simply one more example of the degree to which drama is a visual genre.

Costuming   The playwright normally leaves the details of costuming to the director of a particular performance. But there are three different approaches which he should consider before he writes even the first line of dialogue: Are the costumes to be period, symbolically significant, or merely street clothes? These choices correspond roughly to the division of realism, expressionism, and bare staging already discussed.

The great majority of plays specify in the introduction that the costumes are of the period and are true to nationality and class. Certain differences, of course, can be suggested on the basis of personality. But the pattern remains: Most realistic plays employ realistic costumes.

Realistic costuming is also often used in highly expressionistic plays. Ionesco's *The Bald Soprano,* for example, is a totally expressionistic sequence of dreamlike incidents, yet the hero, Mr. Smith, is described with comically realistic detail as "an Englishman, seated in his English armchair and wearing English slippers, is smoking his English pipe and reading an English newspaper, near an English fire." And Mr. Zero in Elmer Rice's *The Adding Machine* dresses conventionally in spite of the expressionistic set, as do the characters in *The Sandbox.*

Symbolic or what might be called expressionistic costuming is, however, occasionally used as a natural extension of the distortion we see in the action and setting of expressionistic plays. In Adrienne Kennedy's dark nightmare of a play, *A Rat's Mass,* the scene is simply described as "The rat's house." As for costume, she specifies that

> Brother Rat has a rat's head, a human body, a tail. Sister Rat has a rat's belly, a human head, a tail. Rosemary wears a Holy Communion dress and has worms in her hair.

She uses somewhat the same technique in *A Lesson in Dead Language,* a short and bitter play set in a school classroom. The pupils are all in "white organdy dresses"—a minor symbolic suggestion of their conformity and innocence. The real distortion is the teacher, who is costumed as an enormous white dog. Kennedy is working in dead earnest with both religious and racial themes in this play, and the result is a grotesque, relentless fantasy.

Expressionistic costuming can also be used in otherwise realistic plays. Such was the case in the 1955 Noguchi production of *King Lear* which I described earlier. Lear first appears in a flowing robe which, although it suggests no period and no particular country, is clearly regal. And it is decorated with a pattern which vividly resembles the distinctive peacock's tail complete with rainbow-colored eyelike spots. The symbolic association between the proud King Lear and the peacock is both startling and completely natural, but it is only a beginning. In the next scene the costume is so similar that the audience hardly notices that the center portion, the "eyes," of the design are no longer a part of the cloth itself; they are small holes. This is the point in the play when Lear's pride first begins to damage his position.

In the next scene, these holes have grown noticeably. And with each succeeding scene the costume seems to fall apart progressively as if some acid were working its way into the fabric. When Lear's ruin is absolute and he has at last been stripped of all pride, his costume has dissolved into great loops of dung-colored rags. At this point in the play, one remembers the Lear of Act I, and has the distinct impression of having seen a man go through a lifetime. Rarely has costuming in any production created such an effect on the audience.

Street clothes are more commonly associated with readings rather than full productions. Like the bare stage, it is an easier approach and a less expensive one. One of the more famous productions, however, was Orson Wells's adaptation of Shakespeare's *Julius Caesar* in 1937. The modern dress in that case helped to draw a comparison between Caesar and Mussolini.

Lighting   Lighting is the newest of all dramatic techniques. The Greeks depended on the sun and so did the Elizabethans. And from the time of the first enclosed theaters in the late sixteenth century until 1914, lighting consisted of a glare of footlights designed simply to illuminate actors.

In 1914 the first spotlights were hung on the balcony rail of Wallack's Theater in New York. It is a sad fact that a number of Broadway theaters have made no major improvements since then.

An increasing number of colleges and universities, however, have installed multistage light-control systems. Such equipment allows the operator to set up a combination of lights on one "bank" and then, on cue, let that combination take over automatically while he arranges the next scene on the other bank. In addition to ease of control, these lighting boards offer the widest range of color, intensity, and angle.

Returning to the playwright, there is no point in including extensive directions for lighting effects if the play is being written without any particular stage in mind. But the number of plays which are written for college competitions with the hope of production in a specific modern theater is growing every year. For this lucky group, lighting should be considered as important a visual effect as costume and most certainly should be included in the script.

The three factors which must be kept in mind are color, intensity, and angle. Little can be said about any one of these without taking the other two into account. Orange, for example, is a soft light and ideal for a gentle scene. Yet an orange light beamed from directly overhead gives the actor a demoniac look. Low intensity (that is, a dim stage) can lend itself to, say, a love scene if the angle is normal and the coloring on the warm side; but the same low intensity becomes eerie and grotesque if the light is flat-white and from above.

Specific details like these are left to the directors of individual productions, but playwrights often include in the opening of the script some overall guidance about the lighting. In *The Sandbox*, for example, Albee specifies at the opening that "the background is sky, which alters from brightest day to deepest night." The play begins with "brightest day" and passes through night in which Grandma dies (though she still does not realize it), and then it turns to day again.

The script may also indicate how the lighting is to be used to highlight a specific part of the stage. This is particularly important with sets such as those in *Death of a Salesman* and *The Collection*. The illustrations on page 356 show how effectively a simple shift in lighting can appear to change the scene.

In the same way, emphasis can be redirected from one character to another. Miller's *After the Fall*, for example, is intended to give the illusion of being a sequence of memories and reflections. The playwright states in the script that his characters must "appear and disappear instantaneously, as in the mind; but it is not necessary that they walk off the stage." Although the use of lighting is not specified, it is clearly being required.

Like so many aspects of drama, lighting is a set of conventions. When the lights dim slightly during a scene, the audience reacts as it would to background music, expecting a serious moment. But if instead they dim down to a darkened stage, everyone knows that this signals a passage of time or a change in the setting. How do they know this? From seeing many other plays. It is a language which most theatergoers respond to unconsciously. But if the playwright is to use it fully, he must study it consciously.

Mixed

Media   This technique combines legitimate (live) theater with a number of other visual and auditory stimuli—cinema, slides, flashing signs, taped recordings, and the like. One of the earliest and most elaborate examples was a Czechoslovakian show called *Laterna Magica* (*Magic Lantern*). It was produced in New York in 1966 and at Montreal's Expo the following year.

The primary device of the show was to mix cinema and legitimate theater in almost equal proportions. To do this they had two screens on stage and a great deal of film footage depicting actors who also appeared in person. These actors entered the stage and then ducked behind the screen on which the film was just then projecting their own image in natural size. The pace was so rapid and the timing so accurate that it soon became difficult to tell which were live actors and which were the filmed images.

In one comic chase scene, a succession of characters ran across the stage and darted behind a pillar (real) and emerged (filmed) in different costumes only to hide again and reappear (real this time) as different characters altogether. In another skit, a roller skater skidded across the stage (live) and suddenly found himself hurtling down a San Francisco street (filmed) and almost out into the (real) audience.

Like the very first motion pictures, this show concentrated on the use of a new technical achievement. There was no real plot or theme. It attempted nothing but light entertainment. Dramatists have also been experimenting with the use of film clips, slides, and tape recordings, but they have to be careful to keep such devices from taking over the show. As a result, there is a tendency to use mixed media with restraint.

A good example of this is Lee Kalcheim's *Who Wants to Be the Lone Ranger?* The play involves a couple whose marriage is breaking up. By projecting film sequences, the playwright is able to superimpose their happy first year together in somewhat the same way a novelist might use flashbacks. In addition, he uses a sequence of color slides to introduce, as if through a photo album, the many boys she used to date.

Twice the plot takes a happy turn, bringing the couple back together in a joyful reunion. But just as the audience breathes a sigh of relief, two large electric signs on either side of the stage begin flashing in red: "FANTASY! FANTASY!"

Reading about such tricks, there is a temptation to start devising more and more elaborate variations. But before one begins blasting the audience with artificial smells and soaking them with fabricated rain (both have been done), it is worth remembering that any over-used device soon becomes a distracting gimmick. Although comedy, which thrives on surprise and incongruity, can absorb a wide range of tricks, drama which is serious in tone can be destroyed if it begins to be dominated by mere trickiness.

The Playwright's
Visual Imagination
Most of the weaknesses in unsuccessful play scripts can be attributed to the fact that the playwright has read more plays than he has seen. Put more directly, he writes a play as if its primary purpose was to be read.

This lack of visual imagination can lead to both sins of commission and sins of omission. He can, for example, clutter his stage or require superhuman set changes for no good reason or ask for impossible tricks. It was an almost classic sin of commission on the part of my freshman who ended the final scene of his adaptation of *Winesburg, Ohio* with the stage direction: "Our hero takes one last look at the town and then hops on the rear of a moving freight train."

But the sins of omission are almost worse, for they do not stand out clearly. They cannot be laughed at. We finish the play with the vague feeling that it lacked "dramatic punch." The playwright may point out that he has had a man die of cancer and his sister pass into a catatonic fit, but such incidents are elements of plot and not necessarily samples of action. If the stage is not kept alive with meaningful things to see, the play may well be in danger.

There are, of course, plays which run this danger without ruin. But these are as rare as successful poems without assonance or novels without chapter divisions.

Drama has always appealed to the eye. Contemporary drama offers a wide range of possibilities both in the movement of actors, such as was discussed in the previous chapter, and in the use of the set, costumes, and lighting. If the playwright is to fullfill the potential of his art, he must master the ability to *see* each scene, each instant of his play, as he writes and reviews his own work.

33

REVISING A PLAY

The *three steps* necessary to evaluate one's own play:
an uninterrupted *silent reading,* a *spoken reading,* and
a *group reading* to imitate the effect of a full production; the *four critical questions* concerning the *dramatic
impact,* the *theme,* the *dialogue,* and the degree of
originality.

There are three basic steps in analyzing one's own play.
One should use all of them before even considering the possibility
of producing the work on the stage.

The first is reading the play silently. One has, of course, been doing
this through the course of writing. What I am referring to here is a
complete, uninterrupted reading from beginning to end. This is not
always easy to do—students are apt to have roommates, parents have
children, and everyone has Very Important Things to do when the
alternative is reading a work which one has wrestled with for months.

Yet such a reading is essential. Most plays are not only more
intricately structured than stories but longer as well. Because of this,
the playwright tends to think in terms of scenes, and his creative
energies are focused singly on first one and then the next. The uninterrupted, silent reading is necessary to unify one's view of the play.

This silent reading has an advantage over a spoken reading because it is faster. But to be effective, it should be conducted literally without a single interruption. This means not taking notes or even making the simplest mechanical correction. Those can be done later. This is not a proofreading nor is it a critical reading. In many cases, it is the playwright's first introduction to the totality of his creation. Think of it as the foot soldier's first aerial view of territory which he once fought for day by day and town by town.

The second of these three steps is reading the play out loud. Ideally, this too should be uninterrupted; but it is not as important at is was for the silent reading because the intent is different.

One mechanical purpose is timing. The total playing time can be estimated fairly accurately if one allows for those few scenes in which silent action takes place. This information will be needed if the play is to be entered in a contest. More important, it is a way of judging the nature of the work itself. If it turns out to be a long one-act play, it may be worth expanding into a full-length work. If, on the other hand, it is a three-act play which runs only eighty minutes, one should consider either expanding the work or cutting it back to one act.

The difference between a so-called one-act play and a full-length play is about as vague as the distinction between a short story and a novel. A one-act play can be divided into several scenes which may resemble acts, and a full-length play can replace the traditional three acts with a number of scenes which structurally resemble the one-act play. Greater length allows for greater complexity in plotting, but it does not demand it. For these reasons, plays are classified by playing time. The so-called one-act play usually runs from ten to sixty minutes; the full-length play, from two to four hours. In between there is an awkward length which, like the novella, is discriminated against for purely commercial reasons. Playing time is both a practical bit of information and a way of defining the work.

It is also helpful to have a record of how long each scene takes. If a scene is tedious, it is important to know whether it is disproportionately long or merely seems that way.

In addition to these mechanical concerns, the spoken reading is one of the most effective ways to judge the quality of the dialogue. Most of the concerns discussed in the last chapter and reviewed at the end of this one are best analyzed through a spoken rather than a silent reading.

After corrections and revisions, one is ready to take the final step in self-criticism: the informal group reading. The readers should be quite familiar with the script, but there is no need to memorize the lines. If possible, the reading should be taped for further study. Naturally, some of the parts will appear better or worse depending on the talent of the reader, but no matter how informal the performance may be, it provides the playwright with his first real conception of what the play might be like in full production.

It is pleasant to have a small audience of friends for such a reading, but it is not at all essential. The real value comes from translating the written script into something close to what it is intended to become: action and dialogue on the stage. If possible, allow time after the reading for a discussion of the play's dramatic impact, its theme, or any of the four critical questions suggested below. Those who have participated in a reading are apt to have insights into the work which the playwright had never considered.

The Four
Critical Questions

Because a play is created for public performance, the analysis and evaluation of it tends to be oriented toward audience reaction. If one does not do this, the criticism can become pedantic. But exclusive concern for the audience turns the playwright into a commercial writer, a manufacturer of entertainment as a product. For most, some kind of balance is necessary. The four questions are designed for use by the writer himself and by discussion groups as well, and they should help to maintain that sense of proportion.

First, *does the play have dramatic impact?* Specifically, does it pose a dramatic question and does it develop enough conflict between characters to maintain interest? One should also determine whether the play employs irony, satire, or shock. If any of these devices have been used, there is then the question of whether they are effective. If they are excessive, they may have turned the play into melodrama.

These concerns were placed early in the drama section because they are so crucial. But the two chapters on visual details at the end of the section are also aspects of dramatic impact. One should analyze the way the arrangement of scenes maintains the pace, whether characters get about on the stage, and how the set and costumes are utilized. In short, would the play come alive as a production?

Second, *what is the play saying thematically and how does it make these suggestions?* Here one shifts from the practical matter of stimulating the concern of the audience to artistic and literary concerns. If the play is satiric, what is it satirizing and just how effective is the tone? If it is serious and direct, what kind of themes are being suggested and do they reach the audience through the action as well as by pronouncement?

It is here that one must also consider the symbolic elements. Are there symbolic details which are too blatant or even hackneyed? Or are they so subtle that no one but the playwright and his best friend can interpret them? And do they contribute to the overall statement of the play?

Questions like these do not have to be asked if the play is considered as a product. Neither Broadway musicals nor most television dramas bother with more than a cursory attention to theme. Nor do those spontaneous dream plays which undergraduates occasionally write for the fun of it—and which should not be confused with Strindberg's highly symbolic work. But those are by definition simple forms of drama and this text is, as I pointed out in the first chapter, directed toward sophisticated creativity. To create drama of this type, intricacy of theme is essential.

Third, *is the dialogue effective?* Effective for what? That depends on the type of play. In the case of realistic drama, the dialogue must be capable of making the characters credible. One should end with the sense of having met someone new and also memorable. In the case of comedy, the dialogue must be funny—and the most helpful critics are those who are precise about which lines succeed and which do not. In expressionistic drama, the critic as well as the playwright himself must first determine what is going on thematically and then judge each character's lines individually. For example, if one examines the couple in *The Sandbox* it is clear that they are intended as satiric figures. They are cardboard-thin compared with Grandma. A good critic should judge the lines given to Mommy and Daddy in terms of their effectiveness as satire of a type. But when he turns to Grandma's lines, he must use a different standard. She is a much more fully drawn character and her lines work toward our understanding of her.

Finally, *does the play show real originality?* This should be asked about any work, but it is a particularly critical question in the case of drama. Playwrights are more strongly influenced than other writers by what is "in" during a particular half-decade. If they are not careful, their work will be a faded version of whatever plays are currently in favor.

Complete originality probably doesn't exist. One writes in a tradition even if one is determined to reshape it. With this in mind, one should never condemn a play merely because there are elements of plot or technique which echo other plays. What one has to guard against, however, is that feeling that one has seen the whole play before.

We have just survived, for example, a period in which an extraordinary number of student-written plays were echoes of Beckett (*Waiting for Godot, Endgame*), Ionesco (*The Chairs*) and Albee (*The American Dream, Tiny Alice*). What made the student plays so obviously derivative was the fact that the overlapping occurred not only in situation but in treatment (expressionistic) and in theme (existential) as well.

Some students feel that they shouldn't read too much so as to guard against imitating others. This is unwise and ultimately self-defeating. The route to real originality is reading so much drama—volume after volume—that one is not overly influenced by any one. From this rich background in the genre, the writer can develop his own unique voice and his own personal statement.

PART FOUR ∗∗∗

Appendices

A

SUBMISSION OF MATERIAL
FOR PUBLICATION

Unfounded *myths* about publishing; the *tests* of whether
one is ready to submit material; *mechanical considerations* of the manuscript itself; *what to submit; where* to
submit; the *vanity presses;* the use of *personal contact;*
the dangers of *double submissions;* the value of *agents;*
placing a play; and the reasonable approach to publication.

     The number of novice writers who submit material long
before there is any chance of publication is almost as large as the
number of those who refuse to submit even after they should enter
the public market. This absurd situation exists because so few writers
analyze their work or the problem of marketing with any degree of
rationality.

     The field is cluttered with unfounded myths. One hears, for ex-
ample, that nothing is published without "pull," that neither fiction
nor drama can succeed without sex, that poetry must be unintelligible,
that agents are generally dishonest, and that Madison Avenue has a
death grip on every phase of publication. Equally fanciful is the claim

that if a piece of writing is "good" it will eventually be published without the slightest effort on the part of the writer.

In addition, there are a number of personal delusions which occur so frequently that they are almost archetypal. This country is full of pathetic individuals who have lost a trunk, suitcase, or even a crate of manuscripts which, if it were found, would astound the literary world. Meanwhile, they populate writers' conferences. And then there are those who have written a brilliant work which was "stolen" and published under another title with "only minor revisions."

There are two essential facts to remember: First, publication is no more fair than life itself; there will always be good works which are not accepted as well as thoroughly rotten material which is. Second, if talent, practice, and a practical system of submission are combined, one can alter the odds in one's favor.

The test of whether one is ready to submit material is twofold. First, one should have written in that particular genre for some time. So-called "first novels" are usually preceded by considerable practice in short stories and quite frequently by three or four unpublished novels. This may be partly due to the timidity of publishers, but in many cases it is a great blessing.

In addition, one should be perfectly familiar with the publications to which one is going to submit. This is particularly true for poets. Those who live in large cities should buy little magazines from bookstores; those in smaller cities may find the local library helpful; and those who are not near a city should order magazines and journals by mail. Titles are listed in *Writer's Digest,* a monthly, *Writer's Market,* a complete directory, and others. Even small libraries should have these.

If one has passed these two tests of creative maturity, one is ready for a long, sometimes agonizing program of submitting material.

Mechanical
Considerations The manuscript must be typed with a dark ribbon on a good grade of standard typewriter paper (16- or 20-lb. weight with at least 25% rag content). The type should be pica (not elite or the new varieties). The margins at left and at the top should be $1\frac{1}{2}$ inches, the bottom one inch, and the right roughly one inch without excessive hyphenation. All material except name and address should be double spaced. The title should be placed about one-

third of the way down the first page together with the writer's name, address, and brief explanatory material as shown here:

A WINTER'S NIGHT

Joseph P. Author   A short story
50 Bellweather Place   Approx. 4,500 words
Chicago, Ill. 60600

The story begins two double spaces below this. Only in the case of novels or plays should the title be placed on a separate sheet. For poems, indicate the number of lines instead of the number of words. For plays, substitute the total playing time.

The pages should be numbered in Arabic numerals which together with the last name of the author should be placed in the *upper right* corner of every page after the first: Author 2, Author 3, and so on.

Do not place the manuscript in a folder or binder, and do not staple it. A simple paper clip will do. Novels should be sent loose in a box. Covering letters are not at all necessary, but if you do include one, make it brief and factual. Never defend your own work.

If all this seems rather restrictive, remember that originality belongs in the art form itself, not in the manuscript.

For mailing, the envelope should be large enough so that the manuscript need not be folded. This applies to single poems as well. If one buys $9\frac{1}{2}'' \times 12\frac{1}{2}''$ envelopes for sending, one can include a self-addressed, stamped $9'' \times 12''$ envelope for its return. If this is too complicated, merely fold the second $9\frac{1}{2}'' \times 12\frac{1}{2}''$ envelope so that it can be placed inside the first with the manuscript. In either case, be sure that your address and proper postage is on it. Failure to do this not only infuriates the editor but increases your chances of never seeing it again.

Poems may be sent first class. Heavier manuscripts should be labeled "SPECIAL FOURTH CLASS—MANUSCRIPT" so that they will be sent at the more economical book rate. A letter may be enclosed if you state this on the outside and add the extra postage.

Allow about four weeks for poetry and short stories and an agonizing three months for novels. Resist that temptation to enquire about work sent until at least twice the expected time has passed.

If you know no one on the staff, merely send the manuscript to the fiction or poetry editor at the address given in the magazine. But if you have met or have corresponded with an editor or even a junior reader, send it to him.

Keeping records is extremely important. It is impossible to remember what went out when and to which magazine. In addition, it is invaluable to have a record not only of which editors had a kind word or two but of which magazines sent specifically worded rejection slips. The lowest level of rejection slip is merely a printed statement saying that they appreciated receiving your work and were unable to use it. In addition most magazines have one or two special slips with wording like "this was of particular interest to us" or "we hope to see more of your work." Take these seriously. Next on the scale is the penned comment on the bottom of the slip like "good dialogue" or "try us again." These are infuriatingly brief, but they are worth recording. Be careful, however, not to inundate a magazine with weekly submissions. An editor who has commented on one poem is not going to be impressed with a flood of inferior material. Treat him as a potential ally who deserves only your best work.

The highest point on this scale is the *letter* of rejection. Even if brief, this is close to acceptance. If they suggest specific revisions which seem wise, revise and resubmit. If not, send your next really good piece. These are two situations in which you should definitely include a short covering letter.

What to Submit

This decision must rest ultimately with the author. Although the advice of other serious writers is often helpful, beware of being influenced by friends who do not know what you are doing. For example, if a classmate or neighbor never reads contemporary poetry, he is the world's worst critic. The same applies to fiction or drama. Every writer has many friends who know nothing whatever about literature—just as lawyers or doctors associate with those who have never been introduced to even the terminology of law or medicine. It is pleasant enough when such friends enjoy something you have written, but one should not either send material out prematurely or file manuscripts away on the basis of such judgment.

Poets should select a group of four to six poems. Writers of fiction should limit each submission to one story. Once the choice is made, keep sending the work out repeatedly. A single editorial rejection means absolutely nothing. A manuscript is not "dead" until it has been turned down by at least ten magazines. The best approach is to send the work out on the very day it is returned—otherwise you are apt to lose courage. As a practical matter, just as many manuscripts are accepted after six or eight rejections as after only one. This is largely due to the fact that so many nonliterary factors go into selecting a work for publication, such as the number and kind of manuscripts on hand, the balance of a particular issue, and the personal preferences of the first reader.

There is no easy rule concerning what should be sent out; but once the decision is made, stand by it until you have cumulative proof that the work is unpublishable.

Where
to Submit   The writer should keep a file of those magazines which seem to be interested in his particular kind of writing. Addresses can be found in *Writer's Market*. Listings like these include a large number of commercial publications, so it takes a good deal of time and care to find good literary markets. Non-commercial magazines like *Poetry* and the various university periodicals often provide a good launching platform for new works.

Never submit material to a magazine on the basis of these listings alone. Always review at least one issue of several magazines and make your marketing decisions on the basis of these.

Novels can be handled in the same way. A good way to become familiar with which houses publish what kind of material is by reading the book sections of any large newspaper. Generally speaking, book publishers are more catholic in their literary standards than are magazines. For this reason, most writers simply work their way through the list of thirteen to fourteen major publishers without much regard to order. This takes about three long years—time enough to complete the next novel.

Circulating a novel raises four points which in various degrees apply to placing other types of writing as well. First, don't be seduced by the so-called vanity presses unless absolutely desperate. The vanity press is one which charges the author a percentage either for publication costs or for revisions. Some of them are perfectly honest, but it is rare indeed that a vanity press with its minimal system of distribution can do much with a novel which has been rejected by the major publishers. Collections of poetry are sometimes handled in this way and distributed by the poet himself. This is legitimate and honorable —though the poet should make sure he understands the contract even if (or perhaps *particularly* if) the editor is a friend. Novelists, however, should remember that good publishers are searching for good manuscripts. If a new novel is rejected by thirteen major publishing houses, it is time to shelve it.

Second, never be too proud to make use of a personal contact at a publishing house or magazine. It will not, generally, get a bad manuscript published, but it may bypass that first reader who has a great many manuscripts to review. In the case of rejections, the writer is apt to receive a lengthier comment if the reader has some personal interest. I can testify to the fact that such personal contact is not a prerequisite for having stories or novels accepted; but it is neither unethical nor a waste of time to make use of any interested reader or publisher.

Third, never submit copies of the same work to different publishers at the same time. This applies to stories and poetry as well. And with novels, one should not even have two *different* works in circulation at the same time. The publisher assumes that if he accepts a novel, he is investing in an author. Standard contracts insist on a first refusal not only of later works but of book-length manuscripts already written. This is true only of novels, and it is perfectly ethical to have any number of stories or poems out at the same time as a novel.

This is frustrating and, to my mind, unfair to the writer who has two novels which he would like to circulate. But it is one of the facts of the publishing world. It is simply not worth trying to violate what editors so nicely call "publishers' ethics."

Finally, there is the world of agents to consider. Reputable agents charge a flat ten per cent of all material sold through them and make no other charges whatever, regardless of how much postage or time they may spend. In return they expect to see *all* your work. If an author is unpublished, it is sometimes difficult to find an agent who will be willing to handle his work. But it is not impossible. Once an agent has decided to handle a particular client, he is often willing to maintain faith through a decade of absolutely profitless submission.

Certain "agents" charge for reading each manuscript. Some of them may be of help to those in specialized fields like juveniles or mysteries, but any writer whose interest is at least partially literary will have little to learn from them. More serious, some of these agents have a way of flattering incompetent writers into paying one fee after another for such services as "editorial analysis" and "professional revision" which end up finally with an expensive offer from a vanity press. The only way a writer can be sure that he is dealing with a reputable agent is to have an agreement in writing which makes no financial demands but the flat ten per cent for work sold.

There is not much point in seeking an agent if one plans to submit primarily to little magazines. Placing material in such publications is an honor well worth struggling for, but they pay very little and most agents cannot afford to work for love alone.

There is, however, an argument for submitting to agents if one has a reasonable body of fiction (five or six potentially publishable stories) which might be considered by quality magazines and the slicks. Manuscripts submitted to magazines through agencies usually receive more careful scrutiny by a mature reader with more authority.

There is an even stronger argument for working with an agent if one has written a novel. Not only does one reap the benefits mentioned above, but in the event of acceptance, one receives invaluable legal advice regarding the contract. Although magazines do not offer contracts (you merely accept the rate offered) publishers do. And *all contracts are negotiable.* Those without an agent should hire a lawyer, and it is not easy to find one who is familiar with this rather specialized field. These contracts contain three or four pages of very fine print covering, not only a graduated scale of royalties, but highly complex agreements concerning serial rights, film rights, translation rights, and the like. Since you should turn to an agent at this point to protect your rights, you might as well have him handle the submissions from the start.

But this should not deter a writer who is unable to find an agent who will handle his work. Many first novels and stories have been accepted directly from an author.

All this has only partial relevance to the problem of marketing a play. There are several directions the playwright can take—none of them as neat and simple as the methods of submitting fiction and poetry.

First, the playwright can try working through an agent. Most large agencies have drama departments, and some small agencies specialize in this field. Second, he can try every drama contest in the country—

and there are many. Announcements of contests are usually found on bulletin boards in colleges and universities. Third, those who are fortunate enough to be on campuses with a good stage and an active drama group can try to have their work produced locally. This may not be Broadway, but the satisfaction is deep and lasting. It is also professionally valuable. Fourth, it is worth submitting to those publishers who specialize in plays; though here is it much more important to know exactly what their editorial policy is than it is in the case of novels. Most of these concerns have a particular type of play which they consider acceptable for publication. Fifth, one-act plays can sometimes be placed in magazines like *New World Writing*. It is worth writing a letter of inquiry first. Finally, one can try to find a producer directly. There is probably no other branch of the arts which is more committed to personal contact than drama. To put it more brutally, "pull" is extraordinarily valuable. If you know a producer, director, actor, or even a stagehand, write him. This situation is not merely a matter of commercial corruption. The fact is that although book publishers come to know potential writers through little magazines (which they read with professional care), producers have little contact with the young playwright whose work has not yet appeared on the stage. This situation will continue until there are more little magazines willing to specialize in original plays and more low-budget stage companies in the smaller cities. Meanwhile, the playwright must struggle with this particularly difficult task of presenting his material.

The writer who is serious about his art must be realistic when considering publication. It is naive to assume that the word *marketing* is crass and beneath him. Publishers have no way of discovering a writer who does not make his work available. Yet, on the other hand, a mania to publish at all cost can easily become a poison to the creative process. It leads first to imitative and conventionalized work, and finally to the most negative type of self-delusions designed to protect one's ego. To avoid these most unrewarding routes, one must begin with an honest evaluation of one's own work and follow through with a planned, long-range program of submissions. There are, of course, writers who achieve wide recognition very suddenly; but this is rare and not always a blessing. Ideally, creative work is a way of life, and the effort to publish is an important but not a central portion of that life.

B

GLOSSARY-INDEX

This appendix may be used both for quick review of literary terms and as an index. The explanations are limited to the way terms are used in this text. Numbers refer to pages; those in italics locate lengthier treatment. Italicized expressions indicate cross-references either in the same or a closely related form, e.g., *metered* may be found under **meter,** *rhyming* under **rhyme,** etc.

Allegory, 242. A literary work in which all the characters and often aspects of the *setting* and the *plot* represent abstract concerns or institutions. Examples include Bunyan's *Pilgrim's Progress* and Orwell's *Animal Farm.*

Alliteration, *27,* 35. See *sound devices.*

Ambiguity, 86. That which suggests two or more different meanings. Ambiguity in theme which is not resolved frequently leads to obscurity, a form of *simple writing.* But ambiguities can be effective when the two alternative meanings join to make a broader, more profound suggestion or when they are harmonious as in Levertov's "To the Snake" (p. 120) in which the snake can be seen either as sexuality or knowledge in a general sense.

Anapestic foot, 41ff. See *meter.*

Antagonist, 209. See *protagonist.*

Archaic diction, *80ff.* Words which are primarily associated with an earlier period and are no longer in general use.

Assertive writing, *4, 129ff.,* 169. See *descriptive writing.*

Assonance, *27,* 35. See *sound devices.*

Automatic writing, *142.* See *stream of consciousness.*

Ballad, 101. A *narrative poem* often written in quatrains (see *stanza*) of alternating iambic tetrameter and trimeter *rhyming abcb.* "Folk ballads" are often intended to be sung and are relatively *simple.* "Literary ballads" are a *sophisticated* use of the old form.

Black humor, 238, 322. Macabre, grim, or tragic events treated in a comic fashion so that the reader (or audience) is caught between laughter and *shock.* The technique is seen in the works of James Purdy, Joseph Heller, Bruce Jay Friedman, and Roald Dahl. It is sometimes referred to as "dark humor" to distinguish it from works written by black authors.

Black theater, *309ff.,* 335. Plays written by black Americans. Although playwrights like Langston Hughes, Ossie Davis, and Lorraine Hansberry wrote hundreds of works in the 1930s and 40s, the term is most frequently used to refer to those who have come into prominence in the 1960s and 70s like LeRoi Jones, Paul Carter Harrison, Lonne Elder III, and Adrienne Kennedy.

Black verse, 59. *Verse* written by black Americans like Lucy Smith, David Henderson, LeRoi Jones, and Conrad Kent Rivers (see p. 120).

Blank verse, 41. Unrhyming iambic pentameter (see *verse* and *meter*).

Breath units, 53. See *rhythm.*

Business, *343ff.* See *stage business.*

Caesura, 39. A pause or complete break in the *rhythm* of a *line* of *verse* frequently occurring in the middle. It is particularly noticeable in Old English alliterative verse such as *Beowulf.* It is also found in *metered verse.*

Canto, 100. A relatively lengthy unit, often numbered, found in both *metered* and *free verse.* It may consist of several *stanzas.*

Central concern, 15, *235ff.* See *theme.*

Characterization, *194ff.* The illusion in *fiction* or *drama* of having met someone. The illusion depends on consistency of details, complexity of insight, and on individuality. *Simple* characterization stresses consistency at the expense of complexity and often results in a *stock character,* a form of *simple writing.*

Cinquain, 32. See *stanza.*

Cliché, 17, *75ff.* A *metaphor* or simile which has become so familiar from overuse that the vehicle (see *metaphor*) no longer contributes any meaning whatever to the tenor. It provides neither the vividness of a good metaphor nor the strength of a single, unmodified word. "Good as gold" and "crystal clear" are clichés in this specific sense. The word is also used to describe overused but non-metaphorical expressions such as "tried and true" and "each and every."

Commercial writing, 134. *Prose*—both *fiction* and nonfiction—which is *simple* and conforms to certain rigid *conventions* of *plot* and *character* usually for the sake of publication and profit. Fictional forms include the "pulps" (confessionals such as *True Romance*) and the "slicks" (*McCalls*, *Redbook*, and the like). The so-called slick magazines, however, have also published a great deal of *sophisticated fiction*.

Conflict, *210ff.*, 287ff. See *tension*.

Connotation, 82. The unstated suggestion implied by a word, phrase, passage, or any other unit in a *literary* work. This term includes everything from the emotional overtones or associations of a word or phrase to the symbolic significance of a character, setting, or sequence of actions.

Consonance, 27. See *sound devices*.

Convention, *12*. Any pattern or device in literature which is repeated in a number of different works by a number of different writers. It is a broad term which includes basic devices like *plot*, *dialogue*, *meter*, the division of a play into acts and *scenes*, and the division of a *sonnet* into *octave* and *sestet*. It also refers to general patterns in subject matter like man alienated from society in fiction, girls compared with apple blossoms in poetry, and the recognition scene in drama. *Convention* includes everything which is not unique in a work of *literature*.

Cosmic irony, 87, *219*, 289. See *irony*.

Couplet, *32*, 97. See *stanza*.

Creative writing, 5, 147. Any form of *sophisticated literary writing*. This term is generally used to describe college courses in the writing of fiction, poetry, and drama, or any combination of these. It excludes courses in expository writing, assertive writing, and (usually) *commercial writing*. Although all forms of writing require creativity in the broad sense, *creative writing* normally applies to *literary* as opposed to *descriptive* writing.

Curiosity, *215ff.* A form of *tension* in which withheld information is played against the desire to find out.

Dactylic foot, 41ff. See *meter*.

Descriptive writing, *4*, *129ff*, 169. Any verbal system in which meaning is ultimately linked with the real world and so can be judged as generally valid or invalid. This is in contrast with *literary writing* which contains its own system of *internal logic* and cannot be judged as valid or invalid. *Descriptive writing* is synonymous with "assertive writing" and includes such forms as the essay, thesis, editorial, article, text, and the varieties of journalism.

Deus ex machina, 223, 316. Literally, "god from a machine," formerly used to describe stage machinery which was designed to save a character at the last moment. It now refers to any artificial or improbable event or device used in a play to turn the plot in the desired direction. It is often used in *simple fiction* or *drama*. It lacks *internal logic*.

Dialogue, 133, *203ff.*, *326ff.* Any word, phrase, or passage which quotes a character's speech directly. It normally appears in quotation marks to distinguish it from thoughts. "Monologue" is reserved for relatively lengthy and uninterrupted speeches. "Soliloquy" refers to monologues spoken in plays. "Indirect dialogue" (p. 204) is the same as "indirect discourse"; it echoes the phrasing of dialogue without actually quoting. Dialogue and thoughts constitute two of the five *narrative modes*.

Diction, *73ff*, 106, *243ff*. The choice of words in any piece of writing. Diction is a major factor in determining *style*. "Poetic diction" is a special term used by those who argue that certain words are appropriate for poetry and others are not.

Dimeter, 42. See *line*.

Distance, 239. That aspect of *tone* which describes how closely identified an author (or narrator) appears to be to his fictional character. Highly autobiographical and subjective works tend to have very little distance. *Metamorphosing* the *protagonist* or adding an *ironic* or humorous *tone* increases the *distance*.

Doggerel, 42. A form of *simple verse* in which *meter* and *rhyme* are made blatant and the *tone* is comic.

Double rhyme, 29. See *rhyme*.

Drama, *257ff*. That form of *literary writing* intended primarily for presentation by performers speaking and acting on a stage. Drama is characterized, generally speaking, by the following: it is a "dramatic art" in the sense that it has an emotional impact or force; it is a visual art; it is an auditory art; it is physically produced on a stage; it moves continuously; and it is intended for spectators.

Dramatic conflict, *210*, 287. See *tension*.

Dramatic irony, 87, *219*, 288. See *irony*.

Dramatic question, 258, *284ff*. The emotional element in a play which holds the attention of an audience before the *theme* or thesis becomes clear. The dramatic question (or series of questions) is usually a *simple*, emotional appeal based either on *curiosity* or *suspense*. When the dramatic question is stressed at the expense of *theme*, the result is usually *melodrama*.

Dream fiction, 128. See *stance*.

End-stopped line, 44. See *run-on line*.

Epiphany, 162ff. The moment of awakening or discovery on the part of a fictional character, the reader, or both. This use of the term was suggested by James Joyce. It is generally limited to *fiction*.

Expressionism, 318. See *realism*.

Eye rhyme, 34. See *rhyme*.

Falling meter, 43. See *meter*.

Feet, *40ff*. See *meter*.

Feminine rhyme, *29.* See *rhyme.*

Fiction, *125ff.* That form of *literary writing* which tells an untrue story in *prose.* It may be very *simple* like most *commercial writing* or it may be *sophisticated.* In either case, it establishes its own special world which is guided primarily by *internal logic.* Fiction is also classified by length and breadth: The short story is usually less than forty manuscript pages and explores the lives of only one or two characters; the novel is usually over two hundred manuscript pages long, frequently develops more than two characters, and explores a wider variety of themes. The novella is an ill-defined term designating works of fiction which fall between the story and the novel.

Figure of speech, *62ff.* See *image.*

First person narration, 172. See *person.*

Flashback, 158. See *plot.*

Focus, *177ff.* The character or characters who are the primary concern of a story. When it is a single individual, he is also referred to as the *protagonist.* If he has an opponent (especially in drama), this character may be referred to as the *antagonist.*

Foot, 40. See *meter.*

Formula, 139. Popular *conventions* which characterize *simple fiction* and *drama.* These conventions are usually patterns of *plot* combined with stock characters. Sample: The-sincere-brunette who competes with The-scheming-blonde for the attentions of The-rising-young-executive who at first is "blind to the truth" but who finally "sees the light."

Frame story, *159ff.* See *plot.*

Free verse, *47ff. Verse* which is written without meter, depending instead on *rhythmical* patterns derived from *typography,* syntactical elements, the repetition of words and phrases, *syllabics,* or breath units. Free verse contains no regular *rhyme,* depending instead on *sound devices* such as assonance, consonance, and alliteration.

Genre, 125, 129, 258. Any of several types of *literary* writing. In common usage, genres refer to *fiction, poetry,* and *drama.* Classifications like "mysteries," "Westerns," and "science fiction" are often referred to as "sub-genres," though the word does not yet appear in most dictionaries.

Gimmick, 141. A somewhat colloquial synonym for *convention* or literary trick, usually applied to *plot.* Although this word is generally used in its pejorative sense as a too-clever or contrived twist of plot, it is occasionally used to describe any unusual element in a piece of fiction.

Guerrilla theater, 313. Strongly political plays dominated by a thesis. The term comes from the Spanish, *guerrilla,* "little war," and is generally limited to work which has appeared in the 1960s and 70s.

Hackneyed language, 77. A broad term which includes cliches as well as non-metaphorical phrases and words which have been weakened by overuse. Such language is closely associated with *sentimentality* and with *stock characters*.

Haiku, 95ff. Originally a Japanese verse form. In English it is usually written as a three-line poem containing five syllables in the first line, seven in the second, and five in the third.

Heptameter, 42. See *line*.

Hero, 180. See *protagonist*.

Hexameter, 42. See *line*.

Hyperbole, 64. A figure of speech (see *image*) employing extreme exaggeration usually in the form of a simile or *metaphor*.

Iambic foot, 41ff. See *meter*.

Image, 16, 56*ff*., 106. Any significant piece of sense data in a poem. It may be used in a literal statement, as a symbol, or in a figure of speech. A figure of speech (also called figurative language) uses an image in a stated or implied comparison (see chart on p. 69). *Metaphors* are the most common figures of speech. When several contain images which are closely related, the result is an "image cluster" (p. 65). Other figures of speech include similes, *puns*, and *hyperbole*.

Indirect dialogue, 204. See *dialogue*.

Internal logic, 4. A system of consistencies within a literary narrative which determines what is possible, impossible, likely or unlikely for that particular piece. In this way, each piece of literature "creates its own world." This is an inductive system which makes use of every detail in a work—action, *dialogue*, descriptive material, *style*, and the like. It is a writer's primary method of establishing credibility.

Irony, *87ff*., *217ff*. A form of *tension* in which the literal statement or actual event is contrasted with the intended meaning or expected outcome. Irony can take three forms. The first is "verbal irony," in which the author or speaker knowingly expresses himself in terms that are literally the opposite of his meaning (like the man who says, "Great day for sailing" as his house is washed out to sea). The second is "dramatic irony," in which events, not words, are reversed (like the messenger who promised "Good news" when unknowingly he brought disastrous information). The third is "cosmic irony," which is usually thought of as a reversal on the part of fate or chance (like the fireman who dies from smoking in bed).

Journalistic writing, 4, *129*, 169. See *descriptive writing*.

Legitimate theater, 257. Plays performed by actors on a stage as contrasted with television drama, cinema, and the like.

Line, 5ff., *42ff*. A unit of *verse* which when printed normally appears in a single row the length of which is determined by the poet alone. The inclusion of the line as a part of the art form rather than merely a printer's concern is one of the fundamental distinctions between *verse* and *prose*. In *metered verse*, lines usually contain the same number of feet (see *meter*); in *sprung rhythm* and *alliterative verse*, lines are linked by having the same number of stressed syllables; and in *free verse*, the length of lines is more of a visual concern (see *typography*). The following represent eight types of lines used in metered verse: (1) monometer (one foot), (2) dimeter (two feet), (3) trimeter (three feet), (4) tetrameter (four feet), (5) pentameter (five feet), (6) hexameter (six feet), (7) heptameter (seven feet), (8) octometer (eight feet).

Literary writing, 4, 129. Any verbal system in which meaning is ultimately self-contained because it has created its own system of logic (see *internal logic*) which may or may not resemble that with which we interpret aspects of the real world. In essence, literary writing creates its own universe, as opposed to *descriptive writing* which is designed to explain or comment on some aspect of the real world. Literary writing, a synonym for *literature*, is a nonevaluative term and includes both *simple* and *sophisticated* samples of *fiction*, *poetry*, and *drama*.

Lyric, 39. Originally a Greek term referring to verse to be accompanied by a lyre. Today, it generally refers to a short poem which presents a single speaker who is concerned with a strongly felt emotion. Thus, poems of love, observation, and contemplation are "lyrics" in contrast with *ballads* and other types of *narrative poetry*. "Lyrical" is often used loosely to describe poetry which sounds musical because of its *sound devices* and *rhythm*.

Means of perception, 168ff. The agent through whose eyes a piece of fiction appears to be presented. This character is also the one whose thoughts are revealed directly. The term is synonymous with "point of view" and "viewpoint." It is generally limited to a single character in short fiction.

Melodrama, 140, 212. *Simple writing* (usually drama or fiction) which is dominated by *suspense*. *Sophisticated literature* also uses suspense, but melodrama does it blatantly and at the expense of other literary concerns. It usually makes use of *stock characters* as well.

Metamorphosis, *145ff.* Radical transformations of an experience or of an existing draft of a story or play in order to create fresh literary work. This process can be either conscious or unconscious. It is usually employed either to clarify existing patterns or to break up patterns which appear to be too neat or contrived. It may also help a writer to regain control over an experience which in its original form is still too close to him.

Metaphor and **simile,** *62ff.* A simile is a figure of speech (see *image*) in which one item is compared with another which is different in all but a few significant respects. Thus, "He fought like a lion" suggests courage but not the use of claws and teeth. The item being described is called the tenor (the true subject) and the one utilized is the vehicle. (Terms originally suggested by I. A. Richards.) A metaphor implies rather than states this same sort of comparison and so becomes a statement which is literally untrue, but when successful, figuratively stronger than the simile. "He was a lion in battle" is not taken literally because the reader recognizes it as a literary *convention*. In both cases, the base or starting point is the tenor. The reverse of this—using the vehicle as base and merely implying the tenor—is a *symbol* ("It was the lion, not the lamb that ruled England in those years").

Meter, *40ff.* A system of *stressed* and unstressed syllables which creates *rhythm* in certain types of verse. The *conventionalized* units of stressed and unstressed syllables are known as *feet*. Metered verse normally contains the same number of feet in each *line* and the same type of foot throughout the poem. The effect, however, is usually muted by substituting other types of feet occasionally. The following six feet are in common use, but the iamb is the most popular form in English. Those which end on a stressed syllable are called "rising meter"; those which end on an unstressed syllable are called "falling meter."

iamb	(iambic)	ĕxcépt
trochee	(trochaic)	Mídăs
anapest	(anapestic)	dĭsappoint
dactyl	(dactylic)	háppĭlў
spondee	(spondaic)	héartbréak
pyrrhic	(pyrrhic)	ĭn thĕ

Mimetic fiction, 126ff. See *stance*.

Mixed media, 364ff. The use in *legitimate theater* of other visual and auditory devices such as cinema, slides, flashing signs, taped recordings, and the like.

Modes, 131. See *narrative modes*.

Monologue 331. See *dialogue*.

Monometer, 42. See *line*.

Mood and **tone,** 237. See *tone*.

Narrative modes, 131ff., *207ff.*, 245. The five methods by which *fiction* can be presented: *dialogue*, thoughts, action, description, and exposition. Most writers use all five in varying proportions.

Narrative poetry, 100ff. Verse which tells a story. This may take the form of the *ballad*, the epic, or a tale in verse such as Snodgrass's "A Flat One" (p. 116) and Hecht's "Lizards and Snakes" (p. 110).

Octave, 32ff. An eight-lined *stanza* in *metered verse*. Also the first eight lines of a *sonnet*.

Octometer, 42. See *line*.

Off rhyme, *29*, 34. See *rhyme*.

Omniscient point of view, 168, *172ff.* The *means of perception* in which the author enters the mind of all major characters. "Limited omniscience" restricts the means of perception to certain characters. Most short fiction and a majority of novels limit the means of perception to a single character.

Onomatopoeia, 27. See *sound devices*.

Orientation, *224ff*. The sense in *fiction, drama,* or *narrative poetry* of being somewhere specific. This includes awareness of geography, historical period, season, and time.

Overtone and **connotation,** 82. See *connotation*.

Pace, *160ff*, 246, 332ff. The reader's sense that a story or play "moves rapidly" or "drags." This is determined by the *rate of revelation* and by the *style*.

Paradox, 89, *221*. The form of tension found in a statement which on one level is logically absurd yet on another level implies a reasonable assertion. Example from Heller's *Catch-22:* "The Texan turned out to be good-natured, generous, and likable. In three days no one could stand him."

Pentameter, 42. See *line*.

Person, *172ff*. Any of several methods of presentation by which fiction is given the illusion of being told by a character, about a character, about the reader and the like. The third person ("he") is the most common; the first person ("I") can be written either in a neutral *style* or "as-if-told" style. The second person singular ("you") and the third person plural ("they") are seldom used. *Person* is how a story is presented; the *means of perception* is who appears to present it.

Plot, *157ff*. The sequence of events, often divided into *scenes* (p. 337), in any *literary* narrative. This may be chronological, or it may be nonchronological in any of three ways: by flashback (inserting an earlier scene), or by multiple flashbacks (as with Vonnegut's *Slaughterhouse-Five* and Conrad's *Lord Jim*), or by using a frame (beginning and ending with the same scene).

Poetic, 5ff. In addition to being an adjective for "poetry" (see *verse*), this term is used to describe fiction or drama which makes special use of *rhythm, sound devices, figurative language, symbol,* and compression of meaning and implication.

Poetic diction, 73ff. See *diction*.

Poetry, 5ff. See *verse*.

Point of view, *168ff*. See *means of perception*.

Pornography, 140. A form of *simple* writing which, like *propaganda,* is designed to effect only one emotional response. The objective distinction between pornographic works like *Story of O* and *literary* works like *Ulysses* is the difference between writing which is simply concerned with eliciting a single emotional response and that which utilizes a wide and *sophisticated* range of literary effects only one of which may involve sexual words or scenes.

Premise fiction, 127. See *stance*.

Propaganda, 313. The quality in *simple writing* which is dominated by a strong message or *thesis* (312). Sophisticated forms of writing can also present political, social, or religious theses; the distinguishing characteristic of propaganda is its simplicity—its failure to do anything *but* argue a case.

Proscenium arch, 359. See *stage designs*.

Prose, 5. Those forms of writing in which the lines are continuous and have nothing to do with the statement or the form. This is in contrast with *verse*.

Prose rhythm, 7, 47ff., *50.* See *rhythm*.

Protagonist, *180,* 209. The main character in a piece of *fiction*, play, or *narrative poem*. He is often opposed by an antagonist. The term is broader than "hero" which suggests greatness. Protagonists who are perpetual victims are sometimes referred to as "anti-heroes."

Pun, 65, 90. A figure of speech (see *image*) in which two different but significantly related meanings are attached to a single word. Most *sophisticated* uses of the pun are a form of *metaphor* with the tenor and the vehicle combined in a single word as in the case of Dylan Thomas's "some grave truth."

Pyrrhic foot, 41. See *meter*.

Quatrain, 32. See *stanza*.

Quintet, 32. See *stanza*.

Rate of revelation, 161. The rate at which new information or insights are given to the reader regarding character, theme, or plot. It is one of the primary factors which determine *pace*.

Realism and expressionism, 126ff., 316ff. Realism is the literary illusion that the various aspects of a play or piece of *fiction* reflect what we might see and hear in actuality. In fiction, this has been described as the mimetic *stance* (p. 126). Expressionism is used to describe the purposeful and overt distortion of action, dialogue, and the like in *drama*. (For other uses of these terms, see chart on p. 317.)

Recurrent stanza, 99. See *stanza*.

Refrain, 22, *100.* A phrase, line, or stanza which is repeated periodically in a poem.

Reportorial style, 130, *169ff.,* 177. The style of writing used in newspaper articles (see *descriptive writing*) and in fiction which echoes this style.

Resonance, 242. That aspect of *tone* in *sophisticated writing* which is created by the use of *symbolic* and suggestive details. It is a layering of meaning and implication not found in *simple writing*.

Rhyme, *29ff.* A device found exclusively in *verse* and consisting of two or more words linked by an identity in sound which begins with an accented vowel and continues to the end of each word. The sounds preceding the accented vowel in each word must be unlike. This is "true rhyme." "Slant rhyme" and "off rhyme" use similar rather than identical vowel sounds. "Double rhyme," also called "feminine rhyme," is a two-syllable rhyme as in "running" and "sunning." In an "eye rhyme," the words look alike but sound different. "Rhyme scheme" is a pattern of rhymed endings which is repeated regularly in each *stanza* or *metered verse*.

Rhyme royal, 32. A stanza form of metered verse in which each septet is rhymed *ababbcc*.

Rhythm, 7, *38ff*, *47ff*, 107. A systematic variation in the flow of sound. In *metered* verse this is achieved through a repeated pattern of stressed and un-stressed syllables. In "alliterative verse" and "sprung rhythm" the pattern is determined by the number of stresses in each line without regard for the unstressed syllables. In "syllabic verse," the number of syllables in any one line matches the number in the corresponding line of the other *stanzas*. In "free verse," rhythms are achieved by *typography*, repeated syntactical patterns, and breath units. Rhythms in prose are achieved by repeating key words, phrases, and syntactical patterns.

Rising meter, 43, see *meter*.

Run-on line, 44. *Lines* in *verse* in which either the grammatical construction or the meaning or both are continued from the end of one line to the next. One function of this technique is to mute the rhythmical effect of *meter*. It is con-trasted with "end-stopped lines," which are usually terminated with a period or a semicolon.

Satire, 91ff, 221, 289, 323. A form of *tension* in which the "reasonable" view of characters, places, or institutions is played against an exaggerated view for the purpose of criticism or ridicule. At least some measure of exaggeration (if only through a biased selection of details) is necessary to be effective.

Scanning, 41ff. The analysis of *meter* in a sample of verse, identifying the various feet (see *meter*) and the type of *line* used.

Scene, 157, 291ff., 337ff. In *drama*, a formal subdivision of an act marked in the script and shown to the audience by lowering of the curtain or dimming of the lights; or a more subtle subdivision of the plot marked only by the exit or the entrance of a character. The former are here called "primary scenes" and the latter "secondary scenes." In *fiction*, the scene is a unit of action marked either by a shift in the number of characters or, more often, a shift in time or place.

Sentimentality, 138. A form of *simple writing* which is dominated by a blunt appeal to the emotions of pity and love. It does so at the expense of subtlety and literary *sophistication*. Popular subjects are puppies, grandparents, and young lovers.

Septet, 32. See *stanza*.

Sestet, sextet, 32ff. A six-lined *stanza* in *metered* verse. Also the last six lines of the *sonnet*.

Set, 350. See *setting*.

Setting, 226ff. Strictly, the geographic area in which a *plot* takes place; but more generally, the time of day, the season, and the social environment as well.

In most cases, geographic, temporal, and social settings are emphasized un-
equally. In *drama* the setting is usually specified at the beginning of the script.
What the audience sees on the stage (excluding the actors) is the "set" (p. 350).
Set design of *The Collection* appears on pp. 356–357.

Shock, 222, 290. A form of *tension* in which the incredible is made credible.
If misused, it results in melodrama. When successful, it has been prepared for.

Short story, 4ff. See *fiction.*

Simile, 62ff. See *metaphor.*

Simple writing, *8ff., 130ff.* Writing in which the intent is made blatant, the
style is limited to a single effect, or the *tone* is limited to a single emotion. It
includes the adventure and horror story (*melodrama*), many love stories, most
greeting card verse (*sentimentality*), most patriotic *verse* and politically partisan
fiction and *drama* (*propaganda*) and that which is single-mindedly sexual or
sadistic (*pornography*). It also includes work which is so personal or so obscure
that its intent fails to reach even a conscientious reader. The antonym for
simple is *sophisticated.*

Slant rhyme, *29,* 34. See *rhyme.*

Sonnet, *33.* A metered poem of fourteen lines usually in iambic pentameter.
The first eight lines are known as the "octave" and the last six as the "sestet."
The Italian or Petrarchan sonnet is often rhymed *abba, abba; cde, cde.* The
Elizabethan sonnet is often thought of as three quatrains and a final rhyming
couplet: *abab, cdcd, efef, gg.*

Sophisticated writing, *8ff.,* 130ff. Writing in which the intent is complex,
having implications and ramification, the *style* makes rich use of the techniques
available, and the *tone* has a range of suggestion. It is normally unified with a
system of *internal logic.* It is the opposite of *simple writing.* Not to be confused
with the popular use of "sophisticated."

Sound clusters, 28. See *sound devices.*

Sound devices, 6, *26ff.,* 35, 107. The technique of linking two or more words
by alliteration (similar initial sounds), assonance (similar vowel sounds),
consonance (similar consonantal sounds), onomatopoeia (similarity between the
sound of the word and the object or action it describes), or *rhyme* (29ff.). In
addition, "sound clusters" link groups of words with related vowel sounds
which are too disparate to be called true samples of assonance.

Spondaic foot, 41. See *meter.*

Sprung rhythm, 40. A technique of *rhythm* in *verse* which is based on the
number of *stressed* syllables in each *line,* disregarding those which are unstressed.
It is primarily associated with the work of Gerard Manley Hopkins (see "Pied
Beauty," p. 113).

Stage designs, *359ff.* The "conventional stage" has a raised playing area
which is set behind a "proscenium arch" from which a curtain is lowered between acts and *scenes.* The effect is like seeing a performance in an elaborate

picture frame. At the opposite extreme is "theater in the round" or "theater in the square" in which the playing area is a center arena as in a small circus. Compromise designs include a variety of pie-shaped stages with audiences on three sides.

Stage business, *343ff.* Activity on the part of an actor in a play not involving relocation. This includes such actions as sewing, biting fingernails, and the like.

Stance, 126ff. An analysis of fiction on the basis of the author's (and reader's) assumptions about what can and cannot be expected to happen. There are three stances: "Mimetic fiction" is "realistic" in that events follow what we think of as the laws of nature and probability. "Premise fiction" breaks those assumptions with a single exception (such as having a character turn into an insect). "Dream fiction" imitates the apparently arbitrary occurrences of dreams, though it usually follows the logic of association.

Stanza, 31ff., *97ff.* A division within a poem consisting of a certain number of lines. In *free verse* the stanzas vary in length like paragraphs in prose. They are "nonrecurrent." In *metered verse* the stanzas are usually of the same length ("recurrent") and, where *rhyme* is used, of the same *rhyme scheme*. These are the more common types: couplet (two lines); tercet or triplet (three lines); quatrain (four lines); quintet or cinquain (five lines); sestet or sextet (six lines); septet (seven lines); octave (eight lines).

Stereotype, *139ff.*, 212. See *stock character*.

Stock character, 139ff., 212. Characters in *fiction* or *drama* which are *simple* and which also conform to one of a number of types which have appeared over such a long period and in so many different works that they are familiar to readers and audiences. Their dialogue is often *hackneyed* and their presence can reduce a work to the level of *simple fiction* or *drama*.

Stream of consciousness, 142, *176.* Fiction in the form of a character's thoughts directly quoted without exposition. Although wandering and disjointed, it is designed to reveal character. This is in sharp contrast with "automatic writing" in which the writer's goal is not *characterization* (or even *fiction*), but self-exploration.

Stress, 39ff. The relative force or emphasis placed on a particular syllable. In "awake," the second syllable is stressed. See *meter*.

Style, *243ff.* The manner in which a work is written. It is determined by the author's decisions, both conscious and unconscious, regarding diction (the type of words used), syntax (the type of sentences), *narrative mode* (relative importance of dialogue, thoughts, action, description, and exposition), and *pace* (the reader's sense of progress). It is closely connected with *tone*.

Substitution, *43ff.* The technique in *metered verse* of occasionally replacing a foot (see *meter*) which has become the standard in a particular poem with some other type of foot. A common form of substitution is the use of a trochee for emphasis in a poem which is generally iambic.

Suspense, 217. A form of tension in which hope for a particular outcome is played against the fear that it will not turn out that way. An excess of suspense tends to create *melodrama*.

Syllabics, 52ff. See *rhythm*.

Symbol, *66ff.*, 241, 304. Any verbal detail such as an object, action, or state, which has a range of meaning beyond and usually larger than itself. "Public symbols" are those which have become a part of the general consciousness—the flag, the cross, and the like. "Private symbols" are made public slowly either through single works or from a series such as Dylan Thomas's use of the color green. In most cases, the reader is first introduced to the vehicle (see *metaphor*) and then slowly perceives the tenor or true concern. This is in contrast with similes and *metaphors*, wherein the writer is apt to work directly with his tenor and then pause briefly to suggest a provocative vehicle.

Synecdoche, 64. A figure of speech (see *image*) and a form of *metaphor* in which a portion of something (the vehicle) represents the whole (the tenor) as in "a town of four hundred souls," "field hands," and "motors and rails" used to designate types of corporations.

Syntactical rhythm, 50ff. See *rhythm*.

Tenor, 64. See *metaphor*.

Tension, *83ff.*, 108, *209ff.*, 287ff. A force and a counterforce within a work of literature. In *verse* this can take the form of thematic conflict, *irony*, or *satire*. In *narrative poetry*, *fiction*, and *drama* it may also be created through a sense of *curiosity*, *suspense*, and *shock*. "Conflict" (or "dramatic conflict") is that form of tension which is generated when one character opposes another character or some other force such as society or nature.

Tercet, 32. See *stanza*.

Tetrameter, 42. See *line*.

Theater in the round, 359. See *stage designs*.

Theater of the absurd, 321. A somewhat loosely defined dramatic "school" in the *expressionistic* tradition beginning in the 1950s. Shared convictions are that life is "absurd" in the sense of lacking ultimate meaning and that the intellect cannot determine truth. Shared techniques include the use of *expressionistic* fantasies, dark or *black humor*, and a tendency to develop a static quality rather than a *dramatic plot*. Examples include works by Ionesco, Beckett, Pinter, and some of Albee, Genet, and Adamov. (For a chart showing its relationship with other dramatic traditions, see p. 317).

Theme, 15, *235ff.*, *302ff.* The primary statement, suggestion, or implication of a *literary* work. The term is used here interchangeably with "central concern." It does not have the moral implications of "message" nor the didactic element of "thesis." A thesis states or clearly implies a particular conviction or recommends a specific course of action. It is often *propagandistic*. Most *sophisticated* writing is unified by a theme rather than a thesis.

Thesis, *312ff.* See *theme.*

Third person narration, 174. See *person.*

Tone, *237ff.*, 334ff. The emotional quality of a literary work itself and of the author's attitude toward his work as well. Some critics prefer to separate the two aspects of this definition, but most writers tend to think of them as two forms of the same quality. Tone, then, is described with adjectives like "exciting," "sad," "gay," "eerie," or "depressing" as well as with terms like "satiric," "sardonic," "ironic," and "dramatic."

Trimeter, 42. See *line.*

Triplet, *32,* 98. See *stanza.*

Trochaic foot, 41ff. See *meter.*

Typography, *48ff.* The technique in *verse* (and particularly *free verse*) of arranging words, phrases, and lines on the printed page to create a rhythmical effect.

Vanity press, 377. A publisher who charges the author a part or all of the printing costs. Regular publishers assume all costs themselves and pay the author a percentage (generally between 10% and 15%) of the sales.

Vehicle, 64. See *metaphor.*

Verbal irony, *218,* 289. See *irony.*

Verse, *5ff.* That form of *literary writing* which is exclusively characterized by utilizing the length of the *line* as an aspect of the art, and characterized more generally by a concern for the *sound* and *rhythm* of language and by compression of statement and implication. *Verse* is occasionally used as a synonym for a *line,* a *stanza,* or a *refrain.* More frequently, it is used as a general synonym for "poetry." Some, however, prefer that "poetry" be used only with reference to work which is truly *sophisticated.*

Viewpoint, *168ff.* See *means of perception.*

Visual rhythm, 48ff. See *typography.*